LIBERATING LITERATURE

Liberating Literature is the first book to focus on both African-American and white women writers in the US, and to chart the connection between women's political fiction and the social movements and cultural debates of their time. Covering sixty years of political fiction, Lauret challenges hitherto unquestioned assumptions about gender and writing, and about the relation between realism and postmodernism.

Liberating Literature is a book about feminist writers, readers and texts. But it is much more than that. Maria Lauret looks with fresh vision at the American Civil Rights movement of the 1960s, socialist women's writing of the 1930s, the emergence of the New Left and the second wave of the Women's Movement and its cultural practices.

Written with great insight and wit, *Liberating Literature* will be enthusiastically received by feminist readers everywhere.

Maria Lauret is a Lecturer in English at the University of Southampton.

LIBERATING LITERATURE

Feminist Fiction in America

Maria Lauret

London and New York

First published 1994
by Routledge
11 New Fetter Lane, London EC4P 4EE

Simultaneously published in the USA and Canada
by Routledge
29 West 35th Street, New York, NY 10001

© 1994 Maria Lauret

Typeset in Baskerville by
Ponting–Green Publishing Services, Chesham, Bucks
Printed and bound in Great Britain by
TJ Press (Padstow) Ltd, Padstow, Cornwall

British Library Cataloguing in Publication Data
A catalogue record for this book is available from
the British Library

Library of Congress Cataloging in Publication Data
Lauret, Maria.
Liberating Literature: Feminist Fiction in America /
Maria Lauret.
p.   cm.
Includes bibliographical references and index.
1. American fiction – Women authors – History and criticism.
2. Feminism and literature – United States – History –
20th century.   3. Women and literature – United States –
History – 20th century.   4. American fiction – 20th century –
History and criticism.   5. Political fiction, American – History
and criticism.   6. Sex role in literature.   I. Title.
PS374.F45L38   1994

813'.5099287 – dc20   93-48839

ISBN 0–415–06515–1 (hbk)
ISBN 0–415–06516–X (pbk)

In memory of my father

C. H. C. Lauret

and for my mother

C. E. A. Lauret-Jonk

Nobody can live on a bridge
or plant potatoes
but it is fine for comings and goings,
meetings, partings and long views
and a real connection to someplace else
where you may
in the crazy weathers of struggle
now and again want to be.

(from 'Bridging' by Marge Piercy)

CONTENTS

PREFACE

Books do change lives. This book is about the role of literature in social movements, about fiction that has designs upon its readers, about writing that changed the lives of individual women by giving them a sense of collectivity, of movement, and a vision of social change. Books like Kate Millett's *Sexual Politics*, Marge Piercy's *Small Changes* and Alice Walker's *Meridian* helped to bring about the profound social changes effected by the Women's Movement. They also made sense of my personal and educational history in ways which could not have been anticipated by their creators, whose cultural context is so different from my own; *Liberating Literature* is then, in its turn, the result of reading books which changed my life and my mind.

Marge Piercy told me once that writing does not come solely out of other writing, it comes out of life, and I believe this to be true of academic writing as well as fiction. This book would not have been written were it not for my living as a woman and an émigrée in Britain, for my past and present of work in lowly and highly jobs, and for my efforts to try and understand my own experience through that of others – fictional and historical, political and personal. This dynamic relation between literature and life, in which each transforms the other, became the subject matter of *Liberating Literature* and inspired its argument regarding a feminist, counter-hegemonic aesthetic.

Personal motivations aside, however, the question arises whether the world needs another study of feminist fiction. It seemed to me, when I started researching eight years ago, that it did, because there were hardly any such studies and I still believe so, although there are now quite a few. Literary criticism does not take place in a vacuum, a space of pure reason or absolute judgement, but in a cultural-political environment where, at a certain time, certain problems need to be addressed in new ways. I was very aware, whilst writing this book, of the evanescence of such 'newness' in an intellectual culture which is also a marketplace. As new studies of feminist fiction were being published, I had continually to shift my perspective in order to benefit from and speak to the most recent scholarship on a (still very recent) body of fictional texts. Even so, I found that the new theory-informed approaches to feminist fiction could only guide me part of the way to an answer about how the relation between literature and life in this body of texts actually works. Theory has its own history, and the history of poststructuralism, for example, is that of formalism and the modernist avant-garde, whose aesthetic precepts are radically at odds with those of the literature of the Women's Movement. I retained the sense that a different approach was required to understand American feminist fiction, both in its cultural specificity and in its cross-cultural appeal. Much as this book is about political women's writing it is, therefore, also about the standards by which that writing has been judged or might be judged in a different, more historicist paradigm. I address certain critical problems which seem to me important ones to resolve if feminist criticism is to remain innovative and eclectic, rather than become submissive to the lures of theoreticism and postmodern political *skepsis*. Those problems concern the historicisation of women's writing, the increasingly habitual privileging of formal over other kinds of literary innovation in feminist criticism, and the place of realism in contemporary critical thought. In this dialogue with other feminist critics, I undoubtedly make evaluative (counter-)judgements of my own which at times may seem controversial or contradictory. But I hope that at the very least it will be clear how and why I arrived at them, so that they can be checked and argued with.

ACKNOWLEDGEMENTS

My first debt to be acknowledged is to the critics and writers upon whose work this book is based. I thank especially Marge Piercy, who agreed to talk to me and provide me with unpublished materials, and whose writing inspired my own.

Grateful acknowledgement is made to publishers and individuals for permission to reprint the following: fragments from the poem 'To Be of Use' and from the essay 'A Dark Thread in the Weave'; reprinted by permission of Marge Piercy. Lines from 'Bridging' from *Circles on the Water* by Marge Piercy; copyright © 1982 by Marge Piercy; reprinted by permission of Albert A. Knopf Inc. Lines from 'Making Peace' from Denise Levertov, *Breathing the Water*; copyright © 1987 by Denise Levertov; reprinted by permission of New Directions Publishing Corp. Portion of 'Ann Burlak' by Muriel Rukeyser from *A Rukeyser Reader*, W. W. Norton, New York, 1994; copyright © William L. Rukeyser; reprinted by permission of William L. Rukeyser. Every effort has been made to contact the copyright holder for permission to reprint extracts from 'The Blue Meridian' by Jean Toomer.

Thirdly I want to thank my family, friends, and colleagues who have witnessed the years of mostly solitary work that goes into the writing of an academic book. There were people who gave me books, people who gave me ideas, people whose job it was, people whose job it wasn't, people who listened, people who forgot, people who read, people who disagreed, people who had to be convinced. Against tradition, there were none who typed the manuscript, cooked the meals or kept the study free of interruption; time and money were, as always, scarce commodities.

I thank the British Association for American Studies for financial support which enabled me to travel to the United States, Sue Dare for giving me ideas as well as books, and my colleagues at the University of Southampton who were generous with their thoughts and their time: in particular Tony Crowley, Eileen Dreyer, Peter Middleton, Jonathan Sawday, Erica Carter and – more particularly still – Ken Hirschkop.

Of the people whose job it was, I am grateful to Gayle Greene, who read the manuscript for Routledge and provided me with invaluable criticism and comment. She deserves credit for several enormous changes-at-the-last-minute which resulted from her report, without, of course, bearing responsibility for them.

Pete Nicholls gave my research and writing the rigorous critical attention it needed; it is difficult to overestimate his part in shaping this book both as a supervisor and as a friend.

The same is true of Cora Kaplan, whose intellectual example continues to inspire me. If ideas were copyrighted, *Liberating Literature* would be much slimmer and much slighter; I owe many of the best ones to her.

I cannot, finally, express my thanks to Matthew Forster in my own words. The lines from Marge Piercy's 'Bridging' are for him.

Southampton, November 1993

INTRODUCTION
American women's writing and social movements from the 1930s to the 1980s

In 1963 Norman Mailer wrote a review of a 'lady-book', Mary McCarthy's *The Group*: '[McCarthy] is not a good enough woman to write a major novel; not yet; she has failed, she has failed from the centre out, she failed out of vanity' (Mailer 1963: 82).

Feminist fiction emerged in the mid to late 1970s, on the crest of the Second Wave Women's Movement. Following the example of Kate Millett in *Sexual Politics*, who turned the tables on Mailer and exposed him as not a good enough man to treat women decently in literature, feminist writers inverted the logic of a literary-critical establishment which had regarded the 'lady-book' as, at best, a sub-literary genre of its own and at worst as an upmarket version of popular romance. Feminist fiction transformed the literary arena and wilfully made it a gendered, political space in which women's issues could be discussed and a feminist readership constituted. In the work of Marilyn French, Marge Piercy, Alice Walker, Kate Millett, Rita Mae Brown, Alix Kates Shulman and a host of other new writers, the political discourses of Women's Liberation and Black feminism informed imaginative reconstructions of the condition of women in American society. Here was a body of texts which took feminism seriously, which spoke to women's contemporary concerns, voiced their discontents and envisioned their dreams. Here also was a mode of writing which reinserted women into the literary domain and demanded that they be taken seriously as imaginative and political writers.

American feminist fiction of the 1970s and 1980s was a liberating literature, a female body of texts which sought to liberate both women and writing from the constraints of masculinist double standards in literature and in life. It threw its bra in the trash-can of conventional femininity and refused to corset itself in prevailing notions of literariness, thus setting free the loose baggy monster of misogynist critical cliché in big rambling novels where women were, unashamedly, at large.

Of all the Women's Movement's achievements in changing perceptions of gender difference and dominance, its impact on the cultural sphere is

1

perhaps the most marked. Twenty years of feminist fiction has firmly established feminist literary discourse as a force to be reckoned with. But a rereading of the feminist fictions of twenty years ago also marks a considerable historical difference between then and now, a difference which enables a critical vantage point informed by almost as many years of feminist theory and criticism, not to mention social change. The question inevitably arises: how do we read the texts of twenty years of political and literary debate around gender in the light of present concerns, with consciousnesses raised and at a safe distance from the trials and tribulations of being feminists in the making?

'Texts come before us as the always-already-read', Fredric Jameson writes in *The Political Unconscious*, 'our object of study is less the text itself than the interpretations through which we attempt to confront and to appropriate it' (Jameson 1983: 9).

Taking American feminist fiction of the 1970s and 1980s as my object of study, I want to create new meanings for that body of texts as well as to relocate them in their historical moments. Like many others of my generation, I was formed as a feminist and as a critic in the social and political movements of the 1960s, 1970s and 1980s, of which cultural activism was an integral part. I continue to be formed by the changing climate of the 1990s, but it is because I still regard myself as a cultural activist that I also want to examine the 'inherited interpretive tradition' of feminist fiction. I don't think that feminist criticism to date has treated the imaginative literature of its own – that of the Women's Movement – very well, and I therefore want to present my own readings of this literature as an alternative and corrective.

Feminist fiction did not, for a long time, receive the critical attention it so richly deserved. Early feminist criticism, in its enthusiasm for women's writing in general, concentrated on the urgent task of forging a female tradition of women's literature through the ages. It did not pay much attention to the distinctiveness of Women's Movement fiction, because it regarded all women's writing as by definition 'political'. And for a second generation of feminist critics, which made its presence felt in the academy in the early 1980s, feminist fiction as a mode of political writing likewise held little interest. Critical imperatives inspired by poststructuralist and psychoanalytic theory tended to draw attention away from the social functions of literature, obliterated history (at least for a while), and concentrated the critical mind instead on questions of signification and female subjectivity. Having passed through the mirror stage, feminist criticism became its own subject and turned inward to examine its earlier assumptions about the universal category 'woman', the nature of language and representation, and the question of what a female aesthetic might mean. Separated from its mother's body – the Women's Movement – feminist criticism inserted itself into the symbolic order of theoretical correctness and repressed, for the moment, its more anarchic social and political impulses. In the reception of feminist fiction a gap opened up between an early and rather unreflective celebration of women's writing in general on one hand, and subsequently a stringent and often dismissive critique of the literature of the Women's Movement on the other – a political unconscious, indeed.

Due to the hegemony of new theoretical concepts which challenged the referentiality of language and the stability of gender identity, sex/textuality and the role of the unconscious in subjectivity and signification were emphasised. Feminist fiction – especially in its popular, realist manifestations such as French's *The Women's Room* – now came to be regarded as naïve in its belief that it could speak for women and represent the real conditions of American women's lives in literature. Feminist realism, it was argued, was still embedded in traditional conceptions of identity and referential modes of representation; it merely reproduced conventional constructions of reality instead of challenging them. Yet the question of whether feminist realist fiction actually fitted this bill of the conventional and traditional was never examined in detail. Here, for example, is Jane Gallop writing about the politics of experience in relation to the female body, as cited by Alice Jardine in support of a poststructuralist conception of feminism:

> Belief in simple referentiality is not only unpoetic but also ultimately politically conservative, because it cannot recognize that the reality to which it appeals is a traditional ideological construction, whether one terms it phallomorphic, or metaphysical, or bourgeois, or something else. *The politics of experience is inevitably a conservative politics*, for it cannot help but conserve traditional ideological constructs which are not recognised as such but are taken for the 'real'. [my *italics*]
>
> (Gallop 1983: 83; Jardine 1985: 155)

The conflation of realism, and especially feminist realism, with 'traditional ideological constructs' and of referentiality with 'simple' referentiality is indicative of the reductivism which has characterised recent critiques of realism. It is as if, for poststructuralist critics, contemporary feminist writing was still located at the cultural conjuncture in which Virginia Woolf wrote her anti-realist manifesto in 'Mr. Bennett and Mrs. Brown'.[1] This view takes no account of the possibility that a feminist (or a working class, or an African-American) realism might be different from that of the nineteenth century bourgeois novel. It ignores, conveniently, the possibility that there might be a polemical realism which contests, precisely, the 'traditional ideological constructs which are not recognised as such but are taken for the "real"'. And whenever such traditional ideological constructs are challenged with an alternative version of the 'real', even if it is posited as the 'real real', we are in the domain of power, not of simple referentiality signifying nothing.

It is this reductivism, and the trivialisation and depoliticisation of feminist fiction it often entails, that I want to question and redress in the chapters which follow.

Building on the insights that psychoanalytic and poststructuralist feminist criticism also – to be sure – afford, but widening their focus on textuality and female subjectivity *per se* to include historical specificity and the dynamics of literary production and reception, I want to revitalise the political meanings of feminist fiction, because I believe that they pose questions (and answers) which are still relevant for feminism today.

I also believe, however, that we need to regard feminist fiction not as an intrinsically female genre, but as a set of diverse cultural practices which contest both dominant meanings of gender and established standards of 'literariness'. I want to make connections, therefore, between feminist fiction and the writing of other social movements, in order to show their common ground as oppositional literatures of non-dominant groups.

The first, and possibly the most unexpected, connection is that between 1930s socialist women's writing and feminist fiction of the 1970s and 1980s, a connection which I sketch out in order to contextualise recent feminist fiction in American literary history and to place it in a tradition of American women's political writing. Lines of ancestry from the 1930s to the 1970s and 1980s can be traced not only in conscious influence and explicit acknowledgement, but also in a more submerged common strategy arising from the problems posed by a cultural practice which seeks to represent the unrepresented.

In an article on Zora Neale Hurston, Lorraine Bethel explains the difficulty:

> Zora Neale Hurston's work . . . exemplifies the immense potential contained in the Black female literary tradition for the resolution of critical aesthetic and political problems common to both the Afro-American and the American female literary traditions. Foremost among these problems is the question of how Black/female writers can create a body of literature capable of capturing the political and cultural realities of their experience while using literary forms created by and for white, upper class men.
>
> (Bethel 1982: 177)

Bethel sets up an interesting dichotomy between white upper class male literary form on the one hand, and Black, female (and, we might add, working class) realities on the other. Such a dichotomy has become all too familiar in recent feminist criticism where it has simplistically been re-interpreted as an opposition between art and experience, as we saw in the Gallop quotation above. Bethel, by contrast, links this opposition to the aesthetic problems of non-dominant representation, or in bell hooks' words, of counter-hegemonic cultural practice (hooks 1990c: 4). Of course, problems are never static, just as the 'dominant' and the 'non-dominant' sectors of culture and society are never absolute nor static but continually change in the struggle for cultural and political hegemony, as Raymond Williams has repeatedly shown.[2] But my point is that one constant within this struggle remains: that an oppositional culture of non-dominant groups has to define itself against the practices and ideology of the dominant group (or groups), and this inevitably has consequences for form. Indeed, only a very unsophisticated literary criticism could conceive of form and content as distinct entities.

To give an example: within this oppositional relation it is a common strategic move to make epistemological claims for reality, experience and truth as the privileged domain of the oppressed, whilst the dominant mainstream is debited with (ideological) fiction, artifice and untruth as characteristic of its cultural projects. We see this both in 1970s feminist and 1930s socialist writing, where an epistemological realism on behalf of women and working people respectively is self-consciously articulated in realist modes of literary representation against a dominant of modernist and postmodernist writing. Yet it is important to stress that valid claims to political radicalism can (and were, and are) made for (post)modernist modes of representation as well; the virulent debates within Marxist aesthetic theory of the 1920s and 1930s (and those of today) demonstrate that realism – in a different context – is as easily equated with bourgeois ideology as it can be enlisted in the service of revealing 'the real conditions of our existence'. The question is what kind of realism we are talking about, and what its position vis à vis the dominant is. Terry Lovell concludes rightly in *Pictures of Reality* that there is no necessary connection between epistemological and literary realism; whether they coexist in an oppositional cultural practice depends on the condition of the dominant (Lovell 1983a: 98). Formal experimentation, distantiation, fragmentation, parody and fantasy can, therefore, also have an important politicising role to play in the writing of non-dominant groups; the variety of literary forms and genres employed by contemporary feminist writers is a case in point. But we have to bear in mind that if this is so, then the aesthetic solutions adopted by non-dominant groups in their project of self-representation need to be studied within the oppositional dynamics of a dominant/non-dominant cultural spectrum. In the extract quoted above Lorraine Bethel hints at Hurston's achievement in forging a nonupperclasswhitemale literary discourse. In the case of 1930s socialist and 1970s feminist writers then we are looking for an aesthetic which similarly defines itself in opposition to an historically specific dominant.

This approach clearly demands a recontextualisation of 1930s writing, which I present in the first chapter. I do this not in the naïve belief that an unproblematic foray into the past stripped of contemporary critical insights is possible, but rather to suggest that the relation between 1930s women's writing and that of 1970s feminists consists in the common (not the same) problems of forging a counter-hegemonic cultural-political discourse. The self-identified literature of class and race (socialist and African-American writing of the 1930s and 1940s), when put in dialogue with the literature of gender (feminist writing of the 1970s and 1980s), produces new readings in which these familiar categories of oppression are redefined and seen to be reflecting upon each other. I adapt here to my own purposes what Cora Kaplan writes of literary discourse:

> Class and race ideologies are . . . steeped in and spoken through the language of sexual differentiation. Class and race meanings are not metaphors for the sexual, or vice versa. It is better, though not exact, to see them as reciprocally constituting each other through a kind of narrative invocation, a set of associative terms in a chain of meaning. To understand how gender and class – to take two categories only – are articulated together transforms our analysis of each of them.
>
> (Kaplan 1986: 149)

To sketch such a tradition of political women's writing is to reject the concept of a female aesthetic (even if the possibility of a feminist one remains open). If contemporary feminist writing is to be defined as a mode of political writing motivated by the interests of a social movement (a counter-hegemonic cultural formation), then clearly feminist fiction is studied more usefully in comparison with the cultural practices of other social movements than with, say, the work of other contemporary women writers like Alison Lurie or Louise Erdrich or even Joyce Carol Oates or Jayne Anne Phillips, simply because they are women. This approach differs from that of most recent feminist criticism. Paulina Palmer, Rita Felski, Patricia Duncker, Gayle Greene, Patricia Waugh and Anne Cranny Francis have all published books on what can be loosely termed feminist fiction, but they have seen this writing as specific to the politics of gender. Reading feminist fiction as uniquely the product of the Second Wave Women's Movement, they do not take the cultural practices of other social movements of the 1960s – from which the Women's Movement took its cue – into account. Besides, most of these critics have treated feminism and feminist writing in an international frame, thus eliding differences between specific national cultural traditions and discourses (American, British and European).[3]

In my view American feminist fiction is embedded in a very specific, and very specifically American, cultural and political arena. My aim is not only to outline a tradition of women's political writing in the twentieth century, but also to locate this tradition within American cultural debates, in which realism figures very prominently.

Liberating Literature covers a broad sweep of American women's writing in relation to twentieth century social movements. Starting in the 1930s, it

6

discusses women's writing generated by the literary culture of the Communist Party and that of the Harlem Renaissance, and ending in the 1980s it reads more recent women's texts as backlash fictions which exemplify the defensive retreat of feminism under the impact of economic recession and the ideological offensives of the New Right. An analysis of feminist fiction of the 1970s and 1980s, in conjunction with the histories of Women's Liberation, the Black Civil Rights Movement and the New Left, forms the main body of this book.

Inevitably, such a trajectory through the decades narrativises literary history. The story I want to tell is that of the rise and demise of feminist fiction as an oppositional cultural practice, which shadows and interprets the rise and demise of Second Wave American feminism. At the same time I want to chart the dynamic relation between changing conceptions of politics and changes in modes of representation, because formal aspects of feminist writing are never naturally given nor purely a matter of experimentation – they are textual strategies with political effect.

In the first chapter, I suggest that American feminist fiction of the Second Wave can be read as a personal/political re-writing of socialist-realist women's texts earlier in the century, such as Agnes Smedley's *Daughter of Earth*, Meridel LeSueur's *The Girl*, Ann Petry's *The Street* and Josephine Herbst's *Rope of Gold*. This connection has not to my knowledge been investigated in detail, even if a growing body of criticism on 1930s women writers now does exist.[4] As I see it, the work of individual 1930s figures such as Tillie Olsen and Zora Neale Hurston was claimed by feminist criticism as a literature concerned with gender politics *avant la lettre*, and thus incorporated into a new canon of American feminist writing. But this appropriation of a selected sample of 1930s writing resulted in an historical displacement, a zooming-in on gender which precluded a more wide-angled view of these writers' achievements in the context of the cultural movements of their time. Undoubtedly recent feminist criticism has produced fruitful new ways of reading Olsen and Hurston, but it has also tended to treat each writer in isolation from their concerns with racial and class struggles, and as exceptional in relation to the literature of their period. I want to question this exceptionalism and the underlying assumption that social movements on the whole produce bad writing, because they have a simplistic, instrumental view of the role of culture in social change. Rather, I want to problematise the whole notion of bad writing, and ask: bad for what? bad for whom? bad by which criteria?

I think that the new focus on gender issues obscured a sense of writers like Olsen and Hurston working as part of a social movement, a cultural climate within which they were neither unique nor – in that hackneyed sense – ahead of their time. On the contrary: they were very much of their time and their place, so much so that to trace parallels between their cultural practices and those of 1970s feminists is not to commit the sin of presentism and appropriation all over again, but to elucidate different articulations of similar aesthetic and thematic problems and to locate these differences in their historical moments.

I look at feminist fiction's underlying political discourses in the second chapter, where I chart the history of the Second Wave Women's Movement, and more particularly Women's Liberation, from its beginnings in Civil Rights and the New Left of the 1960s to its demise at the hands of the New Right. I suggest that Women's Liberation's conception of personal politics hampered its development from a grass roots movement into an effective political force, but rendered it extremely successful in the cultural arena.

After this historical excursion, the emergence of feminist fiction as a politically interested cultural practice written for, by and about women is examined in Chapter 3. Drawing on popular forms and female genres as traditionally defined, feminist fiction of the 1970s at the same time subverted these forms and questioned the inscription of women in the literary tradition. Here I engage in greater detail with the critical debate over feminist realism, in a brief survey of feminist fiction's development and reception in relation to the history of the Women's Movement. I read the pseudo-autobiographical novels of Marilyn French, Rita Mae Brown, Erica Jong and others, not as individualist confessional writing – as some recent feminist criticism has dismissively done – but as explorations of feminist subjectivity and the process of coming to consciousness.

In Chapter 4 I support this reading both theoretically and critically, in showing that feminist first person narratives can be theorised as fictions of subjectivity which contest dominant definitions of gender and construct an evolving feminist subject.

Taking issue with feminist critics (Rita Felski and Rosalind Coward among them) who have argued that feminist first person narratives posit a unified and universalised female identity, I demonstrate in my readings of Lessing's *The Golden Notebook*, French's *The Women's Room*, Millett's *Flying*, Maya Angelou's autobiographical *œuvre* and Audre Lorde's *Zami* that feminist fictions of subjectivity are much more diverse and complex than these critics' categorisation of them in terms of the confessional has tended to suggest.[5] What they have in common, and what characterises them as political texts of feminism, is not that they tell the story of 'how I became my own person', in Rosalind Coward's words, but that they assert the need for radical social change, whether that change is envisioned in Utopian fantasy of a feminist future or articulated in a critique of existing gender, race and class relations (Coward 1989).

Since little single-text criticism of feminist fiction is as yet available, and in order to show that such criticism can open up new avenues for a feminist reading practice, I offer in-depth readings of two texts in Chapters 5 and 6. Alice Walker's *Meridian* and Marge Piercy's *Vida* provide good case studies for the aesthetic of counter-hegemonic writing. Chapter 5 is wholly devoted to a discussion of *Meridian*, a novel which returns to the 1960s breeding ground of feminism and examines the cultural and political legacy of the Civil Rights Movement. Walker's imaginative reconstruction of African-American history as well as Black female subjectivity is, I suggest, embodied in the formal fragmentation of the text which intertwines poetic/mythical and realist strands of narrative. Combining historicist criticism with psycho-analytical insights, I read *Meridian* as an hysterical text, which takes the collective working-through of African-American history and culture as its central problematic. In addition, I show that Walker's writing harks back to an earlier moment in the African-American literary tradition and can be seen to interrogate both white feminist fictions of subjectivity and Black male writing from a vantage point closer to that of the Harlem Renaissance than to the Black Aesthetic movement of the 1960s.

An historicist/psychoanalytical perspective also informs my reading of *Vida* in Chapter 6. Like Alice Walker, Piercy in this novel re-writes radical history, as a comparison with recent historiography of the student New Left reveals. There are links with 1930s women's political writing here too, but *Vida*'s realism is a Utopian realism which locates a vision of social and personal change in the feminist future whilst acknowledging the demise of 1960s Left radicalism. In my reading, Utopian fantasy and realism are held in suspense in *Vida*'s figurative frame of paranoia, which functions to articulate the problems of feminism on the threshold of the Reagan era, but displaces it on to the fate of the revolutionary New Left.

Alice Walker's and Marge Piercy's reconstructions of radical history and their visions of a changed social order are contrasted in the final chapter with three texts reflecting on the American 1980s in a cultural climate which was much more hostile to feminism. Margaret Atwood's *The Handmaid's Tale*, Marge Piercy's *Braided Lives*, and Sue Miller's *The Good Mother* all articulate an awareness of changed historical conditions, in which the gains of Second Wave feminism can no longer be taken for granted, let alone extended.[6] The battle over the meanings of radical history continues in these texts, but it now rages over the legacy of Women's Liberation. Utopian realism of the earlier period gives way to dystopian scenarios, notably in Atwood's chilling fantasy of a Christian fundamentalist society but also in Sue Miller's new, old-style realism which posits an existing patriarchal social order as fixed and unchangeable.

This story of American women's political writing might give the impression of narrative closure in the post-feminist present. That impression is counter-acted, to some extent, by my Conclusion, in which I return to feminist fiction as counter-hegemonic writing. It is in the novels of the white, middle class constituency which pioneered feminist fiction that realism and fantasy modes of representation lose their political charge, which again shows that particular literary forms are not in and of themselves radical in the political sense. At the same time the continuing popular and academic demand for new feminist fiction is met by new generations of African-American, Chicano, Latino and Chinese-American writers who in their turn re-envision and reconceptualise the personal and political, the popular and the literary, the various configurations of race, class, gender, ethnicity and sexual orientation in an imaginative engagement with feminism. It is the rise of this new feminist fiction that forces the question of the 1990s: post-feminism? whose post-feminism?

1

'THIS STORY MUST BE TOLD'
Women writers of the 1930s

> My vision is very different from that of most writers . . . I don't think in terms of quests for identity to explain human motivation and behaviour. I feel that in a world where class, race and sex are so determining, that that has little reality. What matters to me is the soil *out* of which people have to grow, and the kind of climate around them; circumstances are the primary key and not the personal quest for identity . . . I want to write what will help change that which is harmful for human beings in our time.
>
> (Tillie Olsen, cited by Deborah Rosenfelt 1985: 245)[1]

If any writer deserves the accolade of spanning two generations of political women's writing, then surely it is Tillie Olsen. She began her literary career in the 1930s and survived those years (but barely) with the demands of paid work, domestic labour, childcare, political organising and writing all competing for her time and energy. In the more comfortable material conditions of the 1950s, McCarthyism created an ideological climate in which her writing could not flourish. It was only in the 1960s and 1970s that Tillie Olsen started writing seriously again and found an audience for her work in the new discursive space that Second Wave feminism had created for women's writing. Her collection of essays, *Silences*, and the short stories in *Tell Me a Riddle* were published and republished and gained a deservedly feminist reputation for the insights into the conditions of women's lives and letters that they offered. Yet *Silences*, unlike Woolf's *A Room of One's Own*, Mary Ellmann's *Thinking about Women* or Joanna Russ' *How to Suppress Women's Writing* is not a book about women and literature, just as the stories in *Tell Me a Riddle* are not about gender politics *per se*. Tillie Olsen's work is, indeed, not like that of most other feminist writers. It spans a much wider range of political concerns, in which class figures prominently as well as race. As the title of her only novel *Yonnondio: from the Thirties* and that of Deborah Rosenfelt's path-breaking essay on Olsen indicates, her motivation and her aesthetic programme always came from the 1930s and remain rooted there.

11

So when Olsen, in a speech in 1974 cited above, opposed the writing of identity and introspection to that of circumstance, she contrasted her own work with bourgeois fiction, and she validated realism against the interiority, in both form and subject matter, of modernism and post-modernism. That Olsen could make her critique of a literature of identity applicable to both the 1930s and the 1970s is perhaps unique to her; that she did so in terms of forces of circumstance and a desire to 'help change that which is harmful to human beings in our time' is characteristic of 1930s socialist writing as a whole.[2]

In the history of American literature the 1930s stand out as the decade of the Left, a time when cultural debate was automatically also political debate, and a time which saw the rise of the socialist realist novel. To be sure, this was not the first time that bottom dog stories were being written, nor was it the first time that non-dominant groups entered the literary arena to write on their own behalf – African-Americans like Frederick Douglass and Harriet Jacobs had done so long before the protest novel or proletarian fiction were even invented. What was new about the 1930s was that writers, readers and critics converged for a few short years in a cultural movement around the American Communist Party, professing their allegiance to a political cause (communism and socialism in the early years, anti-fascism later) and demanding radical change in American society. As Günter Lenz writes:

> It was during the 1930s that for the first time in American history the forms, roles, and functions of 'literature', of 'American' 'culture', of 'documentary expression', of 'modernism', of the institutions of 'Art' were *fundamentally questioned, contested and redefined in the public culture at large as well as in critical thought.*
>
> (Lenz 1990: 95)

Women were integral to this movement as workers, as organisers, and as writers – sometimes as all three. And even when women writers were not literally engaged in all three activities at the same time, they still saw themselves less as artists than as cultural workers whose writing had a role in political organising as well.

> She speaks to the ten greatest American women:
> The anonymous farmer's wife, the anonymous clubbed picket,
> the anonymous Negro women who held off the guns,
> the anonymous prisoner, anonymous cotton-picker
> trailing her robe of sack in a proud train,
> anonymous writer of these and mill-hand, anonymous city walker,
> anonymous organizer, anonymous binder of the illegally wounded,
> anonymous feeder and speaker to anonymous squares.
>
> (Rukeyser 1938: 137)[3]

12

Muriel Rukeyser's poem 'Ann Burlak', from which this passage is taken, was not just a praisesong for a real-life political activist, but also a reflection upon the poet's political role. 'Ann Burlak' enacts in poetic form what Grace Hutchins argues in 'Women under Capitalism', that writers, historians and journalists have a crucial role to play in the elevation of the oppressed to the status of new historical subjects:

> This story of organization and struggle must be told . . . of women workers at home and on the farms, in domestic service, in offices, stores, hospitals and restaurants, and in factories . . . their grievances, their demands, their aspirations for a classless society; the story of their struggles – their defeats and their victories.
>
> (Hutchins 1934b: 334)

Feminist fiction, which took its political cue from Women's Liberation, was the product of a similar conception of the role of writing in social movements. In the 1970s, feminists saw themselves as giving voice to the unrecorded lives of anonymous women in the way that Muriel Rukeyser, Tillie Olsen, Meridel LeSueur and others had viewed their work as part of the class struggle in the 1930s. Like the writers of the 1930s also, feminists defined their cultural practices against that of a literary establishment which had abdicated responsibility for the social and political functions of art and taken refuge in interiority and self-reflexiveness instead. The poet and novelist Marge Piercy signalled the distance between the mainstream of American poetry and the new movement poets when she wrote in 1972 that 'Maybe we could say that the grandfathers and those who came in between were men of letters, whereas we are people of the voice' (Piercy and Lourie 1972: 74).

In contrasting men with people, and letters with voice Piercy highlights both the different class and gender basis of the new poetry, as well as her ambitions to reroot art not in literature but in speech, the soil of everyday life.

On these grounds, Deborah Rosenfelt has drawn parallels between the work of 1930s writers such as Olsen, LeSueur, Josephine Herbst and Tess Slesinger and New Left feminists like Alice Walker, Piercy and Grace Paley. Black feminist writers have, in another connection, frequently acknowledged Zora Neale Hurston's importance for contemporary African-American women's writing, with a similar emphasis on voice and the literary emancipation of the marginal subject.[4] Although Hurston certainly does not belong to the Left, her relation to the cultural movement of the Harlem Renaissance is comparable to the position of socialist women writers in the culture of the Old Left: central, but considered marginal in their day because of their gender and their adaptations of the movements' agendas to their own ends. Hurston's example in the 1930s draws a direct line from the Harlem Renaissance to the current revival in African-American literature.

13

Yet in a more specific sense, the connections – both overt and covert – between New and Old Left and between 1930s and contemporary African-American women writers remain to be uncovered. Contrary to stereotype, the questions which feminist writing asks of literature are concerned not only with matters of content, or with the demand for positive images of women in fiction, but also (and crucially) with the role of culture in movements for social change. These questions echo problems faced by the socialist and African-American women writers of the 1930s. What is the role of literature in socialist/feminist/African-American politics? Can there be a politicising art which is neither facile nor strictly doctrinaire, but which can raise consciousness in an imaginative way? If this art should address itself to the unconverted, does this mean that popular forms and genres should have priority? Or does oppositional writing demand new forms to enable a critique of the conservatism of mass culture?[5] These questions were and are pertinent to a discussion of both 1970s and 1930s women's writing, but they are also questions which in recent years have come to seem slightly old-fashioned. Under the influence of contemporary literary theory modernist, and lately also postmodernist writing has been enshrined into literary history as the twentieth century's dominant paradigms. In John Barth's famous phrase literature would never be the same again after James Joyce; in Jerome Klinkowitz's words a postmodernist art would mean 'an art freed from the demands of representation' (Barth 1967: 74; Klinkowitz 1980: 34). I want to argue here that indeed even realist modes of representation have not been the same since Joyce, but I also want to problematise the hierarchy of literary innovations which contemporary theory has created. Since the demise of Leavisite criticism, fragmentation, distantiation, and textual self-reflexiveness have been celebrated as hallmarks of twentieth century writing. And conversely, the supposedly straightforward realism of the nineteenth century novel has been deplored as signally lacking – not just in textual, but also in ideological self-awareness.[6] Structuralism and post-structuralism's unfortunate heritage in the critical domain is, as I see it, that literary innovation has become equated with formal innovation in the narrowest of terms. Twentieth century realisms have been the major casualty in this critical work. Thus what was new about socialist and feminist realisms in the 1930s and 1970s, e.g. their counter-hegemonic uses of realism, which were by no means unselfconscious, has once more become obscured in contemporary criticism. Far from colluding with dominant ideology and common-sense perceptions of reality, both these kinds of realism challenged the way of the world and either posited or implied a radically alternative social order. And far from returning to nineteenth century literary modes, both these kinds of realism were aware of their status as counter-hegemonic constructions, rather than pictures, of reality. Such awareness points to the radical otherness of socialist, feminist and African-American realisms. It is an otherness which resides in the recognition that

14

non-dominant groups in the twentieth century are travelling in the opposite direction from that of their whitemaleupperclass counterparts: from margin to centre, from absence to presence and from the autonomous to the social text.

RADICAL REALISM: AGNES SMEDLEY'S
DAUGHTER OF EARTH

We start in 1929, the year of the stock-market crash and the official beginning of the Depression. The year also in which Michael Gold, architect of the cultural programme of the American Communist Party, wrote his (in)famous essay 'Go Left, Young Writers!' in which he issued his call to the workers of the world to write:

> Do not be passive. Write. Your life in mine, mill and farm is of deathless significance to the history of the world. Tell us about it in the same language you use in writing a letter. It may be literature – it often is. Write. Persist. Struggle.
>
> (Gold 1929a: 189)[7]

Agnes Smedley's novel *Daughter of Earth* was also published in 1929, and might be taken as an unwitting response to Gold's appeal. Despite its melodramatic passages, and despite its central theme of a woman's struggle for sexual and financial independence, Michael Gold read *Daughter of Earth* as an exemplary proletarian realist novel. Ignoring Smedley's gender politics, so obvious to feminist readers now, Gold stressed the novel's proletarian merits: it was about working class life and it did not 'adorn, stylise or pose' (Gold 1929b: 191). We can measure the distance between contemporary feminist and 1930s socialist critical preoccupations quite effectively when we contrast Gold's judgement with that of Rosalind Delmar in her Afterword to the Virago edition of *Daughter of Earth*. Smedley employs a first person narrator, Marie Rogers, to tell a story which closely resembles that of Agnes Smedley's life and Delmar comments upon the rationale for a fictionalised autobiography:

> Her decision in favour of the novel form marks an important insight: that to attempt such a work of reconstruction, to give oneself a sense of coherence and continuity, requires a creative effort of the imagination and implies some awareness that we are all, to ourselves, fictional characters.
>
> (Delmar in Smedley 1984: 271)

Typically, Gold sees representativeness in the individual's narrative, which is therefore about working class life, whereas Delmar reads textual self-consciousness in the fictionalisation of the self. It is possible that Delmar knew what Gold did not: that the writing of *Daughter of Earth* was inspired by the author's experience of psychoanalysis. Even so, such biographical data need not automatically lead us to an autobiographical reading of this novel; Gold's focus on class has as much validity, as much support in the text as has Delmar's privileging of subjectivity – as we shall see.

Daughter of Earth was written in Denmark, during a stay with Karen Michaelis (Smedley's friend and source for the Karen character in the novel) after Smedley had been in psychoanalysis for a year in Germany with a woman analyst of the Berlin school.[8] If the fictional character of Marie Rogers can be regarded in Delmar's terms as the author's attempt to reconstruct herself in language, then this insight must nevertheless guard us against seeing the writing of *Daughter of Earth* as merely (or even chiefly) a therapeutic exercise. For Smedley had another purpose in mind, much more akin to Gold's conception of the role of culture in politics: 'I do not write mere words. I write of human flesh and blood. There is a hatred and a bitterness with roots in experience and conviction. *Words cannot erase that experience.*' (My *italics* Smedley 1929: 168).

Writing is presented here not simply as an act of individual expression or salvation (although it may be that as well), but as recording suffering which is held to be representative of that of the (female) working class. Only those who believe in the talking cure can believe that 'words erase experience' – Smedley's narrator does not.

During his time as editor of *New Masses* and advocate of proletarian realism as a cultural weapon in class struggle, Michael Gold was a powerful critic, who wielded a poisonous pen whenever he could smell even a whiff of individualism in the literary air. A novel like *Daughter of Earth* would certainly have suffered under that pen, if it had not been for Smedley's invitation in the first few lines of her novel to read it as an indictment of American class society and, along with it, dominant standards of fine writing:

> Before me stretches a Danish sea. Cold, grey, limitless. There is no horizon . . . What I have written is not a work of beauty, created that someone might spend an hour pleasantly; not a symphony to lift up the spirit, to release it from the dreariness of reality. It is the story of a life, written in desperation, in unhappiness.
>
> (Smedley 1929: 1)

This opening introduces themes which are characteristic of counter-hegemonic writing and which have echoed in feminist fiction since. What we have here is no apology for raw writing, but a militant assertion of the political and cognitive function of art as opposed to that of entertainment. Stylistic niceties, associated with the literary, are inappropriate to this project because they cannot convey the harshness of working class life. The opening of *Daughter of Earth* expresses an awareness of the non-literary status of such a life; literature, after all, has overwhelmingly portrayed the condition of the middle classes. Marilyn French uses the same image of the sea to frame her narrative in *The Women's Room*, and narratorial interventions in that novel also serve to explain that literary language will not do to tell a woman's story, tainted as it is by centuries of masculinist abuse in the representation of women. Feminist and socialist literary discourses for Smedley and French demand plain language, but they also require broken-up forms, despite a surface appearance of linear narrative. In *Daughter of Earth*, the writing of Marie Rogers' life is compared with the making of a quilt – the choice is between a blue quilt and a crazy quilt of many colours, both cherished objects of childhood. Gathering up the fragments of a life, the narrator opts for the model of a crazy quilt, thus refusing a smooth blue narrative in which different blocks still create even colour. Alice Walker and Marge Piercy were later to use the patchwork quilt in much the same way, as an image of artistic production, using everyday life and history as its raw materials.[9]

Yet contrary to Gold's prescriptive aesthetic for the proletarian novel, which should document class oppression but also herald the dawn of a socialist future, *Daughter of Earth* offers no release from 'the dreariness of reality' and remains without an horizon, even if the demand for social change is always clear. Perhaps it is here, in the refusal of narrative closure and the absence of political solution, that Smedley's gendered rewriting of the proletarian form reveals itself. The novel ends on a note of despairing escape: 'Out of this house, out of this country' (Smedket 1929: 270) – the last of many hasty and forced departures in a tale restlessly moving from one form of violence to another, one deprivation to another kind of poverty, one source of danger to another den of iniquity. Because of its relentless documentation of such hardships Smedley's novel could be described as radical realism, a realism resolutely opposed to that of the nineteenth century bourgeois novel as much as to early twentieth century modernism. The reality represented here has no redeeming features, and Smedley's construction of it offers no escape, no comfortable truths to soothe the soul. The only comfort that realism can bring in *Daughter of Earth* is to help gain an understanding of the world in order to change it.

Marie Rogers' story, which traces her development from a dirt-poor farmer's child in Missouri into a successful New York journalist, cannot, therefore, be a familiar tale of upward mobility and 'making it'. We might call it an American nightmare: sheer hard work which gets you nowhere, fast, lots of times. Class and gender loom large in this text as the twin conditions governing Marie's life. The father's belief in the American dream, turning himself from a farmer into an entrepreneur, makes for an unstable childhood of endless travel and uprooting, later reproduced in Marie's own – involuntary – restlessness. Poverty leads to domestic violence and the example of a long-suffering and powerless mother inspires contempt for women, for the violent institution of marriage and for femininity itself in the young girl. These forces of oppression are only partially compensated for by the joys of education and the life of the imagination, inspired particularly by the father's storytelling. Early on in the novel a dichotomy is set up between the harshness of women's material and emotional existence (the mother's labour, violence and poverty, reproduction) and the dreams, stories and physical power associated with masculinity (the father's aspirations, capacity for pleasure, and the cowboys' freedom to roam the American West). In opting for the latter kind of existence Marie chooses the adventure of the crazy quilt, but in the end her story testifies to the impossibility of living a man's existence in a woman's body – leading to breakdown and 'craziness'.

The West is important in *Daughter of Earth* as a consistent metaphor, not only for the gender-role transgression of frontierswomen bearing arms and riding around on horseback but also for Marie's identification with the Native American past.

Much is made of the father's Indian ancestry and of Marie's love of the land and of the Indians: 'Arizona penetrated my spirit and I felt no friendship for the American soldiers who had hunted and fought the Apache leader Geronimo . . . The Arizona desert came closer to my spirit than has any place I have ever known' (Smedley 1929: 116).

The fact that she is a 'native American' leads Marie to equate the truly American with the downtrodden – the peasants, the workers, the Indians. Later in the novel this love of the Indians is, by means of an interesting slippage, transliterated into involvement with the movement for the independence of India, and she eventually marries an Indian – from India. But although, as Paula Rabinowitz argues, this involvement briefly aligns Marie as a woman and political activist with the feminised image of non-Western and non-working class men, it does not bring her respite from her gendered existence. She is raped by one of the movement men, and her marriage fails as a result.[10] When her work for Indian independence lands her in jail, Marie is released by a man who exemplifies her ideal of the old, pre-capitalist America: 'A man of the West who fought for the traditions of the days when America was young and believed in freedom for all men' (Smedley 1929: 222).

That this freedom was never extended to the Indians (Native Americans) has, by this point in the narrative, curiously slipped her mind. This amnesia is only partially explained by the fact that Marie now realises that the ideal of the old democratic America has been superseded by the ravages of capitalism. Asked why she puts her energies into the cause of a people on another continent rather than working for her own country, Marie replies that she has no country, and that her countrymen are 'the men and women who work against oppression' (Smedley 1929: 236).

Class, internationalism and sexual politics are, in this way, all bound up in *Daughter of Earth*. Marie's answer is reminiscent of Virginia Woolf's famous statement that as a woman she has no country, and equally dismissive of patriotism as a cause which is alien to women and to the working class.

Smedley's Marie Rogers, however, is no feminist in any recognisable contemporary sense, as Marge Piercy noted in a review on the occasion of the novel's republication in the United States. Piercy complained of the absence of female solidarity in *Daughter of Earth*, and saw it as something that both marks the difference between the Old and the New Left in terms of a politics of personal life, but also as a failure which seriously undermines Smedley's feminist credentials.[11] Piercy is undoubtedly right to draw attention to the lack of an articulated gender politics in *Daughter of Earth*, but she in turn ignores the self-consciousness with which Smedley portrays her protagonist's contempt for (most, other) women. For it is not as if this contempt is presented as unproblematic or justified, for the narrator frequently comments upon and questions herself about her attitude towards other women. What is lacking in the text is not so much an understanding of women's situation (always also shaped by class and race) as a political vocabulary. Marie's refusal of marriage and motherhood are explained as avenues not taken because they would tie her down to yet other forms of enforced labour. But this refusal is not generalised, as it would be later in Marilyn French's fiction, as an insight into marriage as an institution or as a critique of the sexual division of labour; Marie's observations remain implicit and pre-political.

A contemporary feminist reading of *Daughter of Earth* can unearth and rehabilitate these aspects of the novel, and suggest that Marie's self-conscious problematisation of a lack of solidarity with women can be read as a gender-exceptionalism, but also as a recognition of the inevitable tensions that a simple notion of sisterhood entails. *Daughter of Earth* then becomes a deeply ambiguous novel about class (and gender) politics, which at the same time as it dismisses traditional femininity (passivity and victimhood) and indicts class society, nevertheless depicts a revolutionary new female subject whose ability to act on the world is never in doubt. But neither is there any doubt about the cost, both psychic and material, of that active struggle for change. Contrary to Piercy's view this ambivalence about femininity may be a strength of the novel, rather than its weakness.

The history of the conception and writing of *Daughter of Earth* as informed and inspired by Smedley's psychoanalytic experience adds an interesting dimension to the moments of exclusion and persecutory paranoia which increasingly haunt the narrative and create the contradiction between active protagonist and female victim. Originally, Smedley had wanted to title her novel *The Outcast* or *An Outcast* (something which, incidentally, would never have passed muster with Michael Gold).[12] Read in the light of Smedley's psychoanalytic experience, the change to *Daughter of Earth* seems to indicate both an acceptance, after completion of the manuscript, of the bond with the father (metaphorically aligned with earth and the land throughout) and the construction of a more positive gendered identity of a woman rooted in 'the soil in which she grew'. Yet the ambivalence about psychoanalysis in the novel itself to some extent evidences Smedley's uneasiness about publicly proclaiming its benefits; psychoanalysis was, after all, regarded in socialist culture as the notorious individual solution inimical to collective struggle. So, on one hand, the portrayal of gender formation and the consequences of transgression in *Daughter of Earth* is undoubtedly psychoanalytically informed. The West is represented clearly as the breeding ground of a masculine kind of femininity out of step with cultural definitions of gender in other social environments, notably that of the smart set of New York intellectuals, and the circles of the Indian revolutionaries. In a letter to a friend Smedley once explained her 'deep castration complex' at length, and in so many words, as a consequence of growing up in the West and of being the daughter of a 'man of imagination, a Peer Gynt'.[13] Yet on the other hand, *Daughter of Earth* also contains explicit critiques of psychoanalysis in the cynical passages about New York intellectuals who try to explain away Marie Rogers' political commitments by pointing to her father complex. Thus the role of individualist psychology in class struggle is revealed as a middle class defence mechanism, in a manner which does acknowledge possible unconscious motivations for Marie's political stance, but at the same time necessarily subordinates that psychoanalytic view to political consciousness of the workings of capitalism.

Agnes Smedley's *Daughter of Earth* has echoes in much recent feminist fiction. Thematically, lines can be drawn to the movement novels of Marge Piercy (*Vida*), Alice Walker (*Meridian*), and Valerie Miner (*Movement*). Smedley's implied critique of marriage as a form of ownership, her insistence that women's economic independence is a condition of self-determination in every other sphere, and the centrality of the quest for non-alienated work are all themes that we now associate primarily with Second Wave feminism. And the crazy quilt metaphor has been used by many feminist writers as a fitting image of a political use-aesthetic of which formal fragmentation and unevenness is a deliberate and necessary characteristic.

As working class writing, Smedley's novel is also engaged in a critique of mainstream culture, which is another theme taken up by later feminists. Her emphasis on education as liberation (a traditional feature in proletarian fiction) entails an awareness of the class-specific basis of what is regarded as education, or culture. When Karin tries to educate Marie Rogers in poetry, the latter's reaction is one of bewilderment: 'I simply could not appreciate [the poems]. Only if they told a story of endeavour, of struggle, could I understand their purpose' (Smedley 1929: 156).

Similarly, when Marie is taken to the theatre by her friends, she is first confused and then bored:

> The play seemed to be about a married woman who saved up money until she could buy a typewriter and by it earn her own living. Such a silly thing to write a play about! The idea in itself was not sufficient to keep me fully awake.

> (Smedley 1929: 124)

This passage is obviously self-referential, because in a superficial sense *Daughter of Earth* is also about 'a married woman who buys a typewriter to earn her living by'. But despite its irony this scene draws attention to Marie's alienation from bourgeois culture, an alienation which is not solved by inserting herself into this cultural domain on middle class terms. Instead, Marie's alienation implies the necessity of a working class literature of her own, a literature of the kind she describes in her opening lines: not a work of beauty, but rooted in harsh experience. When Marge Piercy was asked in an interview whether 'the piling up of events in a short space of time' was characteristic of working class writing, she replied:

> A lot of the most admired writing of our time has to do with a tremendous paucity of experience – an immense amount of style expended on a paucity of experience. I think that probably both [Judy Grahn] and I respond to that, viewing it in part as a class phenomenon.

> (Piercy 1981–1982: 132–3)[14]

This – the privileging of style over material, over the experience of struggle – was precisely Smedley's fear and impelled her not only to write plainly, but to state that she was doing so. For however necessary writing is to understanding and communication, 'words cannot erase that experience'.

WRITING ON A BATTLEFIELD: TILLIE OLSEN'S *YONNONDIO* AND *TELL ME A RIDDLE*

Like Michael Gold and Agnes Smedley, Tillie Olsen, Meridel LeSueur and Josephine Herbst began their writing careers as journalists. They travelled around the country (and abroad) to document what they understood to be the final crisis of capitalism, and recorded the ravages of the Depression in the lives of working people. Finding themselves repeatedly caught up in industrial conflict, witnessing violence and acute poverty wherever they went, they often had to file their reports amidst chaos and the war-like

21

atmosphere of a world which had spun out of control. Tillie Olsen describes the effect this sense of emergency had upon her writing in 'The Strike':

> Do not ask me to write of the strike and the terror. I am on a battlefield, and the increasing stench and smoke sting the eyes so it is impossible to turn them back into the past . . . If I could go away for a while, if there were time and quiet, perhaps I could do it. All that has happened might resolve into order and sequence, fall into neat patterns of words.
>
> (Olsen 1934: 245)

In this passage Olsen not only literally describes the difficult conditions of reporting, but she also implies that traditional standards of fine writing are inappropriate to the circumstances in which 1930s writers found themselves. This is a recognition, yet again, that words cannot erase that experience, that what is required is a mode of representation and a quality of language which can effectively recreate the *feel* of crisis and deprivation. Michael Gold's aesthetic programme for proletarian realism was designed to do just this, to set the standards by which a truly politicising literature could be produced and judged. These standards included telling the truth about the havoc capitalism had wreaked upon American society, creating an art rooted in the everyday life of ordinary Americans, and employing a documentary realist style, which could be understood by working people: plain truths in plain language. Wilfully straightforward as this sounds, Gold very consciously saw documentary realism as a counter-hegemonic form, conceived in opposition to the vulgarity of mass culture on one hand and modernist individualism and *Angst* on the other. Utz Riese concludes in his study of Gold's aesthetics that the objective of this double strategy was to undermine the dichotomy between high and low culture, but he also notes that Gold used his rhetorical fire primarily for attacks on modernism (Riese 1987: 153). Not only did Gold take issue with the modernists' credo that art should be autonomous, but he also criticised modernism for its alleged subjectivism, despair and loss of agency. Naturally this hostility was expressed in class terms: 'Artists have deemed themselves too long the aristocrats of mankind. That is why they have all become so sad and spiritually sterile', whereas 'the masses are never sterile' (Gold 1921: 65–6).

Clearly, the construction of modernism as mere subjective indulgence or a form of sophisticated escapism was a polemically exaggerated stab at the bourgeois class enemy rather than a judgement based on serious analysis and discussion of modernist works in the Communist press (such as would later take place on the European scene between Lukács, Brecht, Bloch and others).[15] Yet this equation of modernism with bourgeois culture (and, as we shall see, an effeminate bourgeois culture at that) did highlight important differences between avant-garde and realist aesthetic practices. It is because Tillie Olsen, as we saw earlier, largely shared Gold's view that her work should be seen in the light of this anti-modernist stance, which was common to most of the writers of the Left in the 1930s.

Throughout the 1930s, perhaps throughout her writing life, Tillie Olsen's sense of writing on a battlefield meant that she saw writing *as* a battlefield too. *Silences* documents not only the multiple cultural silences of oppressed groups and disadvantaged or simply 'blocked' individuals, but also the silences of her own career. *Yonnondio: from the Thirties*, Olsen's only novel, is both the product and the casualty of a silence stretching from the late 1930s until the early 1960s, when *Tell Me a Riddle* was first published. *Yonnondio* in its present form was put together by the author in 1973 out of fragments from old manuscripts, and the image of patching, of stitching together, is again appropriate for a text that bears the scars of the difficult conditions of its making. *Yonnondio* is set in the early 1930s in a Wyoming mining town, and traces the forced migrations of the Holbrook family from mine to farm to the slaughterhouses of the city. The novel dramatises capitalism's toll on the life of the family, in particular on that of Anna and her daughter Mazie. Because of the suffering dailiness of their existence, represented without pathos or sentimentality, *Yonnondio* is a harrowing read. Its stark realism conforms to Gold's prescription for the proletarian novel (but again without the happy ending), and has a polemical edge to it. Witness Olsen's description of a mining disaster, when wives, children and relatives are waiting at the pit-mouth to retrieve their dead. The narrative abruptly breaks off:

> And could you not make a cameo of this and pin it to your aesthetic hearts? So sharp it is, so clear, so classic. The shattered dusk, the mountain of culm, the tipple; clean lines, bare beauty – and carved against them . . . these black figures with bowed heads, waiting, waiting . . . You will have the cameo? Call it Rascoe, Wyoming, any of a thousand mine towns in America, the night of a mine blowup.
>
> (Olsen 1974: 30–1)

Neat patterns of words, polished writing, Olsen seems to be saying here, aestheticise and thereby anaesthetise readers to the effects of capitalist exploitation. The juxtaposition of the cameo image with human suffering, with the 'accidents' of labour, makes for a bitter contrast between a modernist aesthetic and Olsen's own literary commitment to document the cost of working class life. Michael Gold is not the only influence here, for the passage is also strongly reminiscent of Rebecca Harding Davis's story 'Life in the Iron Mills' so admired by Olsen in *Silences*: the same image of sculpture, the same critique of class relations and exploitation, the same mourning of a waste of creative life. In *Silences* Olsen reads 'Life in the Iron Mills' as a realist manifesto in a way that the highly symbolic dimension of Harding Davis's text does not quite warrant. Davis's story, in *Silences* as in

Yonnondio, is thus enlisted *post facto* in the service of a 1930s Left artistic creed in the battle against modernism.[16]

Not only literature, but language itself, is a bone of contention in Tillie Olsen's writing. A world in which 'race, class and gender are so determining' is also a world in which linguistic battles are fought out, because they embody those social and political power relations. 'Hey Sailor, What Ship?' in *Tell Me a Riddle* provides a good example of language as a battlefield. In this story the uses of polite versus street (or ship) language are related to class as well as gender difference. The sailor Whitey's swearing creates discord in the family with whom he stays whilst on shore leave. Whitey is denied access to the family's house 'because of the children', because it is not good for them to be around a drunk and especially one who speaks *like that*. The adolescent daughter Jeannie feels contempt for Whitey and is ashamed of him in front of her friends – yet she will take his money. Aware of her pretensions to social betterment, in contrast with his tramp's existence, Whitey starts addressing Jeannie as 'your royal highness' (Olsen 1980a: 40). Later Jeannie's mother Helen, a mother who like all Olsen's mothers has to take on the role of conciliator and soother of all ills, explains to Jeannie:

> There are worse words than swear words, there are words that hurt. When Whitey talks like that, it's everyday words; the men he lives with talk like that, that's all.
>   Well, not the kind of men I want to know. I don't go over to anybody's house and hear words like that.
>
> (Olsen 1980a: 44)

Class and gender are linked here through the politics of discursive difference: to Jeannie, Whitey's language is neither ladylike nor polite, but Helen counters that the quality of language is not a matter of absolutes, but of circumstance and situation: Whitey's friends 'don't hear the words, they hear what's behind them' (Olsen 1980a: 44).

That there are words worse than swear words is an insight which informs *Yonnondio* too. Here the passage about the mining disaster is followed by a sarcastic anticipation of the language the newspapers will use in reporting it: '"Unavoidable catastrophe . . . rushing equipment . . . bending every effort . . . sparing no expense . . . to save – or recover the bodies"' (Olsen 1974: 31).

This, we can see by implication, is what Helen would call bad language: the hypocritical euphemisms of the capitalist press are satirised by Olsen and exposed, not only as the platitudes of mass culture, but as a kind of linguistic violence.

In 'Oh Yes', also in *Tell Me a Riddle*, the issue of language and inequality surfaces again, this time as a marker of racial difference which destroys the

24

relationship between a white girl, Carol, and her black friend Parialee. Carol's dramatic confrontation with cultural difference as experienced in a black church service becomes her initiation into a *de facto* segregated social order at the same time as Parialee develops her highly creative and lyrical 'jivetalk and rhythmandblues', which codes her as unable (rather than resisting) to conform to the discursive norm of a standardised language. As a result, Parialee is sorted into an educationally inferior stream in Junior High. The girls experience a painful parting of their ways because of the pressures on each to fit in with their racial and cultural peers. Creativity, Olsen seems to be saying here, as in 'I Stand Here Ironing', is not a matter of talent alone – it is a matter of whether and where that talent can find a place in the culture: 'So all that is in her will not bloom – but in how many does it?' (Olsen 1980a: 23).

In 'Tell Me a Riddle', finally, it is not so much the politics of language itself as of culture, education, and reading which plays an important part in the rift between two elderly people, Eva and her husband David. This story traces Eva's gradual physical decline and regression, not to childhood but to her pre-American existence as an activist in Russia, imprisoned for her role in the 1905 revolution.[17] Eva's loss of control unleashes memories and silences which are finally given voice as her speech disintegrates into involuntary and broken-up monologues. Olsen's rendering of these, combined with shifting point of view and reported speech which reads like serial interior monologue (no quotation marks) rather than conventional dialogue, serve to represent in a highly effective and economical way the battlefield that Eva and David's relationship, their history as immigrants, and their family, have become. They do not communicate, yet Olsen's use of speech (Eva's) and narrative (David's) in confrontation with each other (cyclical dreamspeech versus linear progression and rational argument) in this story achieves for the reader an acute understanding of the subject-position of each. 'Tell Me a Riddle' is in many ways *the* story about the sexual division of labour and the damage it does to male/female relations; it is also a rare and precious representation of old age.

Such understanding and empathy as Olsen achieves in 'Tell Me a Riddle' can only be attributed to a didactic dimension in her writing, again akin to 'I Stand Here Ironing'. Here the mother's discourse, in all its ambivalence and complexity, addresses an undisclosed authority figure in a defence of, or *apologia* for her treatment of, a talented daughter. It is the reader who must – uncomfortably – take up the place of interrogator, only to shift position by the end and become the interrogat*ed*: what does it mean to be a good enough mother? and who is to judge?

Motherhood, in Olsen's work, is mother*ing*: neither idealised nor rejected, but always represented as a *praxis* preconditioned by social definitions of gender and rigidly circumscribed by material and historical circumstance. Women – mothers – are not innocents whose reproductive creativity places them outside of history; in *Yonnondio* Anna's physical disciplining of the children is presented as part of a cycle of violence which extends beyond individual tempers and family relations into the power relations of society at large. Writing motherhood into literature as labour and love, domestic work as real work (if also drudgery), and children's play as a site of universal creative potential is, perhaps, Tillie Olsen's greatest achievement in literary innovation. But it is an achievement, like the Korl woman statue in Rebecca Harding Davis's story, wrought from waste materials. It would take 'A Balzac a Chekhov to write it' as Eva despairingly says in 'Tell Me a Riddle' (Olsen 1980a: 109).

But Olsen has another, American, model too. Just as Michael Gold in the late 1930s recast the literature of the Left as the real American literature (as opposed to the class-tainted Modernism of the emigré set in Europe) and cited that most American of American poets, Walt Whitman, in its defence, so also does Tillie Olsen turn to Whitman as her literary forefather.[18] *Yonnondio* is named for his poem, and its meaning is lament: 'To-day gives place, and fades – the cities, farms, factories fade;/ A muffled sonorous sound, a wailing word is borne through the air for a moment,/ Then blank and gone and still, and utterly lost' (Olsen 1974: n.p.).

In the political context of Communism as twentieth century Americanism, and through the literary link with Whitman, Olsen unwittingly became an American Balzac/Chekhov, whose work documents and mourns the past and the passing of ordinary American lives which have gone hitherto unrecorded in history or literature. Where Agnes Smedley was still ambivalent about her role as a writer and the class mobility that role entailed (because 'words cannot erase that experience'), for Olsen words are an essential tool in the struggle for social change: writing is a battlefield.

SEXUAL DIFFERENCES: MERIDEL LESUEUR'S *THE GIRL* AND *HARVEST & SONG FOR MY TIME*

I have perhaps underplayed, so far, the extent to which Olsen's work was also radically at odds with the proletarian aesthetic; this was not a problem with *Tell Me a Riddle* because it was only published much later, but the very emphasis on gender as well as class that I have drawn out does not fit in well with 1930s Left culture. This is because Michael Gold and other male critics of the 1930s, as Candida Lacey has noted, consistently employed a virulently masculinist rhetoric which associated proletarian writing with virility and strength, whilst bourgeois art (with frequent reference to T. S. Eliot's *The Waste Land*) was equated with sterility, stagnation and death.[19] Any feminist critic of 1930s socialist women's writing is then faced with the question how writers like Tillie Olsen, Meridel LeSueur, Josephine Herbst, Agnes Smedley, Fielding Burke, Mary Heaton Vorse and a host of others who were members or fellow travellers of the Communist Party could articulate their gendered experience in a cultural environment which actively disparaged the feminine. Here, for example, is Philip Rahv:

> In the course of the last few years we have observed the rise of the proletarian movement in literature, comprising a drastic deviation from the 'nice and waterish' diet of emasculated, unsocial writing, perennially engaged in futilitarian introspection and constipated spiritual incubations.
>
> (Rahv, cited in Conroy and Johnson 1973: xiii)

In a similar vein Michael Gold described Walter Pater as someone who wrote 'like a fairy for a fairy' because he had been deprived of the masculine experience of working class life, and saw Marcel Proust as 'the master masturbator' (Gold cited by Aaron 1965: 257; Gold 1930: 206). In Gold's critical discourse, a series of binary oppositions was set up between virility and (effeminate) homosexuality, between collectivism and individualism, and between working class earthiness and middle class degeneracy in order to extol the virtues of proletarian literature and to expose the decadence of bourgeois art. Clearly, there was little legitimate discursive space for women in this battle of the masculinities: women writers who wanted to be taken seriously by their male peers had to insert themselves into the literary domain more or less on these sexist and homophobic terms, or be damned. Had Michael Gold not warned against the political dangers of feminine writing, when he proclaimed that reaction is always romantic and sentimental?

Romantic and sentimental the women writers of the 1930s certainly were not; the two feminists who have done substantive critical work in this area both agree that Tillie Olsen, Josephine Herbst, Meridel LeSueur and others did write their way out of this dilemma without either marginalising themselves as women nor by masquerading as men, nor as genderless workers. But their strategies were complex ones; whilst Candida Lacey argues that different women writers found different ways of subverting the masculinist proletarian aesthetic, Paula Rabinowitz stresses in *Labor and Desire* that gender issues were often unreadable to 1930s male critics, in the sense that they literally 'could not see it' (Rabinowitz 1991: 5). Gold's reading of *Daughter of Earth* as an exemplary proletarian novel demonstrates this, and the critical praise which greeted novels like Fielding Burke's *Call Home the Heart* must indicate a similar gender blind spot. Known as one of a group of strike-novels about the Southern textile mills, *Call Home the Heart* offers also, and crucially, an exploration of a woman's active sexual desire, yet this aspect seems to have eluded its reviewers.

Gold's critique of Modernism-as-subjectivism (as opposed to the documentary, scientific emphasis in Marxist art) is likewise present in such women's writing as Tillie Olsen's, but more problematically so than in the work of their male peers. For if femininity is always already aligned with bourgeois individualism in 1930s critical discourse, it is hard for women writers to have a narrative with a female protagonist which nevertheless conforms to the masculinist strictures of proletarian writing. Smedley solves this problem by projecting a masculinised, exceptional image of femininity in Marie Rogers, whilst Tillie Olsen's narrative perspective in *Yonnondio* foregrounds the experiences of Anna and her daughter Mazie but without allowing them to monopolise the novel. Meridel LeSueur's strategy in *The Girl* is, in a way, more militant than either of these because, as Paula Rabinowitz puts it, 'The mother as link between past and future becomes the metaphor for Communist revolutionary transformation – the birth of the new out of the old' (Rabinowitz 1991: 115).

Yet LeSueur's more outspoken gender politics did not come out of the blue. Women writers had some support in the Communist Party's political thought, too. A body of ideas concerning women's collective needs did exist (it included abortion rights, the availability of birth control and an end to the sexual double standard) and theorists like Grace Hutchins and Mary Inman were developing an analysis of women's subordination which not only informed the cultural work of Olsen, Herbst and LeSueur, but in many ways prefigured the political theory of the Second Wave Women's Movement forty years later.[20] As usual, the party line on women remained largely a matter of theory, of secondary importance, put off 'until after'. Party discipline demanded from its political activists wholesale dedication to the cause regardless of personal circumstances or family commitments, even if the sexual division of labour was being questioned (by women). Both female party workers and women writers who wanted to put their gendered experience on the political and cultural agenda therefore laid themselves open to charges of indulgence and narcissism. This may explain not only why there are so few first person narratives to be found in socialist women's writing of the 1930s, but also why any autobiographical material is carefully (if thinly) disguised in fictionalisations, as in Josephine Herbst's *Rope of Gold* and Smedley's *Daughter of Earth*. We can see the correspondence here between an aesthetic which proscribes subjectivism and a political *praxis* which demands that the personal be subordinated to the political. Long-standing Old Left activist Peggy Dennis, for example, wrote in 1979 of the 'lifetime commitment of Self not to oneself but to a collective activism governed and controlled by a structured organization that commanded total allegiance' (Dennis 1979: 454).[21]

She implied that this allegiance took a heavier toll from women than from men: motherhood and communist activism were incompatible, unless women surrendered their children to a full-time surrogate parent, a sacrifice Peggy Dennis was prepared to make.[22]

In Meridel LeSueur's work maternity takes on a different, rather more Utopian and romanticised hue: it is less a problem than *part* of the solution. She writes in an essay:

The source of American culture lies in the historic movement of
our people, and the artist must become voice, messenger, awakener,
sparking the inflammable silence, reflecting back the courage and
the beauty . . .

Capitalism is a world of ruins really, junk piles of machines, men,
women, bowls of dust . . . and in this sling and wound the people carry
their young, in the shades of their grief, in the thin shadow of their
hunger, hope and crops in their hands, in the dark of the machine,
only they have the future in their hands.

Only they.

(LeSueur 1956: 122, 239)[23]

This Whitmanesque, lyrical statement of Meridel LeSueur's aesthetic creed
(also a feminist rewrite of Gold's exhortation in 'Go Left, Young Writers')
introduces many of the metaphors and themes she was to employ consistently in a writing career spanning most of the century. As a political
activist cum writer, LeSueur was the product of a conjunction of social
movements. Her mother's life-long interest in feminism fed into her work,
as did both parents' involvement in the Farmer Labor Party of the Midwest
during the first three decades of her life. And there was also the International Workers of the World (IWW), which made her think of herself as
a worker-writer and as such severed (she might have said 'liberated') from
her middle class origins.

This quotation needs to be read carefully if we want to pick up the strands
of sexual difference which typify LeSueur's stance. There is an emphasis on
metaphors of birth throughout, there is the dimension of spiritual values, of
a refusal to elevate theory over emotion, and machines over crops, and
there is the notion of giving voice to a collective but silenced sensibility, of
movement. More than Agnes Smedley, more than Tillie Olsen also, Meridel
LeSueur saw herself as one who gave voice, and who would represent the
unrepresented through the use of documentary realism. The latter, as
Charlotte Nekola explains, was the ideal form of writing for a revolutionary
aesthetic because 'it raised political consciousness by linking one person
with larger political movements; it replaced private despair with mass
action' (Nekola 1987: 194). Documentary realism in fiction (what Lukács
called, with similar stress on representativeness, portrayal as distinct from
journalistic reportage) was the successor to proletarian realism in Michael
Gold's career as literary lawgiver, and defined as the writing *of* the masses –
not just *for* the masses. It was truly meant to record the voice of the people,
even if, as we now know in post-poststructuralist days, that voice of necessity
had to be a matter of textual effect.[24]

LeSueur's *The Girl* is a case in point. Its narrative is conveyed vividly and
economically through the girl's first-person voice combined with a good

deal of dialogue, which creates the illusion of conversations overheard. In her Afterword to the 1977 edition of the novel LeSueur enhances this illusion when she explains that the text was produced in collaboration with the people whose experience she wanted to use in the story of the girl: 'They looked upon me as the woman who wrote (like the old letterwriters) and who strangely and wonderfully insisted that their lives were not defeated, trashed, defenseless' (LeSueur 1977: 149).[25]

LeSueur sees her role as a writer here, in 1977, still in the terms that Michael Gold prescribed: as primarily an instrumental one, akin to the scribe, or the reporter who selects and simply tells what is 'there' to be told.

Typically for documentary realism, the girl (who remains nameless throughout to stress her representativeness) is caught up in a familiar cycle of poverty, sexual exploitation, violence and reproductive hazards. But the hopelessness of her condition is untypically offset by a community of women – barmaid, prostitute, an elderly woman who is mentally ill, and a Communist organiser – and by the girl's initiation into (hetero)sexual pleasure. This initiation is rendered particularly well with all its conflicting feelings of fear and violation as well as desire and fulfilment. And characteristically for LeSueur, pregnancy and childbirth are presented as the light at the end of a long dark tunnel. When the women talk about their 'hankering' (for food, shelter, and a better life) political and personal hopes for a better future are connected up in maternity:

> You want a head of lettuce. You think you're crazy and the world is crazy. Just something like lettuce, she said, and you feel like making a world where you can have a head of lettuce when you want it.
> Well, Belle said, you'll just have to make a baby, not a world.
>
> (LeSueur 1977: 124)

The Girl ends on an heroic, woman-identified note when the girl's baby (another girl, naturally) is born amidst the noises of a massive demonstration of women clamouring for food outside and the mimeograph machine spitting out leaflets in the middle of the floor: women, crowds, and writing all generating together and in unison.

Like Agnes Smedley, LeSueur also employs a polarity between masculine fantasy and female reality. In *The Girl*, Butch's classic American aspirations for social advancement are cast in sporting terms ('I'm a natural winner'; 'I like to beat everybody in the world') and the rhetoric of private ownership ('Be my own man. You better go with me I'm a winner' (LeSueur 1977: 7)). This verbosity and fantasising of the male characters though is not valued positively, as in *Daughter of Earth*, but is contrasted with a knowing female silence. The requirement for women to 'reflect men at twice their natural size' (in Virginia Woolf's words) is explored to similar ironic effect in one of LeSueur's short stories, 'To Hell With You, Mr. Blue' in *Harvest & Song for My Time*, where a woman shares a bus ride with a Butch-type character and

30

is regaled by a monologue of masculine self-importance. Put in the classic feminine position of listening and asking interested questions, the woman feeds his neurotic conceit:

> 'I've been around. I've seen things, lady. I've seen 'em come and go. I've been in some pretty important places.'
> 'Have you really?'
> 'Oh, certainly. I'm not a ham . . . I been in the big time. Don't you believe it?'
> 'Oh, sure, certainly, I believe anything you say.'
>
> (LeSueur 1982a: 56)

'Giving voice' would be a literal description of this story (it consists almost entirely of dialogue), only here it is not just a matter of giving voice to a woman's discourse, but more especially to its satire – a kind of double-talk, or speech with a forked tongue, akin to Zora Neale Hurston's bitter ironies.

Harvest presents a fine collection of short stories and some subtle erotic writing. As in *The Girl*, maternity is extolled as the productive force of a new future. In the title story pregnancy is figuratively bound to a nostalgia for the old world of pre-technological organic growth, preferred over the masculine new world phallicism of machinery. It is as if the 1930s and early 1940s, despite Gold's aesthetic prescriptions, provided a congenial climate for LeSueur's more experimental writing on female eroticism and women's communities; the stories in *Song for My Time*, published in the same volume but of a later date, are much less innovative, more stilted and defensive.

At a time and in an environment where definitions of gender were rigidly polarised, Meridel LeSueur then took the opposite course from Smedley in asserting a positive and strong femininity based on motherhood and female friendships – outside the nuclear family. But lest we take this for a feminist textual and sexual politics in the contemporary sense, it has to be said that these visions of female community are never articulated in terms of a demand for an autonomous political space for women, let alone women's sexual desire for each other. It may be that the Communist Left's view of homosexuality as a bourgeois aberration, a hangover from the bohemian Left of the 1920s, was operative here too. This means that if on one level LeSueur's representations of femininity based on difference and her critique of the nuclear family can be read as a cultural feminism *à la* Adrienne Rich *in statu nascendi*, at another it must be remembered that for LeSueur this hidden feminist agenda was always integrated with a materialist analysis. LeSueur's work then demonstrates that the privileging of sexual difference can be a polemical necessity, posited against a masculinist environment in the culture of the 1930s, rather than a sign or symptom of biological essentialism. Furthermore, in another departure from Goldian prescriptions and proscriptions for the 1930s novel, LeSueur is also aware

31

of the political uses of Utopian fantasy as a necessary extension of imaginative space beyond the grim present:

> There is some kind of extremity and willingness to walk blind that comes in any creation of a new and unseen thing . . . a creation of a future 'image', a future action that exists in the present even vaguely or only whispered.
>
> (LeSueur 1935b: 302)

Erotic writing was one of the ways in which LeSueur allowed herself to 'walk blind', and her Utopian communities of women were another. The thread of this feminist/socialist Utopianism has been taken up in contemporary feminist writing in multiple ways, from the feminist Utopias of Joanna Russ and Marge Piercy to Alice Walker's male–female relations and spiritual time-frames, in which all can be ultimately forgiven and redeemed.

A HISTORY OF FEELINGS: JOSEPHINE HERBST'S *ROPE OF GOLD*

Such optimism is lacking in Jospehine Herbst's end-of-an-era novel, *Rope of Gold*, where action and imagination, present and future are once more severed from each other.

> Jonathan had always believed that literature was not argument but the history of men's feelings, the search for the hidden springs of men's actions, and if he turned to farmers now, it was not as a substitute for a job undone.
>
> (Herbst 1939: 40)

Rope of Gold was published ten years after *Daughter of Earth* as the final volume in a trilogy.[26] By 1939 Michael Gold's influence was waning and the anti-fascist drive of the Popular Front allowed for more liberal interpretations of political writing – as proletarian fiction, *Rope of Gold* would certainly not have escaped censure. Herbst presents in this novel a cast of characters from all walks of life, and her scepticism about the probability of revolution is one of its major themes. Elinor Langer succinctly describes the problematic of *Rope of Gold* in the Afterword to the novel as 'the tension between the abstract historical forces and the individual life stories of the different sets of characters' (Langer 1984: 431). In Herbst's fictionalised historiography of the 1930s the Depression years are not just, or not primarily, characterised by economic hardship and industrial strife, but by intellectual and moral crisis with distressing consequences in personal life. *Rope of Gold* has a middle class couple, Jonathan and Victoria Chance, as the protagonists of a fragmented story told from multiple points of view. Walter Rideout states that Herbst had been influenced by the American expatriates in Europe whilst on journalistic assignments there, and this may explain why she uses a montage technique reminiscent of Dos Passos' trilogy *USA* – a modernist device, indeed. Seeing *Rope of Gold* primarily as a novel about the 'decline of the middle classes', it is unsurprising that Rideout should judge it a failure; on a feminist reading, by contrast, *Rope of Gold* comes into focus as an exploration of the tensions between public and private life at a time of political and social upheaval (Rideout 1956: 191, 193). Read like this, the novel questions, but posits no alternative to, Old Left masculinist notions of political agency which demand sacrifice and preclude any kind of private life. Marie Rogers's isolation in *Daughter of Earth*, and Victoria Chance's ultimate loneliness here diagnose – not unwittingly – the problem of personal politics in socialist thought, without being able to articulate that problem in terms of the necessity for both class, and gender, solidarity.

Unlike Meridel LeSueur, Josephine Herbst portrays her women characters as very much caught up in the inexorable and objective forces of history, and this sense of 'being at the mercy of history' (a phrase Marge Piercy uses in the close of her novel *Vida*) is pervasive in *Rope of Gold*. For Victoria Chance there is no supportive community of women to soften the blows, nor is motherhood an option as a way of making a new world. In their efforts to devise new ways of living, a mode of relationship in tune with the political urgencies of the time, Herbst's protagonists come up against obstacles larger than themselves. Amongst many other things, the novel charts the gradual dissolution of the Chances' open marriage where a sexual division of labour no longer exists and the partners are separated by their work for long stretches of time. When her husband decides to give up writing for political activism in the farmers' movement, Victoria steps into his shoes and becomes a journalist, often reporting on the very campaigns that Jonathan is involved with. Personal life soon takes second place, as Victoria tells Jonathan: 'The trouble is the earth's shaking, and we stand here talking about love' (Herbst 1939: 91).

At the same time, Victoria cannot see her writing as on a par with Jonathan's activism, and is scathing (as Marie Rogers was) about her middle class existence in New York intellectual circles:

> Victoria sniffed at them often enough and at what she called 'Marx, fifth hand', and she said a revolution was never fought by 'paper revolutionaries' with a feeling of pride that, though she herself might be working at a job in the city, Jonathan was actually putting his hand to the plow, for better or worse.

(Herbst 1939: 165)

Yet despite their role reversal and support for each other's work, traditional gender boundaries between the public and the private begin to assert themselves. For Jonathan, the classic Old Left masculinist ideal of a man unencumbered by emotional ties, wholly devoted to the cause, becomes a moral imperative:

Was it imagination, or did such men really exist or did they merely hide (as all men did) their troubles daily, those deep and personal woes that gnawed relentlessly at the very roots of a man's being. If such troubles gnawed, it was the act that counted, even as it counted in love or war.

(Herbst 1939: 240)

The problem also surfaces in the case of Steve Carson, the farm-worker and union organiser, but the conflict is cast in class terms as Carson takes a more determined stance against making 'a little nest for themselves and let the rest of the world go by', whilst Jonathan is given to what are presented as middle class doubts (Herbst 1939: 278).

Meanwhile Victoria, on a reporting assignment in Cuba, sheds her feminine city clothes for workman's overalls and mounts a horse to visit the distant *guerilleros*. For her it is not work which represents the puzzling but inexorable logic of history's demands, but psychic life:

They had electrical equipment, they knew history, she thought she understood something of the workings of the world and saw through its shams, but she had no guard against these curious superstitions of the senses, these creeping premonitions of the flesh.

(Herbst 1939: 234–5)

The short-story version of this episode entitled 'The Enemy' puts the issue even more clearly. In Cuba, the protagonist – here called Mrs. Sidney – receives the news that her husband has left her. 'She wasn't just a woman anymore. At that moment it seemed the most important thing in the world to be' (Herbst 1936: 103).[27]

The result is the same in both cases: through the loss of relationship, men are free to do what a man has to do, whereas the woman is defeminised and joins the public world reluctantly but completely, as all pretence at temporariness along with all hope that a dual existence is possible are abandoned. In this respect Herbst is a forerunner of modern feminism, posing throughout *Rope of Gold* the almost impossible dilemma of where social responsibility leaves off and personal life begins. It is the central theme of Marge Piercy's *Vida* and the subject of a major part of 1970s feminist theory. The slogan which redefined the problem in terms of 'the personal is political' (and was supposed to solve it) is, however, firmly tied to 1960s political activism and has little purchase on the situation of women in the Old Left, where masculinist notions of the footloose politico with intact sexual double standard still held sway. Significantly, *Rope of Gold* gives the last word to Steve Carson, the model male activist in the novel, as he faces the National Guard in a strike. By that time Victoria Chance has been left behind, desperately trying to hold on to a sense of agency and hope (and again prefiguring the ending of *Vida*):

I have myself . . . no one can take that away from me . . . But she need cry no more since there were those who shed blood, not tears . . . The road and fields were solid ground and the objects of the earth like sleepy animals were rising to their knees.

(Herbst 1939: 406)

Like Agnes Smedley in *Daughter of Earth*, Herbst's portrayal of Victoria Chance's fate is at odds with the solace found in the land and in a revolutionary future projected in these lines. In common with Smedley also, *Rope of Gold* is a fictionalised autobiography which confines its representation of sexual politics to heterosexuality only. Yet Elinor Langer implies in her Afterword that Victoria's adulterous affair with the German refugee Kurt Becher was based on Herbst's brief lesbian relationship with the painter Marion Greenwood – yet another example of self-censorship perhaps, in the increasingly sexually repressive climate of the Left which by that time had defined healthy sex in exclusively heterosexual terms.[28]

The work of Herbst and Smedley, Olsen and LeSueur challenges any simplistic notions of proletarian writing as a crude and didactic literature of conversion. All four writers shared, to varying degrees, a commitment to Michael Gold's cultural programme which spanned the decade, yet all four also tailored it to their own, gendered, purposes. Their conception of political writing, and their creative solutions in trying to represent the unrepresented enable us to read contemporary feminist fiction from a different and wider perspective than that of gender alone: a perspective which has an eye for both the literature of politics and the politics of literature.

'I WANT THE BOSS'S BED': ZORA NEALE HURSTON AND THE HARLEM RENAISSANCE

Black women's position during the Depression was even more precarious than that of their white working class peers, as Paula Rabinowitz notes in her anthology of 1930s radical women's writing, *Writing Red*. Industrial employment, as well as unionisation, was often denied them, which may explain why proletarian fiction is thin on the ground in African-American women's literature. *Writing Red* does include some writing by black women (such as Marita Bonner, Lucille Boehm, Ramona Lowe, and Margaret Walker, as well as some anonymous essays), but if Olsen's notorious forces of circumstance prevented many white women from substantive literary production, this was even more true of their black sisters. Margaret Walker's slavery novel *Jubilee*, forerunner of Toni Morrison's *Beloved* and Sherley Anne Williams's *Dessa Rose* (as well as polemical counter to *Gone With the Wind*) was not published until 1966, and Ann Petry's *The Street*, which also came out of the cultural orbit of the Communist Party through the John Reed clubs, appeared in 1946. In the 1920s and 1930s it was that other major non-dominant cultural movement of the early twentieth century, the Harlem Renaissance, which generated black women's fiction in the works of Nella Larsen, Jessie Redmon Fauset, and Zora Neale Hurston.

Flourishing (roughly) from 1925 until 1935, the Harlem Renaissance never identified itself as a political or even a social movement, however. When in 1925 Alain Locke wrote 'The New Negro', which became the Harlem Renaissance's founding document, he argued in effect for the elevation of a black élite – W. E. B. DuBois's talented tenth – of artists, intellectuals and literati ('niggerati' in Zora Neale Hurston's phrase) whose cultural achievements should be seen as on a par with those of the white, dominant culture. Locke saw the New Negro movement as a 'spiritual emancipation' and stressed that the Negro had 'American wants, American ideas' and should therefore strive for recognition of those wants and ideas by the white culture (Locke 1925: 514, 520). The Harlem Renaissance eschewed the kind of protest writing that was later to develop in the Communist-affiliated work of African-Americans such as Richard Wright and Ann Petry in the 1940s, and later still in the 1960s Black Arts movement. Confident about their cultural heritage, the theorists of the Harlem Renaissance saw cultural production as a means of bridging the gap of ignorance and racist prejudice that separated, as they saw it, black and white Americans. David Levering Lewis, historian of the Harlem Renaissance, puts it thus, that in the programmatic statements of Alain Locke and James Weldon Johnson:

> the Harlem Renaissance reveals itself to be an élitist response on the part of a tiny group of mostly second-generation, college-educated, and generally affluent Afro-Americans – a response, first, to the increasingly raw racism of the times, second, to the frightening Black Zionism of the Garveyites, and, finally, to the remote, but no less frightening, appeal of Marxism.
>
> (Lewis 1981: xvi)

Although broadly correct, Lewis's emphasis on élitism and anti-Communism to some extent belies the diversity of the artists and writers of the Harlem Renaissance, as well as that of their political affiliations. Central figures like Claude McKay and Langston Hughes for example were also figures of the literary Left, and Zora Neale Hurston certainly found herself at odds with the idea that African-Americans had something to prove to white people. Michele Wallace writes that 'Hurston rejected the racial uplift agenda of the Talented Tenth on the premise that ordinary bloods had something to say, too' (Wallace 1990b: 172).

Yet if we look at Charles Johnson's programmatic editorial in *Opportunity* of September 1925, we can see 'where Zora Neale Hurston was coming from'. Here he argues for encouragement of the reading of literature both by Negro authors and about Negro life, not merely because they are Negro authors but because what they write is literature and because the literature is interesting; ... to stimulate and foster a type of writing by Negroes which shakes itself free of deliberate propaganda and protest

(Johnson, cited by Lewis 1981: 97)

Johnson's slightly defensive insistence on African-American writing as literature parallels Michael Gold's efforts to validate working class writing as art, but what Johnson outlines here is not so much a counter-hegemonic Black culture as one which stands alongside dominant cultural practice. This was also Hurston's view, and she shared Johnson's (and Locke's) stance against protest writing.[29] Criticised by her peers, and by Black male critics today, for having no (or the wrong sort of) politics, for painting an idyllic picture of the folk without showing the devastation of white Southern racism, yet celebrated by 1980s feminist critics for her representations of African-American folk culture and black women's self-determination, Hurston's work stands at the centre of African-American critical controversy. Undoubtedly the most difficult to pin down of the Harlem Renaissance's major writers, Hurston is also the most commented upon and fought over female figure in the African-American tradition.[30] What I want to contribute to this debate is that Hurston fails the test of a Black aesthetic only if she is read through a 1960s conception of Black cultural and political militancy; within the emancipatory programme of the Harlem Renaissance her notoriously controversial views on race, her anti-Communism in the 1950s and her cultural practices, rooted in African-American folklore, fit and make sense.

Hurston's championing of the African-American woman, especially in *Their Eyes Were Watching God*, has been taken to be a major departure from earlier representations of the tragic mulatto in the passing novels of Nella Larsen and Jessie Redmon Fauset. Yet as Deborah McDowell points out in her introduction to Fauset's *Plum Bun*, it is possible to read the passing theme as itself a mask. McDowell argues that a double-voiced narrative of racial disguise in *Plum Bun* might veil an underlying concern with definitions of gender and with African-American literary production in this period. Angela Murray's self-disguise (and self-deceit) when living as a white person then brings in its train a host of other disguises and deceits, pointing to restrictive feminine roles but also restrictive modes of feminine writing (the romance) and the restrictions imposed by a system of white literary patronage. [31] Read like this, Hurston's Janie Crawford (also a mulatto, with long straight hair as the distinctive mark of her feminine beauty) is perhaps not so different from Fauset's and Larsen's heroines, except for the fact that Hurston does not allow her protagonist to worry too much about conforming to a stereotype of wanton black femininity. Janie is, indeed, more confident and more at ease with herself as a light-skinned black woman who goes for what she wants. At the same time she is related to the dreamy and languid Southern women Jean Toomer had created in *Cane* long before Janie found her voice in Hurston's novel.

Without wanting to detract then from Zora Neale Hurston's importance for the current revival in African-American women's writing, it is important to situate her also intertextually in this earlier historical moment of the Harlem Renaissance, and that goes for her views on racial identity too. 'I am not tragically colored', Hurston proclaims in her fiendishly forked-tongued self-portrait 'How It Feels To Be Colored Me', only to deconstruct the whole notion of racial identity in the rest of that essay, as Barbara Johnson argues. 'How It Feels . . .' (the very irony of that title already spells trouble) cannot be taken at face value; it is not the racial (self-)respect of DuBois nor that of 1960s Black pride which is asserted here. Just as Jean Toomer saw himself not as an African-American but as a member of a new race, the American, so Hurston explains:

> I have no separate feeling about being an American citizen and colored. I am merely a fragment of the Great Soul that surges within the boundaries. My country, right or wrong.
>
> (Hurston 1928: 155)

This complex and relativist conception of race is also articulated in Hurston's fiction, for example in *Jonah's Gourd Vine*. When John Pearse's father rejects him because of his light skin, his mother protests: 'He ain't he onliest yaller chile in de world. We'se uh mingled people' (Hurston 1934: 23).

In Barbara Johnson's view, the much lauded authentic voice in Hurston's work is not one of self-identity but of self-difference. This division within the category of race, even within the one person, is articulated formally in Hurston's work as well through the use of first and third person narration, standard and dialect discourse, and free indirect speech.[32] I would add to Johnson's argument that it is this conception of race – as never pure, always and necessarily 'mingled' (or hybrid, as we would now say) – and its formal translation into a double address through 'lying' ('the art of conforming a narrative to existing structures of address while gaining the upper hand' – Johnson) is the most important part of Hurston's legacy for contemporary African-American women writers. It left its mark on Toni Morrison's work in her use of 'nigger jokes', for example, and prepared the ground for Alice Walker's (equally controversial) view of racial identity and double-voiced textual address (to white readers as well as Black). When Walker writes in the essay 'In the Closet of the Soul': 'We are black, yes, but we are "white" too, and we are red', she writes about African-Americans as a 'mingled' people (Walker 1987: 82). In another essay, Walker relates racial identity as a cultural and historical construction to the troubled question of what it means to be an American:

> Americans, even (and perhaps especially) genetically, have been kept from acknowledging and being who they really are. There are few 'white' people in America, for instance, and even fewer 'black' ones . . . In all our diversity we have been one people – even when the most vicious laws of separation have forced us to believe we are not. I, too, sing America.
>
> (Walker 1984: 128)

Walker said this in a speech at the première of the film *Seeing Red*, an oral history of the Communist Party of the USA, and her statement is a startling (and no doubt witting) rewrite of the Party's 1930s slogan: Communism is twentieth century Americanism. Walker, as it were between the lines, replaces that slogan with her own brand of 1980s multiracial multiculturalism, thus setting up an unexpected link between the two strands of 1930s women's writing, socialist and African-American, discussed in this chapter.

As a black woman, an anthropologist and a writer, Zora Neale Hurston had 'American wants, American ideas', yet her Americanism was not that radically redefined Americanism of the 1930s Communist Party. When Hurston writes, in the uncensored Appendix to her autobiography *Dust Tracks on a Road* that she 'wants the boss's bed', she does so in her characteristically funky, sassy way, but she also does it as an anti-Communist who denounces class struggle as a European idea antithetical to the spirit of America (Hurston 1942: 345). America, for Hurston, stands for upward mobility and individualism. Hurston's legacy to contemporary African-American women writers then is a complex and, perhaps, a contradictory one. Walker adopts the racial pluralism, the folk and the funk, without adopting Hurston's right-wing political views. Neither does Toni Morrison who develops, in a very different way, Hurston's bitter irony in her strong (and violent) female figures, who are, like Hurston, constantly 'sharpening their oyster knives'. Most of all, both writers build on Hurston's anthropological and literary achievement in giving voice to the Black voice. As Morrison says in 'Unspeakable Things Unspoken', the distinguishing feature of Black writing lies in 'its language – its unpoliced, seditious, confrontational, manipulative, inventive, disruptive, masked and unmasking language' (Morrison 1988: 11).

As in the work of the white socialist women writers of the 1930s, the border between Hurston's fiction and her anthropological researches is often unclear: the 'real' stories collected from her informants in *Mules and Men* often ended up in the short stories (for example, those in *Spunk*) as well, and the linguistic material she gathered was also used to give voice to her folk-characters in the novels such as *Jonah's Gourd Vine* and *Their Eyes*

39

Were Watching God. And just as Michael Gold instructed proletarian writers to dissolve the division between high and low culture through documentary realism, so also did Zora Neale Hurston's transliteration of the African-American oral tradition dissolve hierarchies of speech and writing, art and everyday life.

WRITING IN CIRCLES: ANN PETRY'S *THE STREET*

Their Eyes Were Watching God famously opens with an inversion of the masculine fantasy/female reality opposition we encountered in the work of Agnes Smedley and Meridel LeSueur. Hurston writes 'Ships at a distance have every man's wish on board', but whereas men have their dreams mocked to death by Time, women 'forget all those things they don't want to remember, and remember everything they don't want to forget. The dream is the truth. Then they act and do things accordingly' (Hurston 1937: 9).

Ten years after, Lutie Johnson, the heroine of Ann Petry's novel *The Street*, tries to act on Hurston's American dreams, but fails ineluctably when brought up against the realities of life as a single black mother in Harlem. The contrast between Zora Neale Hurston's romance of the folk and Petry's stark realism is nowhere so clear as in these two novels, which seem almost to belong to different eras – and perhaps they do. Where Janie Crawford's progress is in part that of *embourgeoisement*, the freedom to reject it, and the realisation of female desire, Lutie's development is one of downward social mobility and an awareness of the dangers of female sexuality, with political insight at the end as the sole gain. *The Street* begins with her hopes for a better life in the racial haven of Harlem, and ends with her murdering a black man and having to abandon her child to reform school – the cost of living in a racial ghetto. Petry's Harlem could not be further removed from the cultural capital Carl Van Vechten depicted in his *Nigger Heaven* in the 1920s; this Harlem is closer to a modern, inner city inferno.[33] Commonly described as a protest novel of the Richard Wright school, *The Street*'s political discourse of economic and environmental determinism is reflected formally in Petry's uncompromisingly realist narrative, which inexorably unwinds to its disastrous conclusion.

Yet as Bernard Bell has shown, Petry's novel differs significantly from Wright's *Native Son*. Lutie Johnson is no Bigger Thomas, the narrative focus is not on the protagonist's psychic torment and eventual pathologisation, but on her intelligence and sensibility and her dreams – and nevertheless she is driven to crime.[34] There is a strong case to regard Petry's novel as a counter to *Native Son* rather than as its female equivalent, for in addition to the choice of a female and eminently sane (if misguided) hero, she also opted for a multiple point of view, as opposed to Wright's claustrophobic, single-minded one. This multiplicity enables Petry to explore the determinants of sexual as well as economic exploitation and masculine as well as

female psychic life. If there is pathology in *The Street*, it is located outside
Lutie's consciousness, in working and housing conditions and in the
basements and cellars which, as in Wright's novel, function as a metaphor
for the black man's 'underground' existence. It gradually becomes clear
that Lutie's son Bub will go the same way, is indeed beginning to feel at
home in the Super's basement and will be lost in the world of his deranged
fantasies, unless he is removed from the poisoned atmosphere of the street
– as he is at the end, forcibly, to a detention centre for juveniles.

By this time all Lutie Johnson's nightmares have come true and she is
forced to confront the failure of the American dream that has sustained her
earlier in the narrative. To illustrate the power of bourgeois mythologies,
Petry evokes the spectre of Benjamin Franklin in that archetypal text of
American self-fashioning, *The Autobiography*:

> feeling the hard roundness of the rolls through the paper bag, she
> thought immediately of Ben Franklin and his loaf of bread. And
> grinned thinking, You and Ben Franklin . . . Yet she couldn't get rid of
> the feeling of self-confidence and went on thinking that if Ben
> Franklin could live on a little bit of money and could prosper, then so
> could she.
>
> (Petry 1946: 50)

As Bernard Bell writes, Petry 'de-mythologizes American culture and the
Afro-American character' (Bell 1987: 183). She turns Franklin inside out;
later in the novel she even names a gangster after Franklin's semi-secret
society of public spirited citizens, the Junto. *The Street* must be read as a
critique of African-American belief in and aspirations to social mobility.
Where Hurston voiced the African-American woman's dream, Petry was
more concerned with a gendered version of Michael Gold's truth: the truth
of material conditions that shape black women's lives. *The Street* adds a
stridently political dimension to the African-American tradition of women's
writing, moving beyond the middle class environment of the passing novels
and the romanticised rural settings of Hurston's work into the workaday
world of material survival and parental responsibility.[35]

In common with the white women writers of the 1930s, Petry is at pains to
portray the daily treadmill of housework, childcare and – most of all –
concern for a child's future. Like LeSueur, Olsen and Herbst also, her
allegiance to a counter-hegemonic literary realism is evident throughout,
even if it is a predictable, rather mechanistic version of it. A too-tightly
structured skeleton narrative continually pokes through the thin skin of
Petry's sparse language, and passages such as the following ram the
message home:

> The men stood around and the women worked. The men left the
> women and the women went on working and the kids were left alone

... The women work because the white folks give them jobs ... [and]
... the white folks haven't liked to give black men jobs that paid
enough for them to support their families.

(Petry 1946: 278)

Such overt didacticism reads like something straight out of *The Women's
Room* or *Her Mother's Daughter*; as in Marilyn French's work, there is little
room for the spirit here, nor for the exaltation of motherhood as a saving
grace. And unlike much contemporary African-American women's writing,
there is little self-affirmation or celebration of African-American culture
either, for in Petry's urban environment that culture has been usurped by
the lures of drink, drugs and petty crime. Acutely conscious of the role of
literature in social change, Petry ends *The Street* on an ironic note. Lutie
Johnson draws circles on the window of the train which will take her to
another anonymous city. She is reminded of her schooldays:

> Once again she could hear the flat, exasperated tone of the teacher as
> she looked at the circles Lutie had produced. 'Really', she said, 'I
> don't know why they make us bother to teach you people to write.'
> Her finger moved over the glass, around and around ... The
> woman's statement was correct, she thought. What possible good has
> it done to teach people like me to write?

(Petry 1946: 312)

With *The Street* we come full circle, back to Marie Rogers's open-ended
flight and ostensible hopelessness in Agnes Smedley's *Daughter of Earth*.
Nevertheless, Ann Petry's answer was the same as that of the women writers
of the 1930s: *this story must be told.*

THROUGH THE LOOKING-GLASS: 1930s–1970s

Resolutely realist, unrepentantly referential – yet never 'simply' so, socialist
women writers of the 1930s and 1940s, and feminist realist writers of the
1970s and 1980s, challenge current feminist critical pieties in the problems
of text and context that their work presents. These problems deserve to be
met on their own ground, on 'the soil in which they grew' to cite Tillie Olsen
once more. That soil has been dug over in my discussion of Meridel
LeSueur, Tillie Olsen, Zora Neale Hurston, Agnes Smedley, Ann Petry and
Josephine Herbst, to reveal the roots of more recent feminist writing in the
cultures of the Harlem Renaissance and the 1930s Left. We can now see how
Daughter of Earth engenders *Vida* and *Meridian*, how *Their Eyes Were Watching
God* yields *The Color Purple*, how *The Street* leads to *Linden Hills*, and
Hurston's Eatonville Angelou's Stamps. But we should also be able to see
how Marilyn French adopts similar narrative techniques to those employed
by Agnes Smedley and Ann Petry, and how Victoria Chance's problems in

Rope of Gold prefigure those in the novels of Marge Piercy, and how Michael Gold's invective for working class writers to tell the truth echoes in feminist fiction's claim that it tells the truth about women's experience – as opposed to the artful fictions of dominant literary culture. And so on, and so forth.

Connections and differences between 1930s women's writing and feminist fiction come into focus primarily as strategies in counter-hegemonic writing. Where Tillie Olsen said 'I want to help change what is harmful for human beings in our time', Marge Piercy writes 'I want to change conscious-ness . . . If you don't support alternate ways of imagining things, people aren't going to be able to imagine a better world' (Piercy 1980a: n.p.).

The commitment to cultural work as agency of change stays, even if the means – documentary realism versus 'alternate visions' – vary. And yet of course, such connections and differences become visible only as an effect of reading two generations of American women's writing in tandem: Maya Angelou's autobiographical narratives mean differently if read through the angle of *The Street*, for example – and vice versa.

Feminist criticism has a crucial role to play in this dual process of recontextualising and revitalising women's writing. Inevitably, this project entails a re-evaluation of the critical standards underlying an emerging feminist (counter-)canon. Whereas socialist women writers of the 1930s had a highly prescriptive aesthetic programme to conform to, this was not the case for the Women's Liberationists of the 1970s and the feminists of the 1980s. Feminist literature comes in many forms, from the gritty realism of Marilyn French to the exuberance of Joanna Russ's fantasy modes, and from the *Flying* fragments of Kate Millett's autobiography to the magical realism of Toni Morrison's work. In focusing on realism and in drawing parallels with the 1930s I want to question the aesthetic assumptions which have led so many feminist critics to champion the work of, for example, Fay Weldon, Margaret Atwood, Angela Carter and – lately – Toni Morrison over that of Marge Piercy, Alice Walker, Marilyn French and Maya Angelou. Rita Felski eloquently sums up what these assumptions are:

> The use of realist forms in feminist fiction . . . denotes a concentration upon the semantic function of writing rather than its formal and self-reflexive component. Because many women writers of the last twenty years have been concerned with addressing urgent political issues and rewriting the story of women's lives, they have frequently chosen to employ realist forms which do not foreground the literary and conventional dimensions of the text, but encourage a functional and content-based reading.
>
> (Felski 1989: 79)

On a more than 'functional' reading however, 1930s socialist writers do not lack 'formal self-reflexiveness', any more than contemporary feminist writing of the sort that Felski means (and I shall discuss that later in more detail) is purely 'semantic'. To be sure, self-consciousness in realist fiction is articulated differently from the self-consciousness of the parodic post-modern text or the 'ways of seeing' that modernism offers. Yet as feminist critics should know (and Felski, to be fair, does know it), there is no such thing as literary evaluation pure and simple; women's writing in particular has too often fallen foul of aesthetic judgements based on precisely the formalist (or even Formalist) criteria that Felski slips into here. Nor is there much point, it seems to me, in composing a league-table of women's writing which ranks very disparate cultural practices in order of a spurious feminist literary value without regard to, for example, their political projects and effectiveness, or their polemical engagement with dominant literary paradigms. Penny Boumelha argues sensibly in 'Realism and the Ends of Feminism' that '[w]e should not read realism only as a failure to be or become another mode', e.g. modernism or postmodernism (Boumelha 1988: 82). Nor should we assume that realism is always already reactionary, modernism and postmodernism always progressive and breaking new ground (or indeed, vice versa). In a media age when the techniques which were once pioneered by a cultural and political avant-garde have become the stock in trade of consumer culture, we should beware of such simplistic equations between form and political effect, and between cultural explor-ation and social change.

2

THE POLITICS OF WOMEN'S LIBERATION

It would be easy to represent the difference – and the continuity – between 1930s and 1970s political writing by women in terms of personal politics as the inevitable return of the repressed. We have seen that a concern with gender oppression was constructed as individualistically indulgent in Communist cultural thought in the 1930s, and that political fiction was taboo for the writers of the Harlem Renaissance; neither cultural movement could see gender as a political issue in its own right. Uncovering a feminist agenda in the work of women writers of the 1930s is a matter of reading against the grain of the social movements of their time.

How convenient it would be, then, if we could regard Women's Liberation fiction as an articulation of that previously repressed agenda, as a fiction which finally makes explicit the real conditions of women's existence – patriarchal gender relations – which were masked in 1930s women's writing by the then more legitimate categories of race and class. But neat as it is, the psychoanalytic analogy of a return of the repressed posits too simple a model for the relation between 1970s feminists writing the personal as political and 1930s women writers' treatment of gendered existence. An exchange in *Feminist Studies* between two women who discuss the respective merits of the Old and the New Left in relation to gender and personal life, illustrates the problematic nature of such a model. In 'Women in the Old and New Left', Ellen Kay Trimberger argues that the New Left of the early 1960s consciously rejected the ideological strictures of 1930s Communism along with its authoritarianism. But her assumption that a previously silenced political unconscious of personal life could only find its full articulation in the New Left and – especially – in the personal politics of Women's Liberation, was resolutely refused by Old Left activist Peggy Dennis and dismissed as ahistorical. Dennis counters that the cultures of the Old and the New Left can only be understood in the contexts of their time, in

> the socio-economic realities and the problems for solution those
> realities placed on history's agenda . . . the content of Communist

Party ideology and its concept of 'The Woman Question'; [and] the quality and the impact of that unique, total, long-pull commitment Communists had to ideology and organization.

(Dennis 1979: 451)

Where Trimberger sought to understand the Old Left in the terms of the New, Dennis pointed to ineradicable historical difference and showed, with Fredric Jameson, that we must always historicise.[1]

I cite this example by way of a lesson in historicism, a lesson which has some bearing on my engagement with feminist fiction and especially with the importance of personal politics in it. Wanting to find out where feminist fiction came from, I had to look at literary/political practices earlier in the century, in order to establish its historical rootedness in the aesthetics of other social movements. Turning now to feminist fiction's more immediate cultural and political origins, I find myself drawn to an analysis of personal politics as located in that particular configuration of the American 1960s which links the Old Left with the New, with the Black Civil Rights Movement and Women's Liberation. For, contrary to popular opinion, the concept of the personal as political, which underlies feminist fiction as a mode of political writing, was not invented by the Women's Movement. Nor did it represent a sudden coming-to-consciousness of transhistorical gender oppression, a buried knowledge that women have always had. Instead it was with the Port Huron statement, the New Left's manifesto of 1962, that the 'personally authentic' made its re-entry into American politics, to emerge in a radically transformed way as 'personal politics' in the Women's Liberation Movement some ten years later. The intricate trajectory that led from Peggy Dennis's party-based 'total, long-pull commitment' to a libertarian-socialist Leftism of the personally authentic, and from there to the personal and eventually the identity politics so characteristic of post-1960s social movements, is a difficult one to chart. Yet I make this foray into the conceptual history of personal politics in order to explore the conditions that made feminist writing possible, not just as a mode of literary/political intervention *per se*, but as a site of feminist authenticity *par excellence*. In *Changing the Story: Feminist Fiction and the Tradition* Gayle Greene argues that Women's Liberation was primarily a movement of education:

> If feminism was a 'teaching movement', it was also a 'reading movement' and a 'writing movement', for it was feminist writing – fiction, poetry, and nonfiction – that transformed confusion to consciousness, enabling women to understand the changes they were living through and to interpret their 'relative deprivation' as a collective phenomenon rooted in inegalitarian social, economic and political structures.
>
> (Greene 1991: 50)

Greene here makes very clear how cultural work came to take on a politicising role in Women's Liberation through the concept of personal politics. I want to add to that insight an historical dimension, which compares and contrasts Women's Liberation's emphasis on culture with developments in other social and political movements of the 1960s, of which the search for authenticity was one – with all the problems that notion entails.

FROM THE 1930s TO THE 1960s: FROM THE OLD TO THE NEW LEFT

An expanding economy, a generation of post-war babyboomers entering higher education, and a resurgence of Black Civil Rights activism in the mid to late 1950s fuelled the rise of that amalgam of 1960s social movements which has come to be known as the New Left. The 'socio-economic realities' that Peggy Dennis spoke of could not have been more different at the turn of the 'rebellious decade' from what they had been during the Depression; yet, as in the 1930s, they were the realities of late capitalism. White middle class America benefited from the economic impact of the arms race and enjoyed the fruits of post-war consumerism. If the 1930s had not quite been forgotten, it certainly seemed as if prosperity had a more stable base in the post-war period and that more Americans had a share in it than ever before. But when Michael Harrington published *The Other America* in 1962, that reality was redefined as illusion. Harrington exposed the underside of what J. K. Galbraith had termed 'the affluent society' of the 1950s, in revealing a divided America where urban deprivation, disenfranchisement and poverty were rife. Harrington's book succeeded in breaking the reigning consensus of the end of ideology, and of American pragmatism and economic success as a model for the rest of the world.

Such a challenge to 1950s social and political complacency was also characteristic of the emerging New Left, whose articles of faith were set out in the Port Huron statement, published in the same year as Harrington's path-breaking study of poverty. Drafted by Tom Hayden, but officially authored by a committee consisting of Hayden and fellow students Bob Ross and Al Haber, the Port Huron statement was presented as an open document for discussion, which signalled its anti-authoritarian stance from the outset. What was Port Huron all about? Hayden argued that American politics needed a new infusion of radicalism in order to deal effectively with its internal social problems rather than expending its resources and energies on the Cold War, economic imperialism in the Third World, and the arms race. 'We are people of this generation, bred in at least modest comfort, housed now in universities, looking uncomfortably to the world we inherit', he began, only to deliver a ringing indictment of American society and Kennedy's New Frontier in the subsequent fifty-odd pages of the document (Hayden 1962: 329). Intensely critical of the social conformism

47

of the 1950s and of corporate America, the statement voiced the student movement's concerns in an equally intensely American rhetoric of authenticity and independence:

> The goal of man and society should be human independence: a concern not with image of popularity but with finding a meaning in life that is personally authentic; a quality of mind not compulsively driven by a sense of powerlessness, nor one which unthinkingly adopts status values ... but one which has full, spontaneous access to present and past experiences, one which easily unites the fragments of personal history, one which openly faces problems ... This kind of independence does not mean egotistic individualism – the object is not to have one's own way so much as it is to have a way that is one's own.
>
> (Hayden 1962: 332)[2]

Self-confident and idealistic in tone, the statement presented a searing critique of the military-industrial complex, replacing the class analysis of the Old Left with a theory of institutional and state power. It also proposed a programme for action: community projects, alliances with labour and Civil Rights organisations, popular empowerment and a move to 'start controversy across the land' were to be points on the agenda for a broad movement of primarily young people (liberals and socialists, but explicitly excluding communists). The university, as one of those mammoth institutions which merely seemed to be processing bright young people for their role as a cog in the wheels of corporate society, was to be a primary site of struggle.

Central to the New Left's programme for change was the concept of participatory democracy, which offered a new vision of political process. First pioneered in the Student Non-Violent Coordinating Committee (SNCC) by the great leader and organiser Ella Baker, participatory democracy became the new catchphrase to mobilise young people.[3] James Miller explains its appeal thus:

> It combined a patriotic aura with a revolutionary ring. Because it remained open to different interpretations, it could unite people with different interests in a common political quest ... Used both as an empty slogan and as a more or less clearly defined idea, the notion of 'participatory democracy' became the lodestar of America's New Left. Contradictions and all, it defined what was *new* about this left.
>
> (Miller 1987: 152–3)

Much like personal politics later, participatory democracy grew from humble beginnings into a major mobilising force in the politics of the 1960s. It began as a local, small-scale decision-making strategy of interpersonal communication and consensus. But it quickly developed, as Miller also states, into an alternative to the established political process of representative democracy, and ended up as a powerful slogan betokening all-purpose rebellion against any form of authority and hierarchy. Although distinct generational threads of continuity between the Old and the New Left (the 'red diaper babies') did exist, as well as a common culture of commitment to a political cause, participatory democracy signalled a profound ideological and strategic break with the hierarchical traditions of 1930s Communism. As a new definition of political process, the idea was indebted to the Christian-inspired redemptive community of the Black Civil Rights movement. The suffering of activists dedicated to the principles of collective direct action and non-violence, said John Lewis, Chairman of SNCC in the mid-1960s, 'if necessary, may itself help to redeem the larger society' (Lewis in Cluster 1979: 7).

For the early student New Left of Port Huron, the process of participatory democracy represented just such a vision of community as agency of social change, as well as a site of personal authenticity. It was in this promise of a personally fulfilling political activism that its redeeming and exemplary power was supposed to lie. Even if the authors did not at any point acknowledge the Judeo-Christian values underlying Port Huron's moral concerns, this idealistic spirit is evident throughout.

But there was another, sharper edge to the New Left's programme too. Through participatory democracy the Port Huron statement sought to marry American individualism with a renovated version of collectivist Marxism, whilst at the same time distancing itself decisively from Communism. In their attempt to create a new social and political agenda for the 1960s, the students did not want to turn to old models, to an Old Left which in any case had been decimated by the witch-hunts of the McCarthy era. In a breathtaking tightrope act, they attempted to both critique McCarthyism and assert an anti-Stalinism of their own in a firm rejection of Old Left 'dogmatism' and the 'labor-metaphysic', as New Left ideologue C. Wright Mills called it. With the refusal of Communism, the working class as primary agent of change disappeared too. In 1960 Mills had written in his 'Letter to the New Left': 'Who is it that is thinking and acting in radical ways? All over the world – in the bloc, and in between – the answer is the same: it is the young intelligentsia' (Mills 1960: 90).

Inspired by Mills and other cultural critics of the late 1950s such as Herbert Marcuse and Paul Goodman, the Port Huron statement thus launched Students for a Democratic Society (SDS) with a manifesto which stressed the potentially revolutionary role of students and intellectuals. SDS, together with the young Civil Rights activists in SNCC, came to form the major organised part of the New Left.

This emerging new Left of SNCC and SDS differed from the Old Left then not only in its conception of agency, of the roles of the state and of political process. It was, as James Miller and others have noted, also a deeply moral new Left, inspired as much by religious sentiments, the evident injustices of racial segregation in the South and widespread urban poverty, as it was also embedded in a long tradition of American Utopianism.[4] In 'New Left, Old America' James Gilbert draws numerous parallels between the spirit of the 1960s and the age of perfectionism of the 1830s and 1840s, both periods dominated by a belief in the perfectibility of man (and I do mean man). The anti-materialism of SNCC's short, anonymous founding statement and that of Port Huron illustrate this. Where SNCC speaks of love, justice and the moral nature of human existence (humanist terms largely absent from the Old Left's vocabulary), Port Huron has a section devoted to values, which contains a strong defence of Utopianism – one of the Old Left's strictest taboos. Port Huron's critique of capitalism meanwhile focuses on the vacuity of alienated labour and the *Ersatz* satisfactions of consumer capitalism – but significantly not on class divisions.[5]

Where SDS wanted to define itself against the Old Left, the young Black people participating in SNCC's direct action programmes were taking a stance against the strategies and values of established moderate Civil Rights organisations such as the National Association for the Advancement of Colored People (NAACP).[6] Both constituencies of the New Left firmly believed that, if the past could not be erased, at least the mistakes of their elders could be avoided. Murray Bookchin has argued in this vein that 'the 60s are particularly significant because they tried to deal with problems that 30s radicalism left completely unresolved' – meaning in particular the need for an American Left that could articulate American dreams of Utopia-on-earth in political terms (Bookchin 1985: 248–9).

Such dreams were cruelly shattered in the mid-1960s. The escalation of the Vietnam war, and the brutality of law enforcement which greeted the non-violent sit-ins, marches and freedom rides in the South, propelled the New Left into a different mode of political analysis and strategy. Both SDS and SNCC gradually abandoned non-violence and grass-roots organising and moved towards an increasing militancy and ideological rigour. When Stokely Carmichael published his SNCC position paper 'What We Want' in 1966, he argued for Black Power and against racial integration, which he saw as a 'subterfuge for the maintenance of white supremacy'. Whites had no business in the Black movements any longer: 'it is black people I must speak to first. It must be the oppressed to whom SNCC addresses itself primarily, not to friends from the oppressing group,' Carmichael wrote (Carmichael/SNCC 1966: 141). SDS similarly adopted a much more strident, revolutionary stance and concentrated its efforts on anti-war activism and retaliatory violence, culminating in the Days of Rage at the Democratic convention in Chicago, 1968. Both organisations adopted Third World and anti-colonial struggles as their theoretical and strategic models. Love and community were now left to the counter-cultural hippies, whilst the real 'politicos' began to perceive themselves as guerilla soldiers and revolutionaries. Sectarianism was rife, and SDS spawned its own band of urban *guerilleros* in the shape of the Weather Underground. Meanwhile in the autonomous Black movement, the Black Panthers' grass roots activity in community organising lost ground to factional violence, in part induced by FBI infiltrators. The *débâcle* of the Days of Rage and the disastrous ending of the Black Panthers' involvement in prison revolts (Alcatraz, Attica) signalled the apotheosis of 1960s radicalism; by the end of the decade, the New Left's ego-ideal had shifted 180 degrees from youthful idealism to violent all-out rebellion.

'The "new left" was literally straitjacketed by its ideologues into a sleazy Leninism', writes Murray Bookchin:

> what subverted the 60s decade was precisely the percolation of traditional radical myths, political styles, a sense of urgency, and above all, a heightened metabolism so destructive in its effects that it loosened the very roots of 'the movement' even as it fostered its rank growth.
>
> (Bookchin 1985: 250)

Thus, ironically, the New Left's wilful initial rejection of the discourses and practices of the Old Left resulted in their reappearance at the turn of the decade. Along with the masculinism of 1930s political practice – the 'sense of urgency' that Tillie Olsen identified in the 1930s – resurfaced the 'politics of the act' that Josephine Herbst deplored in *Rope of Gold*. And with it returned the confrontational, macho style of activism whose effectiveness was questioned by Meridel LeSueur. So what was new? What was left of the New Left?

Both the Black and the white sections of the New Left counted numerous women activists among their ranks, but the increasing emphasis on armed struggle, vanguardism, revolutionary discipline and the concomitant suppression of personal needs gradually forced women on to the margins of what had, after all, also been their movement. The New Left, like the Old, made its own mistakes in its own time, and in this volatile, hothouse climate Women's Liberation took root. Rejecting once more the 'old-fashioned class and party politics of a "totalizing" kind', as Fredric Jameson put it, Women's Liberation strongly reacted against the new-fashioned machismo and sectarianism of both the Black and white youth movements (Jameson 1985: 192). Alienated by the revolutionary posturing of their male peers, sidelined in war-protests, and increasingly aware that the new slogan of 'organising around your own oppression' could be applied to gender oppression as well, women began to use to their own advantage what they had learned in SNCC and SDS. 'The personal is political', an insight which derived from participatory democracy and the search for authenticity, community and personal fulfilment of early SDS and SNCC, now became

51

their guiding principle. And just as Black Power had appropriated 'brotherhood' to signify the commonality of racist oppression, 'sisterhood' now came to mean solidarity between women.

ORIGINS OF WOMEN'S LIBERATION: THE 1960s

Women's Liberation was not coextensive with the Women's Movement in America – this distinction must be made first of all. As a specific branch of the Women's Movement – its Special Branch, we might say – with its own practices and modes of organisation, it was different from women's rights organisations such as the National Organization for Women (NOW), whose structure was top-down and whose political strategies were, by and large, those of traditional lobbying and interest groups. The Women's Liberation Movement, by contrast, was not really an organisation with a formal leadership and structure of representation at all, but an amalgam of groups and individuals. Women's Liberationists rejected formal structures in the belief that they merely mimicked a male model of hierarchical power-mongering; they kept the legacy of participatory democracy as an alternative and more democratic model of 'doing politics' alive.

As Ferree and Hess explain in their overview of the history of the American Women's Movement, NOW and Women's Liberation's differences can be traced back in part to their origins in different political traditions and age groups. Whilst the founding of NOW is usually ascribed to the impact of Betty Friedan's *The Feminine Mystique* in the mid-1960s, the ground for a resurgence of a liberal feminism of equality had already been prepared by the President's Commission on the Status of Women, which began its work in 1961. *American Women*, the Commission's report of 1963, reinforced many of Friedan's conclusions and recommendations (especially with regard to women's employment) in *The Feminine Mystique*.[7] Furthermore, Title VII of the Civil Rights Act was passed in 1964, adding 'sex' to 'race, color, religion and national origin' as illegal grounds of discrimination in employment and public services. Ferree and Hess comment that frustration with the lack of enforcement of Title VII contributed to the need for a women's rights movement at a time when more and more women were entering or returning to the labour market. NOW was founded in 1966 and the name, at the time, said it all.[8]

Through the influence of Friedan's book, which named 'the problem that has no name' as the predicament of the housewife engaged in full-time domestic labour and childcare, NOW attracted a membership of married women in their thirties and forties. Women's Liberation's connections with the New Left made for a different constituency of younger, often single and college-educated, women. But different political origins and age cohorts did not preclude occasional joint ventures and mutual influence between Women's Liberation and NOW. The latter, for example, adopted – albeit reluctantly – a more radical, sympathetic stance on lesbianism in the early 1970s, and tried to reconcile the ideals behind participatory democracy and sisterhood with its more traditional structures and procedures. Women's Liberation in turn made common cause with NOW in campaigns for abortion-law repeal and in support of the Equal Rights Amendment (ERA). Still, a major difference between the two remained: NOW was primarily pragmatic and effectiveness-oriented, whilst Women's Liberation was at least as much concerned with the means of change (sisterhood, democracy, openness) as with concrete ends. These different modes of organisation meant – paradoxically – that NOW, through its national networks and the relative anonymity of its participants, could attract a wider variety of membership than Women's Liberation with its more communal, inter-personal style of organising. So, despite a public image of white middle class liberalism, NOW probably counted more working class and Black women among its ranks than its more radical sister did.[9]

Broadly speaking, Women's Liberation stood in relation to NOW as a feminism of difference (but a non-essentialist one) to a feminism of equality. Women's Liberation conceived of women as an oppressed caste or class, rather than a social group merely behind on its constitutional rights. From the very beginning, Women's Liberation took the route of extra-parliamentary action, of working outside the system like the New Left before it. By analogy with the New Left also, the liberation in its name derived from liberation struggles of the 1950s and 1960s in Africa (Algeria, Angola, Mozambique) and Indo-China and took Chinese and Vietnamese women as its revolutionary role models. Male domination was conceived as the colonising force for women to liberate themselves from; Women's Liber-ationists envisioned their revolution as a decolonisation of mind and body, a freeing from male values, male modes of behaviour, and most of all male power structures. Instead of aspiring to equality as NOW did, which would mean minimising or at least de-emphasising gender difference (including what were perceived as women's strengths), liberation implied a process of authentic, gendered self-definition. That ideal of self-definition was in its conception rather similar to what Black men and women in SNCC had begun a few years earlier, when they decided to develop an autonomous authentic Black culture and politics.[10] Working in small groups of women only – something which had also been pioneered in SNCC – would enable women to speak for themselves and to establish mutual trust and intimacy. It would give them individual and collective agency without the need – in theory at least – for leadership and hierarchy.

The more concrete (rather than conceptual) beginnings of the Women's Liberation Movement in Civil Rights and the New Left have been docu-mented by various feminist historians, most notably by Sara Evans in *Personal Politics*. Evans's study gives a useful account of how a generation of women whose political sensibilities were nurtured in SNCC and SDS graduated to Women's Liberation. Wini Breines sums up the main point in a review of *Personal Politics*:

> [Evans's] book suggests that the ideas and ideals of the civil rights movement, the New Left, and the counterculture offered women political images of equality, autonomy and community at the same time that these women were being ignored or mistreated by movement men.
>
> (Breines 1979: 497)

This contradiction between the ideal and the real of life in the New Left fuelled the rise of Women's Liberation, which is as far as Evans's study stretches. But familiar as the argument that Evans puts forward in *Personal Politics* now is, it is less often observed that just such a perceived gap between the professed ideals of a social movement and its *praxis* later caused rifts within Women's Liberation as well.[11] Mary Rothschild shows for example that the shift towards Black self-determination in SNCC as a result of racial divisions was repeated in the move towards lesbian separatism and Black feminism within Women's Liberation. And for the same reason: a lack of understanding of and solidarity with the racial and sexual Other – as defined by the movement's white heterosexual members. Splits between Black and white feminists of the early 1970s had in turn been prefigured, Rothschild argues, in the highly traumatic interracial class and sexual politics of the Freedom Summers, which had caused conflicts between Black and white activists.[12] Here, as in the case of the Old and the New Left, it is not so much that history repeated itself (it doesn't, exactly) but that ways and means of understanding that history – political discourses – repeated themselves in different circumstances, under different conditions. Women's Liberation's inherited belief in autonomous organisation around your own oppression led to an increasingly splintered identity-politics. For, once 'your own' comes to be defined by race, class and sexual orientation as well as gender, then sisterhood, which is based on gender *per se*, and autonomy can no longer be reconciled. Despite its commitment to and validation of women's common experience, Women's Liberation then already carried the seeds of fragmentation within it.

EARLY ACTIONS, DEBATES AND THE MYTH OF UNITY

1964–1967

Such fragmentation however was obscured in the early years by the presence of an identifiable common enemy: movement men. The earliest manifestation of an emerging group-consciousness of budding feminists can be dated back to an unsigned paper submitted to the 1964 SNCC conference entitled 'Women in the Movement'. This paper bears out Evans's point about women's mistreatment by movement men: it tried to put the sexual division of labour in SNCC on the agenda and for the very first time signalled the 'assumption of male superiority' which, the authors asserted, relegated women to clerical work and excluded them from decision-making.[13] The argument for more equitable treatment of women elicited from Stokely Carmichael (then one of SNCC's leaders) the infamous response that 'the position of women in SNCC is prone'.[14]

Although Carmichael's dictum gained particular notoriety for its categorical offensiveness as well as its rhetorical effectiveness, such reactions were not untypical of the white male Left either. When Casey Hayden and Mary King tried to present a paper addressed to the women in the movement in 1965, they got a similarly hostile reception. It was not until two years later that women in the New Left – which was by then a mass organisation of students and affiliated groups – began to assert themselves in larger numbers at the Conference for a New Politics (appropriately named, as it turned out) in Chicago. This time, despite derogatory comments and heckling ('take her off the stage and fuck her'), the women managed to get a motion passed which called for SDS 'to work on behalf of all women for communal childcare, wide dissemination [sic] of contraceptives, easily available abortions, and equal sharing of housework' (cited in Freeman 1975: 58).

This resolution also asked for men to 'deal with' their chauvinist attitudes towards women and demanded that the SDS journal *New Left Notes* solicit articles on and by women. In true sexist form, the journal responded by publishing the women's motion with an illustration of a girl in baby-doll pyjamas carrying a picket sign 'We want our rights and we want them now!'.[15]

But the beginnings of Women's Liberation were not as purely reactive as these episodes in its early history might suggest. More important perhaps than the battle with men was the debate between New Left women over the question as to how fundamental women's oppression was. Should it be seen as part of the larger struggle for an end to all kinds of domination (racism, capitalism, imperialism)? This was the view of the 'politicos' (mainly Marxist women). Or was women's oppression more fundamental than all of these – after all, women hold up half the sky, as the Chinese saying goes. Or, alternatively, did not women's oppression encompass all others, too? And did that insight not warrant separate organisation? This was what the 'feminists' argued. Although many of the 'politico' women later joined the Women's Movement, the issue of the primacy of women's oppression over race and class has remained an important site of difference between feminisms, dividing radicals from socialists and white liberals from Black feminists.

Women's Liberation then began as a caucus within the New Left. Like the SDS of the Port Huron statement, it saw itself as breaking wholly new ground, rejecting the past and embracing the future as a *terra incognita.* Wini Breines argues that what made the American Women's Movement so unique in the West was the fact that

> the civil rights movement and the New Left were not traditional, centrally organized, disciplined left-wing party formations . . . The earlier movements . . . were conducive to a self-activity and creativity that enabled people to organize around their own issues and create their own movements. Thus, there was little doctrine or discipline that constrained the women's movement.

(Breines 1979: 501)

Although this is undoubtedly an accurate reflection of the New Left's and Women's Liberation's self-perception, it was also a rather naïve view of political organisation and activism. For Breines fails to see that self-activity and creativity were not new but, in fact, deeply engrained in American political thought and practice from Franklin onwards. Secondly, Breines ignores the fact that self-activity creates its own myths, most notably that prevalent 1960s illusion of radical breaks with the past and the viability of working outside the system. This New Left legacy of wishful thinking, however attractive and well-intentioned, would cost Women's Liberation dearly in the years to come.

1968–1974

From 1967 onwards Women's Liberation began to grow in a manner which Jo Freeman has described as 'the mushroom effect': local groups were forming everywhere until they amounted to a national movement, with campaigns and women's centres all over the country. So called zap actions, such as the crowning of a sheep at the 1969 Miss America contest and the Burial of Traditional Womanhood at a 1968 peace demonstration, attracted a lot of media attention. Performance and street theatre of this kind had been inspired by 1960s counter-cultural groups such as the Yippies and the Merry Pranksters, who in turn had modelled themselves on the Amsterdam Provos. Despite hostile or uncomprehending media coverage, zap actions helped spread the movement's notoriety and added to the spectre of anarchy which suburban America saw paraded before it on TV every night. Suddenly Women's Liberation was everywhere: in the streets, on the campuses, at cultural and political events, under and in people's beds – even in the pages of *Ladies Home Journal,* a concession won after Women's Liberationists had staged a sit-in at the journal's editorial offices.

Most of these actions are now primarily memorable for their wit and daring, but they did serve important ends at the time. For one, they dramatised the institutionalised and all-pervasive nature of sexism. Secondly, they emphasised that the cause of Women's Liberation demanded not just political change but a wholesale cultural revolution, radically undermining received notions of a woman's place and challenging existing standards of femininity. And thirdly, of course, they demonstrated that feminists did have a sense of humour.

But even at this early stage there were misgivings about this type of agitation within Women's Liberation as well as outside of it. Carol Hanisch argued in an extensive critique of the Miss America protest that the rejection of traditional femininity 'harmed the cause of sisterhood'. Feminists, she believed, needed to take themselves and their cause more seriously, and not use other women as the butt of their feminist jokes (Hanisch 1968: 132–6).

It seems that in the context of the Sexual Revolution, which had exercised the media for some time, Hanisch had a point. Zap actions might be exhilarating to do and to watch, but they could be misunderstood: women's protests against the cultural rituals of the homecoming queen and beauty contests were easily appropriated by the media for an already sexualised and trivialising discourse which constructed feminists as bra-burners and college 'chicks' marching for multiple orgasms. The feminist vocabulary of sexual exploitation and sexual politics was ambiguous because of its ostensible association with the Sexual Revolution, which in the popular mind meant sexual permissiveness. And if anything, feminists were against that kind of permissiveness and their political analysis went well beyond that of sexuality *per se* all the way to patriarchy as an all-encompassing system of gender oppression.[16]

So, whilst zap-activist groups such as WITCH (Women's International Terrorist Conspiracy from Hell) kept the press busy, other feminists were beginning to construct a comprehensive analysis of women's subordination, such as the *New York Radical Women*, *Redstockings* and *The Feminists* in New York, *Bread and Roses* in Boston and various other, similarly named groups in other cities. Most of these groups had a relatively short life-span; few survived for longer than a year or two and died of natural causes, only to resurrect themselves in different ideological configurations to continue the work of theory-building and local activism.

By the late 1960s, 'politico' women began to leave SDS in droves for Women's Liberation, which seemed to offer them a more legitimate and constructive political space. Determined to start with a clean slate, feminists pledged their allegiance to the principle that the personal is political, to participatory democracy and skills-sharing, and to a leaderless movement of autonomous groups. Yet despite Women's Liberation's commitment to going back to basics, to start from the rock-bottom ground of women's experience, the ideological shackles of New Left thinking and the psychic habits of policing others for the correctness of their politics proved hard to shake off. Former New Leftists soon reintroduced the revolutionary rhetoric and Leninist analyses of their recent past, which alienated newer converts.

Conflicts continued to centre on the primacy of gender oppression and how to theorise it: were women a subordinated class, or should any form of analysis rooted in Marxism be abandoned? Was consciousness-raising a bourgeois activity, a form of therapy or, on the contrary, an essential tool in the process of self-education for revolution? Were working class and Black women more oppressed than white middle class students? Should lesbians, because of their wholesale political and personal commitment to women, be the vanguard of Women's Liberation?

> It is important to keep in mind the fact that the women's movement was breaking new ground in every direction it went. No one knew, from either history or personal experience, what all the implications of a new organizational form or theory might be.
>
> (Hole and Levine 1971: 140)

Judith Hole and Ellen Levine wrote in their analysis of the conflict-ridden history of *Redstockings*.[17] True, but this was by no means the whole story. For if – with the benefit of hindsight – one gets the impression that these conflicts were squabbles between factions which had far more in common with each other than they seemed to realise, then that impression obscures the underlying issues of an identity politics in the making. From the vantage point of the 1990s, it is obvious that a new politics cannot be made from scratch, and that experience is as problematic a basis to start from as any already existing political or theoretical framework. For who has the power to name and define what counts as 'women's experience'? What constitutes gendered experience is, after all, far from self-evident and always already presupposes a theory which determines which experiences are significant and which are not, and – of course – what their significance, their political meaning, is. Secondly, it was in the process of consciousness-raising that different meanings of experience had to be addressed and contested, and it was in the process of consciousness-raising also that divisions about what it meant to 'organise around your own oppression' became apparent. Was women's experience of sexual violence, for example, a symptom simply of their oppression as *women*? Or was it, in certain cases, clearly a form of sexual retaliation against lesbians, part of a whole scala of heterosexist measures to keep sexual dissidents in line? Or could it alternatively be seen as part of a long tradition of racist violence (lynching men, raping women) against black people? Who was to decide? And on what grounds? Which were the general cases, which the 'specific cases' relegated to marginal status as exceptions to the rule? Different modes of asserting authority and different analyses created divisions within and between Women's Liberation groups around questions such as these.

If the common identity of womanhood was not enough to sustain a small group in the longer term, it was certainly not sufficient to generate an all-encompassing theory of women's condition and how to change it. Small, collectivist groups required a certain degree of homogeneity to survive for any length of time, but the assumed homogeneity of sisterhood, of all being women together, was in fact systematically being questioned (along the lines of race, class, sexual orientation, ethnicity, age, marital status, motherhood, etc.) in any group which took consciousness-raising seriously.[18]

Some further examples may clarify this crucial point. In 1970 conflicts arose around the so-called 'pro-woman line' developed by *Redstockings*. The group stated programmatically that women were in no way to be held responsible for their own oppression and were entitled to sisterhood-solidarity no matter what the conditions of their lives. Other Women's Liberationists countered that this principle would logically lead to a cult of victimhood which denied women agency and was, therefore, ultimately self-destructive. Later arguments in feminist theory (and history) about the determining nature of patriarchy as a totalising system, versus those stressing women's resistance to or collusion with male domination, took off from here and went to the heart of the question whether women do, after all, really and necessarily have shared interests in every situation and at all times.

A second example of early controversy was the publication of Anne Koedt's article 'The Myth of the Vaginal Orgasm' (1970), which initiated a debate that was to throw all kinds of assumptions concerning women's sexuality – and more especially heterosexuality – into question. Koedt's exposure of the vaginal orgasm as a myth seemed to pose the possibility of sexual autonomy for women and legitimised the clitoral orgasm and therefore, *pace* Freud, lesbian sexuality in particular. Besides, as Lillian Faderman explains with reference to the Sexual Revolution: 'Because non-reproductive sex outside of marriage had become more and more acceptable, it made less sense than it had earlier to condemn lesbianism on the grounds that lesbian sexual pleasure did not lead to reproduction' (Faderman 1992: 201).

As an indirect consequence of this debate, lesbianism became a hot topic in Women's Liberation. In a reversal of the previous dominance of heterosexual issues in the movement, lesbianism now took on vanguard status. The argument that all true feminists are lesbians, and that 'all women are lesbians except those who don't know it yet' was hard to resist for those heterosexual women who felt guilty (or merely confused) about their continuing ties with men. Enter Radicalesbians' concept of the woman-identified-woman and the disputes between 'realesbians' and 'politica-lesbians', for whom lesbianism was less a matter of sexual identity than of feminist conviction. Ten years later Adrienne Rich's influential article 'Compulsory Heterosexuality and Lesbian Existence' tried to put this debate on a more theoretical footing, and proposed the conciliatory idea of a lesbian continuum in female sexuality.

Even if we don't submit to the fantasy that Women's Liberation conjured up its new theories out of thin air, it must be remembered that these debates were conducted in a predominantly young, educated, white movement before the 1970s had even really begun. Clearly the idea that there was once, in a mythical past of only twenty-odd years ago, a mass Women's Movement which was united and knew where it was going does not even have a toehold in the actual history of American Women's Liberation, let alone in the history of the Women's Movement as a whole. But that hindsight's benefits can be gratuitous ones must not be forgotten either. In recent years sisterhood and the idea of a common female identity have had a rather bad press from feminists, on the theoretical grounds that such sisterhood presupposed a unified and homogeneous female identity which we now know, *post*-Lacan and *post*-bell hooks, does not exist. My analysis here proposes something different than the usual dismissal of Women's Liberation's racism or *naïveté*. I think that on one hand it was absolutely necessary for Women's Liberation to try and forge a political identity for women as women, especially in the context of women's experiences in the New Left. Secondly, it is indisputable that for a number of years and for a great number of women the *ideal* of sisterhood had real resonance and produced real political results (for example in the Rape Crisis and Women's Refuge movements). On the other hand however we must not forget that, whilst trying to forge this common identity, Women's Liberation was also engaged in a rigorous critique of traditional femininity and heterosexual relations, and arguing over new, more authentic self-definitions. It was only logical that this desire for a more and more refined authenticity led to increasingly diversified forms of identity politics, in which gender came to be theorised as intertwined with race, ethnicity, sexual orientation and class. It is undoubtedly true that Women's Liberation theory had a tendency to universalise the white middle class woman's experience into the condition of womanhood; this universalised image was certainly the one that circulated in the media and in many of the movement's publications. But it is also true that this universalising image belied the actual pluralism in Women's Liberation's multifarious groups. Despite appearances the category 'woman' in Women's Liberation practice was, in fact, never a hard and fast and self-evident common identity, but always denoted a political position: woman was in effect shorthand for feminist, and any woman could choose to be one of 'us' (whether radical, socialist, lesbian, Black, etc.). That the reasons why she might not do so were inadequately analysed and understood was a failure on the part of the Women's Movement as a whole, which meant that it was ill-prepared for the anti-feminist onslaught *by women* which hit the public arena in the 1980s.

THE 1970s: PERSONAL POLITICS AND CONSCIOUSNESS-RAISING

All Women's Liberation groups, whatever their differences, adopted 'the personal is political' as their founding principle, the basis from which they engaged in activism and began to theorise women's discontents. It meant a new conception of the relation between private and public life: in redrawing the boundaries between self and society and analysing their lives in new ways women sought to establish what was, indeed, personal to them and what might be an effect of social structures larger than themselves. To the dominant strand of white, middle class Women's Liberationists, personal politics also signalled disaffection with working on behalf of other people, that is: working in Black Civil Rights, draft resistance, community organising and anti-war protests, as many had done before they came to Women's Liberation. They felt, *pace* Frederick Douglass, that this was the women's hour. The logic of a politics emanating from experience thus led them to a redefinition of their own identity – 'others' were split off as Black, or male, or working class. For those who had come to Women's Liberation through the New Left, morality and self-sacrifice were out, but collectivism and authenticity were still in. Yet the definition of the 'personally authentic' of the Port Huron statement was considerably narrowed; the earlier belief, that what was good for the most oppressed (Black people, the working class, the Vietnamese) would make for a better world and a better America (including women), now no longer held: sisters were doing it for themselves.

Initially, the concept of personal politics enabled women to see themselves and their lives as in part determined by power structures operative in society as a whole. Another crucial discovery, besides that of a condition-in-common (for example of women who felt themselves to be 'trapped in marriage') was that of agency. The assumption was, as Rochelle Gatlin puts it in New Left style, that 'political action changed the involved individual. By connecting with a larger community, the person gained a new source of strength and a different relationship with history and society' (Gatlin 1987: 88).

Feelings, rather than morality or ideology, were recognised as legitimate motives for political involvement. This put the subjective (Port Huron's search for personal fulfilment) back into politics after the militant New Left and Black Power had rejected it in the mid to late 1960s as sentimental and self-indulgent. What had previously been defined as women's personal hang-ups was now understood as admissible empirical evidence of women's subordination. Consciousness-raising strategies were designed to help women make this transition from the personal to the political, by giving them a vocabulary to name their experience of anger and discontent in feminist terms. From this conception of the personal as also political it was an easy step to what Rochelle Gatlin calls the third stage, in which the definition of the realm of politics was expanded to subsume personal experience almost entirely. Here the personal tended to become a substitute for the political.[19] Obviously this extension was a highly problematic one, even if it forced the meaning of personal politics (e.g. the personal equals the political, or a politics – merely – of personal life) to its logical conclusion. The tendency to confuse politics out there, as a system for the distribution of resources and power, with changes in attitudes and consciousness, was especially pronounced in the cultural feminism of the 1980s.[20] Wont to mistake the concerns of middle class white college students for those of universal womanhood, cultural feminism elided differences of race and class as well as generation – material differences in an important sense. But these tendencies had already been evident in 1970s radical feminism, too. In 1971 Judith Hole and Ellen Levine wrote in their preface to *Rebirth of Feminism*: 'the movement is at present almost as much a state of mind as it is a movement', but a state of mind did not pay the bills, stop the abuse or provide for childcare (Hole and Levine 1971: x).[21] Such confusion was widespread and sometimes led to offensive inverted hierarchies of oppression, as in the statement from Leah Fritz in 1979 that 'the epitome of female slavery is the First Lady' or 'There is a vantage point from which a lovers' quarrel and the ERA carry the same weight, are the same battle' (Fritz 1979: 178, 116).

The potential for individualism and voluntarism was, as we have seen, already implicit in the politics of personal fulfilment of the early New Left. Rochelle Gatlin observes that 'Feminists of the 1970s believed like the hippies of the 1960s that voluntary actions of consciously transformed individuals could create fundamental social change' (Gatlin 1987: 138).

What later was to be called lifestyle feminism ('living the revolution') was personal politics taken absolutely literally. *New York Radical Feminists* for example entitled their manifesto 'Politics of the Ego'; its central tenet was that women were oppressed as a gender-based class, but that 'the purpose of male chauvinism is . . . to obtain psychological ego satisfaction', hence for women 'self-assertion is a political act' (Ware 1970: 58, 18).

Women then could set up collective enterprises, join rural communes, become writers or artists, or simply change their minds about what makes the world go round and believe that they were therefore politically active. This meant that any notion of the political as residing in some form of organised collective action was shifted to collective consciousness, and from there to individual consciousness and action: in changing your own gender role you challenged that of all women.

The flip side of this philosophy was the policing of other feminists' lives to check that they were doing the same. British feminist Kathryn Harriss looked back on this phenomenon in 1989:

oppression came to be seen as a dynamic between individuals rather than as a structural system . . . [T]his had the effect of placing the responsibility for social change on the shoulders of individuals within the WLM, to the disregard of the social policies and practices outside it where institutional power was wielded.

(Harriss 1989: 38)

Such individualisation of political activism was, in fact, fundamentally at odds with Women's Liberation's original analyses of the institutional nature of gender oppression. Yet it must be noted that to some extent individualism went hand in hand with the drift towards organising around your own oppression (identity politics) and – crucially – also with the narrowing of liberal political space during the 1970s and 1980s. Particular uses of consciousness-raising were a third contributing factor in the slide into individualism, as a closer look at its history and radicalisation in Women's Liberation groups shows.

Consciousness-raising, like personal politics, has a longer history than that of the Women's Movement. The first women's groups started as 'rap groups' on the model of some sections of the New Left which in turn had borrowed the Maoist technique of 'speaking bitterness' from Chinese and Vietnamese revolutionaries. Speaking bitterness was a form of testifying to one's experience of oppression; like the later New Left's criticism/self-criticism sessions, it was designed to make political activists aware of their own histories and interpersonal tensions, so that they would work together better without individual neuroses getting in the way. But as Cellestine Ware shows, consciousness-raising had an unexpected precedent also in industrial psychology, where T-groups (Training groups) were used for business executives to air and analyse their personal problems as a way of improving performance (Ware 1970: 108). Women's Liberation rap groups developed into consciousness-raising groups only when generalisations were beginning to be made from women's individual experience to their situation in society at large – a quantum leap from the personal in here to the political out there. This, and not the idea that the personal was political in itself, was Women's Liberation's great innovation: rejecting the New Left's extrovert, self-dramatising politics of the act, feminists prioritised self-scrutiny and the formation of theory over more pragmatic goals in the public arena. Without raised consciousness no understanding of the world, and without understanding no agency to change it. Generalisations would lead women to a new understanding of their history and subjectivity, no longer in the self-blaming terms of popular psychology, but in a theoretical framework of male power and institutionalised sexism. A fully-fledged theory of women's oppression would mobilise women to take action in their own – and

63

therefore all women's – behalf; consciousness-raising was to be the royal road to revolution.

As I have already indicated, it did not always work out that way. Different groups used consciousness-raising to different ends; some used it primarily to build trust and intimacy among its members in order to conduct effective campaigns and actions, others left it to their individual members to organise women in their own workplaces, colleges, neighbourhoods and unions after consciousness-raising had come to the end of its useful life. Groups like *Redstockings* had no activist agenda at all, but concentrated on theory-building alone. Yet another set of Women's Liberation groups regarded consciousness-raising as an end in itself: once you had attained complete awareness, once all the modes of sexist oppression had been exposed to the brutal light of day, anger could be mobilised for a more creative, authentic way of life. New, 'revolutionary' lifestyles would resist and transcend patriarchy at the same time. And once the stage of being able to live the revolution had been reached, that revolution would, in effect, have arrived.

THE 1980s: THE PARADOX OF PRO-FAMILY 'FEMINISM'

But if the revolution did ever seem just around the corner, that corner was never turned. Instead, by the end of the decade, feminists had to fight harder to hold on to their gains than ever before. Hard-won abortion rights of the early 1970s had already been abridged by the Hyde Amendment of 1977. At the same time, women of all classes and colours were getting poorer – and single mothers were the hardest hit of all. The history of consciousness-raising exemplifies contradictions and ambiguities inherent in personal politics, which can in part explain these phenomena. Unlike the National Organization for Women, Women's Liberation groups did not direct their energies at the established political process to better the material conditions of women's lives. In that sense, Drude Dahlerup is undoubtedly right in defining the small-group women's movement as a social rather than a political formation:

> A social movement is a conscious, collective activity to promote social change, representing a protest against the established power structure and against the dominant norms and values. The commitment and active participation of its members or activists constitute the main resource of any social movement.

(Dahlerup 1986b: 277)

Women's Liberation had no paid-up membership, no official leaders or policies and no resources other than its activists. Although various groups did act collectively in mass demonstrations and joint campaigns with NOW, Women's Liberation maintained its commitment to working outside the system. As a result of its dedication to a different (community-based, democratic) way of working, it generated numerous innovative projects in public services, health care and education, and founded essential alternative institutions such as women's refuges and health clinics. But, always precariously and inadequately funded, these projects became increasingly vulnerable to the economic and political changes of the 1970s. As a generation of Women's Liberation pioneers aged and the economic recession of the mid-1970s took hold, the climate for social change became rapidly colder and harsher. Radical practices, lifestyle experiments and workplace organising continued, but the time of Utopian possibility to provide adequately for women's shared needs was over. Institutional power forced itself on to the Women's Movement's agenda with even more urgency than before at the moment when cuts in public services under Nixon and ideological counter-offensives from the New Right began to make themselves felt. In this shrinking political space, increasingly unresponsive or even hostile to feminist demands, cultural practices seemed to offer more promising avenues for authentic self-fulfilment than political activism – at least for the privileged, educated women in Women's Liberation. Cultural and academic feminisms developed out of this configuration. Women's Liberation faded into the Women's Movement, which in turn by the late 1970s fizzled out into a wide variety of different and sometimes mutually contradictory feminisms (socialist, radical, liberal, cultural, Black, lesbian and various combinations thereof). The strengths of diversity contained in personal politics now manifested itself as a disabling fragmentation, a lack of a forceful feminist public presence to counter the pernicious influence of the New Right, which was gaining ground at an alarming rate. This public silence was not to be undone until the early 1990s, with the publicity surrounding the Hill–Thomas case and with Bill Clinton's presidential campaign.[22] In the intervening years, American feminists witnessed the rise of a new pro-family feminism which, with an appeal to a new (rightist) common sense, relegated any notion of the need for women's liberation to the dustbin, where we put away childish things.

In 1987 Sylvia Ann Hewlett published what was in many ways a timely book, *A Lesser Life: the Myth of Women's Liberation*, which focused attention on the contradictory pressures in American women's lives between the demands of career-making (as distinct from 'just' waged work) and those of motherhood and childcare. But, as the second part of the title indicates, this was also an *untimely* book. Whilst Hewlett sought reasons to explain women's worsening economic situation, she used 'the myth of women's liberation' as a rhetorical sleight of hand in the service of a thoroughly reactionary argument: women were not only not liberated, they were not liberated *because* of Women's Liberation. Hewlett adopted the strategy of denouncing Women's Liberation in the name of all those moderate, normal middle class white women who once had subscribed to feminist values of economic independence and self-assertion, only to find that it had landed them with an impossible double burden. Hewlett blamed feminism for the fact that career women still had little access to childcare, for rising divorce rates and for the feminisation of poverty, and launched into a diatribe against the 'extremism' of Women's Liberation: 'The modern women's movement has not just been anti-men; it has also been profoundly anti-children and anti-motherhood' (Hewlett 1987: 149).

This, one would have thought, must have come as a surprise to all the mothers who turned to feminism precisely because they found that patri-archal society had no legitimate place for them, other than as unpaid nannies and housekeepers – and usually inadequate ones at that. In the reasonable voice of a new, sensible, middle-of-the-road feminism, Hewlett's analysis came out against the Equal Rights Amendment, against no-fault divorce, and for the nuclear family (with a mother in paid employment). Her 'facts' about American women's suffering due to the Women's Move-ment's mistakes, says Susan Faludi, 'were close to tabloid fare'; Hewlett did almost no empirical research to support her foregone conclusions (Faludi 1992: 348).[23] Besides, *A Lesser Life* did not for a moment question the sexual division of labour, and accepted – as Lynne Segal points out – that women are and always will be (should be?) the sole childcarers. Hewlett demanded from the state what Women's Liberationists had demanded primarily of men and of their communities: communal childcare and shared domestic responsibilities.[24]

But Hewlett's book was not in a middle class of its own. In a similar vein, formerly prominent figures in the Women's Movement like Betty Friedan also published their troubled thoughts on the legacy of Women's Liberation in the early and mid-1980s, questioning primarily the movement's hostility to the nuclear family (invariably constructed as hostility to motherhood) and to normative sexual practices (constructed as hostility to hetero-sexuality). Backlash texts like Friedan's *The Second Stage* demonstrated both generational shifts in priorities and fragmentation within feminism, but they also had their rationale in the paucity of political options available to feminists in the 1980s: blaming Women's Liberation was the easiest outlet for the voices of discontent and disappointment.[25]

Such discontent and disappointment during the Reagan and Bush years was all too real for American women across the land, who saw their working conditions deteriorating, their welfare and healthcare cut or withdrawn, and their employment prospects decreasing. Yet the hypocrisy of white middle class feminists like Friedan and Hewlett must also be noted. White, middle class women who previously had seen the Women's Movement as their movement, now spoke out against it on behalf of so-called ordinary women. Yet it was white middle class American womanhood also which had been the least responsive to the demands of these 'ordinary' women from different ethnic, racial and class backgrounds in the recent past, who now suffered the most from the feminisation of poverty. By the time white middle class pro-family feminists began to articulate their disillusionment with Women's Liberation, Black feminists and women of colour had been doing so, for different reasons, for a number of years. It was their critique of Women's Liberation which had challenged middle class dominance in the Women's Movement, and it was their critique which had pointed directions for progressive change, directions which the backlash tendency chose to ignore – if it was aware of them at all.

BLACK WOMEN AND WOMEN'S LIBERATION

The relatively privileged socio-economic position of white Women's Liber-ationists, as well as their tendency to universalise their own condition, had alienated many Black women from the beginning. As Constance Carroll has written, Women's Liberation 'attempted to transcend rather than confront the racial tensions and complexities resulting from the Black woman's involvement in the movement' (Carroll 1973: 122–3).[26]

Sisterhood did of course extend to Black women, but all too often, it seemed, only on white women's terms. For some Black women, feminism became altogether co-terminous with white women's bourgeois aspira-tions. The poet Nikki Giovanni for example writes bitterly: 'And we watch white women really getting into what they're all about with their liberation movement. The white woman's actions have been for an equality move-ment first of all and secondly have been patterned after Black men's' (Giovanni 1971: 144).

Yet the relation between Black and white women's images of female agency had once been very different. In 1955 Rosa Parks had triggered the revival of Civil Rights activism in Montgomery, Alabama. An 'ordinary' older Black woman (also an NAACP organiser) she became a role model for Black and white women activists in SNCC along with other Black women leaders in Civil Rights – Ella Baker, Fanny Lou Hamer, Flo Kennedy and Ruby Doris Smith Robinson among them.[27] Robinson in particular was seen as an example by white women in SNCC who later became involved in Women's Liberation; for a long time it was assumed that the anonymous discussion paper 'The Position of Women in SNCC' had been written by Robinson, because it was believed that only a Black woman would have the courage to take such a stand against movement men. Given this precedent of Black women as role models, why were they not also prominent in Women's Liberation?

First of all, women-only groups existed in the Black movements as caucuses before Women's Liberation even came into being. That Black women did not enthusiastically join the autonomous women's movement therefore did not necessarily mean that they had no interest in feminist issues. Secondly, professional middle class women had been active in NOW since its inception in the mid-1960s, with Shirley Chisholm (member of the House of Representatives for New York State) taking up a prominent position. Thirdly, many Black women, because of their position in the labour market, found their interests better represented by the Coalition of Labor Union Women (CLUW), a multiracial working class women's organisation. More Black women joined CLUW than ever involved themselves with Women's Liberation.[28] Of those who did join Women's Liberation groups, some chose to make common cause with white women in the battle against male domination; others saw capitalism as their main target and tried to develop an analysis which theorised racial oppression along with that of gender and class, whilst a third cohort were mainly concerned with their position as Black women in a predominantly white movement.[29] Frustrated with their lack of progress, the latter group went on to organise autonomously: the National Black Feminist Organization (NBFO) was founded in 1973. A year later, the Combahee River Collective began to meet, launching its influential manifesto 'A Black Feminist Statement' in 1977:

> The most general statement of our politics at the present time would be that we are actively committed to struggling against racial, sexual, heterosexual, and class oppression and see as our particular task the development of integrated analysis and practice based upon the fact that the major systems of oppression are interlocking. The synthesis of these oppressions creates the conditions of our lives.
>
> (Combahee River Collective 1977: 13)

This conception of interlocking systems of oppression may still have been news to some white Women's Liberationists, but it was the common ground upon which most feminisms of colour would stand. Furthermore, the Combahee River Collective's statement positioned itself first and foremost in a tradition of Black female activism, and only secondarily in relation to the Women's Movement and Black politics. In this way, Combahee established its historical precedents as well as its political alliances.

Still, many Black women shared Nikki Giovanni's distrust of Women's Liberation as a movement for white self-advancement which had taken its cue from the Black struggles of the 1960s in the first place. Historians have put forward various other reasons for this distrust, ranging from the practical consideration that Black women, because of their socio-economic position, simply had less time to devote to political activism than white college students, to Jo Freeman's theory of relative deprivation (Black women might not share the aspirations of their white sisters because they identified primarily with the plight of Black men).[30] Paula Giddings's argument as to why Black women were under-represented in Women's Liberation is more convincing to me. White middle class women's history of racial insensitivity (to put it mildly) in the Abolitionist and suffrage movements, as employers, and as Southern belles, says Giddings, precluded Black women's identification or solidarity with an all-embracing feminist sisterhood. A deep distrust of those women who had gained their political stars in Civil Rights and were now turning that experience to their own advantage, and the idea that sexism, not racism, was the fundamental blight on women's existence further inhibited interracial alliances. Citing Toni Morrison, she adds that there was 'no abiding admiration of white women as competent, complete people' Black women regarded them as 'wilful children, mean children, ugly children, but never as real adults' (Giddings 1984: 307).[31]

Black feminist Michele Wallace confronted the question of Black women's relation to Women's Liberation from yet another, but related angle. Many Black women in the early 1970s were engaged in their own process of raising consciousness, but consciousness of racial pride. 'Being feminine', she wrote in 1975, '[had] *meant* being white to us', and constructing a new identity as Black women necessitated the rejection of white femininity (Wallace 1975: 5).[32]

With this rejection of the white Women's Movement and white femininity in place, Black feminists began to discuss what their own priorities might be. In 1970 Toni Cade edited one of the first collections of articles on black feminism, *The Black Woman*, which gives an invaluable insight into the current debates of that time. Cade asked in her introduction:

> Are women after all simply women? I don't know that our priorities are the same, that our concerns and methods are the same, or even similar enough so that we can afford to depend on this new field of experts (white, female). It is rather obvious that we do not. It is obvious that we are turning to each other.
>
> (Cade 1970: 9)[33]

The experts had defined gender oppression in terms of male domination and violence, marriage, the family and the social organisation of repro-duction, but these were not necessarily problem areas for Black women's liberation – or not in the same way. Critiques of the family as a restrictive and oppressive institution for example had a rather different resonance in the Black community: in a hostile world the family was often a stronghold for support. Besides, the whole issue of the Black family had been a controversial one from slavery onwards and remained so in the historiography of African-American existence. Controversy over the Black family had been aggravated with the publication of the Moynihan report in 1965, which not only saw the Black family as dysfunctional, but partially put the blame on Black women as matriarchs – an old stereotype of white racism and black sexism.[34]

White feminist treatment of male violence in studies such as Susan

Brownmiller's *Against Our Will* obscured the history of racism and per-petuated a dominant American myth of the black rapist, whilst paying scant attention to institutionalised white male violence against black women under slavery and beyond.[35] bell hooks then is right when she asserts in 'The Politics of Radical Black Subjectivity' that 'the theoretical groundwork for all reconsiderations of the category "woman" which consider race . . . was laid by women of color' (hooks 1990d: 21).

Long before recent theories of fragmented female subjectivity and the Other gained currency in Anglo-American feminist circles, Black feminists had begun to question the universalist assumptions of white women's definitions of what it meant to be female. This questioning was more radical than the by now familiar French feminist paradigm of gender binaries, for Black feminists did not confine their critique to gender alone. They saw Woman as Other to other women, and as Other even to herself. For, as Louise Adams remarks, Black feminists forced white women to confront their reluctance 'to come to terms with the whole of their identities – oppressor as well as oppressed' (Adams 1989: 29).

Easy as it is to recognise and analyse past mistakes, the question remains whether it would have been possible at that historical stage in the de-velopment of racial and feminist consciousness to find enough common ground for a genuinely multiracial Women's Liberation movement. White middle class women who had come through the New Left tended to theorise their bad experiences there in terms of male domination rather than race or class. Politicised Black women were pulled this way and that between their allegiance to the male-dominated Black struggle on one hand and a sisterhood of feminists which could not or would not recognise difference on the other.[36] The Combahee River Collective's 'Black Feminist State-ment' was of historic importance precisely because – despite its professed identity politics – it recognised difference not as something absolute, but as a matter of socially constructed and historically shifting definitions and positionings.[37] Where I think Women's Liberation groups failed all too often, was that they did not move beyond a moral or theoretical notion of sisterhood on to a political *praxis* based on solidarity and empathy rather than identification (which is where 'your own oppression' shades into self-interest, pure and simple). The 1970s Women's Movement campaign for abortion law repeal, for example, would have gained more Black support if, rather than focus on the single issue of a woman's right to choose (abortion or not), it had heeded CARASA's demand for a comprehensive package of reproductive rights and services. After all, whilst white women fought for abortion rights, Black, Puerto Rican and other women of colour were subject to enforced abortions and sterilisation abuse.[38] As we have seen, this failure on the part of white Women's Liberationists to think bigger and wider, beyond their own immediate concerns, was part and parcel of the contradictory and endlessly stretchable meanings of personal politics. Whilst Black women's political experience had been informed by the communal struggle and interracial as well as intersexual conflicts of SNCC, some white women's lifestyle feminism seemed to replace political action with bad old American individualism.

WOMEN'S LIBERATION: THE FAILURE OF SUCCESS AND THE SUCCESS OF FAILURE

As a social, rather than a political, movement *proprement dit*, Women's Liberation was more concerned with means and values than with ends, and more effective in achieving attitudinal and cultural change than in gaining lasting benefits for women in the traditional political arena of power, resources and legislation. However, it would be a mistake to subordinate the importance and lasting effect of that attitudinal and cultural change to the lack of lasting material gains. Nor would it be appropriate to attribute the failure of the Women's Movement in the late 1970s and 1980s to extend women's rights legislation (or even to hold on to it) solely to the personal politics of Women's Liberation. For, whilst it is true that the Women's Movement as a whole began to lose momentum from the mid-1970s onwards, this loss of steam had much more to do with the economic climate of that period than with the movement's organisational and ideological troubles.

From the beginning of the 1970s onwards, feminist demands – jointly articulated by NOW and by Women's Liberation groups – for new legislation and provisions which often relied on increased federal or state funding, faltered because of the wholesale collapse of liberal values in public policy-making.[39] In an important sense the Women's Movement had not just been an ideological product of the 1960s but also, in its expectations and demands, an economic one insofar as those expectations and demands had, in effect, presupposed continuing economic growth and an expanding welfare state. From this illusion the unexpectedness of the oil crisis in 1974, the ensuing recession and the gathering momentum of the New Right provided a rude awakening. The notorious backlash of neo-conservative and religious-fundamentalist anti-feminism got into its stride in the mid-1970s, and was most spectacularly successful in the eventual defeat of the Equal Rights Amendment in 1982. In the sphere of sexual politics and reproductive rights the New Right managed to change the terms of debate from a woman's right to bodily self-determination to that of the right to life – a concern with protection of the weak and vulnerable not otherwise evident in its social policy proposals.[40] Furthermore, the Women's Movement had been an effect as well as a cause of changes in American society during the 1960s and 1970s. The President's Commission on the Status of Women had made wideranging recommendations for the improvement of

71

women's socio-economic position as early as 1963, motivated by the demands of an expanding economy as well as those of a comprehensive civil rights programme.

Women's Liberation then radicalised and accelerated these developments, but it was only one factor in a complex web made up of a changing social climate, extreme economic imperatives (first due to growth, then to the massive public expenditure on the Vietnam war and later to the recession), and political upheaval. According to Drude Dahlerup, a social movement is still alive so long as it continues to challenge society in its values and organisation.[41] The overwhelming impression of the American Women's Movement in the late 1970s and 1980s was one of feminism forced into retreat (along with all the other radical practices and ideas originating in the 1960s). As the 1990s began however, it was clear that issues of race, class, gender and sexual orientation had not gone away, but merely underground. The Clinton presidential campaign was the first to address the proliferating crises of mass unemployment, AIDS, urban unrest, and the feminisation of poverty in terms reminiscent of the New Left and Women's Liberation. Hopes that the feminist retreat might have been a matter of *reculer pour mieux sauter* seemed to have had more of a hold on the American political imagination in the early 1990s than they had had for a long, long time.

This must be because Women's Liberation's political failures during the 1970s and 1980s contained a spectacular measure of success within them: the success of personal politics as a mobilising concept, of grass roots participation, of consciousness-raising, and of creative visions – however Utopian at times – which literally changed countless women's lives for the better. Women's Liberation genuinely did create a social and cultural revolution which permeated every aspect of American society, and was kept alive in the collective consciousnesses of the women who created it – and passed it on to their daughters. In this process, the role of the feminist media cannot be overestimated. It would not be an exaggeration to say that Women's Liberation as a leaderless amalgam of dispersed groups and practices was held together not by organisation, but by an infrastructure of magazines, touring speakers, broadsheets, films and exhibitions and – last but not least – creative writing. For many more women than were initially active in the movement, politicisation was the result of media-aroused curiosity and reading of movement literature. National conferences (the last one was held in 1977) were important, but they were not accessible to the vast majority of women. It was through the feminist journals, starting with *Voice from the Liberation Movement* in 1968 and culminating in the publication of no less than 135 feminist journals in 1975, that the wide and popular dissemination of feminist ideas was achieved. Sara Evans cites an illustrative example of a woman who began to read and hear about the Women's Movement:

Her days became consumed not only with diapers but also with news of feminism. 'By the time my husband walked in the door all hell would break loose. He was responsible for all the evils of the world and especially responsible for keeping me trapped . . . I knew that if I ever met Gloria Steinem we would be best friends . . . *Ms.* magazine, I read it totally uncritically. I didn't care what kind of bullshit articles were in there, it was my magazine'.

(Jan Schakowsky, cited in Evans 1979: 227–8)

For this woman, as for so many others, *Ms.* magazine had a politicising function in the absence of a consciousness-raising group or local feminist campaigns. As the imaginative embodiment of personal politics, American feminist fiction came to fulfil a similar role for countless more women, and their sisters and daughters and mothers, at home and abroad.

3

LIBERATING LITERATURE

There can be little doubt that literature is one of Second Wave feminism's greatest success stories. The impact of the Women's Movement – and more particularly of Women's Liberation – on the cultural arena is succinctly summarised by Nicci Gerrard:

> Feminism has encouraged writers who might never have written at all. It has validated writers who, before they found feminism, felt they had no 'right' to write. It has given a whole new subject area to literature, demonstrating that women's lives are important and their fictions exciting and readable. It has produced presses to publish women's writing. It has encouraged readers who were, often unknowingly, hungry for women's writing. It has meant an enormous increase in the richness and range of fiction. And it has been a vital tool for the women's movement.
>
> (Gerrard 1989: 76)

Constructing feminist fiction as the Women's Movement's bestseller, Gerrard here accurately describes its success in the literary marketplace, but the political role this fiction played in many readers' lives is added only as an afterthought. In my analysis of feminist fiction as a liberating literature, Gerrard's postscript becomes the main plot. Without losing sight of the dynamics of production and reception, I want to ask with Rosalind Coward, 'What is the relationship of the practice of reading . . . with political movements, in what way are texts effective, and most important, which ones are?' (Coward 1980: 236).

To Gerrard's list of new writers and readers, new fiction, and what Rita Felski has called the constitution of a feminist counter-public sphere, we could add the emergence of a powerful, influential and still proliferating feminist criticism and literary theory, courses in women's writing, and ongoing lively debate about what a feminist aesthetic might mean. The Women's Movement created nothing less than a new, gendered discursive space in which all women's writing would henceforth be written and read, whether it had allegiances to feminism or not. Coward's question originates from this perceived change in the layout of commodity culture; she argues, importantly, against indiscriminate consumption of women's writing and for a feminist reading practice which is self-conscious about its political interests.

But perhaps other questions need to be asked first. Why was fiction so central to the American Women's Movement? What exactly was the relationship between feminist fiction and Women's Liberation theory and practice? In which 'dominant' did it intervene and to what extent did that determine its forms as well as its subject matter?

LITERATURE AND AMERICAN FEMINISM

Women have traditionally been regarded as the reading sex, and from the time women gained access to higher education, literature has drawn them in greater numbers than any other discipline. This was no less true of the post-war generation of baby boomers who came to academic study in the 1960s. Many of the women students who were involved in the New Left were literature majors, whose experience of alienation in the classroom was a politicising factor in their shift towards feminism. Like their female peers in sociology, psychology and history, literature students were faced with a heavily male-dominated curriculum, overwhelmingly devised by men, taught by men, assessed by men. During the 1960s, the Civil Rights Freedom Schools and Black Studies programmes had raised the issue of the political determinations of school and university curricula, so that Women's Liberationists already had a model to work from. And because of the nature of their trade, women literature students were, perhaps, more likely to perceive the discrepancy between a liberal arts education which demanded on one hand a personal response, and on the other denied or trivialised it if that response was at all gender-, or rather female-specific. Part Three of Kate Millett's pathbreaking *Sexual Politics* was clearly written out of this experience of alienation, and Judith Fetterley expresses the same disaffection, or even anger, on behalf of women students confronted with an almost exclusively male literary canon: 'the female reader is co-opted into participation in an experience from which she is explicitly excluded; she is asked to identify with a selfhood that defines itself in opposition to her; she is required to identify against herself' (Fetterley 1978: xii).

For aspiring women writers the situation was no better: their efforts were often ridiculed or relegated to the inferior women's league (or 'lady-book', in Norman Mailer's terms).[1] Women's Liberation gave these writers the impetus and the confidence to articulate a different experience for women readers to identify with or have personal responses to. As Lindsy Van Gelder put it: 'Come the women's revolution, an awful lot of talented women are going to be hauled away from their steno pads, research jobs, and fashion columns – to explain it in print' (Van Gelder 1970: 93).

Explain it in print they did, notably and at length in fiction. Here, at least, women had historical precedents and role models. Women have had access to writing as a profession when other occupations (and arts) were closed to them, and this is especially evident in the history of the novel – literature's Women's Room, as it were. Terry Lovell argues that the commodification of literature in the late eighteenth century strengthened women's role as both producers and consumers in the literary marketplace whilst lowering the status of the novel as a literary form; the aggressive marketing of so-called Women's Lib fiction in the mid-1970s produced the same result.[2]

Some literary genres have lent themselves particularly well to the exploration of women's issues insofar as these were still perceived to be confined to the private sphere in the eighteenth, nineteenth and the best (worst) part of the twentieth century. Women writers have been relatively over-represented in the epistolary novel, the diary, the *Bildungsroman*, and the popular novel by comparison with the more highly valued literary forms of poetry, drama and the epic.[3] It was no accident then that in their assault upon standard literary values Women's Liberation writers sought to revive and valorise these 'female' forms (previously regarded as sub-literary) first of all.

We must be aware furthermore, with Lovell, that feminism has always associated itself with literature, from Wollstonecraft via de Beauvoir and Millett to present day feminist theory and criticism. Wollstonecraft targeted women's reading of (romantic) novels as a problem, to be solved through the process of a more useful and rational education for women, whereas Millett and de Beauvoir turned their attention to the representation of women (or Woman) in canonical male texts. Implicit in the work of all three is the idea that there is a strong relationship between what women read (whether it is romantic fiction or D. H. Lawrence) and what women feel themselves to be: irrational and subordinate beings, embodiments of the eternal feminine, and sexual objects – respectively. The analysis of women's relation to literature has thus from the outset been seen in feminist theory as crucial to an understanding of female subjectivity. Catherine Belsey's Althusserian statement that '[t]he interpellation of the reader in the literary text could be argued to have a role in reinforcing the concepts of the world and of subjectivity which ensure that people "work by themselves" in the social formation' was thus in essence already understood by Mary Wollstonecraft, who worried about the ideological effect of romantic reading on women's subjectivity. And the point that '[o]n the other hand, certain critical modes could be seen to challenge these concepts, and to call into question the particular complex of imaginary relations between individuals and the real conditions of their existence' was well taken by de Beauvoir in *The Second Sex* and by Millett in *Sexual Politics*, as well as the novelists of Women's Liberation who sought – precisely – to question these 'imaginary relations' in the dominant culture of literary canons (Belsey 1985: 51).

In the national frame of the American 1960s and its emphasis on a politics of authenticity and cultural revolution, and in the traditional linkage of women and literature, the centrality of fiction to American feminism can be explained. Women's Liberation writers consciously chose to challenge the literary standards and representational strategies which they had encountered as 'the dominant' in American culture. Not only did writing promise the freedom of self-definition in the search for a female authenticity, not only would feminist writing liberate its readers to recognise the real conditions of their existence, but it might also serve to liberate literature itself from restrictive and prescriptive male-determined standards of good and serious writing.

WOMEN'S LIBERATION FICTION: ROOTS IN CULTURAL REVOLUTION

What did feminist writers perceive to be 'the dominant' in American culture when they entered the literary arena in the early 1970s? If they were – like the socialists of the 1930s – writing in the service of an oppositional social movement, then what were they reacting against as well as acting for, and what models did they have?

Oppositional movements such as Women's Liberation which situated themselves outside the political system of Western representational democracy, had to create their constituency rather than finding it ready-made in the world of traditional politics. This means that they had to forge a new political subject in order to be effective, and this in turn required the crucial work of raising political consciousness. Women's Liberation magazines, path-breaking theoretical works like *Sexual Politics*, *The Dialectic of Sex*, *Sisterhood Is Powerful*, *The Black Woman*, *Against Our Will: Men, Women and Rape* and – slightly later – novels like *The Women's Room* played an important part in creating a constituency for feminism. The dictum that the personal is political undoubtedly enabled women writers to join up traditional female concerns and genres with a political aesthetic of counter-hegemonic writing. But this is not to say that feminist fiction sprang fully-fledged from the ideas of Women's Liberation, for the ground had been thoroughly prepared by earlier social movements such as 1930s Communism, the Black aesthetic and the cultural revolution of the 1960s.

A 1930s notion of representativeness for example returns in this poem by Marge Piercy, which dedicates her first volume of poetry, *To Be of Use*, 'to the movement':

For the give and take
for the feedback between us
for all the times I have tried in saying these poems
to give back some of the energy we create together
from all the women who could never make themselves heard
the women no one would listen to
to all the women who are unlearning not to speak
and growing through listening to each other

(Piercy 1973: flyleaf)

The individual who takes on the collective voice, who speaks from and for a disenfranchised group: this is characteristic of the writing of oppositional social movements, including Women's Liberation. Unlike the 1930s however, when documentary realism was the preferred form for oppositional writing, the American 1960s proved fallow ground for realist political fiction. The parodic, highly self-conscious novels of Thomas Pynchon, Norman Mailer, Joseph Heller and Kurt Vonnegut, which were still part of a literary underground which sought to challenge cultural and political complacency in the early 1960s, had been elevated to the status of high literature by the time Women's Liberation fiction came along in the mid-1970s. But Mailer, Pynchon, Vonnegut, Heller and other critics of American society did not earn their place in literary criticism's heaven because of their social concerns, but because of their metafictional tendencies, which had been elaborated into a high art in the work of postmodernists like Barth, Barthelme, Coover, Gass, Sukenick and a host of others.[4]

The rebels of the early 1960s thus paved the way for a properly postmodern fiction characterised, as Morris Dickstein observes, by an increasing 'emotional withdrawal' from the social and political spheres (Dickstein 1977: 226).[5] By the time postmodernist writing-about-writing writing came to be regarded as the new paradigm in American literature, the 1960s were at an end and Christopher Lasch's culture of narcissism was well under way.[6]

Thus it was not surprising that Women's Liberation novelists who chose to 'explain it in print' in linear, realist first person narratives (such as French's *The Women's Room*, Rita Mae Brown's *Rubyfruit Jungle* and Alix Kates Shulman's *Burning Questions*) were greeted with derision by mainstream critics. This was not so much, or not only, because they were profiled by their publishers as so-called Women's Lib writers, but because they were writing against the grain of what literature was supposed to be: self-referential, preoccupied with the problems of representation and autonomous fictionality rather than asserting, as women writers did, the necessity of a literature rooted in the social.

Just as 1930s socialist writers had defined themselves against what they saw as bourgeois interiority in modernism, feminists of the 1970s rejected their 'dominant' of an entrenched, canonical male modernism and a newly enshrined masculinist metafiction.

And yet – feminists had models for a reassertion of presence and voice in 1960s writing as well. Women's Movement politics learnt much from the Civil Rights movement and the New Left, and so also did the cultural branches of these social formations engender feminist writing. African-American culture had, as Michele Wallace argues, been

> crucial in forming the aspirations of the New Left, as well as minority revolutions – not so much by its considerable political activism – but precisely by its counterculture. While this 'minor' culture may sometimes be difficult to explicate as protest, it was always clearly formed in the spirit of subverting a majority culture that tried to choke it at the root. Precisely by its sex, drugs, dance, dress, music and style, it kept the records of its discontents accurately and well.
>
> (Wallace 1989: 105)

As Wallace reminds us, that other, earlier protest against an increasingly hegemonic modernism, the Beat aesthetic of the 1950s, had been indebted to the performance style and the way of life of black bebop and jazz musicians. The Norman Mailer of 'The White Negro' (1957) had unashamedly appropriated that heritage, mixing existentialism with black street culture for a model of a new philosophy for the 1960s:

> With this possible emergence of the Negro, Hip may erupt as a psychically armed rebellion whose sexual impetus may rebound against the anti-sexual foundation of every organized power in America, and bring into the air such animosities, antipathies and new conflicts of interest that the mean empty hypocrisies of mass conformity will no longer work.
>
> (Mailer 1957: 102–3)

What happened in the 1960s was all of the above, of course, with Mailer being a crucial and witting conduit of such rebellious energies, as manifested themselves in the American 1950s, and already very clearly formulated in terms of a sexual politics, – albeit very different from Kate Millett's some fifteen years later.

African-American street culture also informed the literature of the Black movements of the 1960s, which was often patterned on the rhythms and imagery of black speech (jive talk, signifying, lying, sermonising). In its efforts to reproduce and represent orality and non-standard speech, African-American writing challenged the dominant notion of good, literary writing, just as feminists were to do ten years later.[7] Marge Piercy's opposition between the new poetry of voice and an older modernist tradition of (élitist) letters thus reiterated a theme already prevalent in African-American writing of the 1960s.

It is certainly arguable that for the youth movements of the 1960s music (folk and blues, soul and rock later) was a far more important oppositional

79

cultural force than literature ever was, or could be. Nevertheless, the white New Left did have a literature of its own, notably in poetry and increasingly experimental forms of journalism. As in the 1930s, journalism, much more than 1960s fiction, offered Women's Liberation writers a model of the writer as both observer of social change and participant in it, but with this difference: the observer/participant was now also concerned with the 'personally authentic' nature of her work. Sara Davidson's account of three women's destinies through the 1960s and 1970s, *Loose Change*, is a kind of docu-fiction in which the author/narrator tries to weigh up what the 1960s meant to her; Davidson frequently comments on the overlap between fiction and journalism. And Nora Sayre's journalism in *Sixties Going on Seventies* traces the author's gradual awakening to Women's Liberation through her professional involvement with the movement as a female reporter. In poetry, women had role models in political poets like Diane DiPrima, LeRoi Jones, Gary Snyder, Nikki Giovanni and – most importantly of all – Allen Ginsberg. Ginsberg's 'HOWL' (1956) had long been a formative text in the cultural revolution, challenging the pieties of an academically enshrined New Criticism and the conformism of the literary establishment of the 1950s. The work of these poets and others were frequently heard in performance at anti-war demonstrations, whilst political journals such as *Ramparts* and *New Left Notes* also published them, alongside the latest position paper on the latest sectarian split.[8]

Autobiographical discourse, whether in Ginsberg's poetry, Tom Wolfe's and Hunter S. Thompson's New Journalism, or in Malcolm X's *Autobiography*, permeated the counter-cultural writing of the 1960s. Despite the masculinist – if not outright misogynist – preoccupations of much of this literature, it did not fail to encourage women to tell their stories in this personal/political way too. Black feminist Michele Wallace describes how 1968 and Black consciousness turned her life around:

> My dust-covered motto, 'Be a nice well-rounded colored girl so that you can get yourself a nice colored doctor husband', I threw out on the grounds that it was another remnant of my once 'whitified' self. My mind clear now, I was starting to think about being someone again, not some*thing* – the presidency was still a dark horse but maybe I could become a writer. I dared not even say it aloud: my life was my own again. I thanked Malcolm and LeRoi – wasn't it their prescription that I was following?
>
> (Wallace 1975: 66)

Clearly Wallace saw race as more of an obstacle on the path to cultural recognition than gender, but it is worth noting that writing here is represented in the terms of a search for authenticity: not just something to *do*, but also to *be* – a new identity. By the turn of the decade, at the very point when American postmodern male writers began to feel less secure about their previous status as privileged observers and interpreters of American culture and turned inward to examine the processes of writing and the role of narrative authority itself, Black and white women writers assumed their mantle as engaged writers, as cultural and political critics.[9] Experience could once more be mobilised in the service of art as it had been in the 1930s and mid-1960s, and art and politics became 'the avenues to authentic selfhood' for feminists. Women's Liberation writers then took the personal is political as their aesthetic as well as their political programme, and in reaction to masculinist literary norms and forms they sought to (re)create a literature of presence and voice. They felt they were beginning to write themselves into being, not so much as authentic, unified and universal female selves but as authentic and legitimate political subjects hungry for change. The anguish of Plath and Smedley, the artistry of Lessing and Woolf, the double-edged wit of McCarthy and Hurston, the political commitment of Petry and Olsen would now, unequivocally and explicitly, be harnessed for the cause of writing women's liberation.

WOMEN'S MOVEMENT WRITING

Like the movement activists then, feminist writers wanted to wipe the slate clean upon which woman had so long been inscribed by men, and begin again. As in the 1930s – but for different reasons – they turned against modernist impersonality and revived realist modes of writing. As in the 1930s also, they were concerned with truth – but feminist truth – experience – but understood in feminist terms – and representativeness, as well as documentation of women's suffering at the hands of patriarchy.

Through its validation of experience, personal politics legitimised a return to literary realism and first person narrative, but there were also elements in Women's Liberation's political thought which militated against a mode of feminist writing which would do no more than testify to victimisation and defeat. (Arguably, pre-feminist women writers like Joan Didion and Sylvia Plath had already produced such testimony in *Play It As It Lays* and *The Bell Jar.*)[10] Utopianism, a taboo in Old Left aesthetics and politics, returns with a vengeance in 1970s feminist writing. Terry Lovell articulates the necessity of a vision of the good society in the literature of oppositional movements:

> Marx dismissed as 'utopian' any form of socialism which was not based on a scientific analysis of the 'laws of motion' of the capitalist mode of production. But successful political struggles always depend on their ability to connect with utopias – with the belief that things might be better.
>
> (Lovell 1983b: 24)

A literal interpretation of 'living the revolution' soon faltered against the stumbling blocks of everyday reality, but it was nevertheless a powerful fantasy for feminist writers to pursue in fiction. As a consequence, the what if? scenario became a trope in the writing of the Women's Movement, a fertile opportunity to explore the vagaries of female desire and fantasy, often with the political rationale of envisioning change so as to better direct the struggle to bring it about. Nor did this what if? script only appear in overtly Utopian or science fiction writing by feminists; one of the distinguishing features of feminist realism is a Utopian dimension to even the grimmest tale of women's suffering.

Popular perception has stereotyped all feminist fiction as straightforwardly dogmatic blockbusting novels in the realist mode, but feminists have, at different stages in the history of feminist writing, opted for science fiction and fantasy as well as third person and first person realism. What these diverse textual strategies had in common, however, is that they all defined themselves against the canon of male writing. Joanna Russ explained her reasons for choosing science fiction in her essay 'What Can a Heroine Do? Or Why Women Can't Write' in these terms: if plots are made of culture and culture is male, then a good narrative cannot be produced by mere reversal of gender, because a woman protagonist cannot realistically take up a man's place in traditional cultural scripts. Literature does not have women *personae* in it, but only images of women, that is, woman as Other, and the Other 'is not a person at all, but a projected wish or fear' (Russ 1973b: 6). There are only two sorts of narrative in which a woman, hitherto, could be a credible protagonist, argues Russ: in the story of 'How She Fell in Love' and in the story of 'How She Went Mad'. Few options then remain for the feminist writer who does not want to marry her heroine off or reduce her to hysteria. She can produce non-narrative texts which will only find a limited audience; she can use a lyrical mode without chronology or causation (as in Virginia Woolf's novels); or she can turn to genres where gender transgression is already part of the convention, such as detective fiction, fantasy and science fiction. For Russ, the latter is preferable because SF lends itself to political writing, allied as it has always been with allegory and parable and other didactic forms. It is because Russ wants to reassert the cognitive function of fiction that she states at the end, despairingly, that forty years ago people who read books read fiction, whereas nowadays they turn to popular psychology and anthropology. In a ringing indictment of the American novel *anno* 1973 she concludes that 'perhaps current fictional myths no longer tell the truth about any of us' (Russ 1973b: 20).

But not all feminist fiction writers chose Russ's radical departure from realist fiction. In the same year, Doris Lessing remarked in a new introduction to *The Golden Notebook* that

ten, or even five years ago ... novels and plays were being plenti-
fully written by men furiously critical of women ... portrayed as bullies
and betrayers, but particularly as underminers and sappers. But these
attitudes in male writers were taken for granted, accepted as sound
philosophical bases, as quite normal, certainly not as womanhating,
aggressive or neurotic. It still goes on, of course – but things are better,
there is no doubt of it.

(Lessing 1962: x) [11]

Russ's advocation of abandonment of both literary tradition and realist
narrative, and Lessing's reminder of the widespread misogyny of mainstream American and English literature, together give us some idea of the
climate in which the new feminist fiction was conceived and received. I
believe that the much disparaged aspects of feminist fiction of the 1970s –
uses of realism, consciousness-raising as framing device, sexual exploration
and the role of the woman writer as protagonist – must be seen as complex
cultural responses to the predicament of writing as a woman, and a feminist
at that, in a politically and aesthetically hostile environment. But as complex
cultural responses, they were by no means unique in the history of literary
realism. Amy Kaplan adds an historical dimension to my argument in
defence of feminist realism in her book on realisms in the work of William
Dean Howells, Edith Wharton and Theodore Dreiser. In *The Social Construction of American Realism*, Kaplan disputes the romance-thesis put forward
by Richard Chase in *The American Novel and Its Tradition*, which argues that
the American novel has never been comparable to its European counter-
part, because American heroes embark 'on a melodramatic quest through
a symbolic universe, unformed by networks of social relations and unfettered
by the pressure of social restraints' (Kaplan 1992: 2).

Kaplan dismisses this idea as ahistorical, but draws upon its widespread
acceptance to demonstrate – rightly – that realism then came to be seen as
distinctly un-American, both in its associations with the European tradition
but more importantly because of its preoccupations with class and social
relations. In Kaplan's sophisticated analysis, American realism is distinctive
as a contesting mode of representation, a strategic and polemical intervention in America's habit of romantic individualist self-representation.

Realists do more than passively record the world outside; they actively
create and criticize the meanings, representations and ideologies of
their own changing culture.

(Kaplan 1992: 7)

Furthermore, Kaplan shows that American realist fictions contain
Utopian elements which posit the possibility of social change, and that the
frequent foregrounding of the writer as protagonist reveals a level of self-
awareness about the social and textual construction of reality in fiction: 'To

understand realism's struggle with other modes of representation is to restore to realism its dynamic literary qualities', and 'To call oneself a realist means to make a claim not only for the cognitive value of fiction but for one's own cultural authority both to possess and to dispense access to the real' (Kaplan 1992: 13).

I think that this description of early twentieth century realism is appropriate for American feminist realist fiction of the 1970s, too; it provides a fitting counter-argument to the notion that realism is merely a dressed-up version of conservatism and common sense. And it is worth bearing in mind that Kaplan's dissection of the motivations for American realism has much in common with Russ's arguments for science fiction, namely: contestation of the 'dominant', Utopian possibility, and the cognitive function of fiction. Such common ground indicates that perhaps Russ's highly self-conscious fiction, because of its reliance on a feminist epistemology, belongs in the realm of political writing rather than the postmodern or the metafictional.

Lacking a Michael Gold to prescribe what kind of politically useful fiction they ought to write, feminist novelists carved out their own – very diverse – narrative shapes, which is why it is difficult to define feminist fiction as a formally cohesive body of texts.[12] It would be too simple to assume that feminist fiction of the past twenty years provides a step-by-step imaginative rendering of the history of the Women's Movement over that time, or that it merely narrativised in fiction what theory did in theory. But there were two aspects to its counter-hegemonic aesthetic which united realist and fantasy forms nevertheless. The first was an emphasis on fiction as a mode of cognition of the 'real conditions of our existence' (literary as well as literally), and the second was a reliance upon and dialogue with feminist epistemology as articulated in the practices of Women's Liberation and in its major theoretical texts. It is then possible to say that feminist fiction drew upon, and answered back to, the history of the Women's Movement and those major texts as well as feminist theory.[13]

IN SEARCH OF A VANISHING OBJECT: FEMINIST FICTION

Although feminist journals had been printing poetry and short stories by women from the late 1960s onwards, and small feminist presses had published some novels and collections of articles, the distribution of Women's Liberation literature remained largely underground and incidental to the movement in the early years. Before a self-identified feminist fiction could make an impact upon the public domain through these counter-cultural channels, the commercial publishing industry invented it as a marketable concept. By-women-for-women fiction had always been a mainstay of the popular market; it seemed that feminist fiction could be sold as a sexier, more up-to-date variant.

The 'Women's Lib' novel burst upon the cultural scene in the early to mid-1970s with the publication of Sue Kaufman's *Diary of a Mad Housewife* (1970), Alix Kates Shulman's *Memoirs of an Ex-Prom Queen* (1972), the notorious *Fear of Flying* by Erica Jong (1973) and Lisa Alther's *Kinflicks* (1976). These novels were the first of the new women's writing to be widely reviewed in the mainstream press and discussed on talkshows, with the predictable result that they very quickly achieved bestseller status. With the exception of Alix Kates Shulman, none of their authors were movement writers in the sense that Marge Piercy, Kate Millett, Robin Morgan or Rita Mae Brown already were, and it was therefore all the more remarkable that Jong, Alther and Kaufman all of a sudden were hailed as voices of the Women's Liberation Movement. The publishers' hype surrounding these novels suggested a heady mixture of sex and female rebellion, and was aimed, at one and the same time, at women's feminist curiosity and at male voyeurism – after all, these novels promised an insight into 'what it is really like for her', and an answer to that age-old conundrum of what a woman wants. Yet despite their ambivalent (at best) relation to Women's Liberation politics, these novels did fulfil an important function for literary feminism: if nothing else, as cultural zap actions they made incursions into the mainstream which prepared the way for Women's Liberation writers to increase their audiences with a commercial publishing house.[14]

This was important, for although Women's Liberation did spawn a publishing industry of its own, distribution of the literature often proved more difficult. Having learnt some lessons from the 1960s underground press, Women's Liberation was effective at networking and passing on information through informal channels and resource centres, but it maintained its outside-the-system distrust of mainstream publishing. This meant that movement writers who wanted to reach a popular audience of 'ordinary women' often opted to have their books published by the big houses once they had made a name for themselves.[15] Of course, there were commercial interests at stake too. Small feminist publishers like the *Feminist Press* or *Kitchen Table/Women of Color Press* were always at risk from having their most successful authors poached by commercial publishers. As is so often the case, these small publishing houses were the ones to encourage and develop new women's writing, only to lose their most popular authors to bigger concerns.[16] But whatever the business of publishing feminist fiction, there can be no doubt but that its increasing availability created a loyal readership which in numbers vastly exceeded the constituency of women who were ever directly involved in Women's Liberation.

Publishers did not create feminist fiction merely by their marketing methods, however. After the first wave of bestsellers had splashed over America, bathing it in the illusion that 'Women's Lib' was really only the female version of the sexual revolution, a new kind of women's writing appeared which not only addressed Women's Liberation issues more seriously and more assertively but which also took the process of coming-to-feminist-consciousness as a major theme. These were the kinds of novel which could not have been written without the impact of Women's Liberation theory – they were, in a way, historical novels charting the genesis of the movement itself through the story of an individual or a group of women. Its prototype, Marilyn French's *The Women's Room*, traces the struggle of a suburban housewife for economic and personal self-determination, along the lines of Betty Friedan's *The Feminine Mystique*. But the novel also incorporates the tales of other women characters in a collective narrative clearly informed by the politics of Women's Liberation. Because it made many of the ideas of American Second Wave feminism accessible in popular form to a wide audience of uninitiated readers, *The Women's Room*, in spite of its later feminist detractors who dismissed it as a political and literary misconception, was and still remains one of the founding texts of the modern Women's Movement.

How did this self-identified feminist fiction attempt to change dominant cultural definitions of gender? I have so far deliberately avoided any attempt at defining feminist fiction in terms of a particular corpus of texts, set of formal characteristics or thematic concerns, or uses of genre.[17] Because of the variety of forms and genres in feminist fiction, it is not really possible to construct a strictly chronological schema, but I would suggest that we can nevertheless discern a certain pattern in the predominance of particular representational modes at particular times. A first phase of feminist attempts at an *Umwertung aller Werte* can be dated approximately from the early to late 1970s and is characterised by fictional representations of what feminism was fighting *against*. These included for example: restrictive sexual mores, the stifling aspects of middle class suburbia, unwanted pregnancy, abortion, premature marriage, and 1950s-to-1970s trajectories told in a first person voice. In short, the predominant weight of the first phase of feminist novels lies in a charting of change, the story of 'how (and why) I became a feminist'. Examples which broadly fit this description are *The Women's Room, Burning Questions* by Alix Kates Shulman, Sara Davidson's *Loose Change*, and Marge Piercy's *Small Changes*. Personal histories of a later date tend to be written in a different, more self-reflexive vein, such as Audre Lorde's *Zami*, Marge Piercy's *Braided Lives* and *The Color Purple* by Alice Walker, as well as Barbara Raskin's recent, parodic *Hot Flashes*; often they refer back to or contest these early fictions of feminist subject-formation.[18]

A second phase or trend can be distinguished from the mid-1970s onwards, when the feminist subject begins to appear in women's fiction, as it were, fully constituted. This means not only that feminism itself can be discussed and explored in these texts, but also that the feminist subject is naturalised as agent of change – in however circumscribed a fashion. It also means that new narrative strategies emerge which are often at more than one remove from the earlier linear, realist and first person modes. At its most audacious, fiction of this sort has strong elements of Utopian or science fiction, as in Piercy's *Woman on the Edge of Time* and Joanna Russ's *The Female Man* and *On Strike Against God*. At the other end of the spectrum novels like Kate Millett's *Sita* and *Flying*, French's *The Bleeding Heart* and Piercy's *The High Cost of Living* engage in an exploration of a changing feminist subjectivity: what are the psychic repercussions of living the revolution, what are the obstacles confronted daily in a male-dominated public world, but also in the private sphere of sexuality, where the structures of fantasy and desire prove recalcitrant to the demand for feminist transformation?

Such questioning of feminist identity and disappointment with the pace of social change continues as feminist fiction moves into the 1980s. A third group of novels, mostly written at a time when the Women's Movement's public presence is rapidly fading from view, seems to retreat from the realm of personal/political struggle in the present and project its concerns on to the past. In the harsher climate of the Reaganite 1980s, realist writers turn away from contemporary issues and begin to reflect, both nostalgically and critically, on the social movements of the 1960s, as in Marge Piercy's *Vida*, Alice Walker's *Meridian* and *Movement* by Valerie Miner. Subsequently, these writers try their hand at historical novels, seeking to revive a memory of women's agency and resistance during World War II in *Women at War* (Miner) and *Gone to Soldiers* (Piercy). Re-examination, or more accurately, reconstruction of history occurs at the same time in Black feminist writing. But unlike their white peers, Toni Morrison, Sherley Anne Williams and Alice Walker use the past to remember and mourn a brutalised history in *Beloved, Dessa Rose* and – again – *Meridian* and *The Color Purple*. Female violence or retaliation, a powerful site of fantasy in Miner's and Piercy's work, is here confronted in more ambivalent ways, formally represented in the violence of these texts and spilling over into the present despite the containment of an historical setting. Such female violence is channelled in a different way in feminist crime fiction, which begins to burgeon from the mid-1980s onwards in the work of Barbara Wilson, Mary Wings, Sara Paretsky, Amanda Cross and a flood of other new writers. Although blood and guts rarely drip off the page, they do rather disturbingly seep into everyday life: the 1980s world of feminist crime fiction is a dangerously unstable one, only ever temporarily righted through the intervention of strong – but human – feminist women. Agency here is central to generic convention, but limited to individual acts of transgression and heroism with little political effect but that of restoring a wicked world to its own wickedness.[19]

Whilst up until now we have been able to speak of feminist fiction with a reasonable degree of confidence despite the plurality of feminist discourses that these fictions draw upon and engage with, from the mid to late 1980s even a pluralist political designation becomes increasingly problematic. Terry McMillan's *Disappearing Acts*, though clearly informed by feminism, heralds a change of direction in Black women's writing away from collective history and the mythical/political towards personal relations within the parameters of contemporary urban existence. Margaret Atwood's dystopian *The Handmaid's Tale*, hailed as a feminist critique of Christian fundamentalism, in fact inverts many of the values of the 1970s Women's Movement. *The Handmaid's Tale* is a disturbing text less because of its harrowing dystopia than because of its representation of feminism and loss of female agency. The same is true of Sue Miller's nostalgic elegy for the nuclear family, *The Good Mother* and of her second novel, *Family Pictures*.

These novels present us with the problem not just of defining feminist fiction in a way that is both consistent and flexible enough to take account of the changing meanings of feminism itself, but more importantly they pose the question of how political women's fiction can still be produced and read once it is unmoored from its anchor in a social movement. Novels by movement writers in the 1990s, like Marilyn French's *Her Mother's Daughter* and Alix Kates Shulman's *In Every Woman's Life* then begin to look uncannily like pre-feminist family history blockbusters or 1960s portraits of modern marriage, like Alison Lurie's *The War Between the Tates*.[20]

In my analysis, feminist fiction is a dynamic discursive field. It emerged from the larger – already politicised – arena of women's writing, but is distinctive within that arena because of its allegiance to the Women's Movement, which it signals in its themes and underlying discourses of female agency and social change, as well as in its embodiment of a critique of literature itself in its very representational forms. In addition, feminist fiction addresses its readership in ways which seek to challenge prevailing cultural definitions of gender, so that at the same time as it constructs the reader as a gendered subject in conventional ways, it also offers the possibility of new and transgressive positions.

Reading is always, in a sense, a holding operation in the process of signification. That means that our reading of feminist fiction as oppositional writing cannot be static, but must yield meanings which slide and turn about with the shifting sands of historical and cultural conditions. What was written in the 1970s as self-identified feminist fiction had a strong connection with a social movement – was part of it, even. Ten and twenty years later, the situation is much changed: the earlier work, if it is to retain any political significance at all, requires an historicised approach, whilst on the other hand it is unclear what the political meaning of contemporary 'feminist' fiction can be now that the adjective has to be surrounded by inverted commas to indicate its uncertain and fragmented status. It should be clear however that the genesis and development of American feminist fiction, out of 1960s counter-culture and into the 1970s and 1980s, is far more complex and far more specific to American culture than the label 'feminist' in itself would suggest. This is where my engagement with other feminist critics over the political meanings of this fiction begins. Judith Newton writes:

> As feminist critics we speak of making our knowledge of history, choosing to see in it not a tale of individual and inevitable suffering, signifying nothing, but a story of struggle and relations of power. We speak of making our notion of literary texts, choosing to read them not as meditations upon themselves but as gestures toward history and gestures with political effect. Finally, we speak of making our model of literary criticism, choosing to see in it not an ostensibly objective reading of a text but an act of political intervention, a mode of shaping the cultural use to which women's writing and men's will be put.
>
> (Newton 1987: 124)

I take Judith Newton's emphasis on history as struggle, literature as political, and literary criticism as a mode of intervention to heart as also my critical credo, when I look at the question of how critics and reviewers have tried to shape the cultural use of feminist fiction. I think that feminist criticism has skipped a stage in its engagement with American feminist fiction: it has not, so far, historicised it in relation to developments within the Women's Movement (and later feminism), nor has it read American feminist writing in the context of 1960s (counter-) cultural debates and the American literary tradition. Two phases can be distinguished in the reception of feminist fiction: first, an attempt to read feminist novels within the frameworks of traditional literary criticism and genre theory, and second, critical readings which bring the insights of poststructuralism and psychoanalysis to bear on feminist realism. Differences between these approaches are very marked, so that we can, perhaps, speak of two generations of feminist critics, whose work reflects not only their different intellectual trajectories in the academy but also historically shifting conceptions of what it means to be a feminist critic working within, or without, a social movement.[21] What they have in common is that they engage almost exclusively with white women's writing, which dominated the developing sphere of feminist criticism until well into the 1980s.

GENDER, GENRE AND LITERARY THEORY IN THE RECEPTION OF FEMINIST FICTION

One of the earliest attempts to engage with an emerging new feminist fiction is Ellen Morgan's 'Humanbecoming: Form and Focus in the Neo-Feminist Novel', which looked at texts such as Unna Stannard's *The New Pamela* and Alix Kates Shulman's *Memoirs of an Ex-Prom Queen* in terms of the female *Bildungsroman*. Writing in 1973, Morgan did not as yet have many examples of feminist fiction to draw upon for her hypothesis that a radically new kind of women's writing was emerging from Second Wave feminism. But she did note a difference between the traditional women's novel of development, which represents the process of growing up as one of growing down (adulthood is equated with marriage, and marriage infantilises women) on one hand, and the neo-feminist text in which growing up means the achievement of authentic selfhood. Morgan sees this construction of an androgynous authentic selfhood as a political advance for women, a kind of free space transgressing conventional boundaries of gender role, made possible by the recognition that gender difference is socially constructed rather than biologically determined, and therefore amenable to change.

Androgyny, gender role and female authenticity have since come under fire from a more theoretically inclined feminist criticism which has rejected the humanist terms upon which a criticism such as Morgan's was based.[22] Yet her essay does give an astute account of how the 'neo-feminist text' subverts the conventions of a traditional genre, and of the way in which that subversion is informed by Women's Liberation theory.

Building on this reading of the feminist first person narrative as female *Bildungsroman*, other feminist critics such as Linda Huf and the contributors to Elizabeth Abel et al.'s useful collection, *The Voyage in: Fictions of Female Development* could in the mid-1980s look at novels such as *Kinflicks*, *Flying* and *Fear of Flying* as exponents of a new sub-genre, portraits of the artist as a young woman or female *Künstlerroman*.[23] Bonnie Zimmerman's contribution to this project of generic classification was particularly useful, since she showed how lesbian first person narratives combine and rewrite features of a range of traditional genres: *Rubyfruit Jungle* or – again – *Flying* may be categorised as coming-out stories, artists' autobiographical novels and female picaresques all at once.[24]

In exposing the limitations of traditional modes of literary classification, these genre critics were in effect beginning to formulate a new critical methodology in which the social concerns and political function of feminist texts were seen in relation to aspects of form. They, at least, were aware that the writing of feminist fiction was not a matter of pouring new wine into old bottles, but that new themes demanded new forms of representation and new ways of reading, exploding genre conventions and standards of good writing.

Kathleen Dehler's essay 'The Need to Tell All: a Comparison of Historical and Modern "Confessional" Writing' is a good example of interventionist criticism in Judith Newton's sense. Dehler rejects the term 'confessional' when applied to feminist fiction, because of the confession's association with shame and (sexual) guilt. Quoting Kate Millett's dictum that 'a writer ought to be shameless', she argues that a literature which seeks to liberate women's sexuality from its cultural connotations of secrecy, unseemliness and sin cannot seriously be discussed within the terms of a traditional genre such as the confessional.[25] Instead she proposes to read feminist first person narratives as a form of 'sociological autobiography', which absorbs common histories and mediates them through the voice of an individual protagonist. Far from a confession of past sins or a compulsion for self-revelation, this form of writing then represents a celebration of change and a refusal to apologise for deviation from traditional sexual mores.[26]

Although Dehler's essay was still couched in terms of a unified female literary tradition, which saw all women's writing as by definition oppositional in some way, she did note that the neo-feminist bestsellers of the 1970s elicited rather more heated reactions from reviewers than other women's novels of that time, and evidently 'touched a nerve in the culture' (Dehler 1978: 349). An interesting example of such heated reaction in the press, and of the confusion surrounding the meaning of an emerging new 'feminist' fiction, is the contrast between Germaine Greer's judgement of *Kinflicks* and John Leonard's in the mid-1970s. Whereas the latter finds *Kinflicks* an 'oddly invigorating' and 'very *funny* book', Greer describes it as 'gothic drollery': 'Lisa Alther's is not the voice of liberated woman, nor the voice of female wit. To clear the fogged brain of the flicker of *Kinflicks*, 500 words of Dorothy Parker would suffice' (Greer 1977).[27]

For Leonard, who is more aware of *Kinflicks*'s place in the American literary tradition (he mentions Holden Caulfield and Huckleberry Finn as progenitors of Ginny Babcock, Alther's heroine), the lack of a feminist perspective is the novel's greatest merit: '*Kinflicks* is not a long-playing whine, it is, rather, an exuberant yawp'. Furthermore, it has for Leonard 'an energetic intelligence, an absence of self-pity, an appetite for experience . . . making many recent feminist novels seem like clenched fists around the fact of injured self' (Leonard 1976).[28]

Whilst Greer rejects *Kinflicks* on political and satirical grounds, John Leonard's dismissal of 'many recent feminist novels' as self-indulgent and unsophisticated is fairly typical of a criticism which demands that feminist writing conform to the reigning standards of good literature: ironic distancing and pastiche (as in *Kinflicks*) are in, seriousness and political critique (as in so many other feminist novels) are out.

Frederick Karl takes a similar line in his survey of post-war American literature, where he elides the difference between feminist/oppositional and women's writing and disparages realism. In his chapter on women's writing, entitled 'The Female Experience' he argues not only that women authors demand too little for their female protagonists (all the women seem to want to do is break free, then 'curl up'), but also that the novels are marred by an 'unadventurous use of narrative, plot, character', because 'all that counts is subject matter' (Karl 1983: 424, 425, 426). Karl suggests for example that in *The Women's Room* disclaimers about art and literary tradition are designed to undercut anticipated hostile criticism (of precisely the kind that he lavishes on women's realist writing); the possibility that

Marilyn French may be on the offensive with those interjections against dominant literary standards, is not even considered.[29]

Yet Frederick Karl's negative judgement of feminist fiction cannot simply be put down to male chauvinist prejudice, for a feminist critic like Rosalind Coward also suggests that in 'confessional' novels (*The Women's Room*, *Kinflicks*, *Fear of Flying*, *Sita*) feminists use 'conventional forms uncritically':

> Indeed, it could be argued that the emergence of this particular form of 'women's writing', with its emphasis on sexual experience as the source of significant experience, might have the effect of confirming women as bearers of sentiment, experience and romance (albeit disillusioned).
>
> (Coward 1980: 234)

The throwaway phrase at the end is indicative of the source of Coward's misrecognition of what these novels are actually about: to write about the disillusionment of 'sexual experience as significant experience' is quite a big step in women's fiction, and not one to be relegated to secondary, bracketed status. And that is not all: 'Perhaps the kind of writing involved in *Kinflicks* or *The Women's Room* corresponds more closely to the structures of popular fiction rather than satisfying the incipient feminism of the population' (Coward 1980: 232).

This is a remarkable statement on the part of a contemporary feminist critic. Firstly, Coward entirely disregards the fact that for many feminist writers the choice of popular genres is a conscious and strategic one, which taps into existing channels for female pleasure and serves to widen the readership for feminist fiction. Secondly, Coward's questioning of the role of sexuality in 'confessional' writing, – quite apart from the accuracy of that observation – disregards the pleasure these texts afford in their representation of women's sexual agency (for it is not all disillusionment that is being served up here). Reading Coward, there is more than just a whiff of Mary Wollstonecraft in the air: romantic fiction rots the brain, feminist novels may do no better.

I find it interesting to note that what to one group of critics (including myself) seems innovative and challenging about feminist texts (frequent use of first person narrative, sexual transgression, long discursive passages alternating with more conventional fast-paced storytelling) provokes a knee-jerk response of irritation and impatience in others. Frederick Karl takes refuge in a conventional 'broader canvas' criticism that characterises women's writing as narrow and unimaginative, on the unspoken assumption that feminist writers are of necessity newcomers and amateurs who don't yet know what they are doing nor how to do it well. In their critique of *Fear of Flying* Elisabeth Cowie et al., like Rosalind Coward, opt for what might be called the defensive attack: by expressing reservations about what is popularly understood as 'Women's Lib' fiction they can preserve the notion of a pure, serious and properly feminist fiction – of which no examples are given. One problem with this line of argument is certainly that it fails to distinguish between novels which, strictly speaking, belong to the sexual revolution rather than to Women's Liberation: *Kinflicks* and *Fear of Flying* are much more ambivalent in their attitude to the Women's Movement than *The Women's Room* is and these novels therefore do not belong together in the same class. But there is something else at stake as well. Coward's critique of the 'confessional' is typical of the manner in which sociopolitical concerns in feminist criticism have given way to more (or differently) theorised approaches, so that feminist criticism has increasingly come to be read as a sexual/textual (in Toril Moi's phrase) phenomenon rather than as a cultural/political intervention, as in the early 1970s. This is both a gain and a loss in my view.

It is a gain in the sense that feminist fiction is finally, twenty years after its inception, beginning to receive the attention that it deserves; besides reviews and a few scattered articles there was not much critical interest in feminist fiction before the mid-1980s. Recent uses of poststructuralist, psychoanalytical and deconstructionist theory have undoubtedly sharpened feminist critical analysis, questioned traditional conceptions of female identity and drawn attention to the instability of the process of literary signification. As one of the first of this new generation of theory-informed feminist critics to pay attention to the literature of the Women's Movement, Rosalind Coward asked important questions of that literature and its readership which went well beyond the concerns of reviewers and of sympathetic feminist critics like Dehler and Morgan. Coward made a crucial contribution to the debate around the politics of women's writing when she questioned the universalist assumptions which governed the reception of 1970s bestsellers, when she wrote:

> Feminism can never be the product of the identity of women's experiences and interests – there is no such unity. Feminism must always be the alignment of women in a political movement with particular political aims and objectives. It is a grouping unified by its *political interests*, not its common experiences.
>
> (Coward 1980: 238)

The first to signal a necessary distinction between oppositional and conformist women's writing, Coward nevertheless misdirected her polemic in several respects, and this is where the losses contained in a shift towards the textual vagaries of cultural production manifest themselves. The fact that bestsellers like *The Women's Room* were marketed in a certain suspect way and read by some for titillation, does not diminish their importance as an emerging public discourse, by women for women, which politicised issues of personal life and sexuality and treated them *as if* these were indeed legitimate things to discuss in literature. For many a woman reader the

93

charting of sexual experience through personal histories in these fictions represented at least an imagined possibility of self-determining sexual pleasure, as well as an education – should she need it – in the social determinations of sexuality itself. The latter was, of course, especially innovative and liberating in lesbian fictions of development or awakening, such as *Rubyfruit Jungle* or June Arnold's *Sister Gin.*

The hypercritical treatment that realist feminist fiction has received at the hands of poststructuralist critics like Rosalind Coward, Margaret Homans, Meaghan Morris and others such as Elizabeth Wilson and Nicci Gerrard, is largely due to these critics' confused notion of textual politics. Such confusion arises in their tendency to equate, as we have seen, all realist writing with a stereotyped and monolithic notion of the bourgeois nineteenth century novel, as if a feminist construction of reality, informed by feminist epistemology, were no different from hegemonic accounts of the way of the world.[30] Another such confusion is that poststructuralist critics – surprisingly enough – tend to take the rhetorical use of 'voice' and 'experience' in feminist writing at face value, thus denouncing feminist realist fiction as a simplistic mode of signification. Representations of consciousness-raising as a framing device are a case in point. Both Rosalind Coward and Rita Felski, who on the whole is much more sympathetic to feminist realism, equate the consciousness-raising novel with the 'confessional' since it 'signals its intention to foreground the most personal and intimate details of the author's life', according to Felski (Felski 1989: 87). Note how the *trope* of a woman writer (or artist) as protagonist is interpreted here, not as a literary device encouraging identification, but as a statement about 'the author's life' as if there were no distance in women's writing between author and narrator. But consciousness-raising is precisely not a matter of revealing 'the most intimate and personal details' of a person's life for the sake of collective storytelling or confession; it is part of a process of theory-building, which might explain a general discontent. 'Experience' in this context is, of course, always the problematic term, since it is used both to denote the conditions or events producing that discontent *and* the articulation of it in political terms. As feminist critics ought to know however, there is no such thing as raw experience which can merely be recorded to produce (the author's) true-to-life story. When dealing with feminist first person narratives, as Sue Roe has remarked, the objects of study are already interpretations of oppression – the notion of oppression is itself a theoretical entity.[31] I labour this point because it effectively defuses the case against feminist realism, a case which has almost exclusively been made on the grounds that it operates (especially in its first person voice) on a 'naïve' theory of signification. I would argue to the contrary that it is feminist critics who are being naïve when they discuss texts which consciously try to construct a feminist reality and subjectivity and which self-consciously posture as anti-literary in the service of that project (Millett's

Flying, French's *The Women's Room*) in terms of an 'unmediated baring of the soul' as Felski does, or as 'the culture of the solid signified, the hard facts, the true story and Amazing Scenes . . . the literature of "what it's really like for women"', in the words of Meaghan Morris (Felski 1989: 97; Morris 1988a: 67). What is amazing is that feminist critics educated in the highly textually aware paradigms of poststructuralism and deconstruction, having forged an impressive set of critical tools in the service of reading women's writing, cannot bring them to bear on feminist realist texts. There is nothing more spontaneous or natural or unmediated about feminist realist or autobiographical fictions than there is about the – in this paradigm – more fashionable fragmentation of the (post-) modernist text. If feminist critics read them as such they are being ensnared in an illusion of their own making. Nor, finally, is the notion that feminist realism is about 'how I became my own person' (Coward), 'what it is really like for women' (Morris) or the discovery of an 'authentic self' (Felski) tenable in the light of this argument. To be sure, feminist realists do chart the quest for such authenticity, such a reality, such a mode of self-determination. But what characterises them is not that they find it, but that they constantly document the difficulty of that quest, and its inevitable failure under the 'dominant' of patriarchal social relations. If anything, novels such as *Rubyfruit Jungle*, *The Women's Room* and – most notably – *Flying* and *Sita*, map out the fragmentation of female subjectivity into the disparate elements that make up psychic life: conscious and unconscious, political understanding and recalcitrant fantasy, private and public. Not a single one of these texts can, upon careful reading, be said to tell the story of 'how I became my own authentic unified identity'. What they do show is that feminist knowledge gives a better grasp of the real, and that a necessarily fragmented subjectivity does not preclude female agency. It is precisely in the gap between reality as lived and social change as envisioned that their political significance lies.

In its politically confused uses of poststructuralist theory recent feminist criticism has had the effect of both disparaging feminist writers and their popular female readership.[32] Countless women who came to feminism because of novels like *The Women's Room* were constructed by these critics not just as unsophisticated readers but also as women at a primitive stage of political development, or as masochists taking their pleasure from a representation of, in Coward's words, 'a world without fantasy, where women struggle on, often grim, brutalised and victimised' (Coward 1989: 47).

This statement not only misrepresents the (much more diverse and positive) nature of feminist fiction, but it also leaves the crucial role of women's anger at this grim existence out of account. Feminist novels from the 1970s clearly had politicising designs upon their readers, and this meant generating and then mobilising this anger for the cause of radical change. Moreover, it is important for a feminist cultural politics to stress the role of the feminist writer as in control of her material, as consciously setting out to create an illusion of directness and spontaneity in order to forge an intimate relationship with the woman reader. As oppositional cultural practices, these texts try to minimise alienation and aesthetic distance in order to maximise the didactic and interrogative, e.g. political functions of the text. They do this by means of an exploration and critique of cultural definitions of gender as well as literary standards, and by positing female agency in text as well as sex. In this respect, feminist first person narratives are 'fictions of subjectivity', trying to give a voice, shape and form to a story which can bring a notional feminist self into being. This notional feminist self is neither unified nor disablingly fragmented and out of control, as Patricia Waugh points out. As a corrective to other feminist critics' unquestioning accept-ance of the anti-humanist stance of poststructuralism and psychoanalysis, Waugh argues that the Lacanian/Derridean rejection of a unified sub-jectivity is as problematic as the liberal construction of self:

> Much contemporary feminist writing . . . has accommodated humanist beliefs in individual agency and the necessity and possibility of self-reflection and historical continuity as the basis of personal identity. It has modified the traditional forms of such beliefs however, in order to emphasise the provisionality and positionality of gender, and the discursive production of knowledge and power. What many of these texts suggest is that it is possible to experience oneself as a strong and coherent agent in the world *at the same time as* understanding the extent to which identity and gender are socially constructed and represented.
>
> (Waugh 1989: 13)

It is this insight into feminist fiction's project of positing female agency whilst exploring the contradictions of gendered subject formation that informs my discussion of feminist first person fictions of subjectivity in the next chapter.

4

'IF WE RESTRUCTURE THE SENTENCE OUR LIVES ARE MAKING'

Feminist fictions of subjectivity

A voice from the dark called out,
  'the poets must give us
imagination of peace, to oust the intense, familiar
imagination of disaster.
  . . .'
       A line of peace might appear
if we restructured the sentence our lives are making:
shift from affirming profit and power,
questioned our needs, allowed long pauses.
                              (From Levertov 1987b: 41)[1]

In Denise Levertov's poem 'Making Peace' a voice from the dark calls for a new kind of language to articulate a changed, or rather a chang*ing*, world. I have chosen a line from this poem to describe feminist first person narratives of the 1970s: personal histories which attempt to restructure the sentence of women's lives, in both senses of the term 'sentence' – the technical one suggested by Virginia Woolf in *A Room of One's Own*, but also the juridical connotation of the sentence as cultural verdict passed upon women in dominant, masculinist representation.

To 'restructure the sentence our lives are making' was the first project of women writers of the 1970s such as Erica Jong (*Fear of Flying*), Marilyn French (*The Women's Room*), Alix Kates Shulman (*Burning Questions*), Kate Millett (*Flying*), and Rita Mae Brown (*Rubyfruit Jungle*). Later, other writers such as Marge Piercy (*Braided Lives*), Audre Lorde in *Zami* and Maya Angelou in her autobiographical *œuvre* placed themselves in this tradition whilst at the same time critiquing it. That restructuring the sentence was a project, and not just a spontaneous overflow of feminist emotion or narcissistic indulgence, becomes clear when we read feminist first person narratives as self-conscious fictions of subjectivity in which new scripts for women's lives are being written. I use the slightly awkward phrase 'fictions of subjectivity' to signal the common ground between real autobiographies

(Millett, Lorde, Angelou) and fictional narratives in the first person voice (Lessing, French); both forms employ a narrator as protagonist, and both rely on the illusion of presence in their mode of signification. The formal characteristics of this writing – varieties of realism and the autobiographical voice – align feminist first person narratives with the political literature of other non-dominant groups, rather than proving the existence of a gendered textuality. Whilst it is true that feminists sought to revalorise traditionally female genres in their uses of the first person, we must at the same time be aware that there is nothing intrinsically female about forms like the epistolary novel, the novel of development or indeed autobiography – such a designation is an effect of literary history, not of biology.

FICTIONS OF SUBJECTIVITY: THEORISING PERSONAL/POLITICAL WRITING

In her introductory essay to *The Female Autograph*, Domna C. Stanton points to a problem for feminist critics in the reception of women's writing. The 'age-old, pervasive decoding of all female writing as autobiographical', she argues, has effectively served to discredit all women's writing on the assumption that 'women could not transcend, but only record, the concerns of the private self' (Stanton 1987: 4).

I indicated before how a similar presupposition underlies some contemporary feminist critiques of feminist first person narratives, when they are discredited as 'confessional'. It seems that as a result, some of the feminist fictions of the 1970s have suffered the same fate at the hands of feminist critics as has befallen women's writing traditionally. Here I want to develop a theoretical framework for feminist fiction which leaves the autobiographical for the moment out of account, except as a textual effect creating an illusion of presence and directness, in order to avoid this traditionalist danger of equating the writing with the life. I think this is necessary, because the issue of women's writing being read as autobiographical is, of course, bound up with cultural definitions of women as the narcissistic sex. Although such definitions are usually associated with the nineteenth century, they still echo in contemporary writing (both critical and creative), and more especially in connection with the first person 'voice' in literature from the 1960s and 1970s – the latter was baptised the me-decade, after all. Rita Felski suggests in a discussion of the work of cultural critics Christopher Lasch and Richard Sennett that their critique of narcissism can be useful in separating the wheat of legitimate explorations of subjectivity in literature from the chaff of confessional writing. But she rightly concludes that 'whether subjectivity is perceived as radical politics or self-indulgent narcissism is at least partly dependent upon the standpoint from which it is being judged and the context in which it occurs' (Felski 1989: 187).[2]

If we take the context to be that of Women's Liberation, and if we make a political, engaged feminist criticism our standpoint, then clearly we cannot judge feminist fictions of subjectivity simply as self-obsessed. We must engage with them as oppositional cultural practices trying to change the cultural meanings of gender. To theorise this further, it may be useful to refer to Julia Kristeva's argument concerning women's relation to the symbolic order, and more particularly their relation to language as its necessary condition. In 'Women's Time' Kristeva observes that women (feminists, to be more precise) perceive themselves as casualties of the symbolic order, which she describes in Lacanian/Saussurean terms as 'an essentially sacrificial relationship of separation and articulation of differences which in this way [that is: in the articulation of differences, of which 'woman' is one] produces communicable meaning' (Kristeva 1981: 203).

Because outright rejection of the symbolic order would mean either utter silence or insanity, women have to somehow take up a place in it if they want to function in the world at all. Women's traditional place has been primarily to pass on the symbolic order, as mothers, to the next generation; feminists, however, have wanted to intervene in it. Two modes of counter-investment in what Kristeva calls the 'socio-symbolic contract' have presented themselves within feminism: one, to possess and subvert the socio-symbolic contract, and two, to explore its constitution and functioning, preferably in finding 'a specific discourse closer to the body and emotions, to the unnamable repressed by the social contract' (Kristeva 1981: 204).

Kristeva specifically excludes *écriture féminine* and the Utopian dream of a woman's language from the possibility of meeting this latter demand, because she does not believe in a gendered textuality but only in textual qualities reminiscent of a pre-linguistic closeness to the mother's body, at times to be found in avant-garde writing of both sexes. But I think a case can be made for feminist first person narratives to be read in the terms of Kristeva's first mode of counter-investment, that of 'possessing and subverting' the socio-symbolic contract.[3] To put this in more concrete terms, we might look at feminist fictions of subjectivity as a genre which on one hand draws upon a traditional white Western discourse, that of autobiography – a discourse which assumes unified identity and records public achievement (the story of significant lives, by implication those of great *men*). But whilst drawing on autobiographical discourse, feminists also try to subvert it by offering explorations of the social and psychic construction of female subjectivity (what Kristeva calls 'the subject in process'), telling a story of ostensibly private failures (separation, loss, fragmentation) which are then redefined as nevertheless enabling and real because necessary for personal and political growth.[4] Viewed from this perspective, the frequent foregrounding of the writing process and the casting of the woman writer as narrator or protagonist is less a postmodern metafictional device than a way of thematising women's problematic relation to a language and a literature which has traditionally functioned to define and confine them. Emphasis on the struggle with words and narrative structure in the search for female authenticity, the quest to escape the sentence should not then be read as a device signalling the autobiographical ('there is a real writer behind this text whose agonies of signification we as readers witness directly'), but rather as part of an argument about women's relation to the symbolic order in which the reader is implicated as much as the writer: both are engaged in the construction of oppositional meanings.

Of course, such a construction of new meanings is always circumscribed by the socio-symbolic contract, because 'communicable meaning' requires existing forms. In *Writing a Woman's Life* Carolyn Heilbrun lucidly sets out what the problems are in something so superficially simple as the telling of a woman's life story. She concludes that the supposedly self-evident, empirical material of female (auto)biography is almost invariably shaped according to certain dominant cultural scripts, notably those of romance and marriage. Like Joanna Russ in her essay on women's science fiction, Heilbrun shows that these scripts construct certain events and themes as significant at the expense of others, and notes that models for a woman's political life (for a narrative of female agency in the public world) are particularly scarce.[5] We can adapt Heilbrun's notion of existing (auto) biographical scripts for our analysis of feminist first person narratives, to see how the creation of new plots is inevitably mediated through the terms of the old.

In some feminist fictions of subjectivity, such as Marge Piercy's *Braided Lives*, Shulman's *Burning Questions* or French's *The Women's Room*, we can see the construction of a new script – that of 'how I became a feminist' – at work, but its formal articulation is still shaped by familiar forms. Elizabeth Abel's distinction between the novel of development or *Bildungsroman* (journey through childhood and adolescence up to adulthood) and the novel of awakening (crisis in adulthood, which restructures what went before) enables us to differentiate between different scripts in fictions of subjectivity. Within this schema, novels which employ the model of an original outsider (*Rubyfruit Jungle* and *Burning Questions*) are then read as conventional novels of development, whilst texts which represent a gradual coming-to-consciousness (*The Women's Room* and *Braided Lives*) are closer to the novel of awakening.[6] This distinction makes a difference to the construction of subjectivity and its political effectiveness in these texts: if the 'always a rebel' model presents feminist politicisation as a matter of psychic predisposition (from birth!), then feminism appears to be just one of many stages of non-conformism. The script of awakening by contrast usually turns on some dramatic event or series of events (such as the formation of a social movement) which forces the protagonist to re-examine structures and values previously taken for granted. For a literature which seeks to change women's consciousness about their own condition, these latter scripts are far more convincing because they change the terms by which personal life and life history are understood. Feminist novels of development and awakening do have in common, however, as Kathleen Dehler notes, a belief in social change.[7] This belief, and a refusal to apologise for the course of change taken, is a hallmark of personal/political novels, as their explorations of the social determinants of subjectivity and their indeterminate endings show. For unlike conventional scripts of closure (as Joanna Russ put it: romance, madness or death), endings in these texts often leave the protagonist alone, stripped of roles and illusions – including the illusion that feminism is the cure for all ills. However hard the trajectory, feminist endings are open endings, pointing to a yet-to-be-determined future. Often this is a future in which the writer/protagonist is implicated as the author of her own life, whether literally or metaphorically (literally in *Flying, The Women's Room, Braided Lives*). Open endings illustrate that the feminism of these texts is not a matter of a single ideology or theory underlying all; they are not simple narratives of conversion. As we have seen, it would in any case be more accurate to speak of a plurality of feminisms, which inform cultural practices in different ways, and to be aware that feminist first person narratives explore the social determinations (roles) and psychic structures (pleasure, fear, sexuality, fantasy) of female subjectivity rather than that they assert 'woman' as a fixed and coherent identity. Feminist fictions of subjectivity create, on the contrary, a femin*ist* subjectivity which is always positional, provisional, or – in Nancy Miller's words – 'subject to change'.[8]

Rosi Braidotti theorises this phenomenon in 'The Politics of Ontological Difference':

> Speaking 'as a feminist woman' does not refer to one dogmatic framework but rather to a knot of interrelated questions that play on different layers, registers, and levels of the self. Feminism as a speaking stance and consequently as a theory of the subject is less of an ideological than of an epistemological position ... By providing the linkages between different 'plateaux' of experience, the feminist thinker connects, for instance, the institutions where knowledge is formalized and transmitted (universities and schools) to the spaces outside the official gaze, which act as generating and relay points for forms of knowledge as resistance (the women's movement).
>
> (Braidotti 1989: 94)

I believe that we can read feminist first person narratives more productively than feminist criticism has hitherto enabled us to do if we bear this definition of what it means to speak as a feminist woman firmly in mind: a knot of interrelated questions, 'playing on different levels of the self', rather than a set of prepackaged answers. These levels include fantasy and the unconscious, and they include also the different historical layers of subjectivity. As fictions of subjectivity, first person narratives construct a feminist subject who is in the process of becoming a knowing subject, but as often as not the outcome of this process is precisely the knowledge of its own continuity into the future. As the narrator in *Burning Questions* concludes:

> But in the end those weren't the facts that mattered. The significant ones were the intangibles . . .
>
> *Often when people try to sum up the activity of a group or individual and can point to no immediate, tangible results, they conclude that the activity was a failure. But how can you count all the circles made by a stone when you toss it into the water?*

(Shulman 1978: 347)

Still, even if we conclude that feminist fictions of subjectivity often arrive at the construction of a feminist subject-in-process, they do so in the literary discourse of fiction and not in the epistemological mode of Braidotti's feminist thinker. What then is the relation between creative writing and feminism as an epistemology? So far I have only asserted that feminist political discourses ('major texts') inform or underlie fictions of subjectivity, but that notion now needs to be specified. Paulina Palmer writes of the influence of feminist theory upon women's writing – I want to put this more strongly and speak of feminist political theories as authenticating discourses for feminist fiction. This means that the traffic is not, as Palmer's analysis seems to suggest, purely one-way; feminist fiction certainly interrogates and challenges feminist theory as much as it is also informed by it.[9] But the notion of an authenticating discourse of feminist fiction does require further discussion of realism, since it is in realism (not modernism or postmodernism) that epistemological claims for literature have traditionally been made.

IS FEMINIST REALISM DIFFERENT?

Terry Lovell's intricate and sophisticated argument in *Pictures of Reality* offers a useful insight into that most vexed of questions: the relation between realism and referentiality. Realism as a mode of representation, Lovell argues, assumes the existence of an external, material reality beyond discourse. But although this assumption has usually been taken as a prescription for realist literature to 'depict' external reality, there is, in fact, no necessary connection between a belief in extradiscursive reality and an artistic practice that has to render it truthfully. For truth, in Lovell's analysis, requires validation from outside literary discourse:

> Art may express true ideas, and may produce knowledge in the sense that some people may learn these truths through art rather than through historical or sociological analysis. Art may also produce conviction. But the status of its truths *as* valid knowledge is determined

102

elsewhere than in art, in the univocal language of science and history rather than the polysemic language of art.

(Lovell 1983a: 91)

Literature, in its polysemic use of language, can therefore produce knowledge, but it is a different kind of knowledge from that afforded by science, history or – we might add – feminist theory. For Lovell, literature's cognitive function is always secondary; it is not essentially the business of art to tell it like it is – other discourses do that with more validity, with a truth claim behind them. Feminist realist texts then can make no ultimately valid claim to producing knowledge of the real conditions of women's existence, and they have to rely on feminist theory, living memory and the practices of the Women's Movement to do this epistemological work for them. But conversely, feminist fiction does provide imaginative scenarios in which that epistemology is opened up again and exposed to new questions, new challenges. Feminist theory, memory and feminist politics then function as feminist fiction's authenticating discourses.

Clearly feminist texts, as political texts which seek to raise women's consciousness, have to foreground their cognitive function if they are to be politically effective. The question then arises as to what textual strategies are employed to bring this about. I can see two possibilities: firstly, the text tries to limit or control its polysemic processes, or secondly, the text offers particular avenues of pleasure (through its use of plot, or the possibility for identification) in order to simultaneously delight and instruct the reader. This passage from *The Women's Room* suggests that here is a text which tries to control its own meaning:

Do you believe any of this? It is not the stuff of fiction. It has no shape, it hasn't the balances so important in art. You know, if one line goes this way, another must go that way. All these lines are the same. These lines are threads that get woven into a carpet and when it's done the weaver is surprised that the colors all blend: shades of blood, shades of tears, smell of sweat. Even the lives that don't fit, fit.

(French 1978: 269)

Ostensibly a defence against formalist notions of art, this passage seeks to gain the reader's assent to its account of gender relations in contemporary society. Fiction is posited here as false – too orderly, too symmetrical compared with the chaos and repetitiveness of women's lines/lives as lived. Every woman's life, it is asserted, ultimately conforms to a script of victimisation which is being written (or woven) over and over and over again. The terms upon which we usually believe or disbelieve are reversed: it is implied that it is easier to believe in (comforting) fiction than to believe the 'truth' related here, in *The Women's Room*. This inversion is characteristic of feminist realism as an oppositional practice – after all, feminist realism

103

tries to tell us something new in a mode of representation which purports to reflect existing conditions. It just does not always tell us so explicitly that it is doing so – French's tendency to patronise her readers in this way has annoyed many a critic, feminist and non-feminist alike.

The political discourse authenticating French's message that 'All these lines are the same . . . Even the lives that don't fit, fit' is that of *The Feminine Mystique* and *Sexual Politics*, both of which universalise the plight of the middle class white woman as women's condition full stop. But *The Women's Room* as a novel performs this universalising operation by its direct address to the reader ('you', 'we', 'I'), which rhetorically positions her as one who can assent to the text's construction of reality, and experience it as a mode of cognition. In effect, this reader is constructed as white, female and middle class, the 'dominant' in Women's Liberation.[10] This does not mean that the text therefore excludes other readings and other kinds of readers, but it does mean that the particular pleasure of (re-)cognition through identification is denied them. Terry Lovell calls this kind of textual pleasure a social pleasure, because it arises from 'common experiences identified and validated in art':

> Cultural products are articulated structures of feeling and sensibility which derive from collective, shared experience as well as from individual desires and pleasures. The pleasure of the text stems at least in part from collective utopias, social wish fulfilment and social aspirations, and these are not simply the sublimated expression of more basic sexual desires.
>
> (Lovell 1983a: 61)

Contrary to a Brechtian conception of a political art which mistrusts narrative pleasure and prevents the reader/spectator from getting too involved, feminist realism does not reject identification but often actively invites it. The necessary cognitive function of distancing the reader from the everyday world of dominant ideology and common sense is thus not achieved by means of alienation effects and breaks in perspective, but rather by a narrative evocation of the strangeness of reality itself. The passage from *The Women's Room* illustrates this technique: the 'real real' under the surface of individual everyday lives is more alien and more horrifying to women than fiction. Once they can confront it, their anger will surface and they can begin to do something to change it.

Feminist realism, by virtue of its reliance upon extraliterary feminist discourses, is then indeed different from other realisms, whether bourgeois or socialist.[11] Feminist realism does not present a picture of reality which confirms and naturalises the (implied) reader's worldview, nor does it – as in socialist writing of the 1930s – rest content with the documentation of the harshness of that reality. For there are Utopian realisms as well; not all feminist realist fiction is so obsessed with the social determinants of women's lives, and so determined to spell it out as is *The Women's Room*. Rita Felski has coined the term 'subjective realism' to describe American feminist fictions which 'incorporate the depiction of dreams, fantasies, flights of the imagination as part of [their] conception of the real' (Felski 1989: 82).

If subjective realism seems to be a *contradictio in terminis*, then that contradiction is more apparent than real. Subjective feminist realism, after all, only articulates imaginatively what Rosi Braidotti claims is the condition of feminist thought: to connect knowledge with lived experience – and that includes the lived experience of psychic life, of desire, and (often crucially) of Utopian fantasy.

Feminist fictions of subjectivity then seek to intervene in the symbolic order by restructuring the sentence of women's lives, whilst at the same time they are being shaped by existing cultural scripts which limit the reach of the new. They have a cognitive function, but it is feminist theory, living memory and feminist politics which authenticate feminist fiction's claim to truth, mediating between fictional representation and the real conditions of women's lives. Not only is feminist realism different from conventional realisms, but as a subjective realism it furthermore challenges and at times erases the division between inside and outside, subjective psychic life and objective social reality. So far, so good. But what of the difference between real autobiography and first person fictions? For whereas first person fiction should be read as a form masquerading as autobiography, real autobiography is supposed to have a real referent and a real subject – it is supposed to provide, in the real-life person of its author, its own authentication. I stated earlier that I would disregard this difference between real and fictional first person narratives for the moment, but the moment has come to ask whether such an elision is tenable.

USES OF THE AUTOBIOGRAPHICAL VOICE AND THE PARADOX OF TRUE STORIES

An extensive body of theory has developed in recent years on the subject of women's autobiography. Whilst the distinguishing features of true autobiography have always been assumed to be that author, narrator and protagonist are one and the same person, that this person has really existed or still exists, and that the narrative order of the autobiographical text refers to real-life events, these critical axioms have been challenged recently by theorists who reject such empirical entities as 'real-life events' and – indeed – authors.[12] Conventional criticism tended to concentrate its analyses of autobiography on the *auto* and the *bios*, as if textual processes could be disregarded (just as they were, for a long time, in historiography), but more recent studies of autobiography have drawn attention to the *graphia*. It is this shift towards a concern with autobiography as a textual practice as well as a life history that may prove useful for a criticism of feminist fictions of subjectivity.

Feminist critics of autobiography in particular have taken advantage of literary-theoretical developments inspired by post-Saussurean linguistics and psychoanalysis to break open a critical discourse which had largely confined itself to the study of autobiographies by famous men (Rousseau, St Augustine, Benjamin Franklin). By focusing on women's autobiographies, they changed the terms of analysis from autobiography as an account of public achievement to a wider definition of autobiography as a construction of subjectivity. Thirdly, in loosening the previously unproblematic connection between text and referent, feminist critics have been able to show how other literary and non-literary forms of writing (the *Bildungsroman*, the romance, the blues, collective oral history, the family saga) have shaped women's autobiographical texts both as oppositional and as conformist cultural practices.[13] This does not mean, however, that the referent has been abandoned completely either in feminist or in contemporary theory-informed criticism generally. Philippe Lejeune's attempt to solve the paradox of 'true stories' by proposing a *contrat de lecture* for example shifts the responsibility of truth-telling in a Barthesian way from the author to the reader, who contracts to *read* real-life events into the narrative. Lejeune distinguishes between a *pacte autobiographique*, by which we read real autobiographies, and a *pacte fantasmatique* for autobiographical fiction, where author and protagonist cannot be identified with each other (they have different names). The latter signals to the reader 'this says something about me, but it is not me', whereas the former simply states 'this is about me' (Lejeune 1977: 29). Lejeune's distinction enables us to identify the different assumptions we bring to our reading of women's autobiographical texts. Whereas autobiographies of public women, such as Millett's *Flying* or Audre Lorde's *Zami* are approached by the autobiographical pact, a third person fictionalised autobiographical novel such as Agnes Smedley's *Daughter of Earth* is read differently: we take it as a novel, and have to refer to Smedley's biography to authenticate (aspects of) the narrative as auto-biographical. Lejeune's schema is useful, but it is important to note that nothing is said here about rhetorical fictional uses of the first person 'voice' (as in *The Women's Room*), which invoke the autobiographical or fantasmatic contract but cannot be held to it. Because I know nothing in any detail about French's life, and because the speaker of French's novel is, at the end, identified as Mira Ward, the illusion created in *The Women's Room* of an autobiographical voice, a presence which speaks to us directly, is shattered. All we are left with is a fictional construction: Mira, protagonist in a novel.

Neither does Lejeune make judgements about the truth value of first or third person autobiographical narratives – he is only concerned with the reader's attitude to it. It is the reader who does or does not equate the author with the narrator/protagonist, and it is the reader who, in Benveniste's terms, decides to take the autobiographical text as an *énonciation* or utterance in which the speaker refers to him or herself, or merely as an *énoncé* – the sentence or text which is uttered but which does not refer back to its originating instance, the speaker.[14]

Elizabeth Bruss's *Autobiographical Acts* approaches the same problem of referentiality from a pragmatic point of view. Using speech act theory, Bruss argues that because autobiography is not characterised by an intrinsically autobiographical form, its distinctiveness is governed by extratextual factors. Autobiography as a speech act can function performatively as promise, apology or defence, or simply as narration or description. As an illocutionary act however it is always tied to the speaker as authenticator of whatever discourse is produced, so that (at least within linguistic pragmatism) the difference between real autobiographies and fictional ones is maintained: texts do not just have a meaning because of what they say and how they say it, but also because of who identifies herself as the speaker.[15] Bruss's speech act approach, however reductive in other ways, is useful for an analysis of feminist fictions of subjectivity because it explains the appeal and effectiveness of real autobiography in providing role-models and sites of identification for women readers. Maya Angelou constantly signals proud ownership of her autobiography, whereas Marilyn French distances herself from Mira Ward's fictional first person voice. The textual construct 'Maya Angelou', when identified with Maya Angelou the real historical person, can thus become a model of real life possibility whereas Mira Ward cannot – or not in the same way.

Domna Stanton, by contrast with Lejeune and Bruss, emphasises the similarity between autobiography and fiction: 'the excision of *bio* from autobiography is designed to bracket the traditional emphasis on the narration of "a life", and that notion's facile assumption of referentiality' (Stanton 1987: vii).

Whether the assumption of referentiality need necessarily be 'facile' or not, it is clear that Stanton sees all autobiographies as novels (but not vice versa), because they are subject to the same processes of invention of the self through the construction of narrative. As Benveniste wrote: '[i]t is in and through language that man constitutes himself as a subject', and the same goes for woman: there is no such creature as an extradiscursive self (Benveniste 1971b: 223).

Looking at autobiography and first person narratives *en masse* as fictions of subjectivity then is to take Stanton's point on board that there is no textual difference between real and fictional autobiographical voices – both are a matter of textual effect and it is the reader who contracts to believe in the presence of that voice automatically or to suspend disbelief for the duration. I do think though that Stanton's fictionalising approach has to be supplemented with the insights that Bruss, Lejeune, and Benveniste give to the extratextual dimensions of reading autobiography as opposed to reading fiction. For, whilst we may ignore the real life referent of the autobiographer, we should not disregard the pragmatically different functioning of real autobiography (in which author, narrator, and protagonist are assumed to be the same). In its exemplary (role modelling) function, the real autobiography can play an important part in oppositional cultural practices, and more especially in those which rely on a politics of identity; this is a crucial aspect of the way in which they mean.[16]

Thus, in the texts discussed briefly below, the point is not to comment on how the fictional or autobiographical subject relates to one that really existed (or might exist), but rather to look at how subjectivity is figured in relation to feminist discourses, how reality is constructed in oppositional ways, or in short: to look at ways in which the texts 'restructure the sentence our lives are making'. This is a complex enterprise, for, as Sidonie Smith explains '[t]he hermeneutics of self-representation can never be divorced from cultural representations of woman that delimit the nature of her access to the word and the articulation of her own desires' (Smith 1987: 151).

'SO WHY WRITE NOVELS? INDEED, WHY! I SUPPOSE WE HAVE TO GO ON LIVING AS IF . . .': DORIS LESSING'S *THE GOLDEN NOTEBOOK*

Any discussion of American feminist fictions of subjectivity has to begin with *The Golden Notebook*. First published in 1962, Doris Lessing's best known novel raised some dust in the United States, but it was not until republication in 1973 that its full impact was felt. Just as Simone de Beauvoir's *The Second Sex* engendered the Bible of the Women's Liberation Movement, Kate Millett's *Sexual Politics*, so also did *The Golden Notebook* generate other novels exploring the social, political and psychic features of women's subjectivity. Feminist fiction of the 1970s is riddled with references to Lessing's novel, and populated with narrators and protagonists who address Anna Wulf – and quarrel with her – in their own efforts to create a life and a self (and a text) out of fragments.[17]

The Golden Notebook is in several respects a prototype for American feminist fictions of subjectivity. In the new introduction to the novel (1973), Lessing drew attention to its major theme: the predicament of the artist in the modern world – something which undoubtedly appealed to Women's Liberation writers who were struggling with their own predicaments as artists and were, like Anna, in search of female authenticity. But although Lessing constructed a credible female protagonist in Anna Wulf, Lessing herself never put the question in gender terms. She vigorously resisted the idea that the novel was 'about the sex war' and she saw her own concerns as infinitely wider than just feminism in *The Golden Notebook*: to make connections between the dynamics of gender relations, the history of the Left, postcolonial struggles, the nature of love, the insights and limitations of psychoanalysis, and the crisis in literary representation – all at once. The theme of the alienated artist struggling to create order out of the chaos of modern existence was nevertheless taken up by American feminists who, like Lessing and Anna Wulf, saw the struggle with language and traditional modes of representation as a condition for social change. Lessing's formal innovations in *The Golden Notebook* likewise influenced feminist writing. The mixture of first person voice in some of the notebooks, third person fictional narrative in others and the Russian doll-like framing technique of novels within the novel, makes for a complex multilayered text which not only mirrors the many layers of Anna Wulf's subjectivity but also collapses realism into modernism and modernism into postmodernism. In many ways *The Golden Notebook* documents, in its depiction of the many contradictory forces governing Anna's life, the breakdown of the master narratives of psychoanalysis, Marxism and also literary tradition, as well as those of true love and true sex. In the end Anna Wulf refuses the resolution of her psychic fragmentation in madness or death (hitherto the usual fate inflicted by women writers upon their non-conformist heroines), but she does not discover a satisfactory alternative way of being either. *The Golden Notebook* ends in ambivalence, separation, and aloneness: for Anna, the self remains unrepresentable and all there is left to do is to do: work, politics, integration into the everyday world.[18]

The Golden Notebook portrays in Anna the dilemma of a woman writer in search of a form which is adequate to her experience, but it is Lessing who finds that form in this novel, not Anna. It is a form appropriate to 1962, to the pre-feminist era of widespread female discontent lacking a focus and a movement; a period also of literary complacency and New Critical confidence in aesthetic values such as unity and integrity. Lessing exploded these standards of literariness, and held them up to the cold light of day, but she could not quite do the same with her analysis of gender relations in *The Golden Notebook*. At best, Anna Wulf gains insight into the necessarily fragmented nature of her existence, continually torn between personal needs and public demands, past and present, self and others.[19] *The Golden Notebook* is undoubtedly 'about' the personal as political, and about the literary as political, but Anna Wulf lacks the conceptual framework in which that understanding can be articulated. From a contemporary socialist-feminist vantage point, *The Golden Notebook* remains, in its very ambivalence, its fragmentation and its insistence, nevertheless, to connect everything with everything else (and most of all to live with the contradictions), a seminal text of feminism, in which nothing gets resolved but everything is laid open for discussion.

LETTING THE VOICES OUT: MARILYN FRENCH'S
THE WOMEN'S ROOM

What *The Golden Notebook* lacked in feminist analysis, *The Women's Room* provided in lengthy and meticulous detail. 1978 saw the publication of a host of feminist texts (it was a leap year for feminist criticism too), but *The Women's Room* gained – and has probably retained – a reputation as the classic novel of Women's Liberation. Marilyn French explained its impact thus:

> [It] spelt the truth about how a lot of women felt. It wasn't a truth coming to them from the outside; it was a truth they had known, and felt, and never seen reflected in their culture. When they did see it *they recognised it immediately* and suddenly realised that they were not peculiar. The reason they were unhappy was not that they were neurotic or bad, but because these were cultural facts about what happens to women. It empowered them. The possession of truth is always empowering. [my italics]
>
> (French, cited in Gerrard 1989: 137)

French's statement is typical of a view of feminist fiction as straightforwardly reflectionist, telling a truth about women's experience which is both already there and still hidden. This truth can only be recognised once it is put into words, or, more accurately, narrativised, which means articulated in terms of cause and effect. And yet for all its familiarity, this is a peculiar statement in the light of a (re)reading of *The Women's Room,* for the idea that women 'recognised its truth immediately' denies and ignores all the polemical pointers that French incorporated in her novel to ease the passage from old (bad and neurotic) to new truths of female subjectivity (women are victims of male domination, and can only turn to each other for comfort). It ignores, in other words, the ideological/epistemological work that the novel itself performs upon the fictional narrative, both by means of the inclusion of political discussions between the women and also in its aesthetic (meta)discourse of narratorial intervention.

The Women's Room is, like *The Golden Notebook*, voiced in part in the third person and partly in the first. The first person narrative frames a voyage into the past through the familiar terrain of the American 1950s and 1960s and into the present. It is not clear until the very end that this first person narrator is Mira Ward, one of several characters whose personal histories are recounted, even if hers takes pride of place throughout. This de-centring of the narrative focus keeps the reader guessing where the story originates; any of the women could be telling it – and this, of course, is the point.

In speaking about her (past) self in the third person, Mira fictionalises herself within her autobiographical discourse. Thus, in a way Mira Ward's

110

account of Mira Ward's life is a novel within the novel (much like *The Golden Notebook*) despite the illusion of directness. That illusion is created by *The Women's Room*'s constant hailing of the reader with its intimate mode of address: 'Perhaps you find Mira a little ridiculous. I do myself. But I also have some sympathy for her, more than you, probably' (French 1978: 10).

Like Lessing in *The Golden Notebook*, like Erica Jong in *Fear of Flying*, like Kate Millett in *Sexual Politics* and Simone de Beauvoir in *The Second Sex*, French thematises the role of cultural discourses in subject formation, emphasising the epistemological violence that dominant culture wreaks upon women's subjectivity.[20] Paulina Palmer observes that French works with repetition and overstatement, but unlike Palmer – who sees this simply as bad writing – I think French's technique comes out of her realist (i.e. anti (post)modernist) stance.[21] Art here imitates life and life is tedious; in a later novel, *Her Mother's Daughter* French uses realist detail, ostensibly trivial events and tedium as a mimesis of the drudgery of women's lives to even greater effect. To an important extent however overstatement and repetition highlight the cognitive function of *The Women's Room*: the narrator's comments which question conventional narrative and then explain why the story takes the turns that it does represent the novel's epistemological claims to realism – it is 'narrating feminism'. This involves much more than how I became my own person, or even how I became a feminist; *The Women's Room* aspires to nothing less than to write the way 'we' were: the autobiography of a generation. This collective dimension, as both Paulina Palmer and Rosalind Coward have noted, is figured through the consciousness-raising group of which Mira Ward is a member. Early radical feminist theory (Millett, Firestone, Koedt, Brownmiller) is here dramatised for the uninitiated reader: traditional feminine roles resemble nothing so much as a Stepford Wives type of existence – woman as robot or living doll, stowed away in the box of suburban domesticity.[22]

Although the narrator of *The Women's Room* acknowledges that women's experience as remembered in her story is confined to that of white, middle class educated women only, the rape scene towards the end (in which a young white woman is raped by a black man) reveals the novel's allegiance to a political analysis which subordinates all power relations within society to those of gender.[23] Simplistic at best, racist at worst, the politics in *The Women's Room* leave a lot to be desired. But the politics in the text are not necessarily coextensive with those of the text: the very reductionism and simplicity which mar the novel's political analysis also lend it its peculiar rhetorical force and unity. For whatever the appearance of structurelessness, *The Women's Room* is held together, relentlessly we might say, by a vision of unified male power instantiated over, and over, and over again in the collective personal histories of women's victimisation. It is this vision which generates anger – in agreement as much as dissent – and it is this anger which French seeks to mobilise so that women finally confront the real conditions of their existence. Like socialist-realist writing of the 1930s, *The Women's Room* is an urgent act of bearing witness. Its narrator echoes Meridel LeSueur when she writes: 'I feel as if I were a medium and a whole host of departed spirits has descended on me clamoring to be let out' (French 1978: 17).

As in socialist-realist fiction of the 1930s, these voices are represented with as much directness, as much illusion of presence as possible. If, as we saw earlier, dominant literary writing means artificial order and untruth in *The Women's Room*, then the only option is to write in the vernacular of women's language, i.e. speech: 'What's the use? Everything I write is lies. I am trying to tell the truth, but how can I tell the truth? . . . All I can do is talk, talk, talk. I will do what I can. I will talk, talk, talk' (French 1978: 582).

Margaret Homans has remarked that French's novel shows a faith in representational language, which ought to be regarded by those who know better as an 'enabling delusion' (Homans 1983: 190). American feminist writers generally, according to Homans, believe in the adequacy of representational language even if at the same time they thematise women's exclusion from it. This seems to me somewhat contradictory. Clearly French does thematise women's exclusion from the socio-symbolic order, but this does not mean that she sees women as unproblematically able to appropriate language and representation for themselves in order to critique it. *The Women's Room*'s self-conscious passages point precisely to the difficulty in writing female subjectivity, not merely to the necessity of creating new images of women. To say, as Homans does, that French sets up a 'seeming transparency between experience and narrative' is correct, but only if we take 'seeming' as the operative word.[24] After all, the narrator herself constantly disrupts this illusion of transparency and exposes the social construction of experience, as well as the possibility of a different narrative. As, for example, in this passage: '[in the mirror] her self refused to coalesce . . . She could see bits and pieces – hair, eyes, legs – but the pieces wouldn't come together' (French 1978: 9). This picture of subjectivity is mirrored a few pages on with a similar image of textuality:

> you don't have to know anything about writing to teach it. In fact, the less you know the better, because then you can go by rules, whereas if you really know how to write, rules about leading sentences and paragraphs and so forth don't exist. Writing is hard for me. The best I can do is put down bits and pieces, fragments of time, fragments of lives. I am going to try to let the voices out.
>
> (French 1978: 17)

This is early on in *The Women's Room*, when the (as yet unnamed) narrator decides to make sense of her fragmented mirror image by writing the fragments to see if they can form a whole. Experience and narrative are not simply coextensive here: it is the process of writing which has to construct experience in such a way as to 'reflect' back a different, more coherent face of feminism in the mirror. And it is the illusion of commonality with what is to be revealed as a fictional narrator at the end which does this politicising work for the (implied, ideal) reader.

No doubt the Virginia Woolf of *A Room of One's Own* would have disapproved of French's narratorial interventions as Brontëan obstructions of narrative flow, but then an argument with Woolf's modernist, androgynous aesthetic is part of the novel's subtext. Mira Ward's fragmentation in the mirror follows almost to the letter Clarissa Dalloway's dubious efforts to 'draw the parts together' in order to present a public face to the world; Clarissa's fear of disintegration is here confronted and exposed for what it is: a refusal to face up to reality. *The Women's Room* represents what becomes of *A Room of One's Own* in Women's Liberation: collectivism instead of individualism, gender affirmation instead of transcendence and realism instead of modernism. It can be no coincidence that in *The Women's Room*, as in *The Waves*, the sea has the final word: 'I have opened all the doors in my head./ I have opened all the pores in my body./ But only the tide rolls in' (French 1978: 636).

Like the opening of *Daughter of Earth*, this ending leaves the heroine alone on the beach, reflecting on past and future. It not only echoes Woolf's greatest achievement, but it also symbolises the shifting tides of social change and of Second Wave feminism.

LEARNING LESSING'S LESSON: KATE MILLETT'S *FLYING*

With *Flying* we move into the domain of autobiography as we traditionally understand it: the life and times of a famous person opened up for public scrutiny. But this, fortunately, is about all that is traditional in Millett's text. Its cyclical structure, divided up into four parts which could be books in themselves, its clipped impressionistic sentences and likewise truncated scenes, its cut-and-paste method of collating a personal history – these qualities flash 'experimental writing' in large neon letters. And yet, as Annette Kolodny notes, *Flying* was almost universally panned in the press, feminist and non-feminist alike.[25] It does not seem to have occurred to any of these critics that here they might be faced with a radically unassimilable text: subjective realism writ large.

Like *The Golden Notebook*, *Flying* is a lengthy text of, and about, writer's block. Nor is this the only paradox Millett presents us with, for Millett – again like Lessing in *The Golden Notebook* – also succeeds in collapsing the formal differences between realism and modernism, and even post-modernism – at least on a superficial reading. Yet there is one obvious method in Millett's ostensible madness, and that is the cinematic model upon which *Flying* is constructed. It tries to capture filmic techniques in writing, with rapid successions of images, flashbacks, close-ups, jump cuts –

a montage of discrete units which give the illusion of uninterrupted flow –
albeit a turbulent flow. Yet it is in this illusion of random stream of
consciousness that its realism lies; just as French's novel presented us with a
hard to take mimesis of the tedium of ordinary women's lives, so *Flying*
mimics the turbulence of a female psyche-in-distress which goes round in
circles and whose only hope of authenticity lies in the very act of self-
representation. Both are equally demanding on the reader's tolerance, but
in very different ways. Suzanne Juhasz has remarked on the 'seeming
randomness' of *Flying*, and it would take a diligent critic indeed to
disentangle the 'seeming' from the truly random in this whale of a text
(Juhasz 1980: 225).

At one level, it is as if Millett writes over 600 pages of Molly Bloom's
monologue, an anti-novel of epic proportions and a fundamental challenge
to linearity, causality and rationalism. In another way, however, *Flying* is also
an antidote to Joyce's *Ulysses*; Millett's discourse clearly stakes a claim to
representing a truly female discourse in a way that Molly Bloom's chapter
never could or can – because she is, from the point of view of linguistic
pragmatism, always a third person, and the figment of a male imagination at
that. Where in *Ulysses* the Author is always in control, never mind what goes
on in Molly Bloom's head, in *Flying it seems as if* the author is out of control
in writing as well as in life. Every part of *Flying* can stand for the whole:
nothing is central to it, but everything is. Lacking a narrative, the con-
structedness of *Flying* is not so much (self-)evident in linguistic acrobatics as
it is foregrounded in the persistent theme of cultural production (writing,
filmmaking, public speaking, painting, sculpture) as *work*. Besides this
aspect of Millett's counter-hegemonic aesthetic, there is also the not so
mean feat of an autobiography which radically demystifies the female public
figure as heroine. Bella Brodzki and Celeste Schenck argue that female
autobiography takes as given that the self is always already mediated
through existing cultural discourses; what we see in *Flying* is a self caught in
mediation, for to represent Kate Millett is to represent 'Kate Millett' the
public figure.[26] And being Kate Millett then is either to play 'Kate Millett' or
to refuse to do so: the rabid feminist, the lesbian, the woman who practises
what she preaches or fails to live up to one's expectations, the celebrity who
trades on her fame, the celebrity who plays at being ordinary, and so on and
so forth.

Most of all, perhaps, Millett's autobiography is the anti-text to *Sexual
Politics* (usually referred to as 'that book' in *Flying*). It represents the other,
personal side of *Sexual Politics*'s public coin, the vernacular against the
academic, female versus male, exploration instead of argument.

Flying, in Kolodny's words, 'reveals its own organisation' and as an
account of 'Millett' it does the same with female subjectivity: not one single
identity but multiple identi*fications* (Kolodny 1980: 240). If *The Women's
Room* represents the female self as victim/hero (because French's women, as

feminists, never lack agency) then maybe *Flying* can be said to represent the next stage, where woman/heroine, once she has got beyond *Fear of Flying*, becomes victim again – of her own success. And writing is a casualty of that process for Millett. An interview with the expert's expert on writer's block, Doris Lessing, momentarily brings *Flying* into focus. Lessing says about writing:

> 'My problem is wondering why I should.' 'But you are making literature', I protest . . . Of course she has made a grimace over 'literature'. 'And if I were? What does it accomplish?' I have never thought. Art is of itself surely . . . 'Your book does things', she says . . . 'Books like that make change', she insists.

(Millett 1974: 400)

A little later Lessing states that all she is interested in now is 'the expression of women's self'. Her curiosity about what Millett will do in that line sanctions (we gather) the project of Millett's autobiography which is already in process (and which we know we are reading). Millett writes:

> Doing it in the first person which seems necessary somehow, much of the point is lost in my case if I didn't put myself on the line. But feeling so vulnerable, my god, a Lesbian. Sure, an experience of human beings. But not described, not permitted. It has no traditions. No language. No history of agreed values. 'But of course people wish to know', she interrupts. 'And you cannot be intimidated into silence. Or the silence is prolonged forever.'

(Millett 1974: 401)

Lessing, not Millett, is thus the one who gets to speak the significant lines; it is Lessing who 'authorises' Millett's *Flying*. Like Mira Ward, like Anna Wulf in *The Golden Notebook*, and like Isadora Wing in *Fear of Flying* Millett will not let her readers remain in ignorance of what *Flying* is actually for: not 'art for itself, surely' but art for a culture which has marginalised lesbian writing and lesbian experience.

Yet this does not lead her to a writing of positive images or women's community in any simplistic or idealised sense. 'Millett's' support networks are overwhelmingly staffed by women, but if anything *Flying* blasts apart an assumed sisterhood within the Women's Movement (let alone without it). In so doing it highlights both the exaggerated expectations of feminism as a movement for universal female happiness and the difficulties of living up to the status of feminist idol. Rita Felski, who on the whole is very critical of Millett, does value this aspect of *Flying*: 'the very point of feminist confession is to confront the more unpalatable aspects of female experience as general problems, not to present idealized images of women as positive role-models' (Felski 1989: 106).

Agreed, but of course *Flying* does, at the same time and highly paradoxically, present us with a role model which is neither positive nor negative but, we are invited to believe, *real*. This is 'Millett' as role model who despite fame and fortune is still vulnerable, insecure, self-accusatory and so on. In other words: still a real woman. Reading as a woman of the 1990s, I for one find this more problematic than enabling, and more suspect than honest – which is, no doubt, what it is intended to be. Nor is this necessarily a matter of wanting positive images, but rather of wanting to see important women in autobiography take responsibility for their strengths as well as their weaknesses, their successes as well as their failures. This, it seems, 'Millett' as persona cannot do, even if Millett can.[27] With regard to *Flying* as counter-hegemonic autobiography, we then have a problem in that it works against the tradition of male autobiographers' narratives of 'making it' but not much against female autobiographers' difficulty in representing the life of a successful, public, political woman. *Flying* asks what it means to be a feminist and a lesbian – to act, live and write in the service of social change. To Millett's eternal credit, it put some of 'the more unpalatable aspects' of feminist women's subjectivity (ambition, individualism, sexual jealousy, and disillusionment with sisterhood) on the literary map, shunning neither conflict nor contradiction. In this respect, exploring and maintaining the inevitable tensions between public political identification with a cause and personal history, she is the true daughter of the Lessing of *The Golden Notebook*. As an autobiographer who inverts the male tradition of writing a life, however, she paradoxically reverts to an old model of the more palatable aspects of female subjectivity (guilt, insecurity, incessant self-surveillance), thus liberating with one hand what is being tied up by the other.

AFRICAN-AMERICAN AUTOBIOGRAPHY

Amidst the flood of feminist first person narratives of the 1970s there were few written by Black women. Yet the act of bearing witness in the autobiographical voice, and the revalorisation of the African-American oral tradition had in the 1960s led to a glut in political poetry and autobiography (Malcolm X, Eldridge Cleaver, George Jackson). Why then did African-American women writers choose to restructure the sentence of their lives in third person fictions?

Part of the answer must lie in African-American feminists' ambivalent relationship with the white Women's Movement on one hand, and their similarly marginal position with regard to Black politics of the 1960s on the other.[28] White feminist writing of the kind I have discussed so far was widely perceived by Black women as self-indulgent, and dismissed as 'a luxury Afro-Americans cannot afford' (Schultz, citing St Clair Drake 1981: 111).[29] Angela Davis explains in the introduction to her autobiography that the book was, in a way, a product of reluctance since

116

I did not want to contribute to the already widespread tendency to personalize and individualize history . . . When I was writing this book, I was vehemently opposed to the notion, developed within the young women's liberation movement, which naïvely and uncritically equated things personal with things political.

(Davis 1988: x)[30]

Davis's autobiography as a result eschews anything that might be taken for the personal, and reads like what it purports to be: the life of a political activist, written for and about 'the collective power of the thousands and thousands of people opposed to racism and political repression' (Davis 1988: xi).

Selflessness of a different kind had of course been a feature of the early Civil Rights movement, and this erasure of the personal resurfaced as revolutionary discipline in Black Nationalism. Thomas P. Doherty says of George Jackson's *Soledad Brother* for example that it was written as an autobiography, but as one which should be devoid of self so that narcissism and individualism could not detract from its intended political impact.[31]

So, if the exploration of female subjectivity was monopolised in the counter-public sphere by white women's subjective realism, whilst Black men seemed to have a patent on writing Blackness in political auto-biography, African-American women writers would have to turn elsewhere to articulate what it means to be Black and female in America.

As we have seen, the representation of white female subjectivity is itself a complex, multilayered thing requiring revision of traditional narrative practice, but for African-American women the situation was even more complicated, since the cultural definition of gender that white feminists were writing against had never even applied to them in the first place. Elizabeth Fox-Genovese argues that 'for white American women . . . gender constitutes the invisible, seamless wrapping of the self', whereas African-American women have historically been excluded from dominant definitions of true femininity – as Sojourner Truth's question, 'Ain't I a Woman?' so graphically demonstrated. For African-American women writers therefore 'the gap between the self and the language in which it is inscribed looms large and remains fraught with struggle' (Fox-Genovese 1988: 83).[32]

There were African-American women who wrote autobiography during the 1970s, but they tended to be political testimonies *à la* Davis and Malcolm X – Ann Moody's account of her experiences in the Southern Civil Rights Movement for example, *Coming of Age in Mississippi*. Or they were public statements on the aesthetics of Black Nationalist counter-cultural practice, such as those by poets Gwendolyn Brooks and Nikki Giovanni. They both published their autobiographies *Report from Part One* and *Gemini* in the early 1970s as portraits of the artist, and both were at pains to point out that they owed their identities as political poets to Black Nationalism, not Women's Liberation.

Here I have chosen to discuss two slightly later autobiographies by African-American women which connect with the 1960s counter-cultural Black aesthetic but also with white feminist fictions of subjectivity. Maya Angelou's five-volume autobiographical *œuvre* engages white feminism on its own realist and cognitive ground of a personal/political rewriting of African-American history, whilst Audre Lorde's *Zami* can be put in dialogue with white feminists like Millett and French in its polemical reconstructions of lesbian identity and feminist politics. Both writers offer their own restructuring of women's sentence, and both in so doing critique white feminism's 'grammar of justice/syntax of mutual aid', to cite the words to Denise Levertov's 'Making Peace' once more.

'FOR THE BLACK VOICE AND ANY EAR WHICH CAN HEAR IT': MAYA ANGELOU'S AUTOBIOGRAPHICAL WORK

A literary reputation which is almost wholly based on autobiographical writing is a rare thing, but Maya Angelou's achievement in constructing an individual Black woman's life as a significant life and liberating autobiography itself from its subordinate status in the hierarchy of literary discourses, proves that it is possible. Five volumes of Angelou's epic life story have appeared to date: *I Know Why the Caged Bird Sings* (1969), *Gather Together In My Name* (1974), *Singin' and Swingin' and Gettin' Merry Like Christmas* (1976), *The Heart of a Woman* (1981) and *All God's Children Need Travelling Shoes* (1986), of which only the first has received much critical attention.[33] This is not entirely surprising, since *I Know Why the Caged Bird Sings* is by far the most imaginative of the five and the most literary: here Angelou captures the thoughts and speech of a young black girl growing up in Arkansas during the Depression, without the knowing distance which characterises much of the later volumes, where there is an increasing tendency towards a mere chronicling of events and encounters, swinging the balance to a univocal social historiography. Of course, within the parameters of Angelou's Black feminism, this shift is valid in its own right: she provides the reader with a lived history of the major African-American political and cultural movements of the century, from the tail-end of the Harlem Renaissance through *Porgy and Bess* to the Civil Rights Movement and Black Nationalism to back to Africa in the 1970s, at the rate of one decade per volume. This sense of movement is applied literally as well, for the epic of one woman's life takes her across America twice, and then across continents as well (Europe in *Singin' and Swingin'*, Africa in *All God's Children*). Angelou's is, then, a project of personal/political historiography in a very specific sense, that of a woman who has been in the right place at the right time and can speak of African-American politics with the authority of an insider. She explains in an interview with Rosa Guy: 'it's so heartbreaking to me that I also see a generation who will live out that bitter statement, "He who does not learn from his history is doomed to repeat it"' (Angelou 1988: 16), thus revealing her own agenda as – at least in part – providing a history lesson.

Combining novelistic modes with vignettes of Black life (rather reminiscent of Zora Neale Hurston's in *Dust Tracks on a Road*), dashes of social historiography, travel writing and blues, Angelou's *œuvre* presents a formally variegated account of one woman's life in an attempt to restructure the sentence of Black women's history and particularly that of her stereotyped images as saint, sapphire, mother or whore. Resisting dominant cultural scripts for the African-American woman is the *raison d'être* of Angelou's work, positioned not just against a white male dominant, but also in polemical dialogue with white feminist fictions of subjectivity and Black male political autobiography and fiction.

As well as demonstrating the elasticity of autobiography as a form stretching all the way from novel to historiography, Angelou's epic is a good example of a textual practice which demands the reader's collusion with Lejeune's *pacte autobiographique*, for it is the assumption of 'real life' and 'real living history' that lends this narrative its particular force. The historical events can be checked, the life cannot – but the fact that the two are so intertwined (Angelou with Martin Luther King, with John O. Killens, with John Lewis, with Malcolm X on his African pilgrimage) creates credibility. Angelou's autobiography is a performance: it constantly invokes the community of speaker and listeners of the oral tradition, and constructs the life story as an autobiographical act in Elizabeth Bruss's sense. It is only through the use of historical referentiality that Angelou avoids the danger of fictionalisation as incredibility which often comes as an effect of vivid storytelling; if it were not for the reader's assumption of referentiality and the assumption that all five volumes are about the same real historical person, the work would not hold together as a single fiction of subjectivity. It would be difficult, for example, to assume any identity between the rape-ravaged Ritie of *Caged Bird*, the fallen woman Marguerite Johnson in *Gather Together*, the showbiz figure stage-named 'Maya Angelou' of *Singin' and Swingin'* and the African wife Maya Make of *Heart of a Woman* if we as readers did not somehow anchor these personae in the person of Maya Angelou.

In deconstructing stereotypes Angelou in effect represents herself as a series of different incarnations, maintaining a very precarious balance between the Black woman as victim on one hand and superwoman on the other, between representativeness and exceptionalism. Thus the story reads on one level as an archetypal American account of making it, which is then undercut – but not in the end invalidated – by the cumulative effect of trials and tribulations. Together, they highlight both the enormous odds against, and the actuality of, social change for African-Americans in this century.

Clearly, in inviting the autobiographical pact Angelou sets herself up as a role model for Black women:

> So many young Black women are not spoken to by white women. Are not spoken to by Black men. Are not spoken to by white men. And if we don't speak to them, there will be no voice to reach their ears or their hearts.

> (Angelou 1988: 16)

As Sondra O'Neale has argued, Angelou undertakes nothing less than the reconstruction of the Black woman's image from the 1930s onwards, with particular emphasis on the African-American woman as artist (singer, actress, performer, poet, dancer and writer).[34] But it is the combination of this theme with others such as growing up in the South, sexual violence, the role of strong female relatives, single motherhood and domestic work, that links Angelou's work up with that of other African-American women writers like Toni Morrison, Toni Cade Bambara, Alice Walker, and Gloria Naylor. Like Marilyn French and Erica Jong, Angelou furthermore weaves women's writing and its role in the formation of female cultural identity into her narrative. Some critics have observed parallels between Angelou's portrait of Stamps, Arkansas and Hurston's Eatonville in *Dust Tracks on a Road*, for example.[35] I would suggest that Angelou avails herself of Ann Petry's *The Street* as a cultural script which is at least as important as *Dust Tracks*. The 1940s volume, *Gather Together in My Name* invites particularly strong comparison with Petry's novel, which is set in the same era and also depicts a single mother's inexorable slide down the social ladder into poverty and crime. 'Rita' and the protagonist of *The Street* even share the same name – Miss Johnson – which can never be without significance in a tradition which is so highly aware of the politics of naming.

The difference between these texts is marked in large part by their different modes of political analysis: where Petry was at pains to emphasise economic determination in the final instance, Angelou always stresses individual strength and the ability to overcome – as in that famous hymn of the Civil Rights movement from which she draws her inspiration.

Still, the strain of American individualism in Angelou's work does not constitute a single, unified identity, nor is a self-determining subject (whose strength in the end wins through) ever posited. All the incarnations that 'Angelou' goes through carry different names to signify multiple layers of oppression and personal history, as well as the racist habit of calling African-Americans out of their name – right down to the point where 'Maya' is being 'christened' as such by white people.[36] Doubt about one name to denote one self remains throughout the autobiography: 'I wondered if I'd ever feel [this name] described the me myself of me', in *Singin' and Swingin'*, is echoed in *Heart of a Woman* where 'Angelou' discovers Baldwin's *Nobody Knows My Name*: '[it] gave me heart. Nobody seemed to know my name either. I had been called everything from Marguerite, Ritie, Rita, Sugar, bitch, whore, Madam, girl and wife' (Angelou 1976: 96 and Angelou 1981: 224).

Like a modern day 'Song of Myself', Maya Angelou's autobiographical *œuvre* demonstrates just how complex and multiple the notion of *the* African-American woman really is. Identifications as wife, mother, worker, political organiser, performer and writer are constantly interrogated and reconstructed in relation to other existing cultural discourses (of white femininity and feminism, Black masculinity and politics, and national identities). But these are neither choices nor free-floating diversities, for Angelou in the end always anchors her constructions of subjectivity in history – not as yet another discourse, but as lived experience which determines the self, in the final instance.

WRITING THE HOUSE OF DIFFERENCE: AUDRE LORDE'S *ZAMI: A NEW SPELLING OF MY NAME*

Angelou's multiplicity of identifications, her internationalism and her continuing dialogue with dominant and non-dominant definitions of Black womanhood are very much a part of Audre Lorde's *Zami* as well. Lorde writes:

> I see protest as a genuine means of encouraging someone to feel the inconsistencies, the horror, of the lives we are living. Social protest is to say that we don't have to live this way . . . My power as a person, as a poet, comes from who I am . . . Not to deal with my life in my art is to cut out the fount of my strength.
>
> (Lorde 1982: 264)

Evading all existing categorisations, *Zami: a New Spelling of My Name* is a genuinely experimental feminist text, combining myth with realism, sexual with race and class politics, and historiography with a poetic envisioning of the future. Without generalising over much, I think it is possible to say that as the cyclical is to the straight in narrative structure (if nothing else), so Audre Lorde is to Maya Angelou what Kate Millett is to Marilyn French: a different look at difference, a different conception also of Black women's subjectivity and of Black women's history in America. In part Lorde's difference is informed by her invocation of Caribbean cultural heritage, which is distinct from the slave past which writers like Angelou, Morrison, and Walker confront in their writing. But it is also a political and a sexual difference in that, for Lorde, women's community is always primary, not necessarily allied with or generated by feminism, and profoundly rooted in

121

a woman-identified spirituality which her work exalts. Feminist critics Barbara Smith and Chinosole characterise *Zami* therefore as a biomyth-ography, a textual practice which constructs the self through myth as part of a collective history and cultural tradition which stretch back way beyond the memory of lived experience.[37] As a new form which both argues and embodies its distance from white Western discourses of identity, *Zami* nevertheless partakes of several well-established traditions at once. Tropes familiar in the long history of African-American autobiographical writing surface here too, in the issue of naming and renaming, of tongue-clipping and speech, education and literacy, the African diaspora, and matrilinear oral heritage.[38] Feminist themes prevalent in the work of Marge Piercy and Marilyn French emerge also in Lorde's representation of a personal history which takes her through the sexual politics of the 1950s and 1960s and the history of the American Left. The poet's role as one who gives voice both personally and politically is figured throughout in mythic and realist strands of Lorde's text; this, again, is a portrait of the Black woman as artist.[39]

As in Maya Angelou's work, it is the intertwining of these strands into one inextricable knot of connections and interconnections that makes *Zami* a powerful political and literary manifesto, which enhances its lesbian-culturalist credentials by its frequent appeal to an idealised past and future of women's community. At a more down to earth level, *Zami* questions every -ism in the book and uses the critique of one to elucidate another. As the poetic, and sometimes lyrical, italicised passages of Lorde's text rupture the seeming conventionality of the straight autobiographical narrative, so also does her portrait of lesbian existence complicate and shake up any linear notion of progress in gay politics over the past twenty years or so. *Zami* not only critiques the Left in the 1950s for its homophobia (homosexuality was regarded then, as in the 1930s Left, as a bourgeois aberration) but it interrogates in particular white feminists' construction of the 1950s as the era of the feminine mystique, the dark ages of female, heterosexual rivalry before the dawn of Women's Liberation and sisterhood. It does this in its construction of strong Black women as positive role models, thus exposing the familiar, hegemonic image of the 1950s suburban housewife as specific to the white middle class, and it argues with the idea that women's solidarity was invented by Women's Liberation: 'gay-girls were the only Black and white women who were even talking to each other in this country in the 1950s, outside of the empty rhetoric of patriotism and political movements' (Lorde 1982: 225).

As Barbara Smith notes, *Zami* serves in this sense as a history of lesbian community, of the practice of living as a woman-identified-woman 'before we even knew the words existed' (Smith 1990: 243).[40] More than that, Lorde's mythopoeic text is also an experiment in erotic personal/political writing; images of closeness to the mother's body in childhood prefigure lesbian women's intimacy and sexual pleasure in adult life.[41] The scene where 'Audre' experiences her first period whilst helping her mother in the kitchen relies for its erotic effect on the pestle and mortar as male and female sexual symbols. They repeat metaphorically what Lorde states in her Prologue:

> *I have always wanted to be both man and woman, to incorporate the strongest and richest parts of my father and mother within/into me – to share valleys and mountains upon my body the way the earth does in hills and peaks.*

(Lorde 1982: 7)

Here the island of Carriacou, the mother's birthplace, is represented as a sensual paradise of women's community, its magic captured in the one word *Zami*: 'A Carriacou name for women who work together as friends and lovers' (Lorde 1982: 255).

Because there is plenty of hard-nosed politics in Lorde's autobiography, this Utopian aspect of the text (located in mythopoeic past and future but not in a realist present) appears to serve as a dream-like counterpoint to a painful personal history. For Lorde there is no real me nor a new, empowered feminist me, but only 'a new spelling of my name'. This new spelling radically restructures individual subjectivity into a mythical vision of a newly unified self, but the question arises how this self, stripped of troublesome contradictions and negotiations and no longer individual but submerged in a collective creative and lesbian subject, comes into being. Lorde's poetic mode of 'exiting from patriarchy' (to borrow a phrase from Bonnie Zimmerman) aims at transcendence as well as transformation, and exalts the spiritual as well as it asserts the political. Lorde's textual practice in *Zami* then is an effective mode of personal/political counter-hegemonic writing. Lorde explains that she, as

> a young Black woman writer in the 1950s, needed to know (and unfortunately did not) that Angelina Weld Grimke existed, and that she was not only a Black woman playwright and poet but also a woman who loved women.

(Lorde 1990: xii)

Zami ensures in precisely this way that the women of the 1980s and after know Audre Lorde. Or, as she put it in an autobiographical essay: in the event of another bout of literary and political amnesia which obliterates Black lesbian existence, she has made sure that 'My Words Will Be There'.[42]

123

5

HEALING THE BODY POLITIC
Alice Walker's *Meridian*

In 1964 an anonymous woman addressed a paper entitled 'Women in the Movement' to the Student Non-violent Co-ordinating Committee (SNCC), one of the major Black Civil Rights organisations. She wrote:

> it needs to be known that many women in the movement are not 'happy and contented' with their status. It needs to be made known that much talent and experience are being wasted by this movement when women are not given jobs commensurate with their abilities. It needs to be known that *just as Negroes were the crucial factor in the economy of the cotton South, so too in SNCC, women are the crucial factor that keeps the movement running on a day-to-day basis . . .*
>
> And maybe sometime in the future the whole of the women in this movement will become so alert as to force the rest of the movement to stop the discrimination and start the slow process of changing values and ideas so that all of us gradually come to understand that this is no more a man's world than it is a white world. [my italics]
>
> (SNCC 1964: 116)[1]

Drawing parallels between the position of African-Americans and women, which for some time was almost habitual in white feminist political discourse, has been discredited in recent years under the impact of Black feminist theory, to the point where it is now virtually taboo to make comparisons between Black and female oppression.[2] Yet what has become obscured by this guilt-ridden rejection of a discursive alignment of the plight of women with that of African-Americans is the common history of the Black movements of the 1960s and Women's Liberation, a common history which we find articulated here, in the political language of the early New Left.

In 1976 Alice Walker returned to this moment, the genesis of Women's Liberation in Civil Rights, in her novel *Meridian* which presents the story of a young Black woman's progress from an utterly marginal and pathologised existence to political and personal agency. *Meridian* takes the politics of Civil Rights as one of its central themes and uses the development of the Black movement itself as a narrative device. However, to say that the plot of the novel (insofar as there is one) revolves around the main character's involvement in Civil Rights would be to make an obvious and trivial point; far more interesting is the realisation that in telling Meridian's story Walker at the same time charts the historical conditions (political, social and cultural) that made her own discursive practice as a Black woman possible. In other words, the story of Meridian, who saves herself from suicide by becoming politically involved, entails the story of how Civil Rights engendered Black self-affirmation and later the Women's Movement – the two constitutive elements of a gendered Black consciousness which Walker has termed 'womanism' and which informs all of her writing.

It is significant, therefore, that in this novel it is Civil Rights, not feminism, that brings the African-American woman as historical subject and agent of change into being. Walker differentiates her gender politics (womanism) from that of white women (feminism), by invoking a long history of Black female spirituality, suffering and a strength which is rooted in community and folk-culture, which projects a future in which that suffering yields wisdom and self-determination. In this way, Walker also claims back the history of the Civil Rights Movement from its famous male leaders (Martin Luther King, James Forman, Bob Moses, Bayard Rustin) for its female activists and organisers (Ruby Doris Smith Robinson, Ella Baker, Flo Kennedy, Fanny Lou Hamer, Rosa Parks). But she also remembers and re-emphasises the enormous debt feminism owes to Civil Rights for its concepts as well as its strategies; a debt which has remained underacknowledged by white feminism.[3] *Meridian* engages in a political polemic with both Black men (writers and historians) and with white feminists. Questions around the role of the Black woman in the struggle, of non-violence versus armed resistance, of politics and religion and of alliances with white student volunteers, which are historically situated in SNCC's debates of the 1960s, echo unmistakably in *Meridian*'s narrative. These issues are addressed most obviously in the novel through dialogue, in explicit political discussions. More obliquely, the representation of African-American female subjectivity in Meridian's development towards agency and the formal fragmentation of the 'body of the text' are part and parcel of Walker's revisiting of 1960s radical history. This history of struggle and changing consciousness is here represented as the nub of contemporary debates around race and gender: the 1960s are cast as that historical moment in which all of Walker's stock concerns and themes – sexual politics, womanism, spirituality and African-American history – can be articulated.

But if Walker's political critique is firmly located in post war radical history, her aesthetic differences with African-American men and white feminist writers hark back further than 1960s counter-hegemonic culture to the Harlem Renaissance of the 1920s and 1930s. I want to present my own reading of *Meridian* here, before I discuss the larger context of Walker's reception and her position in African-American cultural debates over the heritage of the Harlem Renaissance and that of the Black Arts Movement of the 1960s.

BODY POLITICS: READING THE WOMANIST TEXT

Because of its doubly marginal relation to the (white, male) mainstream of American literature, African-American women's writing has tended to draw on a multiplicity of oppositional discourses working in concert and/or confrontation. This is due not only to the double consciousness which W.E.B. DuBois ascribed to African-Americans at the beginning of the century, but also to a double-voicedness as a result of both Black and female emancipation struggles of the 1950s and 1960s.[4] Despite considerable cultural and political differences between African-American women writers (whether feminist or womanist, or otherwise engaged), all seem to agree that gender alone can never determine a writing tradition, let alone a politics, and in this sense they are radically at odds with many of their white feminist peers. When I explore then the specific configuration of literary, political and historical discourses and practices which inform and authenticate *Meridian* as a political novel, I do so starting from the position that a feminist criticism which focuses purely on the most obvious markers of female oppression (motherhood, sexual violence, victimisation) is reductive. It is likely on one hand to suffer from the dangers of biological essentialism (of us all 'being women together') or from its obverse, cultural exoticism ('Black femininity is irreducibly different') on the other. What I am working towards is a criticism which is informed by contemporary feminist theory and psychoanalysis, but which can nevertheless mobilise the political and historical meanings of Walker's text – with all the methodological problems such a project entails. I want to develop a criticism which treats the history and the politics of race not as an added and optional extra to (white) feminist analysis but as something which should and can be integral to any critique of Black and white women's writing.

Walker's womanism, which we understand as the politics of race and gender intertwined, is figured in the construction of Meridian, its striking, unconventional main character. Immediately we are faced with a problem: Meridian is hardly the prototype of an activist or organiser. In a sense she is not really active at all: her public protests seem enigmatic, and they appear to happen in spite of herself, not as conscious and planned campaigns but rather as performances, stagings enacted in a kind of trance. Her mysterious illness, a central metaphor in this narrative which – in the manner of a patchwork quilt – incorporates many other stories ostensibly unrelated to Meridian's plight, can be diagnosed by any armchair psychoanalyst as a case of hysteria. The hysteric, as Freud discovered, suffers from reminiscences, and these other stories (about slavery, about the Native American burial ground, and about Fast Mary and the Wild Child) highlight the violence and mutilation of African-American history. Just as Meridian's body disintegrates under the pressures of a coming-to-consciousness of this history, so also do these stories disrupt the body of the text. Of course, this is no coincidence in a novel about Civil Rights, a movement which had no other weapons than the human body and whose resistance consisted – precisely – in putting one's body on the line. 'It was a decade marked by dead', *Meridian*'s narrator states (p. 21), and indeed the novel is haunted by the dead, by the victims of racist murder and brutality. To this theme of racial violence Walker adds other images of body politics: unwanted pregnancy, rape, the Serpent burial mound as testimony to the genocide of Native Americans, severed limbs and cut out tongues. And – emphatically at the very beginning – the corpse of a white woman offered up by Meridian for public viewing, signifying the ultimate commodification, but also the demise, of an obsolete icon.

Hélène Cixous and Catherine Clément propose in *The Newly Born Woman*, a theoretical dialogue on hysteria, that the hysteric is steeped in guilt. An original and deeply repressed trauma they say, citing Freud and Breuer, causes physical unconscious pain where there should be mental pain (Cixous and Clément 1975: 40). In Meridian the trauma is that of the African-American past and physical pain manifests itself in/on Meridian's body, with the hysteria staged in public acts of atonement for the suffering of a people. But the physical drama is also a healing process. Freud and Breuer wrote:

> we found, to our great surprise at first, that each individual hysterical symptom immediately and permanently disappeared when we had succeeded in bringing clearly to light the memory of the event by which it was provoked and in arousing its accompanying affect, and when the patient had described that event in the greatest possible detail and had put the affect into words.
>
> (Freud and Breuer 1893: 6)[5]

It is the narrative which here performs this analytical function of 'describing the events and putting the affect into words'; at the end Meridian returns to the world 'cleansed of sickness', Lazarus-like, able to integrate with a community she now recognises as her own (Walker 1976a: 227).

Clearly what we have here is no political novel about Civil Rights in any ordinary sense. Rather, what is presented is a construction of the Civil Rights Movement as an historical crossroads in which various conflicts and contradictions around Black emancipation manifested themselves, re-evoking memories of Reconstruction and of the nineteenth century Abolitionist movement. Walker projects these contradictions on to the figure of

Meridian, who has taken that troubled past into herself and feels guilty for it. For most of the narrative, Meridian embodies these conflicts, and in the end manages to work them through: it is the agency of political work that enables her to externalise her trauma. *Meridian* closes with a poem that finally exorcises guilt and conflict and forces the Black man (Truman) to face up to his task:

> *whatever you have done, my brother . . . know i wish to forgive you . . . love you it is not the crystal stone of our innocence that circles us not the tooth of our purity that bites bloody our hearts . . .*

[Truman] wondered if Meridian knew that the sentence of bearing the conflict in her own soul which she had imposed on herself – and lived through – must now be borne in terror by all the rest of them.

(Walker 1976a: 228)

Bernard Bell in his essay on Walker in *The Afro-American Novel and Its Tradition*, objects to this construction of Civil Rights as also a personal politics, which requires questioning of innocence and ideological purity and asks for a change in interpersonal as well as political power relations. According to Walker according to Bell, Civil Rights was 'a means of spiritual and moral redemption from a guilty past for individuals like Meridian, not a radical new social order in which all could realise their full potential'. He then goes on to argue that 'the social context and symbolic conclusion resound with personal self-indulgence, for Walker does not describe the revolutionary role of the working class in contemporary society' (Bell 1987: 263).

Unwittingly, Bell proves Walker's point. *Meridian*, after all, very deliberately substitutes the revolutionary role of the African-American woman for that of the working class, and replaces the image of the male leader with that of the female community worker. Nor is this change merely a matter of a different politics. Crucially it is a case of a polemic with literary representation, of substituting the lone male protagonist of the Wright-Ellison-Baldwin-Reed tradition who gets all the action and the reader's attention with a heroine who respects and works among the common folk and who refuses victimisation. This literary polemic becomes explicit in the chapter 'The Recurring Dream': 'She dreamed she was a character in a novel and that her existence presented an insoluble problem, one that would be solved only by her death at the end' (Walker 1976a: 115).

This interjection is clearly informed by feminist literary criticism; as a consequence we are aware that this novel proposes a different solution, when it becomes Truman's task to work through the same inner conflict that Meridian has borne for so long. Thus Walker does suggest the 'radical new social order' that Bell asks for, but it is one which significantly entails the repositioning of the African-American (true)man as a condition for 'all to realise their full potential'.[6]

Meridian's hysteria then is not a matter of individual pathology, but a figuration of redemptive suffering in true SNCC style – in that sense (of taking on the suffering of an entire race) Bell is at least right. But maybe there is another, more satirical dimension too. Meridian's catatonic faints can be read as a literalisation of Stokely Carmichael's derisory answer to the question of women's position in the movement, 'the position of women in SNCC is prone'.[7] We have to bear in mind that in Walker's imaginative vocabulary the spiritual and the political are coextensive, as indeed they also were for the Christian mainstream of the early Civil Rights Movement. The prone position is no joke, and Meridian's redemptive suffering is not a manifestation of female masochism but of the collective pain of history inscribed on the African-American woman's body.

THE ELEVATION OF THE OTHER? EXPLORING BLACK FEMALE SUBJECTIVITY

Like *The Women's Room* and other white feminist texts of the 1970s, *Meridian* is a novel of development and politicisation charting a process of personal and political change, from passivity and hopelessness to agency and a wide open future. But this process is represented rather differently from the way it is told in the narratives of white Women's Liberation, and *Meridian* not only transgresses dominant cultural definitions of gender but also con-ceptions of race. How then does Walker construct the African-American female subject in this text? Jean Toomer wrote in 'Blue Meridian':

> Whoever lifts the Mississippi
> Lifts himself and all America;
> Whoever lifts himself
> Makes that great brown river smile.
> The blood of earth and the blood of man
> Course swifter and rejoice when we spiritualize.
> (Toomer 1925: 214)

It is likely that Walker took some inspiration from Toomer's long poem. Meridian spiritually raises the Mississippi and therefore all America; her significance is that she acts as a catalyst around whom various psychosocial conflicts come to the surface and are then fought out. In placing her in a triangle with Lynne (white woman) and Truman (black man), Walker represents a Black female subjectivity which is resolutely positional: Meridian can only be what they, the others, are not. Beginning as non-white and non-male, she moves towards agency, towards becoming female and Black without ever achieving a unified identity; her sense of herself remains relational but becomes more stable, positive and harmonious.

In her incisive analysis of the discourses of ethnicity and race in American women's writing, Mary Dearborn describes this process of self-definition by contrast, the negative which becomes a positive, as the elevation of the Other to the status of the One. It turns an older tradition of ethnic and racial assimilation (always tied up with social mobility) on its head and proposes something akin to a cultural separatism. In *The Color Purple* says Dearborn, 'the other truly prevails' (Dearborn 1986: 192). Pocahontas's story tells of an indigenous woman's marriage to an American colonist and her subsequent success in English society; as in classic romantic fiction, love and social mobility are rolled into one. Throughout her book Dearborn uses the Pocahontas legend as a fantasy of assimilation underlying much ethnic women's writing, but she argues in her conclusion that in Alice Walker's work the obverse of assimilation, the 'prevailing of the other', is less a triumph of ethnic writing than a re-affirmation of Pocahontas's exotic status:

> To claim a mysterious 'otherness' for the literature of gender and ethnicity is to continue the long and sorry tradition of exoticizing, excluding, and ultimately colonizing Pocahontas. It is time that we reclaim Pocahontas and take a second look at her place in American culture.
>
> (Dearborn 1986: 193)

Whilst Dearborn seems to take Alice Walker's construction of difference (at least in *The Color Purple*) to be one of absolutes, i.e. a form of essentialism both biological (woman) and cultural (African-American), it is questionable whether this is the only, let alone the most productive, way that the prevailing of the other in Walker's work can be read. I would suggest that in *Meridian* difference is presented as socially and historically, even linguistically, produced: Meridian is seen as constantly in the process of defining herself against and in relation to her environment. The process itself is charted through particular interpersonal conflicts, which punctuate the narrative at regular intervals.

The first of these concerns Meridian's relationship with Ann Marion, a college friend who at some stage during the 1960s opts for militancy rather than non-violent resistance. When called upon in a kind of criticism/self-criticism session to state categorically that she will 'kill for the revolution', Meridian's voice dries up.[8] 'They were waiting for her to speak. But what could she say? Saying nothing she remembered her mother' (Walker 1976a: 15).

This memory is significant, for it evokes an earlier experience of coercion when Meridian, in church with her mother, is being forced to profess belief in God, a God who is not so much reminiscent of a caring Father as of a ruling patriarch or slave-owner: '"Say it now Meridian, and be saved. All He asks is that we acknowledge Him as our Master" . . . But she had sat mute,

watching her friends walking past her bench, accepting Christ, acknowledging God as their Master' (Walker 1976a: 16).

The conflict with Ann Marion (political differences which result in
separation) is the first to occur in the course of the narrative, but it
echoes the very first such separation from the mother. In both cases the
fear of sanction, of desertion and isolation is paralysing: silence, not
active disagreement, is the only possible response. Subsequently, when
Meridian suffers sexual abuse, silence is robbed even of its power as a
mode of passive resistance when the rapist threatens 'you must promise
not to talk' (Walker 1976a: 60).[9]

Reduced to speechlessness and inactivity, deserted by her best woman
friend and deserting her mother and child for fear of reproducing her own
troubled history, Meridian gets involved with Truman, who as an educated
Black male (and an artist to boot) seems to offer a way out of confusion and
into the big wide world. But Truman proves an unreliable ally in the quest
for self-understanding and agency. With his desire for upward mobility, he
marries a Jewish woman from the North (Lynne) who comes down South to
work on voter registration during Freedom Summer.[10] In sexual rivalry with
Lynne, white femininity intrudes upon Meridian's sense of self for the first
time: 'It was strange and unfair, but the fact that he dated [white women] –
and so obviously because their color made them interesting – made *her*
ashamed, as if she were less' (Walker 1976a: 103). Meridian feels diminished
despite her inner sense of superiority: 'black women were always imitating
Harriet Tubman', whereas 'one never heard of [white girls] *doing* anything
that was interesting' (Walker 1976a: 105).[11]

Conflict with Truman then evolves from his valorisation of white (the *New
York Times*) over Black cultural values and from his shifting politics of Black
manhood. First the assertion of African-American manhood gives him the
'right' to the white woman's body, because the taboo-breaking quality of
interracial sex lends it an aura of political legitimacy, but subsequently Black
masculinity also gives him the 'right' to discard Lynne for Meridian, who is
now seen as the African queen of current trends in Black liberation
philosophy: '*Have* my beautiful black babies' (Walker 1976a: 113).

In this way, Meridian is caught between the demands of Black manhood
for the elevation of the race and those of female solidarity. This becomes
clear when Truman leaves Lynne to return to Meridian and, when she will
not have him, accuses her of taking the white woman's side. Meridian
responds '"Her side? I'm sure she's already taken it. I'm trying to make
the acquaintance of my side in all this. What side *is* mine?"' (Walker
1976a: 137).[12]

The dilemma of what side is compounded, later still, by what in some ways
is the centrepiece of the novel: a discussion of the sexual politics of 1960s
Black activism. When Lynne wants to tell Meridian woman to woman that
she has been raped by a Black man, Meridian turns away. Only too aware

of the history, here evoked, of white Southern femininity in the service of racial violence and coercion, Meridian is unable to position herself as a Black woman except by refusing the speech of her white friend and denying her credibility, in the way she has denied Truman before.

> 'I can't listen to this', said Meridian, rising abruptly and throwing up her hands. 'I'm sorry, I just can't.'
> 'Wait a minute', cried Lynne. 'I know you're thinking about lynchings and the way white women have always lied about black men raping them. Maybe this wasn't rape. I don't know. I think it was. It *felt* like it was.'
> Meridian sat down again and looked at Lynne through her fingers, which were spread, like claws, over her face.
> 'Can't you understand I can't listen to you? Can't you understand there are some things I don't want to know?'
> 'You wouldn't believe me *either*?' Lynne asked.
> 'No', Meridian said coldly.
>
> (Walker 1976a: 153)

At this point Walker's womanist agenda, and her argument with white feminist analyses of rape as violence against women comes into focus.[13] Speechless again, unable to listen, unable to assent, repeatedly unable to align herself with one party or the other, Meridian's plight shows that there are divisions within race along political and religious lines, as much as there are differences between men and women, differences within gender between black and white, Jewish and Black, Northern and Southern, rural and urban, and so on. Meridian's journeying towards subjecthood, her making of herself and her 'cleansing of sickness' thus entails a series of positionings and repositionings, always relative, always changing, never static.

Yet if this is so, it should lead us to a very different conclusion from Dearborn's regarding Walker's exoticism in her representation of the Black woman as other. Far from the elevation of the absolute other to the status of the one, we see in *Meridian* Kristeva's subject-in-process, cutting across and moving beyond existing categories of identity, resisting cultural definitions of gender and race and only ever temporarily and provisionally locating herself in the gaps in between. Cixous and Clément's view of the hysteric as a disturbing figure and disruptive force is apposite here once more:

> there is no place for the hysteric; she cannot be placed or take place. Hysteria is necessarily an element that disturbs arrangements; wherever it is it shakes up all those who want to install themselves, who want something that is going to work, to repeat. It is very difficult to block out this type of person who doesn't leave you in peace, who wages permanent war against you.
>
> (Cixous and Clément 1975: 156)

Meridian allows 'an idea – no matter where it came from – to penetrate her life', the narrator tells us towards the end of the novel (Walker 1976a: 227). This idea is the paradox posed at the beginning, of killing for the revolution: how to bring about social change without resorting to the enemy's weapons, how to live with integrity in a world where duplicity means survival, how to live – in the words of the anonymous writer of the SNCC pamphlet – as a Black woman in a world which is no more a man's world than it is a white world. This, for Walker, is ultimately the question that the Civil Rights Movement posed and that is still waiting to be answered. In asking such awkward questions, specifically of white feminists and of her Black male peers, Walker, like Meridian, 'shakes up all those who want to install themselves, who want something that is going to work, to repeat'.

MERIDIAN: THE BODY OF THE TEXT

Meridian poses awkward questions to the reader in its very form. Composed of three parts and thirty-four short chapters, each with its own title, the novel reads initially more like a collection of short stories than as a coherent narrative.[14] The realist rendering of Meridian's development is interspersed with short episodes whose relevance to the main narrative often appears oblique: the discovery of a bar of gold in the garden; an old Indian burial ground where Meridian has a mystical experience which connects her with her Native American great-grandmother; and the stories of Fast Mary and the Wile Chile, both poor black women whose pregnancies kill.

The most chilling of these half-relevant interruptions of the main narrative is the tale of the slave woman Louvinie, who tells white children in her care a story of such horror that one of them dies of shock. Her trial-by-storytelling is an act of retaliation, a literal sentencing to death of whites for their crimes against African-Americans. In bloody retribution the slave-master then rips out Louvinie's tongue, which is buried only to rise up again in the shape of a tree, the Sojourner. This episode plays on the name of the archetypal self-identified black woman, Sojourner Truth; truth here springs metaphorically from the grave of a black woman's mutilation and silencing.[15]

The story as related in *Meridian* must, I think, be taken as a crucial moment in African-American women's writing in relation to a white readership. It is a moment when language goes beyond innocuous self-expression or compromised double-talk and becomes dangerous: a murder weapon. For the white reader is also in a sense in the position of listening to the Black woman's story; here, s/he is made aware that s/he is historically implicated in the silencing of African-American people. By incorporating such tales in the novel, Walker is thus able at once to thematise the Black woman's discursive power and its suppression, as well as remind her white readers of their peculiar relation to and perusal of Black culture. This relation, Walker would seem to imply, is one of ambivalence which comes from a fascination with otherness on one hand and exploitation of it (whether as voyeurism, psychosexual projection or actual commodification) on the other.

Theoretical insights concerning the politics of certain textual practices and reading-relations are often embedded in feminist creative writing, and it seems that here, in Louvinie's story as an emblem of Black/white discursive politics we have another such example of embedded critique of the 'dominant'.[16] Indeed, the whole of *Meridian* can, I think, be read as an implicit criticism of aesthetic practices which produce seamless narratives of (political) cause and (personal) effect, whether they be those of white feminist writing or the militant masculinist protest fiction of an earlier black male tradition. In disrupting what could otherwise be a traditional *Bildungs*-story of an individual's growth with an assortment of highly symbolic tales, anecdotes and myths, Walker produces a novel on the structural model of the patchwork quilt with every seam showing, flaunting its visible stitched-upness.[17] With each reading/stitching the pattern can be different; there is no singular representation but a mosaic of images whose meanings change, depending on the reader's perspective and the work s/he is prepared to put into it. In *Meridian* the process of making meaning and of the reader's self-positioning in the process of signification is highlighted. This structure then foregrounds discursivity itself, or in Anne Freadman's words, the phenomenon that 'to write, to read or to speak is first of all to turn other texts into discursive material, displacing the enunciative position from which it originated' (Freadman cited in Morris 1988a: 3).

Freadman's insight is a classic statement of poststructuralist and postmodernist conceptions of signification, but *Meridian* does not 'displace enunciative positions' for the sake of it, or to make a point about the postmodern condition. Instead it appropriates and critiques the discourses of white feminism and Black militancy, and puts them in dialogue with each other to create the new epistemology of womanism. Thus, the 'other texts' which have become the discursive material of *Meridian* are existing cultural (and oppositional) definitions of race and gender in which Meridian, like Cixous and Clément's hysteric, cannot 'take place or be placed'. But perhaps the most important of these other texts appropriated and revised by Walker is not a text at all, but the material survival, imagination, memory and lived experience of the African-American woman's body. It is this knowing, suffering, healing body which enshrines an experience and a history that cannot be found in the official text of African-American historiography and politics, but can only be spoken in the body of this text.

HISTORY, HYSTERIA, HER STORY

The living memory of 1960s Civil Rights, and more specifically that of women's involvement in SNCC, permeates *Meridian* and functions as its authenticating discourse. At the same time, the novel's disruptive symbolic strands interrogate official, written historiography of the period which disregards, by its very nature, the lived experience of individuals as well as a history of survival and struggle which stretches far further back than the 1950s and 1960s.[18] In the triangle of sexual politics involving the relationship between Truman, Lynne and Meridian, the novel in effect re-presents the main ideological shifts in the history of SNCC, but from the Black woman's point of view and *as lived*, in the way that only novels, oral histories and autobiographies can. Beginning with a commitment to Christian values of redemption through suffering and the political strategy of non-violent protest and community organising (Meridian's voter-registration activities), SNCC moved to a radicalisation which eventually led to an alliance with the Black Panthers and other organisations involved in armed struggle (Ann Marion's militancy and Truman's).[19] SNCC then survived into the 1970s as a more dispersed but also more consolidated relay point for grass roots community projects (Meridian, and Truman at the end). Although references to SNCC or any other Black political organisation are never overt, this narrative of 1960s social movements must inform a reading of *Meridian* as both an historical and political novel of womanism; without such contextualisation, the novel would indeed be inauthentic, because reduced to a story of individual pathology or eccentric fantasy.

But there is more. SNCC's history is interwoven with other stories of the past, such as that of Native America, by means of Meridian's father's interest in Indian history and his efforts to preserve the burial mounds. Awkward questions are posed here as well. Whilst slavery is figuratively linked with the fate of Native Americans in the memory of joint violation, degradation and destruction at the hands of white colonists, this joint history is not an innocent one, for it is suggested that African-Americans were implicated in dispossession and in the eradication of Native American culture (e.g. the Buffalo soldiers).[20] This connection is allusively made when Meridian's guilt, always evoked by her mother's question, 'Have you stolen anything?', applies not only to the mother's resentment of her daughter (who has 'stolen' her life), but also to the Indian past. Since it is intimated that the very land on which Meridian's family lives really belongs to the Indians, the gold dug up in the garden belongs to them too and has, indeed, been stolen.

A third historical strand running through *Meridian* is obviously that of slavery. This, it seems, has become *the* paradigm of recent African-American women's writing, a locus of representation of the victimisation and resistance of African-American womanhood.[21] In *Meridian*, as we saw in the episode about the slave woman Louvinie, slavery is remembered explicitly in connection with the African-American oral tradition and with the silencing of the black woman's speech.[22] But through the common theme of violation during slavery, this silencing trope is associated with the traumatic history of black motherhood too. When Meridian feels forced to give her baby son away, her guilt deepens:

> Meridian knew that enslaved women had been made miserable by the sale of their children, that they had laid down their lives, gladly, for their children, that the daughters of these enslaved women had thought their greatest blessing from 'Freedom' was that it meant they could keep their own children. And what had Meridian Hill done with *her* precious child? She had given him away. She thought of her mother as being worthy of this maternal history, and of herself as belonging to an unworthy minority for which there was no precedent and of which she was, as far as she knew, the only member.
>
> (Walker 1976a: 87–8)

The slave mother's plight and the status of the black family under slavery are again familiar themes in Black women's writing and African-American historiography. But what is striking here is the associative link between the clipping out of Louvinie's tongue and the loss of a baby. Meridian's voluntary abdication of motherhood entails a form of self-silencing in a rejection not just of maternal history but also of the 'mother tongue'; Meridian's mother's Christian vocabulary of self-sacrifice, designed to induce guilt, is thus yet another discourse that Meridian refuses, and refuses to pass on to her child. Only when at the end, in church, she hears the public testimony of a father's grief for his murdered son, does she find her tongue again and realises that she *could* kill for the revolution, if that is what it takes to prevent or counter such grief.

Racist violence, sexual violence, and coercion to speak in the languages of others (mothers, the Church, the Revolution) all lead to the same result: the Black woman's silence. Her only retaliation is to refuse their dictats and to speak – for herself, in and on her own terms in other ways. Just as Meridian's hysterical symptoms speak the trauma of an internalised guilty past which can only be redeemed through self-sacrificial public acts, so also does the body of the text speak through the gaps of an ostensibly disordered but highly evocative set of different narratives. Symbolic allusions both disrupt and reflect upon *Meridian*'s historicist realism, much in the way that hysterical symptoms, dreams and screen memories act upon consciousness as disturbance and potential source of self-knowledge, and therefore self-healing.

The history of Civil Rights as re-presented in *Meridian* is figured as a story of origins, as a tracing of the conditions which made Black women's political writing possible. This history of 1960s social movements can be seen at work in Walker's novel in the way that Catherine Belsey defines history in literary texts: 'not as background, not as cause, but as the condition of the work's existence as ideology and as fiction' (Belsey 1980: 136).

At the same time, this history is continually problematised by her-story, Walker's complex womanist aesthetic which combines the metaphysics of folk spirituality with the down-to-earth demands of a materialist agenda for social change, realism with myth, and racial solidarity with a feminist sexual politics. Inevitably such a synthesis of disparate positions and traditions is fraught with contradiction. Meridian 'allowed an idea . . . to penetrate her life', and because she is a woman of ideas she literally becomes a site of struggle, a battleground on which all conflicts have to play themselves out. *Meridian* likewise is a novel of ideas, steeped in historical consciousness and suffused with the symbolic and mythical traditions of African-American culture. It is a patched-up tale of the Black woman's progress through the past two centuries, each patch representing a piece of a still-usable past that must be confronted for radical change to be possible.

Given the history of psychoanalysis, and particularly that of hysteria as an affliction of the nineteenth century bourgeois white woman, a reading of Walker's womanist text in these terms is not unproblematic.[23] It might give the impression of (re)pathologising the black woman, inserting her in the discourse of feminist psychoanalytic criticism which has been predominantly white women's domain. I think however that an historical and political reading of *Meridian* is possible, and that hysteria can provide a useful theoretical framework for this reading. Patricia Waugh writes:

> Traditionally, women have always . . . us[ed] their bodies as instruments of protest against their 'feminine' positioning and identification. For Freud's female hysterics the bodily symptom . . . 'speaks' or signifies the conflict produced within the psyche as a consequence of the organisation of sexuality and the acquisition of gender. Hysteria can thus be seen as both a 'symptom' of powerlessness and a form of *resistance* to power.
>
> (Waugh 1989: 174)

Meridian's suffering is in part associated with her ambivalent position as a Black woman, but her physical protest is not just a gender protest. What she suffers from is *his*tory – not just her own, but that of African-Americans in general, of women, and ultimately of America itself. As an hysterical text, *Meridian* not only asks awkward questions of historiography and the literary tradition, but also of feminist criticism, since it so clearly bypasses (white) feminism's critique of femininity and evades established categorisations of 'the' female literary tradition. I would suggest that a psychoanalytical reading of 'inappropriate' texts like *Meridian*, texts which don't fit any particular critical paradigm, can in fact point out strengths and weaknesses of feminist psychoanalytic theory and take the arguments further. Feminist psychoanalytic criticism and theory, however useful in other ways, has more or less remained a white Eurocentric enclave as regards its concerns and practitioners.[24] But it is not quite the case that psychoanalytic feminism is not aware that it has a problem with historical and cultural specificity. In 'Keys to Dora', Jane Gallop observes that

> One of psychoanalysis' consistent errors is to reduce everything to a family paradigm. Socio-political questions are always brought back to the model father/mother/child . . . The family never was, in Freud's texts, completely closed off from questions of economic class. And the most insistent locus of that intrusion into the family circle (intrusion of the symbolic into the imaginary) is the maid/governess/nurse. As Cixous says, 'she is the hole in the social cell'.

> (Gallop 1985: 213)

I think that, in this case, Gallop is right and that there is a task for feminist criticism to widen the scope of psychoanalytic theory and to address those sociopolitical questions in more historical and culturally specific ways. Because Gallop mentions class here but not race, it seems appropriate to close my discussion of *Meridian* as an hysterical text with the figure of the maid/governess/nurse. I want to relate her to the African-American woman as 'threshold figure', positioned within the 'family' of American literature but at the same time outside it. Slave, mammy, domestic worker, and object of sexual fascination and exploitation: the African-American woman's history, the history that Meridian suffers from, can with some validity be compared with Gallop's and Freud's maid. She is the maid who is, in Cixous' words, 'fucked at the door', the maid who figures in every neurotic's fantasy but never gets to tell her own story within the Freudian framework. Perhaps in *Meridian* Alice Walker shows us what happens when she does.

RACE, CLASS, AND GENDER: A CRITICAL DEBATE

The multiple contradictory tensions between and within Walker's politics and her textual practice have provoked as many different and conflictual critical responses. Bernard Bell's essay on Walker, which I cited before, is fairly typical of a masculinist Black aesthetic school of criticism; after lodging the by now familiar complaint about negative representations of Black men, Bell judges *Meridian* self-indulgent, untrue to the historical record of Civil Rights and apolitical (because not about the working class).

But *Meridian* gets an equally hard time from Black feminist critic Hazel Carby, who in her book *Reconstructing Womanhood* puts Walker (quite rightly) in a rural tradition but equates this with a romanticisation of Southern black folk, which for Carby is ultimately regressive because it marginalises the urban literature of the Black working class (Carby 1987: 175). Yet the very same aspects of Walker's work that Carby deplores are celebrated in Barbara Christian's reading of *Meridian*, which stresses the – supposedly – feminine connections between Walker's animism and Meridian's saint-like qualities in her role as nurturing universal mother. For Christian, Meridian embodies the personal as political because she holds to the (supposedly) female values of mothering and self-sacrifice.[25] Susan Willis argues against Christian that *Meridian* is not about mothering at all, but about physical violence habitually inflicted upon the African-American woman throughout history, as well as about the power of language (in its testifying and imaginative functions) to counteract such violence. In *Meridian* all the children die, Willis archly points out, except for Meridian's son and he is saved only because Meridian has him adopted, in the knowledge that she could *not* be a good mother.[26]

Where do these points of critical controversy leave us? Clearly, these four critics bring different criteria to bear on their readings – Bell and Carby seem to demand a more explicit (or a different) political agenda in line with 1960s counter-hegemonic calls for a Black art of protest, whereas Christian and Willis appear to represent different (culturalist versus Marxist) schools of thought within feminist criticism. Rather than directly engaging with these positions, I have presented a different reading of Walker's novel which addresses the relation between spirituality and politics, the roots of feminism in Civil Rights, and different conceptions of African-American identity and Black female subjectivity. In speaking the repressed trauma of black women's historical silencing *Meridian* confronts the past in order to heal present divisions in literary and political, race and gender relations – as indeed do the later novels, *The Color Purple* and *The Temple of My Familiar*, whilst *Possessing the Secret of Joy* widens its political terrain to take in the mutilations of African history and sexual/political practices which continue into the present.

Central to this reading is my belief that the trajectory, which led Walker from the realism of *The Third Life of Grange Copeland* via *Meridian* and *The Color Purple* to the spiritual fantasy mode of the last two novels, reflects an aesthetic journeying back through the century and beyond. That is: a journey back from the overtly political concerns of the 1960s Black Arts Movement to the spiritual modernism of Jean Toomer and Zora Neale Hurston in the Harlem Renaissance, and back beyond that to the oral tradition of storytelling, upon which *The Temple of My Familiar* is patterned.

I am interested in the question of Walker's aesthetic allegiances, because I think that misreadings of her work are in part attributable to a misunderstanding of where Walker places herself in African-American cultural and political debates.

A WOMANIST AESTHETIC: FROM THE HARLEM RENAISSANCE TO THE BLACK ARTS MOVEMENT

Walker's indirect, symbolic evocations of pre-1960s African-American literary and political history are contained in the title of *Meridian*, which is not simply named after its protagonist. In addition to the dictionary definitions at the beginning (highest point, great circle, distinctive character, Southern), which are in themselves telling enough for a story about an eccentric Southern Black woman, 'Meridian' also alludes to a Mississippi town, which was the site of violent race-riots in 1871, and a centre for voter-registration in the 1960s. It was also the place from which three Civil Rights workers, James Chaney, Michael Schwerner and Andrew Goodman, disappeared during Freedom Summer, 1964. They were found, forty-four days later, murdered by a posse of Klan members and Mississippi law-enforcers.[27]

The very title 'Meridian' then sets up a link between the Reconstruction after the Civil War and what Manning Marable calls the Second Reconstruction of the post World War II period. Moreover, Walker refers with this name and this title, as we have seen, to Jean Toomer's poem, which begins:

> It is a new America
> To be spiritualized by each new American.
> *Black Meridian, black light*
> *Dynamic atom-aggregate*
> *Lay sleeping on an inland lake.*
> (Toomer 1925: 214)

With 'The Blue Meridian' in mind, Walker's novel reads as the story of this atom-aggregate's awakening, and of the Black woman's mission to re-spiritualise America. This spiritual mission has increasingly become a bone of contention in Walker criticism; Bernard Bell referred to it as self-indulgence, and *The Temple of My Familiar* has provoked even more extreme responses along these lines. *Temple* is indeed a difficult and often irritating book, but I have to agree with Gina Wisker that hostility to Walker's mysticism outstrips any genuine political objection that critics may have against the turns her writing has taken. Wisker observes that a mixed mode of realism and the supernatural has never been a problem in the work of canonical writers such as Emily Brontë; I would add that indeed, it is a much admired aspect of Toni Morrison's fiction, or that of Isabel Allende or Gabriel García Márquez.[28] Nor can the absence of a specific political solution for the world's ills at the end of the twentieth century be an adequate explanation for Walker's loss of favour with critics and reviewers. Melissa Walker rightly observes that in the latest works personal growth and artistic practices of various kinds seem to take the place of political activism, but then this was always an important part of Alice Walker's aesthetic, and it still keeps faith with that early New Left search for personal authenticity and with the conviction that cultural work is also political work.[29]

It seems then that Walker has a different, special problem in reception, which I think lies in the fact that she does not quite write a magical realism – with all the exotic attractions that has for a reader who is unhindered by any knowledge of its native cultural context – but a didactic, spiritual realism whose authentication in archaeological and scientific discourses is often spurious or controversial.[30] This spiritual realism aligns her with Toomer, whose language of spirituality originated less in some vague personal mysticism (though it may have been that, too) than in the historically specific concerns of the Harlem Renaissance, in which the roots of Walker's literary philosophy can be found. In that movement's founding manifesto, 'The New Negro', Alain Locke called for the 'spiritual emancipation' of the race through cultural production, away from 'the Negro problem' and towards 'a fuller, truer self-expression' (Locke 1925: 514). The aesthetics and cultural practices of the Harlem Renaissance are far more complex and contradictory than I can set out here, but the main point is that it rejected sociological protest writing in favour of true creative writing; that it believed in the spiritual regeneration of America as a multi-ethnic, multicoloured nation; and that it addressed its literature, to this end, to a white as well as a black audience.[31] As such its aesthetic programme stood in vivid contrast not just to the cultural politics of the Communist Party in the 1930s, but also to the explicitly political Black aesthetic developed through the Black Arts Movement of the 1960s. As part of an amalgam of 1960s counter-cultural practices, the Black Arts Movement was deeply entwined with African-American political activism, and more particularly with Black nationalism. Its blueprint for a new Black writing was, like Michael Gold's in the 1930s, characterised by an overriding concern with the role of culture in social change: no more self-expression but protest; no more conciliation and spirituality (unless, maybe, of African origin) but militant affirmation of racial pride; no more art for art's sake, but oppositional cultural practices which would transgress the 'dominant's' distinction between high and low culture (between poetry and performance, between oral and written, between literature and music). Most of all, art should be useful in the Black revolution: it should hail African-Americans in a call to action.[32]

As LeRoi Jones, one of the architects of the Black Arts Movement put it in 1962: 'If there is ever a Negro literature, it must disengage itself from the weak, heinous elements of the culture that spawned it' (Jones 1962: 197).

In many ways this evolving Black aesthetic translated Michael Gold's class-based cultural programme of the 1930s into the racial terms of Black nationalism. But, as in the 1930s also, this programme had little or no place for a politics of gender. Or if it had, it meant the politics of Black masculinity which required the subordination of the 'domineering matri-archal' woman to the Black man's authority. Feminism, as Luisah Teish points out, was regarded by many in Black Liberation as the 'white girls' thang' (Teish 1983: 331).

It was not until the demise of Black militancy in the early 1970s, when African-American feminists began to articulate their critiques of white feminism as well as Black gender relations, that a self-identified Black feminist cultural practice began to emerge in the work of Maya Angelou, Toni Morrison, Toni Cade Bambara, Gloria Naylor, and Alice Walker. Black women poets and playwrights (Lorraine Hansberry, Nikki Giovanni, Gwendolyn Brooks, Sonya Sanchez, Lucille Clifton) had been prominent for quite some time by then, but this new fiction differed from 1960s counter-cultural writing not only in its positive representation of strong black women, but perhaps particularly in its return to the language and rural setting of the American South and West as a 'feminine' space, in contrast to the urban ghettos and street culture where their male literary peers found their inspiration. And just as these male colleagues had taken Malcolm X and Richard Wright as their literary icons, so did African-American women look for ancestors in the female tradition. 'The veneration of foremothers', writes Luisah Teish, 'is essential to our self-respect' (Teish 1983: 333).[33] For Alice Walker this foremother is Zora Neale Hurston, and it is as a revision of Hurston and Toomer through the political and didactic lens of the Black Arts Movement that Walker's work in my view can most fruitfully be read. A short story such as 'Everyday Use', which critiques the elevation of quiltmaking to art and – as in *Meridian* – satirises the idea of the Black woman as African queen, clearly shows Walker's commitment to an art which is an act of imagination, but which is also useful: it doesn't want to be merely an aesthetic object, but also an act of critique or insight. Similarly in 'The Revenge of Hannah Kemhuff' Walker returns to Hurston's work on hoodoo, and affirms the avenging and healing powers of the folk tradition – hoodoo also as an imaginative and useful art. And of course the essay collection *In Search of Our Mother's Gardens* makes this same point in many different ways. *Meridian*, as we have seen, rewrites Toomer's spiritual legacy in the political terms of Civil Rights, whilst *The Color Purple* thematises and politicises the problems of creating an authentic African-American voice and an audience for the Black woman's speech, problems which plagued Zora Neale Hurston's autobiographical discourse in *Dust Tracks on a Road*, and which have since been identified as problems of non-dominant representation in Tillie Olsen's *Silences* and other works of feminist criticism.

Having set herself up as Hurston's main advocate, the critical controversy surrounding the latter's literary and political values has extended itself to the reception of Walker's writing too. Thus Celie's independence in *The Color Purple* is either celebrated as a triumph of the Black woman's survival, much like Janie's in *Their Eyes Were Watching God*, or it is – again, like Janie's fate – denounced as Utopian, or as individualist *embourgeoisement*.[34] Part of this Hurston-induced controversy concerns Walker's race-politics of Americans as 'a mingled people', a hybrid race made up of various colours and ethnicities. This hybridity does not conform to a 1960s Black nationalist conception of African-ness, but derives again from Toomer and Hurston in the 1920s and 1930s.[35] In contesting both white feminism's conception of gender and Black nationalism's race-politics, and embracing ecology, Jungian psychoanalysis and goddess-mysticism, Walker invites, in a sense, the mixed reviews that she has had. For her, the key to America's future (and indeed that of the world, no less) lies in a confrontation with its divisive and oppressive past and present. James Baldwin's credo is shared by Walker: 'I think that the past is all that makes the present coherent, and further, that the past will remain horrible for exactly as long as we refuse to assess it honestly' (Baldwin 1955: 318).

Meridian embodies Walker's complex and misunderstood womanist aesthetic, which consists in an amalgamation of features from the Harlem Renaissance, the Black Arts Movement, Black feminism and the African-American folk tradition. In the later works a strong Utopian dimension enters the fray, and it is this that causes critics – including myself – so many problems. In an interview Walker once said that Zora Neale Hurston 'saw poetry where other writers merely saw failure to cope with English'; it may be that Alice Walker herself is also ahead of her critics in that way. Richard Wright, in 'White Man, Listen!' tried to make a distinction between narcissistic writing and a 'form of things unknown'; it is possible that those critics who regard Walker's work as narcissistic, pure and simple, try to read to the letter of things known, where they might instead look for the spirit, and the form, of things unknown (Walker in O'Brien 1973: 202; Wright cited in Chapman 1968: 45). For as Ola, the African playwright, says in *The Temple of My Familiar*: 'Keep in mind always the present you are constructing. It should be the future you want' (Walker 1989: 262).

6

SEIZING TIME AND MAKING NEW
Marge Piercy's *Vida*

Marge Piercy's *Vida* is in many ways *Meridian*'s twin. This novel also bears the name of its main character – a political activist – as its title, it also returns to the early New Left as the true moment of personal politics, and it also highlights questions of female subjectivity and agency through an engagement with 1960s radical history. Furthermore, in *Vida* as in *Meridian* the personal costs of an activist life lived outside the structures and securities of mainstream politics are dramatised in particularly forceful ways.[1]

Vida revises the history of the white New Left, Students for a Democratic Society (SDS), and its aftermath the Weather Underground, in the way that *Meridian* draws on and rewrites the history of the Student Non-Violent Coordinating Committee (SNCC). But whereas in *Meridian* it is hysteria which provides a useful interpretive grid for Walker's sexual/textual politics, in *Vida* paranoia is the dominant metaphor in a tale of flight, persecution and disintegration of public and private life.

Despite their many thematic and political similarities, *Vida* and *Meridian* are very different novels. In contrast with Walker's cut-up spiritual realism, Piercy's mode of representation is ostensibly more conventional. It sets great store by detailed descriptions of the exigencies of everyday life, and punctuates a fast-moving narrative with dialogue where the ideas upon which the novel is constructed are themselves debated. The latter strategy in particular creates the impression that the novel is self-explanatory, that its meanings are transparent; *Vida*, like most of Piercy's work, wears its ideological colours on its sleeve. But there is rather more to *Vida* than simply the story of a woman activist's journey through the American 1960s and 1970s – good though that story is as a role-reversed picaresque.[2] *Vida* interrogates and rewrites radical history as it explores the origins of feminism in the New Left. It also projects – paradoxically, in what is on the whole a grim tale of bare survival – a strong Utopian vision of a transformed world in a sub-text of fantasy and desire which acts as a counterpoint to the surface narrative of flight and persecution. As a paranoid text, one which not only thematises the psychic reality of vigilance, subterfuge and hyper-consciousness, but which also formally re-enacts it, *Vida* furthermore raises questions regarding modes of personal/political consciousness and organisation that it ultimately cannot resolve. These questions of living the revolution, of collective agency, and of the public and the private, concerned feminism in the early 1980s but are here displaced, or rather projected on to, the New Left of the 1960s and 1970s. In this and every other sense, *Vida* again is a novel about understanding personal and political history in order not to repeat it.

PLACING *VIDA*: THEMATICS AND NARRATIVE STRUCTURE

Vida was Marge Piercy's sixth novel, published in 1980 on the threshold of the Reagan era, after her name and fame as a feminist novelist had been firmly established with the critical acclaim for *Woman on the Edge of Time* (1976a). Within Piercy's work, *Vida* is thematically and chronologically positioned between *The High Cost of Living* (1978) and *Braided Lives* (1982); it reworks the central problematic of *High Cost* in its focus on marginalisation and politics-as-morality, and begins the fictional historiography of the Women's Movement which was to be the basic project of *Braided Lives*. But whereas in the earlier novel Piercy problematised lesbian separatism as a viable position for feminists to take up, in *Vida* the question of a political choice which leads to marginality is addressed through representation of a revolutionary non-feminist politics and its personal costs. And where *Braided Lives* locates the roots of feminism in the repressive social climate of the 1950s and in the sexual politics of violence and reproduction, *Vida* explores feminism's breeding ground in the turbulence of radical social movements from 1967 until 1974, zooming in on questions of agency and the contradictions of living the *socialist* revolution.

By way of a sales pitch, the British Women's Press edition of *Vida* quotes *The Times Literary Supplement*: 'The real strength of the book lies ... in the power with which the loneliness and desolation of the central characters are portrayed ... A powerful novel, written with insight, wit and remorseless energy.'

This judgement evidently rests on an identificatory reading and valorises the emotional impact of the novel, for which 'remorseless' is indeed an appropriate term. Yet I can think of better recommendations than the promise of a depressing read; clearly we are expected to sympathise with Vida's plight, but we are at the same time invited to question the choices which have led her to an existence underground, and to consider the spaces for fantasy and desire that the novel also offers. I would suggest that as a political novel of feminism, *Vida* stands out amongst other fiction written by women in the same period and on similar subject matter. Valerie Miner's *Movement: a Novel in Stories* published in 1982, for example, is much less a text which examines radical politics in the 1960s than a novel of personal development which simply takes that era as its colourful background. For Miner, the 1960s are apparently a closed period, to be remembered with a sense of wonder and a good measure of nostalgia. In *Movement*, as in Sara Davidson's *Loose Change: Three Women of the Sixties*, history becomes largely a matter of style, of food, of clothes, of causes to be involved in. As attempts at writing novels with a collective protagonist (also one of Mailer's aims in *The Armies of the Night*), both texts fail because the burden of sociological detail – carefully worked indicators of the *Zeitgeist*, as in some kind of costume drama – inhibits or displaces any deeper examination of what determines individual and collective consciousness in relation to 1960s social movements. *Vida*, by contrast, seriously interrogates the forms of political organisation, practice and theory associated with those movements, without nostalgia or millenarian sentiments, in a way that is still relevant to feminism today.[3]

In *Vida*, questioning of the appropriateness and validity of New Left politics *vis à vis* feminism is dramatised in the changing relationship between two (half-)sisters.[4] Through Vida and Natalie the emergence of feminist consciousness is played out dialectically as evolving from the early New Left of the mid-1960s and opposing itself to the sectarianism and dogmatism of the revolutionary New Left of post 1968. Thus, in casting Natalie as the feminist and Vida as the revolutionary Leftie, Piercy represents the relationship between Women's Liberation and the New Left not through a gender opposition (female soft-centred personal politics versus male chauvinist Left hard core), but as a difference in political praxis. This is unusual and interesting, because it deviates from feminist historiography of Women's Liberation which has tended to stress the chauvinism of the New Left – as we have seen. In their zeal to present the Women's Liberation Movement as something radically new, feminist historians have found it necessary to underplay the ideological and organisational continuities between Women's Liberation and the New Left.[5] The process of polit-icisation is a theme which Piercy has dealt with time and time again. But here it takes a specific form: both Vida and Natalie are already established as political subjects (through their involvement in the New Left), so that their subsequent development is one of an evolving political conscious-ness, not a consciousness that suddenly emerges out of raw experience. For Vida this means a radicalisation towards guerilla warfare, and for Natalie it means feminism – less dramatic, less visible, but no less radical a political praxis than Vida's revolutionism. Ros Petschesky explains the concept of praxis thus:

> a series of 'negotiations' back and forth between ideology, social reality and desire. These negotiations result not only in a 'decision', a discrete act, but often in an unarticulated *morality of situation, of*

praxis, which incorporates social and individual need into the shifting ground of moral values.

(Petschesky 1984: 387)

Vida's evolving political consciousness is less a product of successful negotiation between 'ideology, social reality and desire' than a damaging internal conflict which results in isolation and the suppression of personal needs. For Natalie, by contrast, that negotiation yields an integrated, situational politics which is effective in the public, and rewarding in the private, spheres of her life. Where Vida's revolutionary radicalisation leads to personal disintegration and political ineffectiveness, Natalie's revolution is a revolution within the self but also within politics, because it unites personal needs with social imperatives. Through its depiction of Vida's increasing isolation, the novel in the end valorises Natalie's chosen feminist path, which harks back to the values of the early New Left, over Vida's heroic self-sacrifice and ideological purity. But this is a conclusion which is achieved with difficulty and a good deal of ambivalence; Natalie virtually disappears from the narrative halfway through and the focus on Vida's development draws the reader's attention more to the social and political determinants of subjectivity than that it posits a simple question of the right or wrong political choice. As in *Meridian*, there is no easy option, no unequivocal celebration of this or that political position, but rather a constant retracing of cause and effect, of 1960s radical history and its aftermath, once the political climate has changed.

Formally this interrogation of the meanings of history is reflected in a non-linear narrative, which intersperses sections set in an indeterminate present (some time in the late 1970s or early 1980s, we assume) with forays into the past: 1967, 1970 and 1974 respectively – significant moments in the history of the student New Left. This formal construction in which the narrative, as it were, continually looks over its shoulder towards the past, mirrors Vida's situation in the present as a political fugitive living underground, feeling hunted, having to resort to dissimulation and subterfuge, haunted by the fear that the past will eventually catch up with her. Unlike Meridian, who needed to confront the past in order to exorcise it, Vida continually tries to erase it in a disavowal of her own history and of her self. Underground existence requires disguise and denial of previous emotional bonds but – paradoxically – it also enables a fantasy existence in which the fugitive, like the actress she is required to be, can reinvent herself over and over again. The paranoia which I mentioned earlier is then as much a label for Vida's mental state, which in Freud's words could be described as 'a pathological mode of defence' to 'fend off an idea that is incompatible with the ego, by projecting its substance on to the external world', as it is also a mode of representation which locks the reader into the closed-circuited consciousness of the protagonist.[6]

Highly effective as a narrative ploy, the paranoid text creates, by means of

147

the gaps in the story of Vida's development, an impression of mystery and secrecy: is Vida's fear of being caught a persecutory delusion or not? And if not, what is her crime? We do not find out until the middle of the novel how Vida, starting as an effective political organiser in 1967, ends up in the nightmare of the paranoid present, and even then her motives remain unexplained (or at best implicit). If Vida's journey is to make sense as a realist narrative rather than a psychopathological case-study, then it should be possible to trace the personal/political disintegration depicted in the closing section of the novel back to a significant, existential moment of crisis or decision on Vida's part, but such a moment is never articulated. It exists only, I think, with reference to the real history of SDS and the Weather Underground, of which the reader is assumed to have some knowledge. Only such knowledge or living memory can realistically (i.e. convincingly, in narrative terms) explain the personal/political path that leads Vida to an existence underground.

In this way historical and fictional narratives merge; they supplement and reflect upon each other, thus keeping the reader oscillating between participation in the text's paranoid discourse and ambivalence about its persecutory fantasy. Because of Vida's ostensible idealism and innocence, it is the persecutory motif that causes problems of credibility in the text for readers who are ignorant of the historical record.

Like *Meridian*'s hysteria, my use of the term 'paranoia' in connection with *Vida* should not just be taken as a diagnosis of its protagonist's mental state, but as a designation of the novel's formal features which position the reader in specific ways, both inside and outside Vida's consciousness. The fact that *Vida* is a paranoid text does not mean that it has no purchase on historical reality; it just means that its truth-claim cannot be grounded without reference to historiography as the novel's authenticating discourse to validate its realism. This discourse concerns the history of the Weather Underground, the revolutionary militant offshoot of SDS whose exploits (bombings and other guerilla-type operations) haunted American political consciousness in the early 1970s. Within the real-life context of those involved in the Weather Underground, paranoia was less a sign of psychosis than a mode of survival in the face of intense and sophisticated state surveillance. In 1970 Bernardine Dohrn, one of the leaders of the Weather Underground, described the state of mind of fugitives like herself thus:

> We're often afraid but we take our fear for granted now, not trying to act tough. What we once thought would have to be some zombie-type discipline has turned out to be a yoga of alertness, a heightened awareness of activities and vibrations around us – almost a new set of eyes and ears.

(Dohrn cited in Sale 1973: 649)

Clearly this is an accurate description of Vida's state of mind in the novel's framing chapters set in the present, too. Where *Meridian* can survive as a novel, if not a political novel, in its own right without readers' detailed knowledge of the history of Civil Rights, *Vida* would be reduced to pure paranoid fantasy, or to a rather ridiculous adventure story, without the reader's acquaintance with the history of SDS to flesh it out and to lend it its stark realism.

RE-PRESENTING THE 1960s: *VIDA* AND THE HISTORY OF SDS AND WEATHER UNDERGROUND

1967

Vida is a member of Students Against the War (SAW):

> History was a sense of urgency, a rush in the blood and a passion to make things better, to push with her whole life on what was. *SAW* was a fiercely, totally democratic organization, open to anyone . . . *SAW* was uncontrollable and lush as a vacant-lot jungle.
>
> (Piercy 1980a: 110)

Vida herself at this point is a sensual woman, who manages to integrate political life with pleasure and the support of a circle of like-minded friends and lovers. She is effective in her role as political organiser – as when she writes the publicity for a demonstration against the war in Vietnam: 'Everywhere her people came together, marching arm in arm and shouting. The demonstration was starting. Some words on a page she had written and people responded' (Piercy 1980a: 128).

The power to bring about action through words is a source of pleasure, even exhilaration for Vida, indispensable to political agency. But this passage has a wider significance than that: at the same time as the text here reinserts women organisers into the history of the New Left – just as *Meridian* does for SNCC – it also posits an ideal of communication modelled on a one-to-one correspondence between intention and response, the ultimate speech act. Later in the narrative this correspondence will break down, to reveal a dramatic split in the closing pages between language and political agency, when political speech has become mere rhetoric and resistance means little more than a refusal to face up to a changed reality.[7]

1967 was, of course, the year of the march on the Pentagon, preserved for posterity in Norman Mailer's *The Armies of the Night*. Regarded by many as the culmination of the 1960s, the year of the summer of love, of Haight Ashbury and flower power, 1967 was also a turning point in the history of the student movement. Kirkpatrick Sale, historian of the white New Left, described 1967 as a time of crisis for SDS. With a larger membership than ever before, SDS's organisational effort for Vietnam summer had elicited a huge response, but harassment and surveillance by the FBI were being stepped up and within the organisation itself ideas about its political direction were changing. At this point, writes Sale, SDS was 'suspended ... between reform and revolution, between personal and political, between action and ideology, between local strength and national promise' (Sale 1973: 351).

Cracks were beginning to show which would later lead to the Big Split within SDS between Progressive Labor (building a mass organisation among the working class and the poor) and Weatherman (militant resistance on the model of that of the Black Panthers, and later guerilla warfare from underground). Clearly, *Vida* charts a similar splitting process in the heroine's personal/political development and in the widening gap between social movement and the isolated existence of a political fugitive.

Importantly with regard to Piercy's novel, 1967 was also a formative year for Women's Liberation, then still only existing as a caucus within the New Left. For the first time SDS Conference passed a motion calling on women to demand full participation in movement work, and asking men to 'deal with' their sexist attitudes.[8]

These historico-fictional parallels, between Vida's involvement in SAW in 1967 and the crisis in SDS, foreshadow the rest of Vida's story and authenticate its realism. What is represented here as political agency and community is no mere projection of an indeterminate feminist future, as in the Utopian elements of Vida's underground existence later in the novel, but a *remembered* alternative to the isolation, ineffectiveness and self-denial that Vida has to practise on the fugitive trail. The 1967 episode in Vida's life is important, I think, because it comes to function within the feminist argument of the novel as an originary moment, a model to be harked back to, of a time when the personal and the political still meshed, when there was a sense of 'history on our side' and of an effective political language.

1970

The second retrospective part of the novel is set three years later than this originary moment, and evokes similar parallels with the history of SDS. Vida's time, May 1970, is sometimes – conveniently – regarded as the end of the 1960s, not so much because of an abrupt end to political activism or the start of the Nixon era, but because what was held to be the spirit of the decade (peace, love, and non-violent protest) came to an end with the acceleration of violence in the streets, with police brutality against anti-war protesters and with their armed retaliation. The shootings at Kent and Jackson State campuses, in which students were killed, made a particularly deep impression. Recorded in bloody detail on network television, the whole world was watching how America treated its young dissenters. 'Don't shoot, we are your children!' – a conciliatory cry still effective at the march on Washington three years before – had a hollow ring to it now; the age of non-violent protest was definitively over.[9]

According to James Miller in his excellent study of the ideas of the New Left, *Democracy Is in the Streets*, May 1970 was something of a watershed for the student movement. Those within SDS who were in favour of violent resistance – like the Weather Underground – had a strong argument for retaliation on their side after the Kent and Jackson State shootings. The Weatherman faction split from the main body of SDS and although its position was denounced by many on the Left as dangerous adventurism and revolutionary posturing, the more moderate mainstream in SDS nevertheless shifted with it towards an acceptance, in principle, of resistance instead of mere protest. It seemed the time was ripe for such a shift. Miller cites Tom Hayden's speech given at the 1968 Democratic Convention rally in Chicago:

> The chief problem is not so much the tendency towards adventurism, to running out in the streets, as it is the tendency in the opposite direction – to look for ways to achieve social change without pain, without loss of life, without prison sentences.
>
> (Hayden cited in Miller 1987: 305)

In other words: self-sacrifice was called for, and political action could no longer be readily integrated with personal life – it demanded dedication, discipline and the willingness to suffer. That was 1968.

After the Kent and Jackson State shootings, Hayden's rhetorical chickens came home to roost. Weatherman began to assert itself with a political ethic of utter commitment to the revolution and a vanguardist politics that could not wait for, let alone create, mass support. Weatherman devised the powerful slogan of 'Bringing the War Home' and professed the belief that America's young activists, the generation that collectively had been nominated *Man of the Year* in 1967 (an irony not lost on the women), were ready to confront the corporate state on its own ground with the same weapons – bombs – as those used to perpetrate US crimes on Indo-China. By 1970, Hayden had changed his mind about the way of social change, and he denounced Weatherman as trigger-happy, politically deluded fantasts who 'in their heads . . . were part of the Third World' (Hayden cited in Sale 1973: 605).

Realising that his own incitements to resistance two years earlier could now with reason be held against him, Hayden decided to draw the line of acceptable political activity at Weatherman, albeit uneasily: 'They would say that I was not seizing the time, that I was not willing to risk everything', he said defensively (Hayden cited in Miller 1987: 310).

How does all this relate to *Vida*? In the 1970 chapter of the novel there is a discussion between the two sisters, which highlights the split opening up between them through Vida's use of political rhetoric. When Natalie enquires about old and established friendships which seem to be falling apart for Vida, the latter explains her feelings about this loss in the public language of 'political differences', of Marxist Leninist teachings, and of (revolutionary) 'seriousness'.[10] Within the value system of the professional revolutionary, seriousness equals commitment equals sacrifice, particularly sacrifice of anything resembling a personal life and emotional ties: 'everything was empty palaver that was not about liberation, not about imperialism, or racism or Third World struggles, about the war, the war, the war' (Piercy 1980a: 191).[11]

Vida thus echoes Hayden's demand for a splitting of the private and the public – a return, in a sense, to an Old Left masculinist model of the political activist who is wholly dedicated to the revolution, unfettered by emotional bonds, bombing his way across America.

The conversation between the sisters is interesting because it invokes between the lines the spectre of the early New Left when, in Stanley Aronowitz's words, people 'shared the belief that they were themselves the new historical subjects', and believed that politics should aim to 'infuse life with a secular spiritual and moral content, to fill the quotidian with personal meaning and purpose' (Aronowitz 1985: 18).

Natalie challenges Vida on precisely this ground, reminding her what it was like when the New Left was new:

'What's the point being a Marxist-Leninist in the US of A in 1970? . . .
You used to laugh at all those factionalists quoting their little red books . . .'
'I'm more serious now than I was then-'
'No, you're just more desperate.'

(Piercy 1980a: 203)

Natalie's (implicit) demand that Vida talk about herself in a language not derived from a theory of past revolutions in Europe, repeats the Americanist principles on which the Port Huron statement was based in 1962, when Tom Hayden and his co-authors were still concerned with 'speaking American' to their constituency of young New Leftists.[12] But by 1970, the American that Natalie wants Vida to speak, the American of a politics with 'personal meaning and purpose' was not only outdated but completely discredited. 'The war, the war, the war' – on the revolutionary Left all talk of finding a meaning in life, and a personally authentic one at that, became taboo. What we see is that in *Vida*, at the point when the New Left is no longer new, feminism (as represented in Natalie's stance) claims the mantle of representing the truly American values of democracy, plain speaking and politics in the service of the pursuit of happiness, and presents women as the new historical subjects.

So 1970 is another turning point in the historical and fictional narrative. On the one hand, with Vietnam protests all attention came to be focused on draft resisters, which left to the women in the movement little except a supportive role towards their either martyred or defiant male peers (Girls Say Yes to Guys Who Say No!). On the other hand, if women in the movement wanted, as they had claimed, an equal share in the action, then they had to prove they were as committed, and as willing to 'seize the time' and to take risks as were the most macho of men – they had to prove their masculinity, in other words. Or they could be real girls, and prove their anti-revolutionary femininity by joining the Women's Liberation Movement, which many New Leftists – men and women alike – still regarded as a bourgeois indulgence 'divisive of the larger struggle'. This Scylla-or-Charybdis choice is replayed in the discussion between Vida and Natalie, where in the terms of the debate of the time Vida takes the politico, and Natalie the feminist, position.[13]

The discussion between Vida and Natalie over political styles also covers interracial rape. At this point sexual and racial politics surface for the first time in the novel, in a talking-through of positions. When Natalie explains her increasing feminist sympathies by stating that she has been raped by a black man, Vida cannot take her seriously and accuses her sister of sounding like a 'Southern Belle racist'. An exchange of political theories concerning violence and armed resistance follows, in which we are clearly invited to concur and sympathise with Natalie's argument that rape is simply rape, a crime against women, no matter what the context or history of interracial sexual relations. Armed defence by women solves nothing. For Vida the issue is not a political one and therefore unimportant; her solution is that if women armed themselves rape simply would not happen (Piercy 1980a: 201–3).

With the precedents of interracial rape in *The Women's Room* and *Meridian* in mind, it looks as though the black-on-white rape discussion is a set piece in American feminist fiction of this period. In all three novels, the issue seems to represent the nub of feminism's conflictual relation to other social movements of the 1960s, an historical trauma no longer repressed but endlessly reworked in the new terms of a gendered race politics, or a raced gender politics. In the 1970 chapter in *Vida* there is on one hand still a close parallel with feminist and New Left historiography, but on the other a gap opens up between the fictional narrative and the historical record: race is erased as an issue of 1960s radical politics in *Vida except for this passage on rape*.[14] In a paradoxical way, Vida and Natalie's discussion of interracial sexual violence is a representation of absence and silence, which points by way of what is being said (rape) to what cannot be countenanced in the text (race). This is important because historical discourses, both those of the actual writing of history and those of remembering it and contesting its

meanings, are *Vida*'s authenticating discourses as well as its central problematic. At the level of representation, this means that the numerous
evocations of historical fact create the effect of a faithful record, a
meticulous realism, thereby obscuring the transformative (imaginative and
ideological) work that fiction enacts upon the material of history and
historiography. The third retrospective moment in *Vida*, and the framing
chapters set in the present, show even clearer traces of this transformative
work as the gap between historical and fictional discourses widens.

1974

In the 1970 section, Vida's crime (she has taken part in a bombing
operation) is disclosed, which provides the rationale for her fugitive status
by 1974. She is now a member of an underground organisation called the
Network, which operates in small, highly secretive collectives. Close historical parallels between the underground cell in which Vida is involved
and the *modus operandi* of the Weather Underground continue in the
third retrospective chapter, set in 1974. Well-documented infiltration of
the Weather Underground by the FBI, for example, corresponds with the
betrayal of Vida's collective by an FBI agent masquerading as an
(over)enthusiastic Network activist. But Piercy's picture of the revolutionary
Network here begins to differ dramatically from historians' judgement of
the nature and significance of the Weather Underground.[15] Sympathetic
historians of the New Left, such as Todd Gitlin, Maurice Isserman and James
Miller uniformly dismiss the Weather Underground as a bunch of misguided hotheads afflicted with delusions of grandeur, a judgement with
which autobiographical accounts by ex-fugitives such as Susan Stern and
Jane Alpert concur.[16]

Piercy, by contrast, portrays a group of flawed but dedicated individuals
who are as much the victims of history as they also still want to see themselves
as the vanguard of change. Sexual and interpersonal doctrines of the
Weather Underground come in for particularly bitter derision on the part
of 1980s historians. Kirkpatrick Sale in 1973 still writes about sexual politics
in the Weather Underground as a veritable frontier of struggle, and cites
with approval New York Weather faction which claimed that 'Women, who
for years had been silent or someone's girlfriend, *in two or three weeks* became
strong political leaders' [my *italics*] as a result of the 'Smash Monogamy'
policy (Sale 1973: 585). James Miller, whose book on SDS came out more
than a decade after Sale's, is much more critical of the Weather Underground
and attributes Sale's credulity to his embeddedness in a revolutionary
rhetoric which 'was still fashionable when he completed his book' (Miller
1987: 379).

Clearly Sale's unquestioning acceptance of the idea that the new men and
women of revolutionist myth can be churned out in a matter of weeks,

illustrates his allegiance to the ideals of the vanguardist New Left, but it also testifies to the powerful hold such fantasies of instant personal/political transformation had on the Left's imagination generally. Piercy exploits this imaginative/Utopian potential in *Vida*, whereas the historians focus on its delusionary and prescriptive aspects. Miller and Todd Gitlin then see the Weather Underground's prohibition on monogamy and its practice of criticism/self-criticism sessions, which were designed to foster revolutionary discipline, quite rightly as inappropriate because derived from Third World revolutionary struggles, but they are interestingly unable to judge them in dispassionate terms. Gitlin gives some examples of the excesses of the Weather Underground's moral strictures, and notes the destructive effect on the mainstream Left of what he calls 'Weatherguilt':

> The Weathermen were a scourge, not an argument . . . Thousands in the movement's most experienced networks bled from weatherguilt. 'Gut-checking' – scrutinizing one another for leftover 'bourgeois attitudes' – became the movement's favorite parlor-game.
>
> (Gitlin 1987: 398)[17]

Yet in *Vida* what we see is a good deal of argument and bitterness between the members of the Network, but also a construction of personal/political relations as a freely chosen plurality of practices in which self-scrutiny can be productive and power relations between the sexes are readily acknowledged as an integral part of sexual desire. *Vida*'s promiscuity moreover – despite some bad experiences with exploitative men – is, by and large, valued positively as one of the few sites of pleasure left within a political morality and revolutionary discipline that allows very little. This picture of an active, self-determining, unvictimised and flagrantly bisexual female desiring subject is an important aspect of the novel, a point where structures of fantasy and a Utopian inversion of social and sexual relations shine through underneath the surface narrative of Vida's increasing marginalisation.

Since the writing of history is always a teleological enterprise, and since the repressive effects of right wing policies against terrorism in the 1970s and 1980s were in large part inspired by the spectre of anarchy which the Weather Underground fostered in American society, Miller's and Gitlin's harsh critiques of the Weather phenomenon was undoubtedly justified. Gitlin suggests that by the mid-1970s Weatherguilt had run its course, and a consensus emerged among ex-New Leftists like himself about the reason for the movement's demise: 'Most of the organizers were convinced that the New Left's fatal mistake had been to burn its bridges to the multitudes whose lives were dominated by scarcity' (Gitlin 1987: 422).

Although in *Vida* the Network reaches the same conclusion in the end, there is no question but that Piercy's construction of the revolutionary underground, by comparison with Miller and Gitlin, is a much sanitised one. *Vida* is certainly – at the very least – ambivalent about the political value of vanguardism and clandestine operations, but it is at the same time sympathetic to the underground's ideals; rather than construct them as violent fanatics, *Vida* emphasises the fugitives' aspirations for social change, their integrity and their isolation. The question then arises as to what purpose this idealised picture of radical fugitives serves in a novel which is, on my analysis, essentially a political text of feminism. I believe the answer lies in *Vida*'s framing chapters, set in the present, because it is there that the paranoid text, propelled by a contradictory combination of persecutory and Utopian fantasies, truly comes into its own.

'THE PRESENT': UTOPIAN REALISM IN *VIDA*

Ostensibly a grim tale of the fugitives' fight for survival, the chapters which treat Vida's existence in the present are, I think, also a site of powerful socialist-feminist fantasy. The so-called guerilla operations in which the fugitives engage, such as the rescue of a battered woman, Tara, are represented as acts of natural justice which turn the logic of existing power relations inside out. In an inversion of the law and order of the society which has forced them underground, Joel and Vida as 'terrorists' become Tara's saviours and guardians, whereas Tara's policeman husband is shown to be the guilty party, the criminal from whom Tara and her children have to be protected (Piercy 1980a: 158). Here *Vida* projects for an instant a vision of a different social and political order, one which is essentially Utopian in this context. For, as Fredric Jameson has written, the guerilla operation, which is apparently an isolated act of desperation, represents at another level a Utopian moment, because it becomes

> a *figure* for the transformed, revolutionary society to come ... This conception of a newly emergent revolutionary 'space' – situated outside the 'real' political, social and geographical world of country and city, and of the historical classes, yet at one and the same time a figure or small-scale image and prefiguration of the revolutionary transformation of that real world – may be designated as a properly utopian space, a Hegelian 'inverted world', an autonomous revolutionary sphere, in which the fallen real world over against it is itself set right and transformed into a new socialist society.
>
> (Jameson 1985: 202–3)

It is this Utopian dimension that marks *Vida* off as a political text of feminism. The vision underlying the narrative of Vida's trajectory through the changing political landscape of America in the 1960s and 1970s keeps the possibility of social change alive and frames that possibility in terms of a feminist politics. Piercy's Utopian realism which juxtaposes an historicist teleological narrative of the past with Jameson's 'inverted world' in the present, can be seen as yet another variant of an oppositional cultural practice which critiques the status quo of existing gender relations and posits the need for radical social change.

It is because the present in *Vida* is a realm of indeterminate time that it can become the realm of Utopian fantasy. There are quite a few such submerged Utopian moments to be found in this novel; apart from instances of political agency, as in the Tara episode, I suggested earlier that the representation of Vida's promiscuity as multifaceted sexual agency offers a powerful image of female desire. Moreover, in its construction of an active female sexuality liberated by 1960s mores, Piercy imaginatively rehabilitates the Sexual Revolution for feminism, writing against an earlier consensus in Women's Liberation that the sexualisation of social relations in the 1960s had merely been exploitative of, and bad for, women.[18]

Behind the predominantly depressing tale of Vida's existence as a fugitive looms a very strong image of a woman who takes up space, who roams across America independently as some avenging angel, and gets away with it – if only just. There are several elements to this feminist fantasy which lend it its peculiar force. One is obviously the idea of space itself, of travel and movement unrestricted by fear of sexual violence. Another, indispensably related to it, is the image of the woman with a gun, a fighter who knows how to defend herself. That she is seen to be fighting the good fight makes the fantasy a permissible one for feminists – much of the novel's political effect depends, after all, on the reader's sympathy for Vida and her sharing of a common dream of female agency and self-determination. This dream, and the image of an independent, mobile woman warrior is strongly reminiscent of Agnes Smedley's gun-toting protagonist in *Daughter of Earth*, except that here the sexual connotations of female mobility and (potential) violence are released and acknowledged, in a way that they could not be in Smedley's novel. For Marie Rogers in *Daughter of Earth* is ashamed of her sexual desires at the same time as she is also uncomfortable with her male-identified public existence; her hostility to other women then can only be explained as a form of self-hatred.

Vida is a feminist rewrite of *Daughter of Earth* in the sense that it takes up that novel's major theme of a public/private, inside/outside split, but without binding the private to sexuality *per se* and without setting up an inexorable incompatibility between femininity and political activism. In *Vida*, unlike *Daughter of Earth*, transgression of gender roles is naturalised and made attractive to the feminist reader; it is not a flight from feminine existence but an expansion of its traditional sphere. Whatever Vida suffers is a result of her political choices and of historical forces, not a consequence of her transgressive bisexuality or of her personal shortcomings.[19]

Another element of Vida's submerged narrative of female desire is that stock ingredient of Utopian fantasy, the pastoral romance: Vida and Joel traverse and come to rest in the countryside where an Eden-like past and future can be envisioned. Vida's compulsive criss-crossing of America is punctuated by such rural idylls, however temporary, and it is no accident that the novel ends with an escape from the forces of law and order (which is also an escape from the urban jungle of New York) to rural Vermont.[20]

Finally, there is love interest, another firm favourite of female fantasy. Here romance is rewritten in a feminist sense as an emotional praxis in Vida and Joel's relationship as comrades-in-arms, whose growing intimacy and sexual passion arise from a common situation and purpose. Neither sudden and overwhelming nor all-encompassing or ever complete – in the end, Vida's closest scrape with her persecutors is the result of Joel's jealousy, and brings about their separation – this romance nevertheless represents a heady mixture of female independence integrated with fulfilment of emotional and sexual needs. Space, movement, political agency, independence, rural retreats, intimacy and sex – taken together, this is about as attractive a scenario for women's liberation in the feminist future as we are likely to get.

READING *VIDA*: CONTRADICTIONS OF THE PARANOID TEXT

But of course in reading *Vida* as a fiction of desire and a reach for Utopian transcendence I am, to some extent, reading against the grain of a much more dominant narrative movement of persecution and flight. The depiction of fugitive existence is a nightmare, equal in power to the fantasy delineated just now, of being lost in the wilds of the city, surrendering self to the false identities required for survival, a picture of desolation, power-lessness and ceaseless tension.[21] It is not insignificant, as Piercy herself indicates in a paper on post-Holocaust Jewish consciousness, that the psychic reality of a political fugitive here concerns a Jewish protagonist. Piercy writes:

> I learned paranoia is often inadequate to the realities of life in our times, but definitely superior to reason as a means of grasping what is going on. That was not the worst preparation for being a writer whose work has a politically conscious dimension.
>
> (Piercy n.d.: 6)[22]

The fact that Vida is a Jew is not particularly foregrounded in the novel, but it may inform our reading in terms of paranoia. As Todd Gitlin observes, a (historically legitimate) paranoia was very much part of the world-view of a post-war generation of Jews, and the living memory of the Holocaust may explain why a disproportionate number of young Jewish people were involved in the New Left:

> The massacre of the Jews was a huge fact lying overturned, square in the middle of the through route to progress. There were some, or many, for whom the Holocaust meant that nothing – neither private

satisfactions nor the nation's greater glory – could ever supplant the need for a public morality. There were christians as well as Jews who concluded that they would never end up 'Good Germans' if they could help it.

(Gitlin 1987: 26)

In connection with *Vida* then, the overriding metaphor of persecution and the notion of resistance-at-all-cost may, at least in part, be read in Jewish cultural and historical terms as the refusal of a generation of Jewish-American activists to be 'Good Germans'.

But there is another dimension too, for we must remember that *Vida* was published at a time when political space for the radical social movements of the 1960s, including feminism, was rapidly contracting. The situation of the Women's Liberation Movement at the end of the 1970s, racked by internal division and a moralistic lifestyle politics on one hand, and lacking political effectiveness in bettering the condition of women's lives on the other, was comparable (if by no means identical) to that of the New Left of a decade before. The heyday of an activist, visible, mass movement of women was over, and feminism could no longer claim a political identity as a force for social change. And in the face of that lack of collective unity, neither could individual feminists posit themselves unproblematically as the new historical subjects. This means that *Vida*, as a paranoid text, can be seen to displace the problems of feminist existence in the un-liberated present of the Reaganite early 1980s on to previous failed experiments in living the revolution; categories of gender, Jewishness and Left wing politics are mapped on to each other as a rationale for Vida's existence on the fringes of American society.

Piercy's own comment on *Vida* in an interview elucidates this mapping-on:

> The experience of becoming a political fugitive, after all, is the experience of being an invisible woman, instead of a token woman . . . As a fugitive, invisible and necessarily anonymous . . . her experiences are much closer to the experience of ordinary women, and she becomes much more open to the ideas of feminism.
>
> (Piercy 1980b: 177–8)

Utopian realism makes for contradictions in the text, held in suspension through the figurative logic of paranoia. Freud writes that paranoia is 'an abuse of the mechanism of projection for the purposes of defence', leading not only to delusions of persecution, but also to megalomania which provides psychic protection against the complete disintegration of personal identity.[23] Obviously, Vida's increasing isolation, her gradual incarceration in the self-legitimising language of revolutionary consciousness, and her refusal to realise the hopelessness of her situation, invite an interpretation in terms of paranoia. But if that were all, her story could easily be dismissed as a comment upon the demise of 1960s radicalism which puts the blame squarely upon the mistakes of the underground Left at the same time as it also constructs this demise as a form of victimisation: a vanguard betrayed and deserted by its foot-soldiers under the imperative of a changing times. Instead, what is offered in the representation of 1967 as an ideal model of political authenticity, and in the Utopian moments of an inverted social order, is a vision of the *possibility* of different social relations, a promise held out to those who will but see beyond the confines of the 'real' present in which the Women's Movement, like Vida's Left, is in decline. This promise is rendered as the memory of the early New Left combined with the feminist future projected in (amongst other things) guerilla operations as megalomaniac fantasies of living in a post-revolutionary world.

We are faced here with a paradox which the novel ultimately cannot resolve, but only stage and re-stage. On the one hand paranoia imprisons the subject – and the text – in a closed circuit of compulsive disavowal of the real conditions of existence, but on the other the situation of the marginal subject – one of Piercy's recurrent themes – creates a heightened awareness, an elevated consciousness which enables the subject and the text to envision social change through the structures of Utopian inversion and desire. In the end, the tension between these two becomes very apparent, as this final scene illustrates:

> I am at the mercy of history, she thought, feeling its force concretely as a steel press closing on her chest, but I can push it too a bit. One thing I know is that nothing remains the same . . . What swept through us and cast us forward is a force that will gather and rise again. Two steps forward and a step and a half back. I will waste none of my life.
>
> (Piercy 1980a: 412)

The passage contrasts a personalised language of loss with a tired-sounding discourse of history and resistance – the rhetoric of the New Left – which has been discredited earlier in the text and is therefore ironised and fails to convince. *Vida*'s ending merely reiterates the (protective) fantasy of radical change at a point where none is possible. The problem is that a resolution in terms of a linear conception of history in the end has to be refused, because it would leave no scope or hope of resistance – there is nothing but historical circumstance for humans to be 'at the mercy of'. But neither can a liberated future be envisioned for a Vida who has cast her personal lot in with a social movement whose time has come and gone. Vida is then as much a tragic heroine, a veritable Antigone, as she is also a powerful figure of female fantasy; this contradiction cannot be reconciled in a satisfactory narrative closure but only restated in an open ending.

160

FEMINIST REALISM AND FICTIONAL
REPRESENTATIONS OF HISTORY

Morris Dickstein writes in his book on 1960s culture, *Gates of Eden*, of an increasing tendency in American fiction from 1968 onwards to eschew political argument and to foreground more and more the writing process itself. It may or may not be coincidental that Dickstein calls the beginning of this development the 'Weatherman phase', whose main characteristic is 'a certain detachment from experience, sometimes to the point of a disintegration of the senses of reality, both in art and politics' (Dickstein 1977: 215).

Norman Mailer's 1968 novel *The Armies of the Night* is a good example of Dickstein's thesis. Mailer's novel is 'about' the anti-war march on the Pentagon in 1967, and is made up of two parts entitled 'History as a Novel' and 'The Novel as History'. With this device Mailer sets up a problematic around the inevitable narrativisation of history in any attempt to represent it, resulting in a textual experiment that abandons all faith in history as (external) reality. Mailer's autobiographical account of the march uses a number of same-but-different narrators: 'the protagonist', 'the historian', 'the novelist', and 'Mailer' (all possible narrative perspectives in fact, except that of the conventional autobiographical 'I'), in order to highlight the inaccessibility of history and to signal the demise of a single unified point of view from which historical events can be comprehended and captured. With all such self-conscious artifice, *The Armies of the Night* offers an essayist exploration of the vagaries and complexities of different modes of representation, to which the march on Washington in the end is merely incidental.[24] Even as such, the novel is less an exploration of representation than an exhibition of a persona called 'Norman Mailer' around whom this universe of discursive practices revolves. As Frederick Karl has written, 'Mailer turns the peace movement into a solipsistic perception: it exists because Norman Mailer was *there*' (Karl 1983: 579).

This is, unfortunately, not the place for an extensive discussion of American literature's penchant in the past two and a half decades for narrative experiments which blur the boundaries between historiography and fiction, but a few remarks may help to place *Vida* as a counter-text within this larger domain. Daniel Aaron is not the only critic who has noted a veritable trend in American literature of pseudo-historical writing with satirical intent and who has been critical of this tendency. Aaron says of writers like Mailer, Robert Coover and E. L. Doctorow that contemporary fictionalisations of the past are designed to attract attention to their authors' textual wizardry rather than that they set out to seriously debate or challenge the meanings of history. For Mailer, or for Doctorow in *The Book of Daniel* (which is ostensibly about McCarthyism and the Rosenbergs, but reaches no conclusion about 'what really happened' and leaves the comforting impression that in history 'everything is elusive'), history is a text

(Doctorow 1971: 42). And if history is a text, it might as well be a literary text which can be endlessly rewritten, refashioned and reread.

The notion that history is a text has become something of a theoretico-philosophical cliché under the impact of poststructuralism and post-modernism. Yet, as Fredric Jameson argues, the realisation that history is not accessible except through signification does not therefore mean that referentiality (and thus epistemological realism) becomes impossible too:

> history is *not* a text, not a narrative, master or otherwise, but . . . as an
> absent cause it is inaccessible to us except in textual form, and . . . our
> approach to it and to the Real itself necessarily passes through its prior
> textualization, its narrativization in the political unconscious.
>
> (Jameson 1983: 35)[25]

I think it is this understanding of history as an absent cause that informs Piercy's Utopian-historicist realism as an oppositional literary practice. Non-dominant groups such as Leftists and feminists do not reject or playfully reinvent a history in which they are only just beginning to inscribe themselves; that history is, in a sense, all too real, all too present, all too much in need of a change in course. This means that if such texts as *The Armies of the Night* and *The Book of Daniel* are regarded as key texts in the fictional construction of radical history, Piercy's *Vida* is to be read against them as a strategic intervention on behalf of socialist-feminism in a mainstream masculinist domain. Piercy's realism in *Vida* is neither trans-parent nor a matter of straightforward referentiality (as in a *roman à clef*), but shot through with Utopian projections of a feminist and socialist future. This Utopian realism is, at this point in American history, a politically necessary realism: necessary to make a claim on history, on women's presence as historical subjects, and necessary as a challenge to the literary practices of 'the dominant'.

In taking political activism and modes of resistance as her subject matter in so much of her work (apart from *Vida*, also in *Braided Lives, Gone to Soldiers, Dance the Eagle to Sleep* and *Woman on the Edge of Time*) Piercy is aware that the transformative powers of imaginative writing *per se*, i.e. apart from social movements, should not be overstated. Michèle Barrett issues a useful caveat along these lines:

> we cannot look to culture alone to liberate us – it cannot plausibly be
> assigned such transcendental powers. Second, since there is no one-to-
> one relationship between an author's intentions and the way in which
> a text will be received, the feminist artist cannot predict or control in
> any ultimate sense the effects of her work. These two points constitute
> an important limitation for the practice of politicized art.
>
> (Barrett 1985: 83)

We know of Marge Piercy's intentions that hers is an outspokenly political aesthetic:

> I write to change consciousness, to reach those people who don't agree already. Cultural work is one of the most effective ways of reaching people. If you don't support alternate ways of imagining things, people aren't going to be able to imagine a better world.
>
> (Piercy 1980a: flyleaf)

Yet we know also that a contemporary readership is unlikely to be familiar with those intentions or with the specific engagement with 1960s radical history that a novel like *Vida* offers. Criticism, however, can intervene in the reception of a work and reradicalise its meanings for the present. A feminist critique should then include consideration of the historical conditions in which the novel was produced, but it should also be aware of the cultural and historical distance between that moment and the present, as Fredric Jameson – again – warns us:

> Our presupposition . . . will be that only a genuine philosophy of history is capable of respecting the specificity and radical difference of the social and cultural past while disclosing the solidarity of its polemics and passions, its forms, structures, experiences and struggles, with those of the present day.
>
> (Jameson 1983: 18)

Only when that distance is measured accurately, as I have tried to do in my elucidation of *Vida*'s historical references, can we establish the common ground between past and present, and articulate the questions that fiction poses for feminism today.

In 1984 Judith and Stewart Albert wrote in their introduction to *The 60s Papers: Documents of a Rebellious Decade*:

> Conservatives, who interpret the sixties, focus overwhelmingly on drugs, riot and streetfighting and diminish the role of ideas. The sixties were much more than an emotional outburst. [They were] a time when truly new ideas were articulated, and everything in our country was up for debate – from foreign policy to sex. Nothing except the need for change was taken for granted.
>
> (Albert and Albert 1984: xv)

Both *Vida* and *Meridian* are, in an important sense, novels which debate the ideas of the 1960s. Fiction does not give us access to the past, or at least not reliably so. Yet at a time when the political climate is as hostile to the spirit of the 1960s as ours has been for more than a decade, and popular memory seems nostalgic merely for the (now heavily commodified) sex and drugs and rock&roll of 1960s culture, fiction and criticism can play a vital role in renegotiating the meanings of radical history in the light of an ever-shifting present. In *Vida* and *Meridian* the significance of the 1960s for radical Left politics and feminism today is represented, however ambivalently, as a time when 'nothing except the need for change was taken for granted'. A feminist reading of these texts in the early 1990s then can mean nothing less – to invoke the rallying cry of 1968 – than seizing that time, and making it new.

7

'CONTEXT IS ALL'
Backlash fictions of the 1980s

Feminist fiction of the 1970s engaged mainstream American culture and society in an aesthetic and political debate over the cultural meanings of gender. Through a range of representational strategies it managed to both mount a stringent critique of dominant modes of representation and project a vision of social change, a vision which transcends the limits of the text to point to the injustice and violence of existing power relations and to the possibility of a feminist or womanist future. The narratives of Marilyn French's *The Women's Room*, of Audre Lorde's *Zami*, of Kate Millett's *Flying*, and of *Vida* and *Meridian* all embodied not just the possibility but the realisation of a feminist literary discourse in textual practices which both thematise and enact the struggle with the language and cultural scripts of a patriarchal social order.

This, however, is no longer unequivocally the case with feminist fictions of the 1980s, as the contradictions of a Utopian/paranoid realism such as that of *Vida* already indicate.

In her essay 'Is Personal Life Still a Political Issue?', Barbara Haber articulates an awareness of changed historical conditions on the eve of the 1980s as the era of a new political 'realism' which was poised to dismantle the gains of the 1960s: 'Now a new day has come. It is time (so soon!) to begin to look at how the world changed and how we changed, and how the two have influenced each other' (Haber 1979: 420).

With the contraction of American feminism's political space, a backlash against the libertarianism of the 1960s brought a reaction against the Women's Movement in its train, which had its effects upon feminist culture and theory too. The backlash fictions of my title then refer to novels which have been read and praised as feminist texts, but which in my view were strongly influenced by, and are in their functioning complicit with, the anti-feminist backlash of America's New Right. A brief discussion of feminist Utopian fiction and its political moment in the 1970s will elucidate this shift from political fictions of feminism to political fictions by women which position themselves post-feminism, or in some cases even against feminism.

FEMINIST FICTION AND THE RISE OF THE NEW RIGHT

Marge Piercy's Utopian/realist novel *Woman on the Edge of Time* is in many ways a pivotal text of the 1970s and marks the transition from predominantly realist to predominantly fantasy (or historicist) modes of representation in feminist fiction.[1]

In writing Utopia, dystopia and realism into *Woman on the Edge of Time*, Piercy in effect sets up a dialogue between the present and different possible futures; the message is that people have a hand in shaping history, even if as individuals they often feel at the mercy of forces larger than themselves. This is true also of Connie Ramos, Piercy's unconventional protagonist whose murderous act in the mental hospital will not set her free; like the woman narrator in Charlotte Perkins Gilman's *The Yellow Wallpaper* her final gesture of defiance is both revolutionary and futile, because self-destructive.[2] Yet any act of resistance in this totalitarian context is better than none, because it establishes Connie's agency, if no one else's. Because of this agency, which is circumscribed but not incapacitated by circumstance, *Woman on the Edge of Time* does not end in defeatism. Connie Ramos's powerlessness in contemporary life (female, ageing, poor, Chicana) is the product of a socially constructed and therefore not inevitable or natural marginality.

The vision of Mattapoisett society in which Connie simultaneously exists (in parallel space) as an incisive informant and enquirer, demands a reconsideration of the reader's initial judgement of her as a mentally unstable and potentially violent social outcast. Categories of gender, race, age, and class have withered away in Mattapoisett's social structure, and even the 'inherent inequality' of biological reproduction has been done away with since it was farmed out to machines (breeders) which manufacture human beings to order.[3] This means that with the shedding of oppressive socially constructed identities and roles, a new person can emerge who both is and is not Connie. Her Utopian double, Luciente, thus fulfils the role of mirror image (or ego-ideal), constructed as she is, in turn, by the ideal values and social relations of Mattapoisett. Inspired by her contact with Luciente's ideal society, Connie, the most marginal of marginal women, becomes the locus and finally the agent of political consciousness-raising and resistance. In this respect, *Woman on the Edge of Time* has much in common with Alice Walker's work and with Maya Angelou's self-construction: all three writers portray the downtrodden woman as bearer of knowledge and agent of change.

The political agendas represented in Utopianism, in *Woman on the Edge of Time* and other feminist novels like Joanna Russ's *The Female Man*, should not, however, unproblematically be read as signs of the Women's Movement's strength in the public arena in the 1970s. They did not, as is sometimes too easily assumed, come out of a particularly optimistic moment in the history of American feminism.[4] Far from it: in a sense it is easier to argue that feminist realism, harsh though it often is, marked a stage in the Women's Movement when radical change seemed a real possibility, than that feminist fantasy (science fiction, Utopian writing and fantasy *tout court*) arose out of a mood of political confidence. Cora Kaplan argues this point in response to an essay by Francis Mulhern, who had claimed that contemporary writing such as *Woman on the Edge of Time* demonstrated a 'cultural dynamism' which could be seen as an object lesson for the Left in the project of constructing 'a socialist politics of culture'. Kaplan's response issued a note of warning both against such an unqualified and decontextualised celebration of American feminist fiction's significance in Britain, and against Mulhern's description of this significance as 'fundamentally the achievement of the women's movement' (Mulhern 1985: 24–6). She writes:

> these particular imaginings of new societies followed from a general weakening and dispersal of libertarian, black and feminist political movements in the late 1970s . . . The anti-realism of these texts . . . masks a shared despair about and disillusionment with the possibilities of political change as a product of mass social and political movements, even as they articulate an inventive optimism about the possibilities of a revolutionized future. They reflect the difficulty of imagining collective struggle in the face of the massive hegemony of the Right in America, as well as the continued need for and capacity to think creatively and practically about the nature of transformed societies.
>
> (Kaplan 1985: 26)

For Kaplan then, feminist flights of fantasy are of an ambivalent nature: both necessary and inspired in the realm of feminist cultural practice, but at the same time a manifestation of the paucity of political options in the United States of the late 1970s. I think, following on from Kaplan, that in 1980s fiction the problem of writing in an environment increasingly hostile to feminism comes to the fore in realist as well as fantasy modes of writing, and that the central question for feminist critics in reading 1980s women's fiction is precisely the often masked influence of 'the massive hegemony of the Right' that she mentions.

Reproductive politics, the family and the role of motherhood in women's lives are the main issues which that conglomerate of social and political interest groups (religious, economic, white supremacist, anti-communist, anti-feminist) known as the New Right placed at the heart of America's political agenda in the mid to late 1970s, thus filling the ideological vacuum left by the impact of the recession and the demise of liberalism and 1960s radicalism.[5] In feminist fiction, these issues are in themselves hardly new.

But in novels such as Marge Piercy's *Braided Lives*, *The Handmaid's Tale* by Margaret Atwood and Sue Miller's *The Good Mother* – imaginative engagements with a changed social and political environment – treatment of these issues takes on a new political hue which reflects and problematises the increasingly contradictory meanings of feminism itself.

In the early 1970s it was still assumed to be self-evident what was good for women (reproductive rights, equal pay, child care provision, self-determination), but by the onset of the Reagan era in 1980 such a consensus no longer existed. With the demise of an identifiable, autonomous Women's Movement and with the rise of a counter-movement of religious and pro-family groups in which women (like Phyllis Schlafly, Anita Bryant and assorted preachers' wives) were prominent, the question of what it meant to be working in women's interest no longer elicited clear answers. Pro-natalist and anti-divorce, right wing anti-feminists insisted on women's 'right' to full-time mothering and first claim on the breadwinner's wage packet. Getting and keeping the man, demanding that he fund the family for a lifetime, in exchange for the delights and soothing powers of traditional femininity, was what the New Right meant by protecting women's interests: patriarchal relations as a protection racket. How could this be? And so soon, as Barbara Haber said?

The New Right was not a counter-hegemonic social movement in the way that Civil Rights, the New Left, or Women's Liberation were. As Sidney Blumenthal describes its formation in his book, *The Rise of the Counter-Establishment*, the New Right was never a coherent political force but arose out of an (un)holy alliance between neo-conservative ideology, monetarist economics, religious fundamentalism and anti-federal regional interests. As such, it constituted itself as a counter-establishment which sought to displace the liberal consensus of the Kennedy, Johnson and Carter administrations. After the *échec* of the Vietnam War and in the midst of an economic recession, the time seemed ripe for an ideological offensive against everything the 1960s had stood for, and neo-conservatives where ready and waiting to seize it.[6] Through its use of electronic media and its exploitation of national networks espousing conservative values (such as Fundamentalist churches and white supremacist clubs) the New Right mounted an extremely effective assault on public opinion, in an appeal to common sense, traditional American values, and people's fear of lawlessness.[7]

Several dramatic reversals of good-for-women legislation marked this ideological change of heart concerning the position of women in American society. The Equal Rights Amendment (ERA), which during the early 1970s had seemed an eminently sensible political goal attracting widespread mainstream support, became a target for the Right as soon as the process of ratification by individual states was set in train. As a result of intensive New Right campaigning, the ERA was defeated in 1982. On the crest of the same wave of anti-feminist backlash the Supreme Court's 1973 *Roe* vs. *Wade* decision which had made abortion legal under certain conditions, was partially revoked in 1977 by the Hyde Amendment and again in 1980 in *Harris* vs. *McRae* through cuts in public funding for abortions and reproductive services.[8] Since the mid-1970s abortion has been *the* most important single issue around which feminist and anti-feminist positions have been defined.

For feminists, free abortion on demand was and is first and foremost a political matter, part of a much larger agenda for change in social and economic relations, but the Right's discourse on abortion was religious and moral. This redefinition of abortion as a moral issue requiring state intervention to safeguard the inviolability of human life, was at the forefront of debate and Republican electoral campaigning for over a decade, and forced feminists into a defensive position. But the Right not only tried to have existing legislation revoked; it also launched offensives of its own. The family, as Betty Friedan put it, became America's new new frontier (Friedan 1982: 89). Paul Laxalt's Family Protection Act for example was designed to reinstate the family as the cornerstone of American society, not by creating support systems such as welfare provisions and tax reform, but rather by further privatising the family by way of welfare cuts. Laxalt's bill included a host of measures to cut public spending, such as withdrawal of funding for school bussing programmes to facilitate racial integration, thus revealing the underlying racist agenda of the New Right as well as its anti-feminist slant. Although the Family Protection Act did not make it into law in the end, it continued to exert ideological pressure on social policy programmes until well into the 1980s.[9]

These examples – abortion legislation, ERA and the various proposals to protect the American family from aberrant women – are only the most public manifestations of the rightward shift in American politics. At least as insidious, if not more so, has been the Right's success in capturing what used to be the middle ground of opinion on social policy. If not a liberal consensus, then at least a groundswell of popular opinion on the desirability of equal rights for women in the 1970s was forced into retreat by the combined appeal of conservative sobriety ('fiscal responsibility', e.g. cuts in public spending) and religious fervour. The middle ground shifted however not only because of expected material benefits (tax cuts) or electoral payoffs, but also because the popular imagination proved highly receptive to a spectre of anarchy, civil unrest and a general breakdown of law and (moral as well as civil) order conjured up by various powerful conservative lobbies and religious groups. Urban unrest, the rise in crime, drug abuse and – later – AIDS were all blamed on the climate of moral degeneracy that 1960s social movements had supposedly created and which liberalism had condoned. Feminism and Black nationalism were singled out for demonisation and held responsible for the collapse of the (white, middle class) nuclear family

169

and, by extension, of all that American society held sacred and dear. On the tidal wave of the Right's exploitation and redefinition of images of the 1960s, liberalism was swept aside. 'Liberal' – let alone 'radical' – became a term of abuse.[10] The Right's discourse then focused on selective memory-making, in which the 1960s, as in the early days of Richard Nixon's presidency, came to stand for sexual permissiveness, drugs, anarchy and general moral lassitude. The débâcle of Vietnam was quickly repressed, except when it suited the Right to draw attention to the plight of the veterans, and to resuscitate the memory of demonstrating hippies who had treacherously refused to treat their fellow Americans to a heroes' welcome upon their return.

Of course, the New Right's ideological offensive consisted in large part in an appropriation of precisely the liberal rhetoric of rights that the new self-styled Moral Majority said should be replaced by duties. In the case of abortion, the rights of the foetus now came to override those of women to bodily self-determination. This exploitation of liberal discourse may explain to some extent the Right's popular success in changing the terms of political debate and keeping them in place, even after its initial legislative successes failed to materialise in a full-scale Republican commitment to a pro-life and pro-family policy programme under Reagan.

For those with a longer than short-term memory, the New Right's obsession with the preservation of life had always seemed rather cynical in the context of its hawkish Vietnam past, and it appeared downright hypocritical when viewed against the backdrop of women's generally worsening economic situation. Welfare cuts, cancellation of affirmative action programmes, and a rising divorce rate all accelerated what came to be known as the feminisation of poverty, which – as usual – hit single mothers, working class women and women from racial and ethnic minorities the hardest. The Right's pro-life and pro-family stance must therefore, as numerous feminist theorists have pointed out, be seen as a symbolic one: it played on fear and on nostalgia for a mythical, more secure and stable pre-1960s normality.[11]

Deirdre English aptly remarks that anti-abortion campaigning for a Human Life Amendment was 'the only issue in which the New Right can claim the cloak of altruism. It sanctifies a movement which is in every other way *anti*-alternative, *anti*minority, *anti*poor, *anti*woman, *anti*gay – and yet calls itself "prolife"' (English 1981: 18).

Contestation of the terrain of post-war history, however, is at least as real as it is also symbolic. The editors of *Social Text* make this clear in their introduction to *The 60s without Apology*, a collection of articles put together precisely to reappropriate the recent-but-distanced radical past and to interrogate popular and personal memory of the period. 'Trashing the 1960s', they write,

has become a strategic feature of the current struggle for hegemony
. . . But visions of history play an enormous – if incalculable – role in
people's political practice in the present: and this all the more when
the interpretation in question is a matter, not of 'attitudes' towards a
bygone age like the era of the Wobblies or the American Revolution,
but rather of people's immediate past. What you finally decide to
think the 60s was is one of the forms in which you affirm or repudiate
a whole part of your own life.

(Sayres et al. 1985: 8)

For the novels I want to discuss here, this latter remark concerning a
refashioning of memory of a part of your own life is particularly relevant,
since this applies to writers and (at least part of) their readership both. Nor
is the rewriting of history, the construction of the times of change in
American women's lives, limited to the legacy and memory of the 1960s.

In *Braided Lives* Marge Piercy sets up a 1950s–1980s dialogue in which the
memory of the era of illegal abortion and political invisibility of women's
issues (including that of women's writing) comes back to haunt contemporary existence as a nightmare vision of history repeating itself, but this
vision is resisted and refused. Atwood's *The Handmaid's Tale* devises a
regressive, nightmare scenario for the future in which almost all the
achievements of (liberal) feminism have been erased. In Atwood's dystopia,
religious fundamentalism dominates the ideological battleground of family
and reproduction and defines the laws of the State. But feminism, and
particularly radical feminism, seems to bear the burden of (unwitting)
collusion in causing this state of patriarchal affairs; the spectre of 1980s pro-
censorship feminists throwing pornographic magazines on the bonfire of
righteous moral indignation haunts the pages of *The Handmaid's Tale*. Sue
Miller's *The Good Mother* presents by extension – and without the distancing
safety net of dystopian fantasy – sexual permissiveness itself as a cause of
malaise in women's personal lives. But where Piercy's protagonist is propelled into action to better women's lot, whilst Atwood's handmaid at least
retains a memory of freedom as well as a nominal faith in the Resistance,
Sue Miller's good mother is completely caught in the terms of the law and
in those of a new, old-style literary and political realism of common sense
and resignation to the way of the world. In Miller's text all sense of Utopian
vision and radical possibility is lost, and a conservative construction of reality
in which law, family and nostalgia are paramount is seen to define and
utterly circumscribe the options for women in the 1980s. For Miller, the
1960s represent an aberration, an era of false hopes and mistaken dreams
which got a whole generation of women into trouble once they woke up to
the 'real world' of post-Left, post-counter-culture, post-feminist America.

As Roger Bromley has argued in his study of Thatcherite popular fictions about the inter-war period, any revisiting of the past in fictional texts is a construction of that past, a process of *Making Memories*, of reification.[12] In Bromley's analysis, as in mine, the making of memories in imaginative writing is a struggle over political consciousness. To render powerless both the positive force of imagination and that of a remembered lived past in which the social climate was more conducive to radical change – this is the subject and the formal project of backlash fictions.

Bromley writes:

> One important strategy that has been used to maintain power at a symbolic level is to 'colonise' people's memory of the past, to obliterate dreams and ambitions that might come from a time when a person could control their own destiny.
>
> (Bromley 1986: 331)

In the fictional debate between feminists and conservatives a battle of the decades takes place, in which images of the 1950s, 1960s, 1970s and 1980s are manipulated to signify a disillusionment with the present which is either constructed as partly the outcome of radical history (Atwood, Miller) or, alternatively, as the product of much more complex and contradictory economic and social forces – 'the massive hegemony of the Right' among them (Piercy). Ultimately, it is this difference in understanding of how we came to be where we are that defines the political – and the literary – tenets of these novels.

'A LONG VIEW BACK': MARGE PIERCY'S *BRAIDED LIVES*

Deirdre English argued in 1981 that the abortion victory of the *Roe* vs. *Wade* Supreme Court decision was in some ways a premature one for the American Women's Movement:

> Despite the best efforts of feminists and others in the late 60s, there had not been enough discussion, enough public awareness and debate, about something which really is part of a revolutionary change. There was a simple, sad, human consequence of this lack of public discussion: the painful stories of many of the women who had been denied safe and legal abortions remained untold.
>
> (English 1981: 31)

The publication of Marge Piercy's seventh novel, *Braided Lives*, in 1982 can be seen as a belated attempt to contribute to the abortion discussion from the inside, that is, with an historical awareness of what it was like before abortion was legalised. A first person realist narrative with reproductive self-determination as its main theme, *Braided Lives* came out of the same sense of political urgency to defend feminist gains in the face of the Right's anti-abortion campaign that generated English's article. But the fact that Piercy in this novel employed the (pseudo-)autobiographical voice is all the more interesting in the light of English's regret that experiential narratives were not told at the time of the Supreme Court's ruling in 1973. For in using the first person voice, Piercy in effect returns to the first wave of self-identified feminist fiction, thereby reproducing in her mode of representation the historical moment of early 1970s Women's Liberation.

Braided Lives combines the centrality of reproductive politics with that of writing itself. Jill Stuart, the novel's main character, who at the age of forty-two decides to reconstruct the story of her life, is a feminist, ex-political activist and poet. Her story is told retrospectively in a linear way, but interspersed, like Vida's, with italicised passages set in the present which comment on and interrogate the story of the past. In this way, the monologism of autobiography is broken up into a dialogue which compares and contrasts Jill's 1950s and 1980s personae.

Jill, the narrator, signals early on in an apologia reminiscent of 1930s fictionalised autobiography, that her project is not motivated by narcissism:

> Too much self-regard has never struck me as dignified: trying to twist over my shoulder to see my own behind. And it is not a mirror I want but a long view back . . . [to] those few years when I became the woman I have somehow in all weathers and all colors of luck remained. I want to visit that burned-over district where I learned to love – in friendship and in passion – and to work.
>
> (Piercy 1982a: 8)

That 'burned-over district' is the 1950s and 1960s, and for 'love' and 'work' we read (bi)sexual pleasure and intimacy, and poetry. The braided lives of the title refer to the friendship between Jill Stuart and her cousin Donna, as well as to Jill's relationships with other veterans of the 1950s and 1960s. But first and foremost the braided lives are a metaphor for the intertwining of personal and political life: sexual politics, cultural politics, bonds between people who have been through the wars together. The polemical under-pinnings of *Braided Lives*'s argument with the New Right become explicit at times, as when in Jill's present 1960s forms of protest have to be revived for another march on Washington in defence of abortion rights. Jill reports an emergency phone call from a woman friend:

> 'Kiddie, it's time to go to Washington again. Faster than inflation we got to move. Those bastards are planning to kill us.' She read me the text of a proposed constitutional amendment to outlaw abortion and then the draft of an ad to be run in protest.
>
> (Piercy 1982a: 262)

Clearly a reference to the New Right's Human Life Amendment, this passage at the same time comments on *Braided Lives* as a political novel, a symbolic march on the powers that be to demonstrate that even what have hitherto seemed to be feminism's firmest gains still have to be argued and fought for, and must not be taken for granted. Histories have to be told and retold, for those who did and those who did not live through them. In that sense, *Braided Lives* is a history lesson, which writes the origins of Women's Liberation into a 1950s climate of anti-communism, repressive sexual mores and the claustrophobia of growing up in a nuclear family – the very 'stability', in other words, that New Right advocates harked back to with nostalgia. In line with this polemic that other mainstay of New Right rhetoric, absolute moral values, is consistently refused and recontextualised in Piercy's novel. Jill's mother's possessive attitude towards her daughter is, we are to understand, a by-product of 1950s domesticity which ties women to their children and imbues them with narrowly determined moral values. The daughter by contrast, who escapes from rigid gender roles through her entry into higher education, learns to live by the demands of the concrete situation or praxis, and to 'find a morality that works for us' (Piercy 1982a: 47).[13]

In *Braided Lives* the fear that 1980s America will be like that of the 1950s haunts the dialogue that Jill conducts between her past and her present. The college boyfriend responsible for Jill's unwanted pregnancy, for example, opposes abortion *not* because it is expensive, illegal and dangerous, but because he sees it as murder. This (no doubt deliberate) anachronism inserts a 1980s discourse of the right to life into a 1950s setting, thus stressing the parallels between these periods. Similarly, the critical standards by which Jill's poetry is judged at college by her teachers and her (male) peers, seem to be the same ones which inform hostile reviews of the forty-two-year-old poet's work. In the 1950s, Jill knows that she is 'not writing the way you are supposed to'; her poems are judged to be formless and too personal; in short, 'not art' (Piercy 1982a: 57, 75, 128).

In the present, such judgements are echoed in a Maileresque review:

> 'Miss Stuart's seventh volume of poetry is crammed with reductionist simplistic snippets of women's lib cant . . . Individual poems stress only the woman's role and anguish, instead of taking a balanced view . . . In art there can be no special pleading for women. Her poetry is uterine and devoid of thrust. Her volume is wet, menstruates and carries a purse in which it can't find anything.'
>
> (Piercy 1982a: 404)[14]

Sexual/textual politics are here writ large in a pastiche of mainstream criticism's treatment of feminist writing, but I think there is more to it than just that. In *Braided Lives* Piercy maintains a dual focus on female sexuality and women's writing, in which the key term is control of reproduction. In the closing section of the novel, which is set in the early 1980s, the narrator explains how women organised a clandestine network (shades of *Vida*) to obtain illegal but safe abortions, and how this network was 'retired' when abortion was legalised. Jill Stuart then asks herself: 'For how long?', and this question obviously concerns the future of a woman's right to reproductive self-determination. But the story of the present then continues with a similar question concerning the future of writing:

> I was writing poems then that everyone ignored. Now I write poems enough people read for them to survive. It feels fragile. The poems have to get printed for people to find them and like them. They have to get distributed. Writing is only the precondition of the life of the poem, but writing is the only part I control.
>
> (Piercy 1982a: 443)

Reproduction, whether biological or mechanical, thus becomes the metaphor which holds both thematic strands together. Just as pregnancy inscribes itself on to the woman's body, so also is writing conceived of as a process of giving life. But the issue is control of either process: forced pregnancy is death, and writing which is not reproduced does not reach its readers, and remains a dead letter. In this logic, writing is like sex: a precondition of life, necessary but not sufficient – social conditions, not the act of writing or fucking itself, determine the viability of a poem, or of a human being.

Braided Lives lends itself, like *The Women's Room* to a reading which sees in Jill's story the autobiography of a movement, a *Bildungsroman* charting the formation of the feminist as new political subject. Despite its privileging of single-issue, radical feminist concerns in the focus on reproduction, at a deeper level Piercy investigates in *Braided Lives* the contradictory and unstable nature of social change and the conditions which make it possible. The fear that the Women's Movement's gains can be undone by political counter-currents necessitates a re-examination of the social determinants of individual subjectivity. This fear is reiterated by Piercy in an autobiographical essay, 'Through the Cracks: Growing Up in the Fifties', where she writes:

> The fifties, I cannot sentimentalize them. I hardly survived them. The idea that they might come back in some form appears ahistorical to me but terrifying, like seeing a parade bearing my own coffin down the street. They were a mutilating time to grow up female.
>
> (Piercy 1974b: 126)

This essay, which provides a running commentary on *Braided Lives*, systematically critiques the New Right's nostalgia for the 1950s, and deconstructs the images of stability and normality upon which Right wing discourse relies. This goes for politics as much as it does for literature: 'Just as there was no community to mediate for me between individual and mass, there was nobody to write for', and

To live in the fifties and think that the way this society distributes
power, money, resources, prestige and dirty work was wrong was to
stand up in a stadium during a football game and attempt to read
aloud a poem.

(Piercy 1974b: 119–20, 128)

To read *Braided Lives* through the cracks of fictional and 'real' autobiographical discourses, is to realise that Piercy's 1950s/1980s dialectic yet
again gives voice to that well-known Marxist adage about understanding
history in order not to repeat it.

'CONTEXT IS ALL': MARGARET ATWOOD'S *THE HANDMAID'S TALE*

'I wait. I compose myself. My self is a thing I must now compose, as one
composes a speech. What I must present is a made thing, not something
born' (Atwood 1985: 76). 'A woman is not born, but made', Simone de
Beauvoir wrote in *The Second Sex*, and Atwood's citation of this central
feminist principle here unmistakably signals the theory-informed status of
The Handmaid's Tale as a reflection on, and critique of, Second Wave
feminism.[15]

As Anne Cranny Francis observes, 'the political sophistication of both the
Women's Movement and feminist literary theory' has increased 'the political
and textual awareness of the writer'; in *The Handmaid's Tale* we have a prime
example of a fictional text which has absorbed many of the insights of
poststructuralist feminist theory (Francis 1990: 142). This is already evident
in the very structure of the novel, in which a first person dystopian narrative
is framed by the academic discourse of that narrative's possible interpretations (in the appended 'Historical Notes'). The narrator's statement
about composition furthermore bears strong Lacanian/Kristevan connotations ('subjectivity can only be constituted in language'), whilst the
radical incoherence of the narrator's first person discourse thematises a
fragmented subjectivity caught in the terms of a patriarchal symbolic order.
Contrary to appearances however, and despite these virtues of sophistication, *The Handmaid's Tale* is not a feminist text in the political, counter-
hegemonic sense which I have outlined so far. Where Cranny Francis
describes it as 'a subversive intervention in the patriarchal discourse which
characterizes contemporary gender ideology' I would suggest, rather, that
Atwood's political critique is misdirected and that the seriousness of that
misdirection overrides whatever 'subversive intervention' is made at the
level of patriarchal language (Francis 1990: 142). The novel's self-reflexive
mode of representation not only incapacitates a projection of female
agency, but it also conforms precisely to the self-conscious metafictional
tendencies of 'the dominant' which previous feminist fictions had sought to

critique. In this sense, and in its dystopian anti-realism, *The Handmaid's Tale* represents a dramatic break with Utopian/realist feminist fiction as an oppositional cultural practice.

That a dystopian novel which clearly sets out to expose the oppressive effects of a patriarchal society on women's lives and sense of self, is nevertheless complicit with some of those values, is by no means obvious. Atwood is widely regarded as a feminist writer, and *The Handmaid's Tale* has probably done more to enhance that reputation than any of her other novels before or since. Yet I think that the misogyny which Gayle Greene finds so disturbing in *Cat's Eye* is already prefigured in *The Handmaid's Tale* as an hostility to feminism.[16] I also believe that, reading backwards through Atwood's work, political confusion reigns in all of her novels, a confusion which is masked by an exquisite literary style and by Atwood's obvious interest in women's problems such as body image, sexuality, violence and victimisation, as well as women's genres such as the romance, the gothic and – here – autobiography. Greene writes about *Cat's Eye* in *Changing the Story*: 'it flirts with a feminist analysis, suggests it as a possibility, but then withdraws it, as though refusing so generalized an interpretation of events which Atwood implies are personal and idiosyncratic' (Greene 1991: 212).

In *The Handmaid's Tale* events are not personal and idiosyncratic, but at a collective level I think that Atwood here, also, flirts with a feminist analysis without really providing one. It seems that the overt critique of the American (Christian fundamentalist) New Right in Atwood's dystopian construction of Gilead, and the novel's focus on that mainstay of feminist fiction, reproductive politics, have blinded feminist critics to the more reactionary aspects of this text which reside at a deeper level of cultural meaning than that of dystopian representation in itself. These aspects are the novel's treatment of feminism, its argument concerning the politics of reproduction, and finally its usurpation of African-American literary motifs for the writing of white femininity. All three – feminism, reproduction, African-American culture – are live issues in American cultural debate of the 1980s and 1990s, and my reading takes off from the rightward shifts of these debates, into which *The Handmaid's Tale* was received. This is a cultural context in which feminism is under attack, women's reproductive rights are being eroded, and moral panics are being induced by the New Right around the decline in the (white, middle class) birth rate, divorce, and race relations. It is, in other words, a context in which a conservative 'dominant', having reconstructed itself as the victim of such terror-tactics as affirmative action and political correctness, seeks reinstatement as the norm, as the silent, Moral Majority of 'most ordinary people' – and *The Handmaid's Tale* plays right into its hands.

The handmaid's tale, as told by herself, is the story of a nameless American woman of about thirty, a mother and wife, who at the beginning of the

177

narrative finds herself radically displaced into a post-revolutionary society. Here she emerges as Offred, handmaiden (surrogate-mother-designate) to the household of a high official (Fred) in the state of Gilead, which is ruled on Biblical, Christian fundamentalist principles. Her daughter and husband have disappeared, and she herself has been subjected to brainwashing which has affected her memory and sense of identity. In Gilead, women of childbearing age are used purely for reproductive purposes; Offred thus becomes reified as a 'womb on legs', her sole purpose in life is to bear children for her proprietor, the Commander. To counter this reification she tells her story, which ends inconclusively in either an escape from Gilead to we know not where, or in execution at the hands of the secret service.

Offred's fate remains unclear in the Historical Notes appended to the autobiographical narrative, which discuss the story's authenticity, its intended audience and its historical dating. These Notes present a pastiche on the discourse of literary criticism, a pastiche which is radically at odds with the ostensibly serious tones of the handmaid's tale. The novel as a whole then is radically split between its dystopian and its parodic parts, and this presents problems for a political reading: if Offred's telling of her story is her only act of resistance, showing that women's discursive agency is still possible even under conditions of extreme duress, the Historical Notes then trivialise and diminish the political status of that act. The handmaid is thus not just reified in Gilead as a human incubator, but in the Notes she is further reduced to a thing, a speech, a set of tapes transcribed and submitted to the scrutiny of academic scholarship. The familiar trope of the writing woman as protagonist in feminist fiction is here literalised into woman-as-text, and all empirical evidence of her existence is erased except for the record she has left behind. But this record cannot be deciphered with any certainty: 'As all historians know, the past is a great darkness, and filled with echoes. Voices may reach us from it, but what they say to us is imbued with the obscurity of the matrix out of which they come' (Atwood 1985: 324).

The Handmaid's Tale is an extremely slippery text, and all this can still be read as a critique of objectification of women, rather than as complicity with it, but only up to a point. The academic discourse in the Notes mimics the language and style of an old boys' literary criticism, but one in which women professors with Native-American-sounding names enthusiastically participate. It is this phenomenon that suggests not just erasure of feminist gains in the academic world of criticism, but feminist critics' collusion in intellectual power games which silence Offred's voice all over again: nothing *really* changes. Read as a more general comment on the chances of survival for women's writing and the nature of feminist criticism, this is a truly dystopian reflection on the state of feminist cultural affairs.[17]

Offred's story of self, composed in a world with few mirrors, her field of vision restricted by a nun-like headdress, is radically incoherent. From a multiplicity of fragmented and contradictory images, memories and ideologies her story is pieced together in scraps – *The Handmaid's Tale* is yet another patchwork text to be stitched up by the reader. Offred composes herself in part out of the Biblical language of Gileadian ideology, which she has internalised as a result of brainwashing. In part she also draws on the memory of her previous life as an alternative normality in which a measure of self-determination was still possible. Contact with a friend from pre-Gileadian days, Moira, who has held on to her feminist outlook on the world, to some extent counters the effect of brainwashing and enables Offred on occasion to see through scriptural/political propaganda.[18] Yet Moira's credibility as a critic of Gilead is severely restricted; from Offred's present perspective, the old feminist desire for sisterhood and women's community has backfired badly, for the sex-segregated society of Gilead may be ruled by men but it is policed by women – thus making a mockery of such dreams of female solidarity. Memories of Offred's mother are similarly tainted by the (unwitting) mistakes of feminism. As a former activist who took part in campaigns for reproductive control and Take Back the Night Marches, Offred's mother is regarded in Gilead as an Unwoman and forcibly exiled to the colonies. In Gileadian thinking, and as a mode of self-justification of its oppressive regime, the mother is seen as part of a movement which left 'nothing for men to work for, nothing to fight for', and because this loss of male agency was a causal factor in the fundamentalist counter-coup, Moira and Offred's mother are both punished in Gilead but they are also, within the logic of this narrative, in fact implicated in Offred's present predicament (Atwood 1985: 221). 'Mother, I think. Wherever you may be. Can you hear me? You wanted a women's culture. Well, now there is one. It isn't what you meant, but it exists. Be thankful for small mercies' (Atwood 1985: 137).

The Handmaid's Tale heralds the return of the 'normal', that is: apolitical, heterosexual, white, middle class female protagonist. Feminists like Moira and Offred's mother (who is throughout portrayed as a bad mother) are shown retrospectively as irresponsible in their desire for female autonomy and lesbian existence; this construction not only leaves the narrator's heterosexism intact but legitimises it. Though Moira is an Amazon heroine of sorts who is prepared to defy the matriarchal (the Aunts) and the patriarchal order of Gilead, her resistance proves self-destructive. And when Offred's mother tells her daughter, in pre-Gileadian days, 'You're just a backlash. Flash in the pan. History will absolve me', we are aware of the bitter irony of such misplaced confidence in a feminist future (Atwood 1985: 131). Offred's existence in Gilead confirms her in a status of innocent victim, and constructs the feminists as extremists who – quite simply – got it wrong. Since there is no alternative voice in the novel to contest this version of how the fundamentalist revolution came about, Atwood's novel is open to the charge of blaming feminism for provoking the backlash of the New Right whose values it at the same time is trying to critique. It is this ambiguity of vision and confusion of political analysis, reiterated throughout the text in its use of irony, which makes *The Handmaid's Tale* such an unpindownable text. If Offred's confused consciousness reflects that of the state of feminism in the 1980s, pulled hither and thither between contradictory claims of who really has women's interests at heart, then Atwood's text provides no clarity but merely confuses the issues further.

As a woman lacking agency and a coherent understanding of history, Offred, like Celie in *The Color Purple*, can do nothing but issue a cry for help into the dark, hoping against hope that it will be heard. Since she cannot act, she can only recompose herself in words, for in a world where the Bible is the only book, where shops no longer have names (only signs), where one's own name is that of property (not a person), and where women's magazines and games of Scrabble come to function as a form of pornography, language stands out as the one thing which promises escape: language becomes the sign of the subversive. This does not mean that language is in any way reliable in 'fixing' the meanings of reality, however. In a passage which evokes (and contests?) Sylvia Plath's poem 'Tulips', the narrator muses on the blurring of distinctions between things through the vagaries of metaphor:

> I look at the one red smile. The red of the smile is the same as the red of the tulips in Serena Joy's garden, towards the base of the flowers where they are beginning to heal. The red is the same but there is no connection. The tulips are not tulips of blood, the red smiles are not flowers, neither thing makes a comment on the other . . . Each thing is valid and really there. It is through such a field of valid objects that I must pick my way, every day and in every way. I put a lot of effort into making such distinctions. I need to make them. I need to be very clear, in my own mind.
>
> (Atwood 1985: 43)[19]

What Offred is looking for is an atomised language, a language which names her valid objects uniquely and unmistakably – denotation without connotation. But this search for perfect correspondence risks losing the world of objects altogether, as the illicit games of Scrabble demonstrate. Words now become objects on the board, meaningless in themselves precisely, meaningful only because they are part of forbidden play: context is all, indeed (Atwood 1985: 154).

Unstable language, fragmented subjectivity, words which mean something only in relation to other words and not in themselves – these are staple themes of contemporary feminist theory. In classic Lacanian/Kristevan fashion, the symbolic order in *The Handmaid's Tale* belongs to the law of the

Father. It is clear who owns the language: men, and who makes a futile attempt to read through the cracks, to 'make distinctions' in order to establish what is what: women. This is not a search for a woman's language, nor a desire to establish a feminist discourse, nor even a desire for communication – far from it: this is a matter of 'being very clear in my own mind' about a field of nameable 'valid objects' without connections, the only stable points in a world otherwise made up of sliding signifiers.[20] As Offred observes, words are precious: 'He [the Commander] has something we don't have, he has the word. How we squandered it, once' (Atwood 1985: 99).

This idea of words as authority or power, 'squandered' in pre-Gileadian days by women, ties in directly with that other squandered resource women once had and now lack: fertility. As in Piercy's *Braided Lives*, the theme of reproductive self-determination and women's writing are thus bound up together, but in very different ways. In the terms of Atwood's dystopia, the hegemony of religious fundamentalism in Gilead was not just enabled by the increasing obsolescence of men because of feminism, but it was also forced by a crisis in human fertility as a result of environmental pollution and women's use of oral contraceptives. In this fundamentalist revolution, it is the means of human reproduction, rather than production, which have been seized to establish a new social order. Yet if Ann Cranny Francis is right in stating that dystopias are not representations of an alternative future, but rather of the present 'stripped of its ideological rationalizations', then Atwood's view of the present state of American (/Canadian) society is a peculiar one indeed (Francis 1990: 141). Far more disturbing than the actual dystopian representation of the handmaid's plight is its underlying assumption of a crisis in human reproduction, which in Atwood's stripped present provides the rationale for Gilead's existence. Coral Ann Howells rightly, but uncritically, points out that *The Handmaid's Tale* is organised around the hypothetical question of what would happen 'if the race were under threat of extinction' (Howells 1987: 65). But 'race' is the operative word here; which race is hypothetically under threat of extinction? Such hypotheses, even in fiction, are never innocent ones, because they arise from particular contemporary concerns. In order for feminist dystopia to function as political critique that concern must be a legitimate one, and here it is not. For whilst it is true that the theme of infertility links in, as Howells also observes, with real fears about a falling birth rate, about AIDS, and about environmental pollution, we have to be very clear, in our own minds, *whose* anxieties these are, and what political purpose is served by pandering to such fears – as I believe *The Handmaid's Tale* does. The idea that the survival of the race (which is, of course, shorthand for the white race) is in jeopardy, is not – to put it mildly – a pressing problem for the Left, nor for feminism, nor for America's non-white population. It is the fear of the white supremacist, anti-feminist New Right.[21]

To be absolutely clear: my objections to Atwood's novel do not stem from the racist and anti-feminist construction of Gilead in itself; after all, this is dystopia and this is part of its critique of the New Right. They arise, rather, from the fact that the dystopia as a didactic form, as a political warning, is premised upon a problem which is only acute in the eyes of a white, conservative and traditionalist middle class worried about its own survival in the face of massive social, racial and ethnic rifts in American society.

Such political misdirectedness, or disingenuousness, is exacerbated by *The Handmaid's Tale*'s literary appropriation of the African-American slave narrative, which is only obliquely and parodically acknowledged in the text and which none of Atwood's admiring feminist critics has noted.[22] The novel's racist assumptions about a contemporary crisis in fertility are thus reproduced in its formal strategy which borrows the generic features of the nineteenth-century slave narrative, but suppresses its African-American origins. *The Handmaid's Tale* once again prioritises gender over racial oppression in its displacement of the political discourse of African-American emancipation on to that of white women's resistance to patri-archy: 'Woman is the nigger of the world', as John Lennon so offensively put it. This appropriation includes the parodic discussion of problems of authentication and audience in the Historical Notes, as well as the trope of oral storytelling and motifs such as the underground railroad (the under-ground 'Femaleroad'), the fugitive trail to Canada, lynching as a public spectacle and the practice of naming people after their owners (Of Fred).[23] We might, to be fair, read Atwood's use of the flight-to-Canada trope as a gloss on her own status as a Canadian writer, and interpret the failure of this flight as a hidden comment on the Americanisation of Canada: there is no 'Canada' any more to escape to. But this still does not resolve the problem of the wholesale subordination of the African-American discourse of slavery to a truly postmodern fiction of speech without presence and history without meaning.

In her book on Canadian women's fiction, Coral Ann Howells praises Atwood's 'acute awareness of the multiple and often contradictory mean-ings' encoded in language and in existing literary forms, and she argues that polysemy in Atwood's work principally results from a reworking of popular genres. Howells and other feminist critics have also observed that Atwood writes and rewrites stories of the woman as victim; clearly, *The Handmaid's Tale* presents yet another such story of victimhood, once more constructs the white middle-class woman as *the* woman, and again creates 'multiple and contradictory meanings' through the use of a borrowed form (Howells 1987: 55, 69–70). Yet if the price for the very literary, highly stylised, and much praised polysemy in this text is the usurpation of African-American literary tradition and the demise of feminism as an imaginative space in which agency and social change for the better can be envisioned, then such riches of the sign is, perhaps, something feminist fiction as a political discourse cannot afford. In the context of the rise of the New Right, that context is, indeed, all.

NEW RULES, OLD GAMES: SUE MILLER'S *THE GOOD MOTHER*

Inscriptions of normality are often the hallmark of reaction. Atwood's narrator is a backlash phenomenon projected into the future as the norm, and Sue Miller trades on a similar notion of normality in her construction of Anna Dunlap, the good mother. The return of the middle-of-the-road protagonist (white, middle class, mother, and wife) in American women's fiction of the 1980s signals a return to an assumed pre-Women's Liberation normality, based on a common sense perception of what 'most' women 'really' want. Sue Miller's Anna is an ostensibly sensible and responsible, get-on-with-things woman, whose cautious attitude to the pitfalls of modern life verges on timidity. This veneer of responsibility hides a sense of helplessness; at heart she is less an autonomous woman than a good *girl* – a child who needs guidance and rules and a fixed morality to live by. Like the archetypal heroine of popular romance fiction, she feels guilty about what she wants, yet innocent and powerless when confronted with the devastating consequences.

Earlier feminist heroines sought liberation from the bonds of marriage and family, whilst keeping hold of emotional ties with friends, lovers and children. Sue Miller creates a protagonist who, conscious of the short-comings of her own marriage and of the authoritarian structure of her mother's family (which is ruled by a patriarch of a grandfather), yearns for the protection of the old-fashioned ways. As a role model of a strong and independently-minded woman of the 1980s the good mother signally fails; she describes herself as 'always only an accomplice in other people's daring schemes' and she confesses, significantly to a feminist friend, that she is 'just an old-fashioned girl, I guess' (Miller 1986: 88, 243).

As a post- or even an anti-feminist realist novel informed by the discourses of the New Right, *The Good Mother* is as yet in a class of its own, even if there are signs of a post-feminist shift in American white women's writing generally and in that of African-American women too.[24] Drawing on the issues of 1980s feminism – most particularly those of the crisis in personal life and the double burden, which have been articulated by feminist theorists in the US in response to the New Right backlash – Miller represents the 'new realism', both in the literary and in the political sense, of 1980s America.[25] This new realism is imbued with the moral and political clichés of 'tightening belts' (public spending cuts), 'return to family values' (pro-natalism and anti-divorce), and 'living with the consequences' (lack of reproductive control). Most of all, perhaps, it is saturated with a nostalgia for a more stable past in which the rules were clear and well-established, a world in which living by such rules meant security, safety and shelter.

The Good Mother starts with Anna Dunlap's divorce from her lawyer husband, which leaves her with the sole care of a young daughter, Molly. For a while the two live out a veritable idyll of mother/child bonding, albeit in a materially impoverished environment. About a third of the way through the novel, this blissful dyad is 'ripped apart' by Anna's affair with a young artist, Leo, whose bohemian lifestyle challenges the values of her bourgeois existence. An encounter between Molly and Leo is misconstrued by the ex-husband and leads to an allegation of child sexual abuse, which hands the rest of the narrative over to courtroom drama. The court case heralds the end of the affair and Anna's downfall as the self-styled good mother; she has to deliver her child into the hands of the upright and law-abiding Father.

The Good Mother plays out an old and established conflict in feminist thought between sexual pleasure and the duties of motherhood, and it does so in a classic middle class white setting. Cross-generational parallels between Anna and her aunt Babe, and contrasts between the family structure of the grandparents (extended), parents (nuclear) and of Anna herself (broken) enable Miller to range from the confusion of the 1980s to the stability of the 1950s and early 1960s, and back via feminism and 1960s permissive sexual mores. In this way, the novel highlights conflicts between old-fashioned familial values and new, more flexible and changeable social relations, with devastation as a result. Although *The Good Mother* can be read sympathetically as an exploration of crisis in family life, of the mechanisms of the feminisation of poverty and of the mother/child dyad, the novel is so clearly suffused with New Right rhetoric that I think a politically neutral reading along those lines would be seriously reductive. Undoubtedly *The Good Mother* is, like *The Handmaid's Tale*, well-crafted and powerfully (if not as subtly) written. Its power however does not derive from its ability to raise important questions but rather, again as in Atwood's novel, from its claustrophobic vision of female subjectivity determined by outside forces, a vision designed to induce fear. Neither Utopian nor dystopian, Miller's realism harks right back to the classic bourgeois novel in which a girl's fate is decided by transgression of or compliance with a social order which is fixed and unchangeable: marry, or die. It is the realism of 'the way of the world', in Franco Moretti's terms (Moretti 1987).

Three discursive strands characteristic of the New Right inform the version of this 'way of the world' plot in *The Good Mother.* Biblical language informs the representation of the grandparents' home as a 'pristine, Edenic' place; Anna feels herself to have 'fallen from grace' after her divorce, and an argument between Anna's father and her grandfather makes her feel resentful towards her mother: 'I wanted her to defend my father, *to cleave only unto him, forsaking all others,* as she and I both knew she should do' (Miller 1986: 41, 197, 45).[26]

Such Biblical phrases are used without irony to signify a moral order older and more stable than the upheaval of the present. This discourse of stability is further legitimised by the narrative development as a whole, in which transgression of the Law, whether real or imagined, is punished, regardless of whether this is the law of the lawyer father, of the patriarchal grandfather, or of the Biblical Father. Liberal values lose out against the pressures of the real world in which Daddy still rules and nothing has changed.

Conforming with the New Right's ideological offensive against the legacy of the 1960s, the second discursive strand which establishes *The Good Mother*'s credentials as a post-feminist text concerns its construction of the 1960s as an era of social and cultural anarchy (permissiveness, rock music, drugs, day care, abortion, narcissism), epitomising the danger of living by other rules than parental/patriarchal ones.[27] Feminism comes under attack, but as in *The Handmaid's Tale* the textual strategy of blaming feminism itself draws upon radical feminist themes. A major part of *The Good Mother*'s critique of feminism is that whilst feminism valorised women's self-determination, it denigrated motherhood and failed to provide viable alternatives to the nuclear family.[28] As Judith Stacey has argued in 'Are Feminists Afraid to Leave Home?', an essay which examines pro-family feminism, this line of thinking cannot just be dismissed as mere reaction or false consciousness on the part of right wing women, but is intimately bound up with stages in the life cycle of feminist women too:

> The pain and difficulties experienced by a generation of feminists who self-consciously attempted to construct alternatives to the family are a major social psychological source of the emergence of pro-family feminism, and one . . . that may fuel the pro-family retreat from sexual politics.
>
> (Stacey 1986: 231)

The Good Mother exemplifies this retreat, albeit not unambiguously. On the one hand the novel employs radical feminist ideas about masculinity, which signal the essential difference of men and link male power with violence; a recurring image is that of the man with the knife.[29] But in a reversal of earlier feminist treatments of the issue of reproductive control, pro-natalism is here writ large: Anna is 'forced' by her lover, not too subtly named 'Leo Cutter', to have an abortion against her will and moral principles. Furthermore, any alternative feminist analysis of the good mother's predicament is rendered dubious because (as in *The Handmaid's Tale*) the voice of feminism is represented by a rather wild and irresponsible friend, an academic, who herself has had three abortions and is doing research into the killing of female babies in India. The feminist is thus constructed in so many words as a hypocrite, driven by a morbid obsession with infanticide in the Third World whilst encouraging it in the First.

Biblical images, and the New Right's attack on feminism and 1960s libertarianism finally tie in with the third strand of right-wing discourse: duty, rules, and guilt. In *The Good Mother*, good American girls were brought up in the 1950s with strict moral codes, lived through the 1960s and 1970s when all the rules changed, only to wake up in the 1980s to discover that – in the real world – the old rules of the patriarchal game still apply. A scene at the very beginning of the novel illustrates this:

> Everyone in my world had been understanding about the divorce, sympathetic, politically correct. But [the notary public] was talking to me as my parents or grandparents might have, and I felt the rebellious, self-righteous fury that *an adolescent feels when she's caught in an act which she knows to be morally doubtful.* [my italics]
>
> (Miller 1986: 28)

Anna thus 'knows' that divorce is wrong, and the association of political correctness with adolescent fury is, of course, not accidental either, for this is the rhetoric employed by right wing critics of the 1960s (such as Bruno Bettelheim, who spoke of student protests as 'infantile temper tantrums'). Similarly, when the feminist friend questions Anna's passivity in the custody fight over Molly and suggests she could have fought her case on other terms than those set by the status quo, her response is that of a guilty person: '"I knew those were the terms ... the judge wouldn't have listened to a discussion on other terms"' (Miller 1986: 330–1).

And so the voice of 'realism' wins out; the guilty party on the stand is not men, not the oppressive institution of the nuclear family, not patriarchal values, not the criminal justice system itself but feminism and the counter-culture which validated, for a time, other terms, other concepts of morality and justice. Like Atwood's Offred, Anna Dunlap sees herself as a victim of progressive social change, caught unawares in the trap that history has set for women: the virgin mother/whore dichotomy is still in force.

A realism without frames, which represents the world as unchangeable, leaves no room for a feminist critique to contest these traditional definitions of gender. *The Good Mother* is a counter-text of a kind, but it is counter to feminism itself. It is less a novel of protest than of resignation, and it enacts Marge Piercy's nightmare of a return to pre-1960s patriarchal values so starkly portrayed in *The Handmaid's Tale* and so strenuously resisted in *Braided Lives*. Miller's novel brings feminist fiction full circle and returns it to its original point of departure in French's *The Women's Room*: in a hostile world where the man with the knife still makes the rules, good girls have no option but to go back to the future of the conformist 1950s: they stay at home, and mind the babies.

CONCLUSION
The future of feminist fiction, or, is there a feminist aesthetic?

Feminist endings are open endings, and this book therefore cannot end on the dystopian note of its final chapter. I have sketched a trajectory for feminist fiction, which moves from feminist realism as a critique of existing gender relations to fictions of subjectivity, which chart a real process of change in American women's lives over the past four decades. From there I have proceeded to discuss a Utopian realism envisioning a revolutionised feminist future and contrasted it with dystopian projections in women's writing, which are at the same time nostalgic for a pre-feminist past.

Any such historical narrative is also inevitably an account of what is left out, what refuses to be forced into the categories that feminist critics like me set up to capture cultural and political practices. Yet these practices are, of course, continually in flux, subject to change and revision. So, neat as the story of *Liberating Literature* is, it obscures the fact that the values and representational strategies of Women's Movement writing continue to flourish, especially in non-mainstream genres such as science fiction, fantasy, lesbian writing and crime fiction. The vitality of women's political writing as a counter-hegemonic practice is, furthermore, evident in the recent proliferation of African-American and ethnic literatures in the United States (Chicana, Mexican American, Native American, Chinese American), which continue to interrogate white feminism and the universalist assumptions of Anglo-American culture generally.[1]

Feminist fiction, like feminism itself, has diversified into a multiplicity of textual practices and political concerns to the point where, as a designation of an oppositional literary movement, it has probably outlived its usefulness. As a generic label, feminist fiction can conceal a multiplicity of sins, as I argued in the last chapter, or virtues, as I showed in the chapters preceding it. From a purely literary perspective (if there is such a thing), there is no reason to mourn the passing of an oppositional writing whose condition of possibility was that of an identifiable Women's Movement and a masculinist literary culture. For, even if we can mourn the passing of that *movement* as a political loss, its achievements in transforming the social

187

and cultural arena are a gain for life, a gain which is all too easily obscured by present perspectives of postmodern fragmentation or post-feminist disillusionment. In Audre Lorde's phrase, again: those words will be there.

It is because I believe that the significance of that gain has been underrated and understated in feminist criticism, and because I think that feminist fiction had a large part to play in feminism's success in redefining the sphere of cultural politics, that I undertook the work which is presented here. I was interested less in making new or different value judgements than in constructing an historical perspective on feminist fiction's project as a political literature. I wanted to look at what these texts were trying to do, how we can read them now in the fullness of time, and how they argue with mainstream literature as well as with each other over what true writing, real art, the right politics, a good woman might actually be. One conclusion that can be drawn from the arguments I have offered is that the appearance of post- or even anti-feminist writing in the 1980s must be taken as evidence – should we need it – that feminist fiction is not coterminous with gender-based cultural practices. A feminist aesthetic therefore cannot be formulated ahistorically, but must be seen as a dynamic *relation* between cultural practices and the shifting terrain of a feminist politics. Such a conclusion need not lead to a wholesale rejection of the idea that there might be such a thing as a feminist aesthetic, however. I think that Rita Felski's polemical title *Beyond Feminist Aesthetics*, for example, is premature because it makes no distinction between a female aesthetic, grounded in the idea that women's writing is different, and an oppositional aesthetic based on the politics of gender, race and class as articulated in the Women's Movement. For Felski, as for me, there is no necessary connection between gender and language, form, or genre, but that does not mean that feminists have not written in ways which are distinctive and which mark them off, at a particular time and in a particular cultural context, from women's writing in general. As I have shown in my comparisons between feminist, socialist and African-American counter-hegemonic literatures, that distinctiveness resides in an aesthetic which seeks to reconnect the realms of politics, art, history and everyday life. According to Christine Battersby, who in *Gender and Genius: Towards a Feminist Aesthetics* has explored the philosophical tradition which severed this connection in the work of Kant and the post-Kantians, it is the task of feminist critics today to begin to question assumptions, first articulated in (male) modernism, about the autonomy of art and its separateness from social struggles concerned with gender (and race, and class).[2] As will be evident, part of my task in this book has been to work, with Battersby and the feminist critics of modernism, towards the formulation of a feminist aesthetic which conceptualises cultural practice as social practice integral to, rather than autonomous from, social and historical relations. I have not been able to do much more here than suggest that such a feminist

188

aesthetic shares much common ground with the aesthetics of other non-dominant groups in the United States. As a large-scale theoretical argument therefore the feminist aesthetic, like most things in life, will have to wait for another book.

NOTES

Only short titles are given in the Notes that follow. For full references, please see Bibliography.

INTRODUCTION: AMERICAN WOMEN'S WRITING AND SOCIAL MOVEMENTS FROM THE 1930s TO THE 1980s

1 Virginia Woolf, 'Mr. Bennett and Mrs. Brown' (1924) rpt in Virginia Woolf (1992) *A Woman's Essays*: 69–87. It was in this essay that Woolf famously wrote 'in or about December 1910, human character changed', thus definitively taking leave of nineteenth century bourgeois realism.
2 See Raymond Williams (1981) *Culture* and 'The Analysis of Culture' in (1961, rpt 1965) *The Long Revolution*: 57–88.
3 Patricia Duncker (1992) *Sisters and Strangers*; Rita Felski (1989) *Beyond Feminist Aesthetics*; Anne Cranny Francis (1990) *Feminist Fiction*; Gayle Greene (1991) *Changing the Story*; Paulina Palmer (1989) *Contemporary Women's Fiction*; Patricia Waugh (1989) *Feminine Fictions*.
4 See for example Paul Lauter's editions of thirties women's novels for the Feminist Press, Paula Rabinowitz and Charlotte Nekola's collection (1987) *Writing Red* and especially Paula Rabinowitz's (1991) *Labor and Desire*, which in its final chapter highlights exactly the link between 1930s and 1970s women's writing that I want to explore.
5 Lessing is included here because of her importance for the genre, and because of her influence on American feminist fiction.
6 Atwood is, of course, Canadian and therefore does not belong – like Doris Lessing in Chapter 4 – to the American tradition I seek to outline. I have chosen to include *The Handmaid's Tale* all the same because of its American subject matter and because I feel this novel has been seriously misread as a political fiction of feminism.

1 'THIS STORY MUST BE TOLD': WOMEN WRITERS OF THE 1930s

1 Deborah Rosenfelt (1985) 'From the Thirties'. Much of what I say about Olsen in this section relies on this seminal article.
2 I use the term 'socialist' here to designate a general Leftist orientation rather than party membership. Many of the women writers discussed in this chapter

were at some time members of the Communist Party of the United States of America (CPUSA), but not all of them, and not at all times. The frequent shifts in CPUSA policy from the mid-1920s to the Hitler–Stalin pact of 1939 caused various factions to form and dissolve and membership numbers to rise and fall dramatically – hence, also, the use of 'socialist' as a broad, catch-all term.

3 Ann Burlak was a young textile worker who became a leading figure in the Trade Union Unity League, and later leader of the Communist Party in Rhode Island.

4 See for example: Lorraine Bethel (1982) 'This Infinity of Conscious Pain'; editors' introductions to Joanne M. Braxton and Andrée Nicola McLaughlin (1990) *Wild Women in the Whirlwind*; Alice Walker (1979b) 'Dedication: On Refusing to Be Humbled by Second Place in a Contest You Did Not Design'; Alice Walker (1975) 'Looking for Zora' and (1976b) 'Saving the Life That Is Your Own' and (1979d) 'Zora Neale Hurston'; Mary Helen Washington (1979) 'Zora Neale Hurston: a Woman Half in Shadow'.

5 Terry Lovell asks a similar set of questions, relating Marxist aesthetic debates to feminist ones, in (1983b) 'Writing Like a Woman': 18.

6 For a discussion of this construction of literary history, see also Raymond Tallis's quirky (and rather reductive) critique of recent theoretical developments in (1988) *In Defence of Realism*.

7 See also, for Gold's importance as *the* critic on the Left in the 1920s and 1930s, Daniel Aaron (1965) *Writers on the Left*; Jack Conroy and Curt Johnson (eds) (1973) *Writers in Revolt*; Walter B. Rideout (1956) *The Radical Novel in the United States 1900–1954*; and most notably Utz Riese (1987) 'Neither High Nor Low'.

  See, furthermore, for a general discussion and overview of changes in Soviet literary policy (which informed those in the CPUSA) Ben Brewster (1976) 'The Soviet State, the Communist Party and the Arts 1917–1936'.

8 See Janice and Stephen MacKinnon's biography (1988) *Agnes Smedley: the Life and Times of an American Radical*: 104–19.

9 Marge Piercy (1982b) *Parti-Colored Blocks for a Quilt*, a collection of essays and interviews, and Alice Walker (1973a) 'Everyday Use', a short story which argues for the use-value of art.

  See, also, for a comparison of Walker's *Meridian* with Smedley's novels, Susan Willis (1987) *Specifying*: 127–8.

10 Paula Rabinowitz (1991) *Labor and Desire*: 12. In this chapter I rely rather heavily on Rabinowitz's scholarship and that of Candida Ann Lacey in her unpublished thesis, (1985) 'Engendering conflict'. I am indebted to both critics for shared and differing insights, and for arousing my interest in this period in the first place.

11 Marge Piercy (1974a) 'Reconsideration: Agnes Smedley, Dirt-Poor Daughter of Earth': 19–20.

12 Janice MacKinnon and Stephen MacKinnon (1988) *Agnes Smedley*: 104.

13 Cited by Janice and Stephen MacKinnon in (1988) *Agnes Smedley*: 94.

14 Marge Piercy (1981–1982) 'An Interview with Peggy Friedmann and Ruthann Robson of *Kalliope*' rpt in (1982b) *Parti-Colored Blocks for a Quilt*: 132–3.

15 See for these European Marxist debates on realism Theodor Adorno et al. (1977) *Aesthetics and Politics* and Michael Sprinker (1987) *Imaginary Relations*.

16 Tillie Olsen (1971, 1972) 'Rebecca Harding Davis' rpt in (1980b) *Silences*: 47–118.

17 See Helge Normann Nilsen (1984) 'Tillie Olsen's *Tell Me a Riddle*: the Political Theme': 163–9.

18 See for Gold on Whitman 'Towards Proletarian Art', where he calls Whitman his 'spiritual grandfather' and 'The Second American Renaissance' which includes

a quotation from *Democratic Vistas*, prefiguring Gold's own aesthetic programme:

> I should demand a programme of culture, drawn out, not for a single class alone, or for the parlors or lecture rooms, but with an eye to practical life, the west, the workingmen, the facts of farms and jackplanes and engineers, and of the broad range of the women also of the middle and working strata, and with reference to the perfect equality of women.
>
> (Michael Folsom (ed.) (1972) *Mike Gold*: 251)

19 Candida Lacey (1985) 'Engendering conflict': 34, 257.

20 See Mary Inman (1940(a)(b)(c)) 'Manufacturing Femininity', 'The Pivot of the System' and 'The Code of a Class', rpt in Nekola and Rabinowitz (eds) (1987) *Writing Red*: 304–7, 308–11 and 312–15; and Grace Hutchins (1934b) 'Women under Capitalism', rpt in Nekola and Rabinowitz (eds) (1987) *Writing Red*: 329–34, which all deal with the politics of housework and the sexual division of labour. Robert Shaffer gives an overview of this literature in (1979) 'Women and the Communist Party USA, 1930–1940'.

21 The exchange between Dennis and Trimberger provides a fascinating illustration of historical difference, as well as of Old and New Left discourses at cross-purposes.

22 This situation was, of course, not all that different from the one in which most working mothers found themselves; Tillie Olsen's 'I Stand Here Ironing' powerfully testifies to their dilemma.

23 Meridel LeSueur (1956) 'The Dark of the Time', rpt in (1982a) *Harvest & Song for My Time*: 122; also in (1982b) *Ripening*: 239.

24 See Georg Lukacs (1932) 'Reportage or Portrayal?' rpt in (1981) *Essays on Realism*: 45–75.

25 Parts of this novel were first published in the 1930s and 1940s, but it was rejected as a novel in 1939 and only printed in its present, full form in 1977.

26 The first volume, *Pity Is Not Enough* was published in 1933, the second *The Executioner Waits* a year later.

27 This Cuban episode appeared as reportage as well in (1935) 'A Passport from Realengo'. Both this and (1936) 'The Enemy' are reprinted in Charlotte Nekola and Paula Rabinowitz (eds) (1987) *Writing Red*: 199–202, 96–105.

28 See Robert Shaffer (1979) 'Women and the Communist Party USA, 1930–1940': 106.

29 Werner Sollors explains Hurston's objections to protest writing (especially her antagonism, a decade later, to Richard Wright) in terms of anthropology versus sociology: 'anthropology was more concerned with "culture", "folk", "tradition", and "adaptation", whereas sociologists looked into "civilization", "an urbanized population", and "modernization", and "conflict"', Werner Sollors (1990) 'Anthropological and Sociological Tendencies in American Literature of the 1930s and 1940s': 37. For much of the century, of course, this opposition also worked as a gender polarisation in African-American writing, between the Hurstons, Walkers, and Morrisons on one hand and the Wrights, Ellisons and Reeds on the other.

30 For overviews and discussion of this critical controversy see Michele Wallace (1990b) 'Who Owns Zora Neale Hurston?'; and Mary Helen Washington (1989a) '"I Love the Way Janie Crawford Left Her Husbands"'.

31 Deborah E. McDowell (1985) 'Introduction: a Question of Power or, the Rear Guard Faces Front'. McDowell makes similar claims, of dual or triple disguise, for Nella Larsen's *Quicksand* and *Passing*, in her postscript to those novels (rpt 1989 London: Serpent's Tail).

32 Barbara Johnson (1986a) 'Metaphor, Metonymy and Voice in *Their Eyes Were Watching God*' and (1986b) 'Thresholds of Difference: Structures of Address in Zora Neale Hurston'. A poststructuralist approach, but this is some of the best Hurston criticism on offer.

33 In *The Narrows*, Petry's 1953 novel about an interracial relationship, there is a similar preoccupation with the determining factors of place, a preoccupation which was later to develop further in the work of Toni Morrison (*Sula*) and particularly Gloria Naylor (*Linden Hills*, *The Women of Brewster Place*). *The Narrows* begins with an explanation of the social geography of The Narrows and its alternative names: 'Eye of the Needle, The Bottom, Little Harlem, Dark Town, Nigger Town – because Negroes had replaced those other earlier immigrants, the Irish, the Italians, and the Poles'(5). Such historical explanations have become a topos in African-American women's writing; Zora Neale Hurston does the same with Eatonville in her autobiography *Dust Tracks on a Road*.

34 Bernard Bell (1987) *The Afro-American Novel and Its Tradition*: 178–83. See also Mary Helen Washington's (1989b) '"Infidelity Becomes Her": the Ambivalent Woman in the Fiction of Ann Petry and Dorothy West'. Washington offers a very different reading of Petry's work from mine (and I think a misreading), but with a similar stress on environmental determinism.

35 Ann Petry disclosed in an interview that *The Street*'s narrative was inspired by a newspaper report of a superintendent in a Harlem building who taught a young boy to steal letters; another source for the novel was Petry's experience as an education officer in Harlem, which caused her concern for the welfare of school-age children. Bub's slide into petty criminality however is not as central to the novel as Petry's stress on this 'documentary source material' might suggest, though it is important. 'Interview with Ann Petry' in Frank Gado (ed.) (1973) *First Person*: 173.

2 THE POLITICS OF WOMEN'S LIBERATION

1 Jameson begins his book (1983) *The Political Unconscious* with this phrase (9). His argument concerning narrative informs much of my thinking in this book.

2 Rpt in James Miller (1987) *Democracy Is in the Streets*. Miller's excellent history informs much of what I say about the New Left in this chapter.

3 I am very grateful to Maureen Cressey-Hackett for pointing this out to me; it is not well-documented in Civil Rights and New Left historiography.

4 See Stanley Aronowitz (1985) 'When the New Left Was New' in Sonya Sayres et al. (eds) (1985) *The 60s Without Apology*: 18; Miller (1987) *Democracy Is in the Streets*: 37.

5 SNCC (n.d.) 'SNCC: Founding Statement': 113; Tom Hayden et al. (1962) 'Port Huron Statement': 331–3, 338.

6 See Cornel West (1985) 'The Paradox of the Afro-American Rebellion': 47.

7 Myra Marx Ferree and Beth Hess (1985) *Controversy and Coalition*: 51. See also Rochelle Gatlin (1987) *American Women Since 1945*: 44–5; Cynthia Harrison (1988) *On Account of Sex*: 134; and Mary P. Ryan (1983) *Womanhood in America from Colonial Times to the Present*: 308.

8 See for Title VII Myra Marx Ferree and Beth Hess (1985) *Controversy and Coalition*: 54; Cynthia Harrison (1988) *On Account of Sex*: 176–80.

9 See for the relationship between NOW and Women's Liberation, Jo Freeman (1975) *The Politics of Women's Liberation*: 99; and Myra Marx Ferree and Beth Hess (1985) *Controversy and Coalition*: 49–50, 118.

10 See for the move towards autonomous Black organisations Clayborne Carson

(1982) *In Struggle*; Manning Marable (1985) *Black American Politics* and (1984) *Race, Reform and Rebellion*; Richard Polenberg (1980) *One Nation Divisible*; Kirkpatrick Sale (1973) *SDS*; and Irwin D. Solomon (1989) *Feminism and Black Activism in Contemporary America.*

11 Although Evans focuses quite a lot on individuals whose personal histories exemplify the trajectory from Civil Rights and the New Left to Women's Liberation, my rather more generalised argument is heavily reliant on hers, and I am indebted to her path-breaking schoalrship.

12 Mary Aikin Rothschild (1979) 'White Women Volunteers in the Freedom Summers'.

13 Anonymous, but attributed to Casey Hayden and Mary King (1964) 'SNCC Position Paper: Women in the Movement', see also Chapter 5. Marge Piercy raised the same issue again in SDS, in (1970b) 'The Grand Coolie Damn', as did Morgan herself in (1970a) 'Goodbye to All That'. See also a Berkeley Sister (n.d.) 'To a White Male Radical'.

14 Cited by Sara Evans (1979) *Personal Politics*: 87–8; Paula Giddings (1984) *When and Where I Enter*: 302–3; and Mary Rothschild (1979) 'White Women Volunteers in the Freedom Summers': 488.

15 Jo Freeman (1975) *The Politics of Women's Liberation*: 58; Rochelle Gatlin (1987) *American Women Since 1945*: 94.

16 See for a discussion of the Sexual Revolution's other meanings my essay (1994) '"It's My Party": Fictions of the Sexual Revolution'.

17 The Redstockings collection (1978) *Feminist Revolution* is a good example of these 'live' debates.

18 See for this point Myra Marx Ferree and Beth Hess (1985) *Controversy and Coalition*: 85.

19 See for an extensive description of the procedure of consciousness-raising Kathie Sarachild (1971) 'Feminist "Organizing" and Consciousness-Raising'.

20 See for a critique of cultural feminism in the context of sexual politics Alice Echols (1984) 'The Taming of the Id: Feminist Sexual Politics 1968–1983'.

21 See also Jo Freeman (1971) 'The Revolution Is Happening in Our Minds'.

22 The Hill–Thomas case refers to the Congressional hearings concerning Judge Clarence Thomas's nomination for the Supreme Court in October 1991. Thomas's candidacy was challenged by Prof. Anita Hill on the grounds of sexual harassment. See for the wider context of this issue and why it attracted so much attention, Susan Faludi (1992) *Backlash*: 201.

23 Faludi performs a searing dissection of Hewlett's book and its sources in (1992) *Backlash*: 246–50.

24 Lynne Segal (1991) 'Whose Left? Socialism, Feminism and the Future': 89.

25 Betty Friedan (1982) *The Second Stage*. For a survey of backlash texts see Linda Gordon and Allen Hunter (1977–8) 'Sex, Family and the New Right' and Judith Stacey (1986) 'Are Feminists Afraid to Leave Home?'. A good general history of the New Right is Sidney Blumenthal (1986) *The Rise of the Counter-Establishment*; see also Chapter 7.

26 Also cited by Rochelle Gatlin in (1987) *American Women Since 1945*: 124.

27 See for a firsthand account of this famous act, 'An Interview with Rosa Parks' in Clayborne Carson et al. (eds) (1991) *Eyes on the Prize*: 45–7. By comparison with their male peers, the great female figures in Civil Rights receive relatively short shrift in this volume.

28 Rochelle Gatlin (1987) *American Women Since 1945*: 118.

29 These three positions are represented in a section on Black Women's Liberation in Morgan's anthology (1970b) *Sisterhood Is Powerful*: Frances M. Beal 'Double Jeopardy: to Be Black and Female': 382–96; Eleonor Holmes Norton 'For Sadie

and Maude': 397–403; Black Women's Liberation Group, Mount Vernon, New York 'Statement on Birth Control': 404–6.
30 See Gloria T. Hull et al. (eds) (1982) *But Some of Us Are Brave*: xx; Jo Freeman (1975) *The Politics of Women's Liberation*: 15, 38–41. Paula Giddings critiques Freeman's theory of 'relative deprivation' on the grounds that despite higher educational achievement, black women's earnings were still consistently lower than those of black men and besides, professional black women were just as likely to compare themselves with white women and men since they were, by and large, more confident of their abilities than their white peers; Paula Giddings (1984) *When and Where I Enter*: 307.
31 Paula Giddings (1984) *When and Where I Enter*: 304–10. See also Frances Beal (1970) 'Double Jeopardy': 393.
32 A few years later Wallace was to subject the image of the strong Black woman as a role model to an equally strenuous critique in her path-breaking (and highly controversial) book (1979) *Black Macho and the Myth of the Superwoman*.
33 See also Gloria Joseph and Jill Lewis (1981) *Common Differences* for a constructive engagement with different analyses and priorities.
34 Frances Beal (1970) 'Double Jeopardy', and Eleonor Norton (1970) 'For Sadie and Maude': 386, 399. See for historical analyses of the Black family Angela Davis (1982) *Women, Race and Class*, and Kum Kum Bhavnani and Angela Davis (1989) 'Complexity, Activism, Optimism'; also Lee Rainwater and William L. Yancey (eds) (1967) *The Moynihan Report and the Politics of Controversy*.
35 See critiques by Angela Davis in (1982) *Women, Race and Class* (Chapter11); bell hooks (Gloria Watkins) in (1982) *Ain't I a Woman: Black Women and Feminism*; and Flo Kennedy (1985) '"It's Damn Slick Out There"'.
36 See Toni Cade's anthology (1970) *The Black Woman* for these debates about the Black woman's 'place'.
37 Combahee River Collective (1977) 'A Black Feminist Statement': 'We believe that the most profound and potentially the most radical politics come directly out of our own identity' (16).
38 See Angela Davis (1982) *Women, Race and Class* (Chapter 12) for an extensive discussion of this issue. 'CARASA' stands for Committee for Abortion Rights and Against Sterilization Abuse; it had a wider agenda for women's reproductive rights than other abortion organisations, but its arguments lost out to the simpler single-issue campaign which could be argued on relatively straightforward liberal grounds.
39 See for a cogent argument regarding the collapse of liberalism, Allen J. Matusow (1986) *The Unraveling of America*.
40 See Rochelle Gatlin (1987) *American Women Since 1945*: 238–9; and for a useful overview Pamela Johnston Conover and Virginia Gray (1983) *Feminism and the New Right*. Midge Decter's (1973) *The New Chastity and Other Arguments against Women's Liberation* is an interesting early example of an anti-feminist tract.
41 Drude Dahlerup (ed.) (1986b) *The New Women's Movement*: 235.

3 LIBERATING LITERATURE

1 Marge Piercy's novel *Braided Lives* (discussed in Chapter 7) convincingly portrays the predicament of an aspiring female poet in a sixties college environment.
2 Terry Lovell (1987) *Consuming Fiction*: 54.
3 See for this point Rosalind Coward (1980) 'Are Women's Novels Feminist Novels?'; Terry Lovell (1983b) 'Writing Like a Woman'; and Rita Felski (1989) *Beyond Feminist Aesthetics*.

4 See for a discussion of the American postmodern novel Patricia Waugh (1984) *Metafiction*; Malcolm Bradbury (ed.) (1977) *The Novel Today*; Jerome Klinkowitz (1980) *The American 1960s*; and Morris Dickstein (1977) *Gates of Eden*.

5 See for changes in the literary 'dominant' also: Marcus Cunliffe (1986) *The Literature of the United States*: Chapter 15; Frederick R. Karl (1983) *American Fiction 1940–1980*: Chapters 8–11; and Jerome Klinkowitz (1980) *The American 1960s*.

6 Christopher Lasch (1979) *The Culture of Narcissism* was highly influential for a while in describing the legacy of the counter-culture and post-1960s consciousness.

7 See for the importance of African-American music and speech as models for writing for example: Maya Angelou (1984) 'Shades and Slashes of Light'; Toni Morrison (1984) 'Rootedness: the Ancestor as Foundation'; Toni Morrison (1988) 'Unspeakable Things Unspoken'; also Gwendolyn Brooks's remarks on 'good poetry' in (1972) *Report from Part One*: 152; and bell hooks's subtle revaluation of oppositional uses of form in black writing in (1990b) 'An Aesthetic of Blackness'. Morris Dickstein describes how the architects of the Black aesthetic, LeRoi Jones (later Amiri Baraka) and Larry Neal 'scorn inwardness as a sterile remnant of bourgeois individualism' – clearly, there's more than a shade of Michael Gold here; Dickstein (1977) *Gates of Eden*: 180. I shall discuss the Black aesthetic of the 1960s further in Chapter 5.

8 See for example Diane DiPrima (1968) 'Revolutionary Letters'.

9 For, as Patricia Waugh helpfully points out: 'For many women there can be no prior subject or self whose fragmentation becomes a political necessity, source of nostalgic regret, or hedonistic *jouissance*.' Patricia Waugh (1989) *Feminine Fictions*: 10.

10 Agathe Nesoule Krouse cites Plath and Didion as examples of what might be called 'negative feminism', because they analyse women's subordinate position but cannot envisage/represent the possibility of change; Krouse (1978) 'Toward a Definition of Literary Feminism'.

11 See for a specifically American angle on this Barbara Ehrenreich, who writes of an 'epidemic of misogyny' as the effect of a 'crisis in masculinity' in (1983) *The Hearts of Men*.

12 There were feminist critics who did voice their demands for a new, properly feminist fiction – predictably, these demands came down to 'positive images'. Nancy Burr Evans for example called for novels which represented the possibility and the process of change in gender relations, whilst Carol Yee emphasised the importance of fictional role models. But a comprehensive programme for feminist fiction was never, to my knowledge, formulated either by Women's Liberation or by feminist writers. Nancy Burr Evans (1973) 'The Value and Peril of Reading Women Writers' and Carol Zonis Yee (1973) 'Why Aren't We Writing about Ourselves?'.

13 It is difficult to say which of these major texts were the most major, or the most influential at what point in feminist fiction. Besides, the designation 'major' has to take into account the differences between political groupings within Women's Liberation. Here is a selection: Friedan's *The Feminine Mystique* became the founding text of Second Wave liberal feminism; Millett's *Sexual Politics* fulfilled that function for radical feminism, whereas socialists were more likely to turn to de Beauvoir's *The Second Sex*, Juliet Mitchell's early essay (1966) 'Women, the Longest Revolution' and her book *Woman's Estate* and Shulamith Firestone's *The Dialectic of Sex*. Radical feminism has probably been the most successful in bringing Women's Liberation theory to a wide audience, with highly influential texts such as Susan Brownmiller's *Against Our Will: Men, Women and Rape*; Andrea Dworkin's *WomanHating* and *Pornography* and Adrienne Rich's *Of Woman Born*.

For lesbian feminism, Lillian Faderman's *Surpassing the Love of Men* and Sydney Abbott and Barbara Love's *Sappho Was a Right On Woman: a Liberated Vision of Lesbianism* were path-breaking works, just as Toni Cade's collection *The Black Woman*, Michele Wallace's *Black Macho and the Myth of the Superwoman* and Gerda Lerner's anthology *Black Women in White America* were important texts for African-American feminism. Anthologies and source books of the 1970s and early 1980s which any feminist worth her salt was likely to have read included: Robin Morgan's *Sisterhood Is Powerful*, Zillah Eisenstein's *Capitalist Patriarchy and the Case for Socialist Feminism*, the Redstockings collection *Feminist Revolution*, Judith Hole's and Ellen Levine's *Rebirth of Feminism*, Cherríe Moraga's and Gloria Anzaldúa's *This Bridge Called My Back: Writings by Radical Women of Color* and one of the first collections of Black Women's Studies, edited by Gloria Hull and others, *But Some of Us Are Brave*. Some of the most popular of Women's Liberation texts translated theoretical insights on the social construction of femininity into practice; the Boston Women's Health Collective's *Our Bodies, Ourselves* was a prime example of this self-help tendency.

14 A good example of how feminist fiction moved out of the closet into the marketplace is the publishing history of Rita Mae Brown's *Rubyfruit Jungle*. This novel attained bestseller status in 1978 as the prototype of a new genre, the lesbian 'raunchy read', a product as much of the sexual revolution as of the Women's Movement. It was 'discovered' as such by Transworld Publishers after it had already been in print for five years in an original edition produced by Daughters Publishing Company, a small feminist outfit.

15 Many of the novelists now associated with the rise of Second Wave feminism had been writing for a long time before they came to prominence as writers of feminist fiction. Marge Piercy had already published two novels, (1969) *Going Down Fast* and (1970a) *Dance the Eagle to Sleep* by the time she made her name with *Small Changes* in 1972; Marilyn French had written two novels and countless short stories before *The Women's Room* was published as a 'first novel'; interview with Marilyn French by Linda Blandford, *The Guardian* January 22, 1986.

16 In Britain, the situation was rather different in that both Virago (founded in 1973) and the Women's Press (started 1978) rapidly developed into highly successful enterprises in their own right. If anything, their success forced mainstream publishers to take women's writing more seriously; many established their own lists and imprints in feminist writing (both fiction and non-fiction).

17 The difficulty of categorisation and definition shows in the variety of approaches adopted by feminist critics. In (1980) 'Are Women's Novels Feminist Novels?' Rosalind Coward categorises feminist fiction very loosely by the explicitness of its allegiance to the Women's Movement, authors' public images as feminists (for example, Kate Millett), or its charting of women's oppression (Doris Lessing, Fay Weldon). Rita Felski almost exclusively focuses on first person narratives, which she divides up into the 'confessional' and the 'novel of self-discovery' in *Beyond Feminist Aesthetics*, leaving other uses of genre and form out of account.

Anne Cranny Francis looks at feminist romance, crime fiction, fantasy and science fiction, but not at realism or autobiographical modes, whilst Paulina Palmer, by contrast, takes in all of these forms, as does Patricia Duncker, but without distinguishing between feminist and women's writing – only between different forms of feminism which can be read into the texts; Anne Cranny Francis (1990) *Feminist Fiction*; Paulina Palmer (1989) *Contemporary Women's Fiction*; Patricia Duncker (1992) *Sisters and Strangers*. All these critics treat feminist fiction in an international frame, without regard for cultural difference and specific national traditions.

18 Examples from outside the US include Anja Meulenbelt (1980) *The Shame Is Over*

(original title *De Schaamte Voorbij*); Verena Stefan (1979) *Shedding* (original title *Häutungen*); and Elizabeth Wilson (1982a) *Mirror Writing*.

19 See for example Amanda Cross (Carolyn Heilbrun) (1981) *Death in a Tenured Position*; Sara Paretsky (1987) *Bitter Medicine* and (1982) *Indemnity Only*; Barbara Wilson (1982) *Ambitious Women* and (1989) *The Dog Collar Murders*; and Mary Wings (1986) *She Came Too Late*. Feminist crime fiction is still a burgeoning genre, with new writers appearing – it seems – week by week.

20 See Gayle Greene's final chapter in (1991) *Changing the Story* for a more elaborate discussion of 1980s (white) women's fiction.

21 See for examples of the first generation: Nina Auerbach (1978) *Communities of Women* (though mostly on nineteenth century women's writing); Cheryl L. Brown and Karen Olson (eds) (1978) *Feminist Criticism*; Susan Koppelman Cornillon (ed.) (1973b) *Images of Women in Fiction*; Arlyn Diamond and Lee R. Edwards (eds) (1977) *The Authority of Experience*; Mary Jacobus (ed.) (1979) *Women Writing and Writing about Women*; Ellen Moers (1977) *Literary Women*; Elaine Showalter (1977) *A Literature of Their Own*; Patricia Meyer Spacks (ed.) (1977) *Contemporary Women Novelists*.

And for examples of the second generation: Rosalind Coward (1980) 'Are Women's Novels Feminist Novels?'; Rosalind Coward (1989) 'The True Story of How I Became My Own Person'; Elisabeth Cowie et al. (1981) 'Representation vs. Communication'; Rita Felski (1989) *Beyond Feminist Aesthetics*; Margaret Homans (1983) '"Her Very Own Howl"; the Ambiguities of Representation in Recent Women's Fiction'; Meaghan Morris (1988a) 'The Pirate's Fiancée'; and Elizabeth Wilson (1989) 'Telling It Like It Is: Women and Confessional Writing'.

22 See for example Toril Moi's highly reductive critique of American feminist humanism in Part One of (1985) *Sexual/Textual Politics*.

23 Linda Huf (1985) *A Portrait of the Artist as a Young Woman*; Elizabeth Abel, Marianne Hirsch and Elizabeth Langland (eds) (1983) *The Voyage in*.

24 Bonnie Zimmerman (1983) 'Exiting from Patriarchy: the Lesbian Novel of Development'.

25 Kathleen Dehler (1978) 'The Need To Tell All': 340. The title of Dutch feminist Anja Meulenbelt's autobiography *The Shame Is Over* was taken from an interview with Kate Millett in *Ms.* magazine, whilst the autobiography itself is modelled to a certain extent on Millett's *Flying*; personal interview with Meulenbelt, 7 April 1989.

26 Jeremy Tambling's book (1990) *Confession: Sexuality, Sin, the Subject* adopts a Foucauldian framework and therefore links the confession with all kinds of modes of surveillance (the panopticon) and self-surveillance. This inevitably entails a widening of the definition of confession, to the point where I no longer found it useful as a critical paradigm for counter-hegemonic writing which, if it cannot ignore the dominant gaze, certainly tries to defy it.

27 Germaine Greer (1977) 'Into the Acid Bath', *The Times*, 19 June.

28 John Leonard (1976) 'Pop Goes the Novel', *New York Times Book Review*, 14 March.

29 Frederick Karl (1983) *American Fiction 1940–1980*: 424–6.

30 See for an excellent analysis of the history of the *Bildungsroman* and its role in asserting bourgeois hegemony Franco Moretti (1987) *The Way of the World: the Bildungsroman in European Culture*.

31 Sue Roe (ed.) (1987) *Women Reading Women's Writing*: 3.

32 These arguments against poststructuralist feminism should not give the impression that such criticism has yielded nothing of use with respect to feminist fiction. But it needs to be said that feminist fiction cannot be read fruitfully as political writing if we merely view it in intraliterary terms and judge it by the

(often unspoken) standards of modernist cultural practices (as Morris, Homans, Coward, and to some extent Felski and Wilson, do). Recent book-length studies such as those of Paulina Palmer, Anne Cranny Francis, Patricia Duncker and Rita Felski have fruitfully tried to combine the insights of feminist literary theory with a critique of feminist fiction's social concerns, and they inform my own critical position throughout this work.

4 'IF WE RESTRUCTURE THE SENTENCE OUR LIVES ARE MAKING': FEMINIST FICTIONS OF SUBJECTIVITY

1 Denise Levertov (1987b) from 'Making Peace' in Denise Levertov (1987a) *Breathing the Water*: 41. Also in Marge Piercy (ed.) (1987a) *Early Ripening*: 137.
2 I would suggest, in line with my proposal to discard the term 'confessional' in relation to feminist writing, to abandon derogatory terms like 'narcissistic' and 'self-indulgent' as well. It is hard to see what purpose they serve other than to put women's writing back into the tradition of its reception which Stanton characterised as focused on women's untranscendable self-obsession. A more precise critical vocabulary which can describe textual features neutrally is surely preferable to moralistic value judgement masquerading as literary criticism.
3 No doubt much against Kristeva's own inclinations, for she is wholly dismissive of self-identified feminist writing, which she characterises as 'naïve whining' (where have we heard this before, and since?) or anachronistic 'marketplace romanticism'; (1981) 'Women's Time': 214. In view of Kristeva's enormous influence, filtered in part through Toril Moi's *Sexual/Textual Politics*, I assume that this negative judgement informs that of other feminist critics, such as those cited in the previous chapter.
4 Kristeva uses this phrase, 'subject in process', in an interview with Susan Sellers (1989) 'A Question of Subjectivity – an Interview'.
5 Carolyn G. Heilbrun (1989) *Writing a Woman's Life*. See also on (auto)biographies of public women: Carolyn G. Heilbrun (1988) 'Non-autobiographies of "Privileged" Women'; Patricia Meyer Spacks (1980) 'Selves in Hiding'; and Elizabeth Winston (1980) 'The Autobiographer and Her Readers'. There are notable exceptions to Heilbrun's generalisation that women autobiographers do not speak with authority on public life. The autobiography of anti-lynching campaigner, Ida B. Wells *Crusade for Justice* (see Chapter 5) is a good example. Dissatisfaction may stem from the way we *read* women's public lives, which, if they confine themselves to career and public achievement, seems to be lacking something: we want to know how they did it.
6 Elizabeth Abel, Marianne Hirsch and Elizabeth Langland (eds) (1983) *The Voyage in*: 12–13. Kathleen Dehler emphasises the role of the older self who interprets and reconstructs the younger in (1978) 'The Need To Tell All'.
7 Kathleen Dehler (1978) 'The Need To Tell All': 345.
8 As in the title of Miller's book, which gives a good theoretical exposé of what makes women's writing feminist; Nancy Miller (1988) *Subject to Change: Reading Feminist Writing*.
9 Paulina Palmer (1989) *Contemporary Women's Fiction*: 2.
10 It is the privilege of the 'dominant', always, to regard itself as the norm. But subordinate groups do make counter-claims to universality: the so-called ordinary woman in fiction (such as Connie Ramos in Marge Piercy's *Woman on the Edge of Time* and Celie in Alice Walker's *The Color Purple*) is figured not as other, but as everywoman in feminist fiction; see also for this point Chapters 5 and 6.

11 See for a discussion, along these same lines, of feminist realism in film Christine Gledhill (1984) 'Recent Developments in Feminist Film Criticism'; and my own (1991) 'Feminism and Culture – the Movie'.

12 Sidonie Smith situates the emergence of autobiography as a distinctive form in the late eighteenth-century revolutionary democratic movements and in romantic individualism; autobiography thus began as a record of the rise of (white Western) public man; Sidonie Smith (1987) *A Poetics of Women's Autobiography.*

13 See for general discussions of women's autobiography: Shari Benstock (ed.) (1988) *The Private Self*; Bella Brodzki and Celeste Schenck (eds) (1988) *Life/Lines*; Estelle C. Jelinek (ed.) (1980) *Women's Autobiography*; Sidonie Smith (1987) *A Poetics of Women's Autobiography*; Domna C. Stanton (ed.) (1987) *The Female Autograph.* For specific discussions of genre: Regina Blackburn (1980) 'In Search of the Black Female Self'; Stephanie A. Demetrakopoulos (1980) 'The Metaphysics of Matrilinearism in Women's Autobiography'; Mary V. Dearborn (1986) *Pocahontas's Daughters*; Nellie Y. McKay (1990) 'The Autobiographies of Zora Neale Hurston and Gwendolyn Brooks'; Elizabeth Schultz (1981) 'To Be Black and Blue'.

14 Emile Benveniste (1971b) 'Subjectivity in Language'.

15 Elizabeth W. Bruss (1976) *Autobiographical Acts.*

16 This exemplary function, which can be used to forge new cultural or social identities, is perhaps especially strong in American autobiography from Franklin onwards. See on this aspect of Benjamin Franklin's *Autobiography* Cynthia C. Jordan's (1989b) *Second Stories*: 27–57. For the general argument about American autobiography as a genre of (national) identity formation see: Sam B. Girgus (ed.) (1981) *The American Self*; Albert Stone (ed.) (1981) *The American Autobiography*; Gordon O. Taylor (1986) *Studies in Modern American Autobiography*; and Margo Culley (ed.) (1992) *American Women's Autobiography.* For women's exemplary autobiographies: Mary Dearborn (1986) *Pocahontas's Daughters*; and Helen Carr (1988) 'In Other Words: Native American Women's Autobiography'.

17 Two notable examples are Millett's (1974) dialogue with Lessing in *Flying* and Isadora Wing's imaginary discussion with Anna in Erica Jong's (1977) *How To Save Your Own Life.*

18 Elizabeth Abel argues that *The Golden Notebook* is a good example of how women's subjectivity is defined in relation to that of other women, but she does not comment on Anna's aloneness at the end; Elizabeth Abel (1981) '(E)Merging Identities'. See also Judith Kegan Gardiner's reply, (1981) 'The (Us)es of (I)Dentity' for a different view.

19 Feminist critics such as Ellen Morgan have objected to this sense of inevitability in *The Golden Notebook* and Lessing's 'failure to represent female authenticity' in Anna. Others have described Anna in terms of masochism and an inability to define herself independently from men. I am almost, but not quite, persuaded by Gayle Greene's argument that Anna does gain some insights by the end of the novel which enable her to write again, and that this makes *The Golden Notebook* a feminist novel; certainly Greene's analysis is the most sophisticated I have read, and it informs my own here. Ellen Morgan (1978) 'Alienation of the Woman Writer in *The Golden Notebook*': 302; Dagmar Barnouw (1977) 'Disorderly Company'; Frederick R. Karl (1977) 'Doris Lessing in the Sixties'; Gayle Greene (1991) *Changing the Story*: Chapter V.

20 The references are multiple: on endings in novels (52, 192); on the 'lies' told in contemporary male fiction (91, 270); on Virginia Woolf and Shakespeare's sister (61); on the failure of art to represent life 'truthfully'(183).

21 Paulina Palmer (1989) *Contemporary Women's Fiction*: 73. Palmer nevertheless

NOTES

gives a good account of French's novel, and is sensitive both to her rhetorical strategies and to the politics of *The Women's Room.*

22 The discussions of the consciousness-raising group likewise read like a teach-yourself-radical-feminism course, as in the speculations upon a future society (498–501) which follow Shulamith Firestone's 'blueprint' in *The Dialectic of Sex* to the spirit, if not the letter.

23 French (1978) *The Women's Room*: 188. See also Chapters 5 and 6 in which this same theme is discussed in relation to Marge Piercy's *Vida* and Alice Walker's *Meridian.*

24 Margaret Homans (1983) '"Her Very Own Howl"': 189. The most we can say perhaps is that, as Homans argues, French critics regard woman as 'the very definition of that which is not representable in language' (187), whereas American writers locate the problem not in language itself but in the modes of organisation of language to signify 'women'. See for this latter argument also Deborah Cameron (1985) *Feminism and Linguistic Theory.*

25 Annette Kolodny (1980) 'The Lady's Not for Spurning: Kate Millett and the Critics'. Estelle C. Jelinek asks why Buckminster Fuller is regarded as an experimental writer but Kate Millett is not, suggesting 'could this be because neither Millett's work nor her life is seen as significant enough to tolerate her eccentricity?'.

Kolodny would answer yes, as would I; Estelle C. Jelinek (ed.) (1980) Introduction to *Women's Autobiography*: 4.

26 Bella Brodzki and Celeste Schenck (eds) (1988) *Life/Lines*: 1.

27 Whenever I have taught *Flying* to female students though they invariably disagree with me on this; that a famous person can also still feel insecure is to them a pleasant (and comforting) surprise. Of course, this is in part the pleasure of demythification. But in another way, this worries me all the more, because this demythification in Millett's case may be another form of remythification; in *Flying* Millett gives only the agony, not the ecstacy of achievement. Does this teaching experience say something about the distance (experiential, educational) between my students and me, or about insecurity as a still-comforting cultural definition of femininity?

28 See for a real sense of this debate over women's place in the Black struggles of the 1960s Toni Cade (ed.) (1970) *The Black Woman.*

29 Elizabeth Fox-Genovese makes a similar point in (1988) 'My Statue, My Self': 71 and says that African-American women have 'eschewed the confessional mode – the examinations of personal motives, the searchings of the soul – that white women autobiographers so frequently adopt'.

30 Toni Morrison expresses similar sentiments about autobiography and individualism in (1984) 'Rootedness: the Ancestor as Foundation': 339–40.

31 Thomas P. Doherty (1980) 'American Autobiography and Ideology': 104.

32 On Black women and definitions of femininity see also Jacqueline Dowd Hall (1984) '"The Mind That Burns in Each Body": Women, Rape and Racial Violence'; and Rennie Simson (1984) 'The Afro-American Female: the Historical Context of the Construction of Sexual Identity'.

33 The limitations of single-text Angelou criticism become clear in a remark such as Nellie McKay's that Angelou 'eschews political narrative for the literary mode of the Bildungsroman', since this only applies to the first volume, *I Know Why the Caged Bird Sings*; Nellie Y. McKay (1990) 'The Autobiographies of Zora Neale Hurston and Gwendolyn Brooks': 265.

34 Sondra O'Neale (1984) 'Reconstruction of the Composite Self: New Images of Black Women in Maya Angelou's Continuing Autobiography'.

201

35 See Sondra O'Neale (1984) 'Reconstruction of the Composite Self' and Joanne M. Braxton (1990) 'Ancestral Presence: the Outraged Mother Figure in Contemporary Afra-American Writing'. Only Angelou herself mentions Petry to Rosa Guy in the interview (1988): 9.
36 As in the episode where white employers want to rename her in *Gather Together*: 76; and in *Singin' and Swingin'* when whites choose a stage name for her: 96.
37 Chinosole (1990) 'Audre Lorde and the Matrilinear Diaspora: "Moving History beyond Nightmare into the Future"'; Barbara Smith (1990) 'The Truth That Never Hurts: Black Lesbians in the Fiction of the 1980s'.
38 See Chapter 5 for the tongue-clipping trope, and Maxine Hong Kingston's autobiographical novel for a cross-cultural reference (1976) *The Woman Warrior.*
39 See for the black woman artist (with or without an art form) also Toni Morrison's *Sula* and *Song of Solomon*, Gloria Naylor's *Mama Day*, Walker's *Meridian, The Color Purple* and *The Temple of My Familiar*, as well as Walker's essays. An illuminating article on this theme is Renita Weems's (1983) 'Artists without an Art Form'.
40 For lesbian subjectivities see also Biddy Martin (1988) 'Lesbian Identity and Autobiographical Difference[s]'; and Bonnie Zimmerman (1983) 'Exiting from Patriarchy'. Adrienne Rich's terminology of the lesbian continuum, as well as her objections to butch/femme role-play inform Lorde's account, despite her polemical swipe here at white feminist theory of the Richian kind; see Adrienne Rich (1980) 'Compulsory Heterosexuality and Lesbian Existence'. For an excellent piece of 'real' historiography see Lillian Faderman (1992) *Odd Girls and Twilight Lovers: a History of Lesbian Life in Twentieth Century America.*
41 Patricia Duncker, in her excellent account of *Zami* in (1992) *Sisters and Strangers* concurs, albeit a little hesitatingly, with this matrophile analysis of the genesis of lesbian desire: 68–71. I find it very problematic, not just for lesbianism but for heterosexual women also. To be flippant: what kinds of monsters of mothers (or fathers!) must heterosexual women *have* to have turned out this way?
42 Audre Lorde (1983) 'My Words Will Be There'.

5 HEALING THE BODY POLITIC: ALICE WALKER'S *MERIDIAN*

1 This SNCC Position paper 'Women in the Movement' was anonymous, but has since been attributed to Mary King and Casey Hayden.
2 See for these critiques for example Angela Davis (1982) *Women, Race and Class*; bell hooks (Gloria Watkins) (1982) *Ain't I a Woman?*; Elizabeth Spelman (1988) *Inessential Woman*, and also my discussion in Chapter 2.
3 See Bernice Johnson Reagon (1983) 'Coalition Politics'; and Michele Wallace (1989) 'Reading 1968 and the Great American Whitewash'.
4 See W. E. B. DuBois (1903, rpt 1968) 'Of Our Spiritual Strivings', Chapter 1 of *The Souls of Black Folk*. I use 'double-voicedness' not in the (much more technical) Bakhtinian sense but in a sense of my own, meaning a dual (race/gender) discourse of emancipation and resistance.
5 Sigmund Freud and Joseph Breuer (1893–1895) 'The Mechanism of Hysterical Phenomena' rpt in (n.d.) *Studies on Hysteria*: 6.
6 This repositioning, prefigured in Grange Copeland's learning process in Walker's first novel, is also a reconciliation between Meridian and Truman, and is repeated rather less convincingly in the Utopian conclusion of *The Color Purple*, and recurs in even more elevated and spiritualised form in *The Temple of My Familiar.*
7 See Chapter 2. Henry Louis Gates describes this ironic reversal of received

images as a trope in African-American writing generally in (1987b) 'The Blackness of Blackness'.

8 There is an intertextual allusion here to Nikki Giovanni's poem 'Nigger, Can You Kill', cited by Michele Wallace in (1979) *Black Macho and the Myth of the Superwoman*: 166.

9 Maya Angelou also uses the familiar trope of rape and silence, which goes back at least as far as Shakespeare, in *I Know Why the Caged Bird Sings*.

10 See for a fascinating account of Freedom Summer and interracial sexual politics Mary King's autobiography (1987) *Freedom Song*, especially 464–5.

11 Harriet Tubman was a nineteenth century black woman, an ex-slave who helped countless African-Americans escape from the South on the Underground Railroad.

12 See also Linda Powell's article (1983) 'Black Macho and Black Feminism', where Powell observes, in a critique of Michele Wallace's book, that Wallace became a feminist because 'there was no language available in the Black movement to explain women's position': 285.

13 See my discussion of Black feminist critiques of Brownmiller's influential book on rape, *Against Our Will*, in Chapter 2 and of *The Women's Room* in Chapter 4. Walker has treated the sexual politics of interracial rape also in the story (1982a) 'Advancing Luna – and Ida B. Wells', which calls up the spectre of the famous anti-lynching activist in an attempt at resolving the contradictions between the history of lynching and feminist insistence that rape is a crime of violence against women – regardless of race. Walker's story reaches no resolution, and comes up only with three different possible endings. The autobiography of Ida B. Wells serves on one hand as an intertextual reference for both 'Advancing Luna' and for *Meridian*, but Walker's texts also critique Wells who allows no ambivalence (along the lines of solidarity with white women) at all – for good historical reasons; Ida B. Wells (1970) *Crusade for Justice*. See for an extensive discussion of 'Advancing Luna' also Valerie Smith's excellent (1990) 'Split Affinities: the Case of Interracial Rape'.

14 Here also Toomer's example is relevant, because *Meridian*'s fragmented, episodic narrative structure is reminiscent of that other text which sings the praises of Southern black women, Toomer's (1923) *Cane*.

15 Henry Louis Gates mentions Janie's 'rhetorical killing' of Joe Starks in Zora Neale Hurston's *Their Eyes Were Watching God* and draws attention to the need for symbolic rather than literal readings of this kind of 'signifying' writing; Henry Louis Gates Jr (1987b) 'The Blackness of Blackness': 241.

16 The 'dominant', as I have noted before, is not a fixed entity but a relative notion; what is perceived as the 'dominant' depends on where people place themselves in the hierarchy of cultural production. This is an example of such relativity: undoubtedly, in more absolute terms white male writing is still more 'dominant' than feminist or black male writing; however, in the context of counter-hegemonic writing Walker perceives white Women's Liberation and Black nationalism as the 'dominant' paradigms in relation to her own practice.

17 See also my discussion of Smedley's *Daughter of Earth*, a novel which Walker knows well, in Chapter 1. See for the relation between this kind of narrative structure and the African-American storytelling tradition Lawrence W. Levine (1978) *Black Culture and Black Consciousness*: 88. See for the quilt as emblem of a useful art Walker's short story (1973a) 'Everyday Use' and bell hooks (1990b) 'An Aesthetic of Blackness' and (1990a) 'Aesthetic Inheritances'.

18 Whilst I think it is right to say that *Meridian* interrogates historiography, it is also true that Walker dedicates her novel to John Lewis and Staughton and Maryam

Lynd, one-time leader of SNCC and historians of the Civil Rights Movement, respectively; she thereby acknowledges their importance. See for the 'dominant' in Civil Rights historiography Clayborne Carson (1982) *In Struggle*; Dick Cluster (ed.) (1979) *They Should Have Served That Cup of Coffee*; Manning Marable (1985) *Black American Politics* and (1984) *Race, Reform and Rebellion*. For feminist historiography Sara Evans (1979) *Personal Politics* and Mary Rothschild (1979) 'White Women Volunteers in the Freedom Summers'; and for personal accounts Ann Moody's (1968) *Coming of Age in Mississippi*; Sally Belfrage (1965) *Freedom Summer* and Mary King (1987) *Freedom Song*.

19 Whether this development towards a more old-style, Marxist and Maoist-inspired revolutionary stance was also more radical in terms of its effectiveness remains a matter for debate; arguably, the redemptive community, participatory democracy and direct action of the early Civil Rights Movement and the New Left were, in a sense, more 'revolutionary', because more innovative and challenging, than the later rhetoric of revolution and armed struggle.

20 Emphasis on and empathy with Native America alludes intertextually to Toomer's 'The Blue Meridian' again, and to Smedley's *Daughter of Earth*. For black collusion with the genocide of Native Americans see Manning Marable (1984) *Race, Reform and Rebellion*: 38. Walker revises her critique of the Buffalo soldiers in a discussion between Suwelo and Fanny in her controversial 1989 novel, *The Temple of My Familiar*.

21 The clearest and best-known example is Toni Morrison's (1987) *Beloved*, but Gayl Jones's (1975) *Corregidora*, Sherley Ann Williams's (1986) *Dessa Rose*, and the forerunner of the current wave of slavery novels, Margaret Walker's (1966) *Jubilee* deal with similar configurations of sexual and racial politics.

22 For a fascinating discussion of literacy and speech as tropes in Afro-American writing see Valerie Smith (1987) *Self-Discovery and Authority in Afro-American Narrative.*

23 Also because there are, of course, more literal ways of reading Meridian's bodily symptoms. Battle fatigue is one explanation which the text itself provides, along with the body politics of Civil Rights. And apparently, the great slave-liberator Harriet Tubman also suffered from mysterious psychosomatic illnesses. An appropriate African-American reading of Meridian's condition further suggests itself in the folkloric tradition of oral storytelling with its miraculous physical phenomena (limbs which can be restored, resurrections, sudden faints and ecstasies), which are usually associated with sorcerers and conjurors. Like Morrison's Sula and Pilate (in *Song of Solomon*), Meridian is a solitary and eccentric figure with elements of the conjure-woman in her; the 'hysteria' then is not, in fact, illness but strength, a sign of her exceptional nature. See the interview with Toni Morrison in Claudia Tate (ed.) (1983) *Black Women Writers at Work*: 117–31; and Luisah Teish (1983) 'Women's Spirituality: a Household Act'.

24 See for this as yet unquestioned Eurocentrism for example collections such as Teresa Brennan (ed.) (1989) *Between Feminism and Psychoanalysis*; Shoshana Felman (ed.) (1982) *Literature and Psychoanalysis*; Shirley Nelson Garner, Claire Kahane and Madelon Sprengnether (eds) (1985) *The (M)Other Tongue*; Juliet Mitchell and Jacqueline Rose (eds) (1982) *Feminine Sexuality*; and Elizabeth Wright's (1984) *Psychoanalytic Criticism*.

25 Barbara Christian (1980) *Black Women Novelists*: 205–38; and (1985) *Black Feminist Criticism*: 211–52.

26 Susan Willis (1987) *Specifying*: 110–28.

27 The disappearance of Schwerner, Chaney and Goodman and the process which led to the discovery of their bodies is well-documented in Civil Rights history. My

source here is Mary King's autobiography (1987) *Freedom Song*, Chapter 10 'Mississippi': 367–98. But it also figures in fiction: Marge Piercy uses it, in fictionalised form, in *Braided Lives*.

28 Gina Wisker's essay (1993b) 'Disremembered and Unaccounted for' productively reads Morrison's *Beloved* and *The Temple of My Familiar* together, to sketch a common ground in their treatment of history/memory and spirituality which is not often acknowledged.

29 There is much more to be said about this, but for those who, like me, had some difficulties with *The Temple of My Familiar* and, by extension also *Possessing the Secret of Joy* and Walker's collected poems in *Her Blue Body Everything I Know*, Melissa Walker's Afterword in (1991) *Down from the Mountaintop*: 199–208 may be useful.

30 For example, in *The Temple of My Familiar* Walker seems to rely a lot on Martin Bernal's pathbreaking, but not uncontroversial (1987) *Black Athena*, a study which relocates the roots of European civilisation in Africa. Even more problematically in *Possessing the Secret of Joy* she appears to take for granted a by now discredited theory of the 'origin' of AIDS, thus passing for 'knowledge' what may be nothing more than a scientific myth.

31 See for the complex nature of Harlem's aesthetics and its heritage Houston A. Baker Jr (1987) *Modernism and the Harlem Renaissance*; Bernard Bell (1987) *The Afro-American Novel and Its Tradition*; Nathan Huggins (1971) *The Harlem Renaissance*; and David Levering Lewis (1981) *When Harlem Was in Vogue*.

32 See for the Black Arts Movement: Nick Aaron Ford (1950) 'A Blueprint for Negro Authors'; Clarence Major (1967) 'A Black Criterion'; Hoyt W. Fuller (1968) 'Towards a Black Aesthetic'; Addison Gayle Jr (1969) 'Foreword' to *Black Expression*: vii–xv; and Reginald Martin (1988) *Ishmael Reed and the New Black Aesthetic Critics*. For women: bell hooks (1990b) 'An Aesthetic of Blackness'; and Gwendolyn Brooks (1972) *Report from Part One*: 21, 84, 183.

33 Alice Walker's essays on foremothers include (1979b) 'Dedication' in *I Love Myself*: 1–6; (1975) 'Looking for Zora' in *In Search of Our Mothers' Gardens*: 93–116; and (1976b) 'Saving the Life That Is Your Own' in the same volume: 3–14.

34 See Bernard Bell (1987) *The Afro-American Novel and Its Tradition*: 259–69; Hazel Carby (1987) *Reconstructing Womanhood*: 7–10; and Joanne M. Braxton (1990) 'Ancestral Presence'.

35 See Chapter 1 for a fuller discussion of this connection.

6 SEIZING TIME AND MAKING NEW: MARGE PIERCY'S *VIDA*

1 These parallels are probably not coincidental, because Piercy wrote an admiring, but not uncritical, review of *Meridian* (she found the ending unsatisfactory); (1976b) '*Meridian* by Alice Walker' in *The New York Times Book Review*, 23 May: 5, 12.

2 I have argued this point at greater length in my article (1989) 'Seizing Time and Making New'.

3 Paulina Palmer describes Miner's novel as a 'fiction of debate'. I am not so sure what that debate would be about, except personal recollection, and it is surprising in this context that Palmer makes no mention of *Vida*; Paulina Palmer (1989) *Contemporary Women's Fiction*: 59–61.

4 Vida and Natalie's sisterhood plays, of course, on Women's Liberation's use of that term, but in many ways their relationship echoes the classical dilemma of Antigone and Ismene in Sophocles's *Antigone*. Margarethe von Trotta treats the

same theme again in her film *Marianne und Juliane* (*The German Sisters*), which is based on the story of Gudrun Enslinn who was a prominent member of West Germany's equivalent of the Weather Underground, the *Rote Armee Fraktion* or Baader-Meinhof group in the 1970s. See for a discussion of von Trotta's film Ellen Seiter (1986) 'The Personal Is Political'.

5 See for this view of Women's Liberation as reactive against the New Left and the Sexual Revolution: Sara Evans (1979) *Personal Politics*; Rochelle Gatlin (1987) *American Women Since 1945*; a Berkeley Sister (n.d., rpt 1984) 'To a White Male Radical' and Robin Morgan (1970a) 'Goodbye to All That'; and Marge Piercy (1970b) 'The Grand Coolie Damn'. For an alternative view which stresses continuity see Genie Plamondon (n.d., rpt 1984) 'Hello to All That'.

6 Sigmund Freud (1966) *Pre-Psychoanalytic Publications and Unpublished Drafts*, Vol. I of *The Standard Edition of the Complete Psychological Works*: 207, 209.

7 This passage might also be read as a self-reflective statement on the nature and function of political fiction: 'some words on a page' whose ideal response results in collective action. See for a fuller discussion of communicative language and political fiction: A. P. Foulkes (1983) *Literature and Propaganda*; and Susan Rubin Suleiman (1983) *Authoritarian Fictions: the Ideological Novel as Literary Genre*.

8 See on this SDS women's motion Sara Evans (1979) *Personal Politics*: 98, 214, and my discussion of its significance in Chapter 2.

9 As in the titles of two studies of 1960s student protest: J. Anthony Lucas (1971) *Don't Shoot – We Are Your Children!* and Todd Gitlin (1980) *The Whole World Is Watching: Mass Media in the Making & Unmaking of the New Left*.

10 Rather like Ann Marion and Truman do in *Meridian*, where the use of political jargon is similarly critiqued.

11 See also the exchange between Ellen Kay Trimberger (1979) and Peggy Dennis (1979) in *Feminist Studies* which I cited in Chapter 2, about the political styles of the Old and the New Left.

12 Michael Harrington reported to James Miller a conversation he had once with Hayden on the question of whether or not a New Left should call itself socialist or communist. Hayden feared this would be seen as un-American; Harrington tells Miller 'what he was essentially telling me was that he wanted to have *a different language*. He wanted to speak American.' [my italics] See James Miller (1987) *Democracy Is in the Streets*: 54.

13 It is no coincidence or mere play on acronyms that Vida's first political organisation is called *Students against the War*, not Students *for* anything. It sums up the difference between Vida's political practice and her sister's: Vida constantly finds herself fighting against forces larger than herself (including her needs for pleasure and intimacy), whilst Natalie is engaged in a quest for herself, in 'the search for personal authenticity' of Port Huron, which she finds fulfilled in the solidarity of women and in the end in a lesbian relationship.

14 Possibly the obsession in white American feminist fiction with black-on-white rape was informed by white feminists' outrage over the sexual politics of some Black male activists in the 1960s, such as Eldridge Cleaver who in (1968) *Soul on Ice* argued that the rape of white women by Black men could be constructed as 'a revolutionary act'. From the perspective of African-American women re-reading the 1960s, white feminists' focus on rape displaces their refusal to seriously engage with racism and with that *other* strand in the history of interracial sexual relations: white-on-black rape. See for this view Flo Kennedy (1984) '"It's Damn Slick Out There"': 356–7 on Cleaver; Michele Wallace (1989) 'Reading 1968 and the Great American Whitewash': 109–10 on Evans, Gitlin, Miller and others; and Toni Morrison (1988) 'Unspeakable Things Unspoken': 12–18 which raises

the general theoretical question of the ideological work required to suppress such African-American presence in literature and history.

15 Vida hears from her husband Leigh, a radical radio reporter, about the COINTELPRO (Counter Intelligence Program) infiltration of the New Left by the FBI: 'They had you coming and going. Infiltrated, recorded and guilt-tripped.' (307)
    Kirkpatrick Sale's history of SDS was published in 1973 and therefore does not cover the aftermath of its breakup, but he does mention infiltration of SDS by the FBI to create paranoia and division on the Left. Sale also documents the ways in which Weatherman, like the Network in *Vida*, was influenced by Women's Liberation and vice versa. Weatherman changed its name to Weather Underground in an attempt at gender neutrality, and on a women's march on the Pentagon in 1971 pictures of Bernardine Dohrn and other Weatherwomen were held high as icons of women-in-struggle by marching feminists; see Kirkpatrick Sale (1973) *SDS*: 652, 654. A blow-by-blow account of a trajectory such as Vida's is Jane Alpert's autobiography (1981) *Growing Up Underground*. First published in 1981, the resemblances to *Vida* are striking. So striking, that I wonder whether Alpert actually modelled her life story on Piercy's novel (although Alpert's exploration of the guerillas' motivation is much less idealised and more personal/psychological than Piercy's construction of it in *Vida*).

16 Susan Stern (1975) *With the Weathermen: the Personal Journal of a Revolutionary Woman*; Jane Alpert (1981) *Growing Up Underground*.

17 For the less savoury aspects of the Weather Underground's interpersonal practices see also Maurice Isserman's (1987) *If I Had a Hammer. . .: the Death of the Old Left and the Birth of the New Left* and again the firsthand accounts of Susan Stern and Jane Alpert.

18 Except for pro-censorship and anti-pornography campaigns which have never deserted the moral high ground of Women's Liberation's critique of the Sexual Revolution, feminist debates on sexuality have moved on from a focus on the sexual exploitation of women to issues of fantasy and heterogeneous sexual identities. See for example *Feminist Review* (eds) (1987) *Sexuality: a Reader*; Ann Barr Snitow, Christine Stansell and Sharon Thompson (eds) (1984) *Desire: the Politics of Sexuality* and Carole S. Vance (ed.) (1984, rpt 1992) *Pleasure and Danger: Exploring Female Sexuality*. See for a re-evaluation of these debates also my essay '"It's My Party": Fictions of the Sexual Revolution'.

19 See also Chapter 1 for a discussion of *Daughter of Earth* and Marge Piercy's review of it.

20 The Utopian setting of some of Vida's rural retreats are reminiscent of Piercy's earlier Utopian novel, *Woman on the Edge of Time* which functions as an intertextual reference for the Utopian elements in *Vida*.

21 American literature has a rich tradition of stories of persecution and fugitive existence, notably in the slave-narratives such as those of Harriet Jacobs and Frederick Douglass, and in their twentieth-century counterparts such as Richard Wright's *Native Son*. The later chapters of Malcolm X's *Autobiography* and that of Angela Davis continue the theme of being hunted, which is also an aspect of Jewish autobiographies of the earlier part of the century, such as the first few chapters of Mary Antin's *The Promised Land* about the pogroms in Eastern Europe.

22 Marge Piercy 'A Dark Thread in the Weave' unpublished version of article in Rosenberg (ed.) (1989). Here Piercy explicitly makes this connection between Jewish paranoia and the Holocaust, as does Morris Dickstein when he writes of Joseph Heller's *Catch 22* as 'paranoia confirmed by history'; Dickstein (1977)

Gates of Eden: 14. In 'Dark Thread' furthermore Piercy explains her fascination with the resistance fighter (a theme revisited in her epic novel of the Second World War, *Gone to Soldiers*) and connects that fascination with being Jewish and with the desire for agency, for fighting back.

23 Sigmund Freud, Vol. I of (1966) *The Standard Edition of the Complete Psychological Works*: 209–10. My (cursory) treatment of paranoia in this chapter is also informed by Vol. XVI of *The Standard Edition*, entitled *Introductory Lectures on Psychoanalysis, Part III* and by a German collection on paranoia, which includes the famous case study of Herr Schreber; Sigmund Freud (1973) *Zwang, Paranoia und Perversion*.

24 Daniel Aaron describes this phenomenon as the use of history as props, in (1980) 'Fictionalizing the Past'.

25 See for an exposition of the argument with which Jameson (and Michèle Barrett in *Women's Oppression Today*) takes issue the collection edited by Derek Attridge, Geoff Bennington and Robert Young (1987) *Poststructuralism and the Question of History*, especially the 'Introduction' by Bennington and Young: 1–11 and Bennington's argument with British Marxism as exemplified in the work of Terry Eagleton in 'Demanding History': 15–29.

7 'CONTEXT IS ALL': BACKLASH FICTIONS OF THE 1980s

1 For criticism of Piercy's *Woman on the Edge of Time* (by far Piercy's most commented-upon novel) see: Nan Bowman Albinski (1988) *Women's Utopias in British and American Fiction*; Anne Cranny Francis (1990) *Feminist Fiction*; Sara Lefanu (1988) *In the Chinks of the World Machine*; Tom Moylan (1986) *Demand the Impossible*; Paulina Palmer (1989) *Contemporary Women's Fiction*; Ruby Rohrlich and Elaine Hoffman Baruch (eds) (1984) *Women in Search of Utopia*; and Patricia Waugh (1989) *Feminine Fictions*. My use of the term 'fantasy' is fairly loose and includes science fiction; for a more discriminating definition see Penny Florence's funny and highly idiosyncratic article (1990) 'The Liberation of Utopia'.

2 Charlotte Perkins Gilman (1892) *The Yellow Wallpaper*. In an interview Piercy said that *Woman on the Edge of Time* should not be read as a Utopian novel, since it does attempt to represent the transition from the old to the new society. Besides, she added, the ideas upon which Mattapoisett society is constructed are not new, but were all (in essence) already being practised in the Women's Movement: 'There is almost nothing there except the breeder not accessible now'; in (1977) 'An Interview with *Sandscript*': 100.

3 This blueprint for a new society in *Women on the Edge of Time* is, I think, modelled on Shulamith Firestone's final chapter in (1970) *The Dialectic of Sex*.

4 Nan Albinski for example writes of 'an infusion of optimism not equalled since the utopian golden age of the late nineteenth century'; Nan Bowman Albinski (1988) *Women's Utopias*: 159.

5 For histories of the New Right and its different ideological currents see: Sidney Blumenthal (1986) *The Rise of the Counter-Establishment*; and Pamela Johnston Conover and Virginia Gray (1983) *Feminism and the New Right*. For the perspective of the New Right see, for example, Midge Decter (1973) *The New Chastity*; and Nathan Glazer et al. (1983) 'Neoconservatism: Pro and Con'.

6 In (1986) *The Rise of the Counter-Establishment* Blumenthal gives an astute and complex analysis of this alliance between right wing thinkers, economic conservatives and Christian fundamentalists. I have had to simplify his account for the purposes of brevity and clarity.

7 See, again, Sidney Blumenthal (1986) *The Rise of the Counter-Establishment* and Susan Faludi (1991) *Backlash*. Gayle Greene gives an excellent account of the New Right's impact on social mores and feminist fiction in the final chapter of (1991) *Changing the Story*.

8 See for these data Rochelle Gatlin (1987) *American Women Since 1945*; Rosalind Pollack Petschesky (1984) *Abortion and Woman's Choice*; Mary P. Ryan (1983) *Womanhood in America*; and for the original documents Mary Beth Norton (ed.) (1989) *Major Problems in American Women's History: Documents and Essays*: Chapter 15.

9 See for a discussion of its genesis Susan Faludi (1991) *Backlash*: 266–78; also Mary Ryan (1983) *Womanhood in America*: 335.

10 As Allen Matusow argues in his history of 1960s liberalism, the process of forging a new anti-liberal consensus had begun long before Reaganism, with the campaigns for Nixon's election in 1968. Once the defence of American values in South-East Asia was no longer viable, the ideological offensive turned on the enemies within; Allen J. Matusow (1986) *The Unraveling of America*.

11 For feminist critiques of the New Right, especially on the abortion issue, see: Andrea Dworkin (1983) *Right Wing Women*; Deirdre English (1984) 'The Fear That Feminism Will Free Men First' and English (1981) 'The War Against Choice'; Susan Faludi (1991) *Backlash*; Myra Marx Ferree and Beth Hess (1985) *Controversy and Coalition*; Nancy Folbre (1983) 'Of Patriarchy Born'; Linda Gordon and Allen Hunter (1977–8) 'Sex, the Family and the New Right'; Virginia Sapiro (1986) 'The Women's Movement, Politics and Policy in the Reagan Era'; Judith Stacey (1986) 'Are Feminists Afraid to Leave Home?'. For an analysis of crisis in masculinity as a contributing factor to the rise of the New Right see Barbara Ehrenreich (1983) *The Hearts of Men*; and for left-wing pro-familism see Michael Lerner (1982) 'Recapturing the Family Issue'; and Barbara Epstein and Kate Ellis (1983) 'The Pro-Family Left in the United States'.

12 Roger Bromley (1986) 'Making memories: Politics and popular writings': 154. A revised version of this thesis was later published as (1988) *Lost Narratives*.

13 See also my discussion of the concept of praxis in Chapter 6.

14 See for the kind of prose that inspired this pastiche Norman Mailer (1963) 'The Case Against McCarthy', which I cited in my Introduction. Thoroughly middle class and highly critical of its women characters, McCarthy's *The Group* was rewritten by Piercy in feminist terms in *Braided Lives*.

15 *The Handmaid's Tale* constantly uses such references to feminist theory and women's writing, and it often uses them ironically and out of context.

16 Gayle Greene (1991) *Changing the Story*, Chapter IX 'Whatever Happened to Feminist Fiction?': 207–14.

17 In a personal communication, Gayle Greene argues with me that the Historical Notes are a warning to feminist critics to be better readers than these old boys and girls. This is, in a sense, the same disagreement she and I have over the role of feminism in Atwood's novel as well. Greene (and Coral Ann Howells) both read the critique of feminism as an argument that 'feminism has not been radical enough'. I wonder what that kind of 'radical' is, exactly, since it doesn't sit very easily with other aspects of *The Handmaid's Tale* (such as the so-called crisis in fertility), nor does it fit in with Greene's own analysis of *Cat's Eye*, where she finds Atwood's treatment of female vs. male power 'inexcusable'. I am tremendously grateful to Gayle Greene for her comments and to Coral Ann Howells with whom I have also discussed *The Handmaid's Tale*, but after careful consideration I think we have to agree to disagree on these points; Coral Ann Howells (1987) *Private and Fictional Worlds*: 65; Gayle Greene (1991) *Changing the Story*: 211.

18 See for example *The Handmaid's Tale*: 128, where Moira asserts that the pornographic films the handmaids are being shown as part of their induction into Gileadian ideology 'aren't real'. This passage draws on the pornography debate which raged in Anglo-American feminism during the early 1980s (pro- and anti-censorship; pro- and anti-alliances with the New Right, which is what Atwood suggests has happened here). See Andrea Dworkin (1981) *Pornography* and Catherine MacKinnon (1987) *Feminism Unmodified* for the pro-censorship position. For the libertarian line see *Feminist Review* (eds) (1987) *Sexuality*; Ann Barr Snitow et al. (eds) (1984) *Desire*; Marion Bower (1986) 'Daring to Speak Its Name: the Relationship of Women to Pornography'; Beverley Brown (1981) 'A Feminist Interest in Pornography'; Carla Freccero (1990) 'Notes of a Post – Sex Wars Theorizer'; Elizabeth Wilson (1983) 'The Context of "Between Pleasure and Danger"'; the papers of that conference, collected in Carole Vance (ed.) (1984) *Pleasure and Danger* and especially B. Ruby Rich (1983) 'Anti-Porn: Soft Issue, Hard World'.

19 Coral Ann Howells also discusses this passage, but again reads it differently; Howells (1987) *Private and Fictional Worlds*: 66.

20 The mock Latin phrase, carved by her predecessor, which Offred discovers in her room and interprets as a sign of resistance, has to be deciphered by the Commander who thus regains control over it ('Don't let the bastards grind you down'). Carolyn Heilbrun mentions in a different context that the poets Anne Sexton and Lois Ames wore this slogan, engraved on gold medallions, around their necks. Significantly Offred's predecessor committed suicide, like Plath and Sexton; Carolyn Heilbrun (1988b) *Writing a Woman's Life*: 72.

21 The history of eugenics in the US has always exploited fears about the disintegration of the family and a declining birth rate for racist, classist and sexist ends; see for example Angela Davis (1982) *Women, Race and Class*, and Linda Gordon (1974) *Woman's Body, Woman's Right*.

22 I am, however, indebted to Cora Kaplan for this idea, who mentioned it in an (as far as I am aware) unpublished paper, presented at the conference 'Feminist Criticism: the Next Decade' at the University of Southampton, 2 July 1988.

23 See for a discussion of the history and generic features of the slave-narratives the editors' introductions to Henry Louis Gates Jr (ed.) (1987a) *The Classic Slave Narratives* and Jean Fagan Yellin's edition (1987) of Harriet Jacobs's (1861) *Incidents in the Life of a Slave Girl*. A scene in which slaves are required to attend a public lynching (similar to the salvaging episode in *The Handmaid's Tale*), occurs in Margaret Walker's slavery novel (1966) *Jubilee*.

24 Terry McMillan's (1987) *Mama* is a realist tale of African-American poverty in which alcoholism and drug abuse, in true Bush/Reagan style, are presented as on a par with 'dependency on welfare checks' (e.g. addictions). The remedy for these ills is, evidently, to 'just say no', which handily brings social deprivation back to individual responsibility. In the final chapter of *Changing the Story*, Gayle Greene gives an excellent account of feminist retreat in 1980s white women's fiction, paying particular attention to the displacement of the woman writer as protagonist; Greene (1991) *Changing the Story*: 193–202.

25 See on the crisis in personal life Barbara Haber (1979) 'Is Personal Life Still a Political Issue?' and Judith Stacey (1986) 'Are Feminists Afraid to Leave Home?'.

26 Anna's narrative is suffused with guilt; she constantly longs for 'the purity of my old life and loneliness': 63.

27 Classical music serves as a metaphor for morality. A classical concert by Anna's students is described in terms of the peacefulness and serenity of a church service, whilst 1960s rock music is associated with sex and guilt; *The Good Mother*: 164, 7.

28 But Germaine Greer writes (in what has otherwise also been read as a pro-natalist/ backlash book): 'Feminists are often accused of downgrading motherhood. The accusation is ridiculous: motherhood hit rock bottom long before the new feminist wave broke. The wave itself was caused by the groundswell.' Germaine Greer (1984) *Sex and Destiny*: 13.

29 Anthony Perkins in *Psycho* is mentioned in so many words (190); others include surgeons, abortionists of course, the grandfather carving meat, and last but not least Leo Cutter, Anna's lover, who 'rips her life apart'.

CONCLUSION: THE FUTURE OF FEMINIST FICTION, OR, IS THERE A FEMINIST AESTHETIC?

1 In *Changing the Story*, Gayle Greene is much more pessimistic about the future of feminist fiction than I am, partly – as she admits- because of the time when her book was written, but partly also, I think, because she concentrates primarily on white women's writing where I agree the 'feminist' of feminist fiction has died a quiet death.

2 See in this context also Terry Eagleton's (1990) *The Ideology of the Aesthetic*, which goes about the question of art's autonomy and a pure, disembodied aesthetic dimension in a different way. For feminist critiques of male modernism, and a re-evaluation of the role of gender in female modernism, see for example: Shari Benstock (1987a) *Women of the Left Bank*; Sandra M. Gilbert and Susan Gubar (1987) *No Man's Land* Vol. I 'The War of the Words' and Vol. II 'Sex Wars'; Gillian Hanscombe and Virginia L. Smyers (1987) *Writing for Their Lives*; and Bonnie Kime Scott (ed.) (1990) *The Gender of Modernism*.

BIBLIOGRAPHY

Primary sources

Alpert, Jane (1981, rpt 1990) *Growing Up Underground*, New York: Citadel Press.

Alther, Lisa (1976, rpt 1977) *Kinflicks*, Harmondsworth: Penguin.

Angelou, Maya (1969, rpt 1984) *I Know Why the Caged Bird Sings*, London: Virago.

—— (1974, rpt 1985) *Gather Together in My Name*, London: Virago.

—— (1976, rpt 1985) *Singin' and Swingin' and Gettin' Merry Like Christmas*, London: Virago.

—— (1981, rpt 1986) *The Heart of a Woman*, London: Virago.

—— (1986, rpt 1987) *All God's Children Need Travelling Shoes*, London: Virago.

Antin, Mary (1910, rpt 1987) *The Promised Land*, Salem: Ayer.

Arnold, June (1975, rpt 1979) *Sister Gin*, London: Women's Press.

Atwood, Margaret (1985, rpt 1987) *The Handmaid's Tale*, London: Virago.

—— (1988, rpt 1990) *Cat's Eye*, London: Virago.

Baym, Nina et al. (eds) (1989) *The Norton Anthology of American Literature*, Vol. I, 3rd edn, London: W. W. Norton.

Belfrage, Sally (1965, rpt 1966) *Freedom Summer*, London: André Deutsch.

Brooks, Gwendolyn (1972) *Report from Part One*, Detroit: Broadside Press.

Brown, Rita Mae (1973, rpt 1978) *Rubyfruit Jungle*, London: Corgi.

Burke, Fielding (1932, rpt 1983) *Call Home the Heart*, Old Westbury: Feminist Press.

Cleaver, Eldridge (1968) *Soul on Ice*, New York: McGraw Hill.

Cross, Amanda (Carolyn Heilbrun) (1981) *Death in a Tenured Position*, New York: Ballantyne.

Davidson, Sara (1977, rpt 1978) *Loose Change: Three Women of the Sixties*, London: Fontana.

Davis, Angela (1988, rpt 1990) *An Autobiography*, London: Women's Press.

Davis, Rebecca Harding (1861, rpt 1989) 'Life in the Iron Mills' in Nina Baym et al. (eds) *The Norton Anthology of American Literature*: 2411–37.

Didion, Joan (1970, rpt 1973) *Play It As It Lays*, Harmondsworth: Penguin.

DiPrima, Diane (1968, rpt 1970) 'Revolutionary Letters' in Massimo Teodori (ed.) *The New Left*: 367–70.

Doctorow, E. L. (1971, rpt 1972) *The Book of Daniel*, London: MacMillan.

Douglass, Frederick (1845, rpt 1987) *Narrative of the Life of Frederick Douglass, an American Slave* in Henry Louis Gates Jr (ed.) *The Classic Slave Narratives*.

Duster, Alfreda M. (ed.) (1970) *Crusade for Justice: the Autobiography of Ida B. Wells*, London: University of Chicago Press.

Fauset, Jessie Redmon (1928, rpt 1985) *Plum Bun: a Novel without a Moral*, London: Pandora.

Franklin, Benjamin (1791, rpt 1989) *The Autobiography* in Nina Baym et al. (eds) *The Norton Anthology of American Literature*: 408–523.

French, Marilyn (1978) *The Women's Room*, London: Sphere.

—— (1980, rpt 1981) *The Bleeding Heart*, London: Sphere.

—— (1987, rpt 1988) *Her Mother's Daughter*, London: Pan.

Gates, Henry Louis Jr (ed.) (1987a) *The Classic Slave Narratives*, New York: New American Library.

Gilman, Charlotte Perkins (1892, rpt 1985) *The Yellow Wallpaper*, ed. Elaine Hedges, London: Virago.

Ginsberg, Allen (1956) *HOWL and Other Poems*, San Francisco: City Lights Books.

Giovanni, Nikki (1971, rpt 1983) *Gemini: an Extended Autobiographical Statement on My First Twenty Years of Being a Black Poet*, Harmondsworth: Penguin.

—— (cit. 1979) 'Nigger, Can You Kill' cited in Michele Wallace, *Black Macho*: 166–7.

Gold, Michael (1930a) *Jews without Money*, New York: Horace Liveright.

Herbst, Josephine (1935, rpt 1987) 'A Passport from Realengo' in Charlotte Nekola and Paula Rabinowitz (eds) *Writing Red*: 199–202.

—— (1936, rpt 1987) 'The Enemy' in Charlotte Nekola and Paula Rabinowitz (eds) *Writing Red*: 96–105.

—— (1939, rpt 1984) *Rope of Gold: a Novel of the Thirties*, New York: Feminist Press.

Hurston, Zora Neale (1924–42; 1985 rpt 1987) *Spunk*, London: Camden Press.

—— (1934, rpt 1987) *Jonah's Gourd Vine*, London: Virago.

—— (1937, rpt 1987) *Their Eyes Were Watching God*, London: Virago.

—— (1942, rpt 1986) *Dust Tracks on a Road*, London: Virago.

—— (1979) *I Love Myself When I Am Laughing . . . and Then Again When I Am Looking Mean and Impressive: a Zora Neale Hurston Reader*, ed. Alice Walker, New York: Feminist Press.

Jacobs, Harriet (Linda Brent) (1861, rpt 1987) *Incidents in the Life of a Slave Girl* in Henry Louis Gates Jr (ed.) *The Classic Slave Narratives*; and ed. Jean Fagan Yellin (1987) *Incidents in the Life of a Slave Girl. Written by Herself*, ed. Lydia Maria Child, London: Harvard University Press.

Jones, Gayl (1975, rpt 1988) *Corregidora*, London: Camden Press.

Jong, Erica (1973, rpt, 1974) *Fear of Flying*, London: Granada.

—— (1977, rpt 1978) *How To Save Your Own Life*, London: Granada.

Kaufman, Sue (1970) *Diary of a Mad Housewife*, New York: Bantam.

King, Mary (1987) *Freedom Song: a Personal History of the 1960s Civil Rights Movement*, New York: William Morrow.

Kingston, Maxine Hong (1976, rpt 1977) *The Woman Warrior*, Harmondsworth: Penguin.

Larsen, Nella (1928, 1929, rpt 1989) *Quicksand and Passing*, London: Serpent's Tail.

Lessing, Doris (1962, rpt 1973) *The Golden Notebook*, New York: Bantam.

LeSueur, Meridel (1935a, rpt 1987) 'Sequel to Love' in Charlotte Nekola and Paula Rabinowitz (eds) *Writing Red*: 36–8.

—— (1977, rpt 1982) *The Girl*, London: Women's Press.

—— (1982a) *Harvest & Song for My Time*, Minneapolis: West End Press and MEP Publications.

—— (1982b) *Ripening: Selected Work 1927–1984*, New York: Feminist Press.

Levertov, Denise (1987a, rpt 1988) *Breathing the Water*, London: Bloodaxe Books.

—— (1987b) 'Making Peace' in Denise Levertov, *Breathing the Water*: 41, and in Marge Piercy (ed.) *Early Ripening*: 137.

Lorde, Audre (1982) *Zami: a New Spelling of My Name*, London: Sheba.

Lurie, Alison (1975) *The War Between the Tates*, New York: Warner.

McCarthy, Mary (1963, rpt 1966) *The Group*, Harmondsworth: Penguin.

McMillan, Terry (1987, rpt 1988) *Mama*, London: Pan.

—— (1990, rpt 1991) *Disappearing Acts*, London: Transworld.

Mailer, Norman (1968) *The Armies of the Night: History as a Novel, the Novel as History*, London: Weidenfeld and Nicholson.

Malcolm X (1965) *The Autobiography of Malcolm X* with the assistance of Alex Haley, New York: Ballantyne.

Meulenbelt, Anja (1976, transl. 1980) *The Shame Is Over: a Political Life Story* (*De Schaamte Voorbij*), London: Women's Press.

Miller, Sue (1986, rpt 1987) *The Good Mother*, London: Pan.

—— (1990, rpt 1991) *Family Pictures*, Harmondsworth: Penguin.

Millett, Kate (1974, rpt 1977) *Flying*, New York: Alfred A. Knopf.

—— (1977) *Sita*, London: Virago.

Miner, Valerie (1982, rpt 1985) *Movement: a Novel in Stories*, London: Methuen.

—— (1986) *Women at War*, London: Methuen.

Moody, Anne (1968, rpt 1974) *Coming of Age in Mississippi*, London: Peter Owen.

Morrison, Toni (1973, rpt 1982) *Sula*, London: Triad Panther.

—— (1977, rpt 1986) *Song of Solomon*, London: Triad Grafton.

—— (1987) *Beloved*, New York: Signet.

Naylor, Gloria (1983, rpt 1990) *The Women of Brewster Place*, London: Minerva.

—— (1985, rpt 1986) *Linden Hills*, London: Methuen.

—— (1988) *Mama Day*, London: Century Hutchinson.

Nekola, Charlotte and Paula Rabinowitz (eds) (1987) *Writing Red: an Anthology of American Women Writers 1930–1940*, New York: Feminist Press at the City University of New York.

Olsen, Tillie (1974, rpt 1975) *Yonnondio: from the Thirties*, New York: Dell.

—— (1980a) *Tell Me a Riddle*, London: Virago.

Paretsky, Sara (1982, rpt 1987) *Indemnity Only*, Harmondsworth: Penguin.

—— (1987, rpt 1988) *Bitter Medicine*, Harmondsworth: Penguin.

Petry, Ann (1946, rpt 1986) *The Street*, London: Virago.

—— (1953, rpt 1988) *The Narrows*, Boston: Beacon Press.

Piercy, Marge (1969) *Going Down Fast*, New York: Fawcett Crest.

—— (1970a) *Dance the Eagle to Sleep*, New York: Fawcett Crest.

—— (1972, rpt 1987) *Small Changes*, Harmondsworth: Penguin.

—— (1973) *To Be of Use*, New York: Doubleday.

—— (1976a, rpt 1979) *Woman on the Edge of Time*, London: Women's Press.

—— (1978, rpt 1979) *The High Cost of Living*, London: Women's Press.

—— (1980a) *Vida*, London: Women's Press.

—— (1982a) *Braided Lives*, Harmondsworth: Penguin.

—— (ed.) (1987a) *Early Ripening: American Women's Poetry Now*, London: Pandora.

—— (1987b) *Gone to Soldiers*, London: Michael Joseph.

Plath, Sylvia (1965a, rpt 1968) *Ariel*, London: Faber and Faber.

—— (1965b, rpt 1968) 'Tulips' in Sylvia Plath *Ariel*: 10–12.

—— (1971, rpt 1972) *The Bell Jar*, New York: Bantam.

Raskin, Barbara (1988) *Hot Flashes*, London: Bantam.

Rukeyser, Muriel (1938, rpt 1987) 'Ann Burlak' in Charlotte Nekola and Paula Rabinowitz (eds) *Writing Red*: 135–8.

Russ, Joanna (1975, rpt 1985) *The Female Man*, London: Women's Press.

—— (1980, rpt 1987) *On Strike Against God*, London: Women's Press.

Shulman, Alix Kates (1972, rpt 1985) *Memoirs of an Ex-Prom Queen*, Chicago: Academy Chicago.

—— (1978, rpt 1980) *Burning Questions*, London: Fontana Collins.

—— (1981, rpt 1983) *On the Stroll*, London: Virago.

—— (1987) *In Every Woman's Life . . .* , New York: Ballantyne.

Smedley, Agnes (1929, rpt 1984) *Daughter of Earth*, London: Virago.

Stefan, Verena (1975, transl. 1979) *Shedding* (*Hautungen*), London: Women's Press.
Stern, Susan (1975) *With the Weathermen: the Personal Journal of a Revolutionary Woman*, New York: Doubleday.
Toomer, Jean (1923, rpt 1975) *Cane*, New York: Liveright.
—— (1925, rpt 1982) 'The Blue Meridian' in Darwin T. Turner (ed.) *The Wayward and the Seeking*: 214–34.
Turner, Darwin T. (ed.) (1982) *The Wayward and the Seeking: a Collection of Writings by Jean Toomer*, Washington DC: Howard University Press.
Walker, Alice (1970, rpt 1985) *The Third Life of Grange Copeland*, London: Women's Press.
—— (1973a, rpt 1984) 'Everyday Use' in Alice Walker, *In Love and Trouble*: 46–59.
—— (1973b, rpt 1984) *In Love and Trouble*, London: Women's Press.
—— (1973c, rpt 1984) 'The Revenge of Hannah Kemhuff' in Alice Walker, *In Love and Trouble*: 60–80.
—— (1976a, rpt 1982) *Meridian*, London: Women's Press.
—— (ed.) (1979a) *I Love Myself When I Am Laughing . . . and Then Again When I Am Looking Mean and Impressive: a Zora Neale Hurston Reader*, New York: Feminist Press.
—— (1982a, rpt 1985) 'Advancing Luna – and Ida B. Wells' in Alice Walker, *You Can't Keep a Good Woman Down*: 85–104.
—— (1982b, rpt 1983) *The Color Purple*, London: Women's Press.
—— (1982c, rpt 1985) *You Can't Keep a Good Woman Down*, London: Women's Press.
—— (1989, rpt 1990) *The Temple of My Familiar*, Harmondsworth: Penguin.
—— (1991) *Her Blue Body Everything I Know: Earthling Poems 1965–1990 Complete*, London: Women's Press.
—— (1992) *Possessing the Secret of Joy*, London: Women's Press Book Club and Jonathan Cape.
Walker, Margaret (1966, rpt 1967) *Jubilee*, New York: Bantam.
Wells, Ida B. (1970) *Crusade for Justice: the Autobiography of Ida B. Wells*, ed. Alfreda M. Duster, London: University of Chicago Press.
Williams, Sherley Anne (1986, rpt 1988) *Dessa Rose*, London: Futura.
Wilson, Barbara (1982, rpt 1987) *Ambitious Women*, London: Women's Press.
—— (1989) *The Dog Collar Murders*, London: Virago.
Wilson, Elizabeth (1982a) *Mirror Writing*, London: Virago.
Wings, Mary (1986) *She Came Too Late*, London: Women's Press.
Wright, Richard (1943) *Native Son*, Stockholm: Jan Forlag.
Yellin, Jean Fagan (ed.) (1987) Harriet Jacobs, *Incidents in the Life of a Slave Girl. Written By Herself*, London: Harvard University Press.

Secondary sources

Aaron, Daniel (1965) *Writers on the Left*, New York: Avon.
—— (1980) 'Fictionalizing the Past', *Partisan Review* 47, 2: 231–41.
Abbott, Sydney and Barbara Love (1972) *Sappho Was a Right On Woman: a Liberated Vision of Lesbianism*, New York: Stein & Day.
Abel, Elizabeth (1981) '(E)Merging Identities: the Dynamics of Female Friendship in Contemporary Fiction by Women', *Signs* 6, 3: 413–35.
——, Marianne Hirsch and E. Langland (eds) (1983) *The Voyage in: Fictions of Female Development*, London: University Press of New England.
Adams, Mary Louise (1989) 'There's No Place Like Home: on the Place of Identity in Feminist Politics', *Feminist Review* 31: 22–31.
Adorno, Theodor, et al. (1977) *Aesthetics and Politics*, ed. Fredric Jameson, London: Verso.

BIBLIOGRAPHY

Albert, Judith Clavir and Stewart Edward Albert (eds) (1984) *The 60s Papers: Documents of a Rebellious Decade*, New York: Praeger.

Albinski, Nan Bowman (1988) *Women's Utopias in British and American Fiction*, London: Routledge.

Anderson, Linda (ed.) (1990) *Plotting Change: Contemporary Women's Fiction*, London: Edward Arnold.

Angelou, Maya (1984) 'Shades and Slashes of Light', in Mari Evans (ed.) *Black Women Writers*: 3–5.

—— (1988) 'Maya Angelou Talking with Rosa Guy', in Mary Chamberlain (ed.) *Writing Lives*: 2–23.

Aronowitz, Stanley (1985) 'When the New Left Was New', in Sonya Sayres et al. (eds) *The 60s Without Apology*: 11–43.

Attridge, Derek, Geoff Bennington and Robert Young (eds) (1987) *Poststructuralism and the Question of History*, Cambridge: Cambridge University Press.

Auerbach, Nina (1978) *Communities of Women: an Idea in Fiction*, Cambridge, Mass.: Harvard University Press.

Baker, Houston A. Jr (1987) *Modernism and the Harlem Renaissance*, Chicago: University of Chicago Press.

Baldwin, James (1955, rpt 1968) 'Autobiographical Notes', in Abraham Chapman (ed.) *Black Voices*: 316–20.

Barker, Francis et al. (eds) (1983) *The Politics of Theory*, Conference on the Sociology of Literature 1982, Colchester: University of Essex.

Barnes, Annette (1977) 'Female Criticism: a Prologue', in Arlyn Diamond and Lee R. Edwards (eds) *The Authority of Experience*: 1–15.

Barnouw, Dagmar (1977) 'Disorderly Company: from *The Golden Notebook* to *The Four-Gated City*', in Patricia Meyer Spacks (ed.) *Contemporary Women Novelists*: 30–54.

Barrett, Michèle (1980) *Women's Oppression Today: Problems in Marxist Feminist Analysis*, London: Verso.

—— (1985) 'Ideology and the Cultural Production of Gender', in Judith Newton and Deborah Rosenfelt (eds) *Feminist Criticism and Social Change*: 65–84.

Barth, John (1967, rpt 1977) 'The Literature of Exhaustion', in Malcolm Bradbury (ed.) *The Novel Today*: 70–83.

Battersby, Christine (1989) *Gender and Genius: Towards a Feminist Aesthetic*, London: Women's Press.

Beal, Frances M. (1970) 'Double Jeopardy: to Be Black and Female', in Robin Morgan (ed.) *Sisterhood Is Powerful*: 382–96.

Bell, Bernard (1987) *The Afro-American Novel and Its Tradition*, Amherst: University of Massachusetts Press.

Belsey, Catherine (1980) *Critical Practice*, New Accents, London: Methuen.

—— (1985) 'Constructing the Subject; Deconstructing the Text', in Judith Newton and Deborah Rosenfelt (eds) *Feminist Criticism and Social Change*: 45–64.

—— and Jane Moore (eds) (1989) *The Feminist Reader: Essays in Gender and the Politics of Literary Criticism*, London: Macmillan.

Bennington, Geoff (1987) 'Demanding History', in Derek Attridge et al. (eds.) *Poststructuralism and the Question of History*: 15–29.

—— and Robert Young (1987) 'Introduction: Posing the Question', in Derek Attridge et al. (eds) *Poststructuralism and the Question of History*: 1–11.

Benstock, Shari (1987a) *Women of the Left Bank: Paris 1900–1940*, London: Virago.

—— (ed.) (1987b) *Issues in Feminist Literary Scholarship*, Bloomington: Indiana University Press.

—— (ed.) (1988) *The Private Self: Theory and Practice of Women's Autobiographical Writings*, London: Routledge.

Benveniste, Emile (1971a) *Problems in General Linguistics*, Miami: University of Miami Press.

—— (1971b) 'Subjectivity in Language', in Emile Benveniste, *Problems in General Linguistics*: 222–9.

a Berkeley Sister (n.d. rpt 1984) 'To a White Male Radical', in Judith Clavir Albert and Stewart Edward Albert (eds) *The 60s Papers*: 517–19.

Bernal, Martin (1987) *Black Athena: the Afro-Asiatic Roots of Classical Civilization*, London: Free Association Books.

Bernheimer, Charles and Claire Kahane (eds) (1985) *In Dora's Case: Freud-Hysteria-Feminism*, London: Virago.

Bethel, Lorraine (1982) 'This Infinity of Conscious Pain: Zora Neale Hurston and the Black Female Literary Tradition', in Gloria T. Hull et al. (eds) *But Some of Us Are Brave*: 176–88.

Bhavnani, Kum Kum and Angela Y. Davis (1989) 'Complexity, Activism, Optimism', *Feminist Review* 31: 66–81.

Black Women's Liberation Group, Mount Vernon, New York (1970) 'Statement on Birth Control', in Robin Morgan (ed.) *Sisterhood Is Powerful*: 404–6.

Blackburn, Regina (1980) 'In Search of the Black Female Self: African-American Women's Autobiography and Ethnicity', in Estelle Jelinek (ed.) *Women's Autobiography*: 133–48.

Blandford, Linda (1986) 'Interview with Marilyn French', *The Guardian* January 22: 24.

Bloom Harold (ed.) (1986) *Zora Neale Hurston*, Modern Critical Views, New York: Chelsea House.

Blotner, Joseph L. (1955, rpt 1979) *The Modern Political Novel*, Westport, Conn.: Greenwood Press.

—— (1966) *The Modern American Political Novel*, University of Texas Press.

Blumenthal, Sidney (1986) *The Rise of the Counter-Establishment: from Conservative Ideology to Political Power*, New York: Times Books.

Bookchin, Murray (1985) 'Between the 30s and the 60s', in Sonya Sayres et al. (eds) *The 60s Without Apology*: 247–51.

Boston Women's Health Collective (1971, 1983) *Our Bodies, Ourselves: a Health Book by and for Women*, Harmondsworth: Penguin.

Bouchier, David (1983) *The Feminist Challenge: the Movement for Women's Liberation in Britain and the USA*, London: Macmillan.

Boumelha, Penny (1990) 'Realism and the Ends of Feminism', in Susan Sheridan (ed.) *Grafts*: 77–92.

Bower, Marion (1986) 'Daring to Speak Its Name: the Relationship of Women to Pornography', *Feminist Review* 24: 40–56.

Boyars, Robert (1985) *Atrocity and Amnesia: the Political Novel Since 1945*, Oxford: Oxford University Press.

Bradbury, Malcolm (ed.) (1977) *The Novel Today: Contemporary Writers on Modern Fiction*, London: Fontana.

Braidotti, Rosi (1989) 'The Politics of Ontological Difference', in Teresa Brennan (ed.) *Between Feminism and Psychoanalysis*: 89–105.

Braxton, Joanne M. (1990) 'Ancestral Presence: the Outraged Mother Figure in Contemporary Afra-American Writing', in Joanne M. Braxton and Andrée Nicola McLaughlin (eds) *Wild Women in the Whirlwind*: 299–315.

—— and Andrée Nicola McLaughlin (eds) (1990) *Wild Women in the Whirlwind: Afra-American Culture and the Contemporary Literary Renaissance*, London: Serpent's Tail.

Breines, Wini (1979) 'A Review Essay' [of Sara Evans' *Personal Politics*], *Feminist Studies* 5, 3: 496–506.

Brennan, Teresa (ed.) (1989) *Between Feminism and Psychoanalysis*, London: Routledge.

Brewster, Ben (1976) 'The Soviet State, the Communist Party and the Arts 1917–1936', *Red Letters* 3: 1–12.

Brodzki, Bella and Celeste Schenck (eds) (1988) *Life/Lines: Theorizing Women's Autobiography*, London: Cornell University Press.

Bromley, Roger (1986) 'Making memories. Politics and popular writings: the representation of the period 1918–1945 in recent popular cultural forms', unpublished Ph.D. thesis, University of Sussex.

—— (1988) *Lost Narratives: Popular Fictions, Politics and Recent History*, London: Routledge.

Brown, Beverley (1981) 'A Feminist Interest in Pornography: Some Modest Proposals', *m/f* 5/6: 5–18.

Brown, Cheryl L. and Karen Olson (eds) (1978) *Feminist Criticism: Essays in Theory, Poetry and Prose*, Metuchen, NJ: Scarecrow Press.

Brownmiller, Susan (1975) *Against Our Will: Men, Women and Rape*, London: Secker and Warburg.

Brunsdon, Charlotte (1986) *Films for Women*, London: British Film Institute.

Bruss, Elizabeth W. (1976) *Autobiographical Acts: the Changing Situation of a Literary Genre*, London: Johns Hopkins University Press.

Cade, Toni (ed.) (1970) *The Black Woman: an Anthology*, New York: Mentor.

Cameron, Deborah (1985) *Feminism and Linguistic Theory*, London: Macmillan.

Carby, Hazel V. (1987) *Reconstructing Womanhood: the Emergence of the Afro-American Woman Novelist*, Oxford: Oxford University Press.

Carmichael, Stokely (SNCC) (1966, rpt 1984) 'What We Want', in Judith Clavir Albert and Stewart Edward Albert (eds) *The 60s Papers*: 117–18.

Carr, Helen (1988) 'In Other Words: Native American Women's Autobiography', in Bella Brodzki and Celeste Schenck (eds) *Life/Lines*: 131–53.

Carroll, Constance (1973, rpt 1982) 'Three Is a Crowd: the Dilemma of the Black Woman in Higher Education', in Glora T. Hull et al. (eds) *All the Women Are White*: 175–82.

Carroll, Peter N. and David W. Noble (1977, rpt 1984) *The Free and the Unfree: a New History of the United States*, Harmondsworth: Penguin.

Carson, Clayborne (1982) *In Struggle: SNCC and the Black Awakening of the 1960s*, Cambridge, Mass.: Howard University Press.

—— et al. (eds) (1991) *Eyes on the Prize: the Civil Rights Reader*, Harmondsworth: Penguin.

Chamberlain, Mary M. (ed.) (1988) *Writing Lives: Conversations between Women Writers*, London: Virago.

Chapman, Abraham (ed.) (1968) *Black Voices: an Anthology of Afro-American Literature*, New York: Mentor.

Chinosole (1990) 'Audre Lorde and the Matrilineal Diaspora: "Moving History beyond Nightmare into the Future"', in Joanne M. Braxton and Andrée Nicola McLaughlin (eds) *Wild Women in the Whirlwind*: 379–93.

Christian, Barbara (1980) *Black Women Novelists: the Development of a Tradition, 1982–1976*, London: Greenwood Press.

—— (1985) *Black Feminist Criticism: Perspectives on Black Women Writers*, New York: Pergamon Press.

Cixous, Hélène and Catherine Clément (1975, transl. 1986) *The Newly Born Woman*, Manchester: Manchester University Press.

Cluster, Dick (ed.) (1979) *They Should Have Served That Cup of Coffee*, Boston: South End Press.

Cohen, Mary (1977) '"Out of the Chaos, a New Kind of Strength": Doris Lessing's

The Golden Notebook', in Arlyn Diamond and Lee R. Edwards (eds) *The Authority of Experience*: 178–93.

Combahee River Collective (1977, rpt 1982) 'A Black Feminist Statement', in Gloria T. Hull et al. (eds) *All the Women Are White*: 13–22.

Conover, Pamela Johnston and Virginia Gray (1983) *Feminism and the New Right: Conflict over the American Family*, New York: Praeger.

Conroy, Jack and Curt Johnson (eds) (1973) *Writers in Revolt. The Anvil Anthology*, New York: Lawrence Hill.

Cornillon, Susan Koppelman (1973a) 'The Fiction of Fiction', in Susan Koppelman Cornillon (ed.) *Images of Women in Fiction*: 113–30.

—— (ed.) (1973b) *Images of Women in Fiction: Feminist Perspectives*, Bowling Green, Ohio: Bowling Green University Press.

Coward, Rosalind (1980, rpt 1985) 'Are Women's Novels Feminist Novels?', in Elaine Showalter (ed.) *The New Feminist Criticism*: 225–39.

—— (1989) 'The True Story of How I Became My Own Person', in Catherine Belsey and Jane Moore (eds) *The Feminist Reader*: 35–47.

Cowie, Elisabeth, et al. (1981) 'Representation vs. Communication', in Feminist Anthology Collective (eds) *No Turning Back*: 238–45.

Cudjoe, Selwyn R. (1985) 'Maya Angelou and the Autobiographical Statement', in Mari Evans (ed.) *Black Women Writers*: 6–24.

Culley, Margo (ed.) (1992) *American Women's Autobiography: Fea(s)ts of Memory*, Wisconsin Studies in American Autobiography, Madison: University of Wisconsin Press.

Cunliffe, Marcus (1986) *The Literature of the United States*, Harmondsworth: Penguin.

Dahlerup, Drude (1986a) 'Is the New Women's Movement Dead?', in Drude Dahlerup (ed.) *The New Women's Movement*: 217–44.

—— (ed.) (1986b) *The New Women's Movement: Feminism and Political Power in Europe and the USA*, London: SAGE.

Davis, Angela (1982) *Women, Race and Class*, London: Women's Press.

de Beauvoir, Simone (1949, rpt 1984) *The Second Sex* transl. and ed. H. M. Parshley, Harmondsworth: Penguin.

Dearborn, Mary V. (1986) *Pocahontas's Daughters: Gender and Ethnicity in American Culture*, Oxford: Oxford University Press.

Decter, Midge (1973) *The New Chastity and Other Arguments against Women's Liberation*, London: Wildwood House.

Dehler, Kathleen (1978) 'The Need To Tell All: a Comparison of Historical and Modern Feminist "Confessional" Writing', in Cheryl L. Brown and Karen Olson (eds) *Feminist Criticism*: 339–52.

Delmar, Rosalind (1984) 'Afterword', in Agnes Smedley, *Daughter of Earth*: 271–9.

Demetrakopoulos, Stephanie A. (1980) 'The Metaphysics of Matrilinearism in Women's Autobiography: Studies of Mead's *Blackberry Winter*, Hellman's *Pentimento*, Angelou's *I Know Why the Caged Bird Sings*, and Kingston's *The Woman Warrior*', in Estelle C. Jelinek (ed.) *Women's Autobiography*: 180–205.

Dennis, Peggy (1979) 'A Response to Ellen Kay Trimberger's Essay "Women in the Old and New Left"', *Feminist Studies* 5, 3: 451–60.

Diamond, Arlyn and Lee R. Edwards (eds) (1977) *The Authority of Experience: Essays in Feminist Criticism*, Amherst: University of Massachusetts Press.

Dickstein, Morris (1977) *Gates of Eden: American Culture in the Sixties*, New York: Basic Books.

Doane, Mary Ann, Patricia Mellencamp and Linda Williams (eds) (1984) *Revision: Essays in Feminist Film Criticism*, Los Angeles: American Film Institute.

Doherty, Thomas P. (1980) 'American Autobiography and Ideology', in Albert E. Stone (ed.) *The American Autobiography*: 95–108.

DuBois, W. E. B. (1903, rpt 1968) *The Souls of Black Folk*, in John Hope Franklin (ed.) *Three Negro Classics*: 209–389.

Dudovitz, Resa L. (1990) *The Myth of Superwoman: Women's Bestsellers in France and the United States*, London: Routledge.

Duncker, Patricia (1992) *Sisters and Strangers: an Introduction to Contemporary Feminist Fiction*, Oxford: Blackwell.

Dworkin, Andrea (1974) *WomanHating*, New York: Dutton.

—— (1981) *Pornography: Men Possessing Women*, London: Women's Press.

—— (1983) *Right Wing Women*, London: Women's Press.

Eagleton, Mary (ed.) (1986) *Feminist Literary Theory: a Reader*, Oxford: Blackwell.

Eagleton, Terry (1983) *Literary Theory: an Introduction*, Oxford: Blackwell.

—— (1990) *The Ideology of the Aesthetic*, Oxford: Blackwell.

Echols, Alice (1984, rpt 1992) 'The Taming of the Id: Feminist Sexual Politics 1968–1983', in Carole S. Vance (ed.) *Pleasure and Danger*: 50–72.

Ecker, Gisela (ed.) (1985) *Feminist Aesthetics*, London: Women's Press.

Ehrenreich, Barbara (1983) *The Hearts of Men: American Dreams and the Flight from Commitment*, London: Pluto Press.

Eisenstein, Zillah R. (ed.) (1979) *Capitalist Patriarchy and the Case for Socialist Feminism*, London: Monthly Review Press.

Ellison, Ralph (1941) 'Recent Negro Fiction', *New Masses* August 5.

Ellmann, Mary (1968) *Thinking about Women*, New York: Harcourt Brace.

English, Deirdre (1981) 'The War Against Choice: Inside the Anti-Abortion Movement', in *Mother Jones*, Vol. VI, no. 11, February–March: 567–88.

—— (1984) 'The Fear That Feminism Will Free Men First', in Ann Barr Snitow et al. (eds) *Desire*: 97–102.

Epstein, Barbara and Kate Ellis (1983) 'The Pro-Family Left in the United States: Two Comments', *Feminist Review* 14: 35–50.

Evans, Mari (ed.) (1983, rpt 1985) *Black Women Writers: Arguments and Interviews*, London: Pluto.

Evans, Nancy Burr (1973) 'The Value and Peril of Reading Women Writers', in Susan Koppelman Cornillon (ed.) *Images of Women in Fiction*: 308–14.

Evans, Sara (1979, rpt 1980) *Personal Politics: the Roots of Women's Liberation in the Civil Rights Movement and the New Left*, New York: Vintage Books.

Faderman, Lillian (1981, rpt 1982) *Surpassing the Love of Men: Friendship and Love between Women from the Renaissance to the Present*, London: Junction.

—— (1992) *Odd Girls and Twilight Lovers: a History of Lesbian Life in Twentieth Century America*, Harmondsworth: Penguin.

Faludi, Susan (1991, rpt 1992) *Backlash: the Undeclared War against Women*, London: Chatto and Windus.

Faulkner, Peter (ed.) (1986) *A Modernist Reader: Modernism in England 1910–1930*, London: Batsford.

Felman, Shoshana (ed.) (1982) *Literature and Psychoanalysis. The Question of Reading: Otherwise*, London: Johns Hopkins University Press.

Felski, Rita (1989) *Beyond Feminist Aesthetics: Feminist Literature and Social Change*, London: Hutchinson Radius.

Feminist Anthology Collective (eds) (1981) *No Turning Back: Writings from the Women's Liberation Movement 1975–1980*, London: Women's Press.

Feminist Review (eds) (1987) *Sexuality: a Reader*, London: Virago.

Ferguson, Mary Anne (1983) 'The Female Novel of Development and the Myth of Psyche', in Elizabeth Abel et al. (eds) *The Voyage in*: 228–43.

Ferree, Myra Marx and Beth Hess (1985) *Controversy and Coalition: the New Feminist Movement*, Boston: Twayne.

BIBLIOGRAPHY

Fetterley, Judith (1978) *The Resisting Reader: a Feminist Approach to American Fiction*, Bloomington: Indiana University Press.

Firestone, Shulamith (1970, rpt 1979) *The Dialectic of Sex: the Case for Feminist Revolution*, London: Women's Press.

Florence, Penny (1990) 'The Liberation of Utopia or Is Science Fiction the Ideal Contemporary Women's Form', in Linda Anderson (ed.) *Plotting Change*: 65–83.

Folbre, Nancy (1983) 'Of Patriarchy Born: the Political Economy of Fertility Decisions', *Feminist Studies* 9, 2: 61–84.

Folsom, Michael (1972) (ed.) *Mike Gold: a Literary Anthology*, New York: International Publishers.

Ford, Nick Aaron (1950, rpt 1969) 'A Blueprint for Negro Authors', in Addison Gayle Jr (ed.) *Black Expression*: 276–80.

Foulkes, A. P. (1983) *Literature and Propaganda*, New Accents, London: Methuen.

Fox-Genovese, Elizabeth (1987) 'To Write My Self: the Autobiographies of Afro-American Women', in Shari Benstock (ed.) *Issues in Feminist Literary Scholarship*: 161–80.

—— (1988) '"My Statue, My Self": Autobiographical Writings of Afro-American Women', in Shari Benstock (ed.) *The Private Self*: 63–89.

Francis, Anne Cranny (1990) *Feminist Fiction: Feminist Uses of Generic Fiction*, Cambridge: Polity.

Franklin, John Hope (ed.) (1965) *Three Negro Classics*, New York: Avon.

Freccero, Carla (1990) 'Notes of a Post – Sex Wars Theorizer', in Marianne Hirsch and Evelyn Fox Keller (eds) *Conflicts in Feminism*: 305–25.

Freeman, Jo (1971) 'The Revolution Is Happening in Our Minds', in June Sochen (ed.) *The New Feminism*: 149–60.

—— (1975) *The Politics of Women's Liberation: a Case-Study of an Emerging Social Movement and Its Relation to the Policy Process*, New York: David McKay & Company.

Freud, Sigmund (1966) *The Standard Edition of the Complete Psychological Works*, Vols I and XVI, transls and eds James Strachey and Anna Freud, London: Hogarth Press and the Institute of Psychoanalysis.

—— (1973) *Zwang, Paranoia und Perversion*, Frankfurt a/M: S. Fischer Verlag.

—— (1981) *On Sexuality: Three Essays on the Theory of Sexuality and Other Works*, Penguin Freud Library 7, Harmondsworth: Penguin.

—— and Joseph Breuer (1893–1895, rpt n.d.) *Studies on Hysteria*, transls and eds James Strachey and Anna Freud, New York: Basic Books.

Friedan, Betty (1963, rpt 1982) *The Feminine Mystique*, Harmondsworth: Penguin.

—— (1982) *The Second Stage*, London: Michael Joseph.

Fritz, Leah (1979) *Dreamers and Dealers: an Intimate Appraisal of the Women's Movement*, Boston: Beacon Press.

Fuller, Hoyt W. (1968, rpt 1969) 'Towards a Black Aesthetic', in Addison Gayle Jr (ed.) *Black Expression*: 263–70.

Gado, Frank (ed.) (1973) *First Person: Conversations on Writers and Writing*, Schenectady, NY: Union College Press.

Gallop, Jane (1983) '*Quand Nos Lèvres S'Ecrivent*: Irigaray's Body Politic', *Romanic Review* LXXIV, 1: 77–83.

—— (1985) 'Keys to Dora', in Charles Bernheimer and Claire Kahane (eds) *In Dora's Case*: 200–20.

Gardiner, Judith Kegan (1978) 'The Heroine as Her Author's Daughter', in Cheryl L. Brown and Karen Olson (eds) *Feminist Criticism*: 244–53.

—— (1981) 'The (Us)es of (I)Dentity: a Response to Abel on "(E)Merging Identities"', *Signs* 6, 3: 436–44.

Garner, Shirley Nelson, Claire Kahane and Madelon Sprengnether (eds) (1985) *The (M)Other Tongue: Essays in Feminist Psychoanalytic Interpretation*, London: Cornell.

Gates, Henry Louis, Jr (1986) *'Race', Writing and Difference*, Chicago: University of Chicago Press.

—— (1987b) 'The Blackness of Blackness: a Critique of the Sign and the Signifying Monkey', in Henry Louis Gates Jr (ed.) *Figures in Black*: 235–76.

—— (ed.) (1987c) *Figures in Black: Words, Signs and the 'Racial' Self*, New York: Oxford University Press.

Gatlin, Rochelle (1987) *American Women Since 1945*, London: Macmillan.

Gayle, Addison, Jr (1968, rpt 1969) 'Perhaps Not So Soon One Morning', in Addison Gayle Jr (ed.) *Black Expression*: 280–8.

—— (ed.) (1969) *Black Expression: Essays by and about Black Americans in the Creative Arts*, New York: Weybright and Talley.

Gerrard, Nicci (1989) *Into the Mainstream: How Feminism Has Changed Women's Writing*, London: Pandora.

Giddings, Paula (1984, rpt 1985) *When and Where I Enter: the Impact of Black Women on Race and Sex in America*, New York: Bantam.

Gilbert, James (1985) 'New Left, Old America', in Sonya Sayres et al. (eds) *The 60s without Apology*: 224–7.

Gilbert, Sandra M. and Susan Gubar (1987) *No Man's Land: the Place of the Woman Writer in the Twentieth Century*, Vol. I 'The War of the Words', Vol. II 'Sex Wars', London: Yale University Press.

Girgus, Sam B. (ed.) (1981) *The American Self: Myth, Ideology and Popular Culture*, Albuquerque: University of New Mexico Press.

Gitlin, Todd (1980) *The Whole World Is Watching: Mass Media in the Making & Unmaking of the New Left*, Berkeley: University of California Press.

—— (1987) *The Sixties: Years of Hope, Days of Rage*, New York: Bantam.

Glazer, Nathan, Peter Steinfels, James Q. Wilson, Norman Birnbaum (1983) 'Neoconservatism: Pro and Con', in Edith Kurzweil and William Phillips (eds) *Writers and Politics*: 302–26.

Gledhill, Christine (1984) 'Recent Developments in Feminist Film Criticism', in Mary Ann Doane et al. (eds) *Revision*: 18–28.

Gold, Michael (1921, rpt 1972) 'Towards Proletarian Art', in Michael Folsom (ed.) *Mike Gold*: 62–70.

—— (1924, rpt 1972) 'O Californians! O Ladies and Gentlemen!', in Michael Folsom (ed.) *Mike Gold*: 117–25.

—— (1928, rpt 1972) 'Ernest Hemingway: White Collar Poet', in Michael Folsom (ed.) *Mike Gold*: 154–61.

—— (1929a, rpt 1972) 'Go Left, Young Writers!', in Michael Folsom (ed.) *Mike Gold*: 186–9.

—— (1929b, rpt, 1972) 'Letter from a Clam-Digger', in Michael Folsom (ed.) *Mike Gold*: 190–3.

—— (1930b, rpt 1972) 'Proletarian Realism', in Michael Folsom (ed.) *Mike Gold*: 203–8.

—— (1941, rpt 1972) 'The Second American Renaissance', in Michael Folsom (ed.) *Mike Gold*: 243–54.

—— (1972) *Mike Gold: a Literary Anthology*, ed. Michael Folsom, New York: International Publishers.

Gordon, Linda (1974, rpt 1976) *Woman's Body, Woman's Right: a Social History of Birth Control in America*, Harmondsworth: Penguin.

—— (1979) 'The Struggle for Reproductive Freedom: Three Stages of Feminism', in Zillah R. Eisenstein (ed.) *Capitalist Patriarchy*: 107–32.

—— and Allen Hunter (1977–8) 'Sex, the Family and the New Right: Anti-Feminism as a Political Force', *Radical America* 11–12: 9–25.

222

Greene, Gayle (1991) *Changing the Story: Feminist Fiction and the Tradition*, Chicago: University of Chicago Press.

Greer, Germaine (1977) 'Into the Acid Bath' [review of Lisa Alther's *Kinflicks*], *The Times* 19 June.

—— (1984) *Sex and Destiny: the Politics of Human Fertility*, New York: Harper & Row.

Guy, Rosa (1988) 'Maya Angelou Talking with Rosa Guy', in Mary Chamberlain (ed.) *Writing Lives*: 2–23.

Gwaltney, John Langston (1980) *Drylongso: a Self-Portrait of Black America*, New York: Random House.

Haber, Barbara (1979) 'Is Personal Life Still a Political Issue?', *Feminist Studies* 5, 3: 417–30.

Hall, Jacqueline Dowd (1984) '"The Mind That Burns in Each Body": Women, Rape and Racial Violence', in Ann Barr Snitow et al. (eds) *Desire*: 339–60.

Hanisch, Carol (1968, rpt 1971) 'What Can Be Learned: a Critique of the Miss America Protest', in Leslie B. Tanner (ed.) *Voices from Women's Liberation*: 132–6.

Hanscombe, Gillian and Virginia L. Smyers (1987) *Writing for Their Lives: the Modernist Women 1910–1940*, London: Women's Press.

Harrington, Michael (1962) *The Other America*, New York: Macmillan.

Harrison, Cynthia (1988) *On Account of Sex: the Politics of Women's Issues*, Berkeley: University of California Press.

Harriss, Kathryn (1989) 'New Alliances: Feminism in the Eighties', *Feminist Review* 31: 34–54.

Hayden, Tom, et al. (1962, rpt 1987) 'SDS: Port Huron Statement', in James Miller, *Democracy Is in the Streets*: 329–74.

Heilbrun, Carolyn G. (1988a) 'Non-Autobiographies of "Privileged" Women: England and America', in Bella Brodzki and Celeste Schenck (eds) *Life/Lines*: 62–76.

—— (1988b) *Writing a Woman's Life*, London: Women's Press.

Hewlett, Sylvia Ann (1987) *A Lesser Life: the Myth of Women's Liberation*, London: Sphere.

Hirsch, Marianne and Evelyn Fox-Keller (eds) (1990) *Conflicts in Feminism*, London: Routledge.

Hole, Judith and Ellen Levine (1971) *Rebirth of Feminism*, New York: Quadrangle.

Homans, Margaret (1983) '"Her Very Own Howl": the Ambiguities of Representation in Recent Women's Fiction', *Signs* 9, 2: 186–205.

Homberger, Eric (1986) *American Writers and Radical Politics, 1900–1939: Equivocal Commitments*, London: Macmillan.

hooks, bell (Gloria Watkins) (1982) *Ain't I a Woman: Black Women and Feminism*, London: Pluto Press.

—— (1990a) 'Aesthetic Inheritances: History Worked by Hand', in bell hooks, *Yearning*: 115–22.

—— (1990b) 'An Aesthetic of Blackness: Strange and Oppositional', in bell hooks, *Yearning*: 103–13.

—— (1990c) 'Liberation Scenes: Speak This Yearning', in bell hooks, *Yearning*: 1–14.

—— (1990d) 'The Politics of Radical Black Subjectivity', in bell hooks, *Yearning*: 15–22.

—— (1990e) 'Saving Black Folk Culture: Zora Neale Hurston as Anthropologist and Writer', in bell hooks, *Yearning*: 135–43.

—— (1990f) *Yearning: Race, Gender and Cultural Politics*, Boston: South End Press.

Howe, Florence (1973) 'Feminism and Literature', in Susan Koppelman Cornillon (ed.) *Images of Women in Fiction*: 253–77.

Howe, Irving (1957) *Politics and the Novel*, Cleveland, Ohio: Meridian.

Howells, Coral Ann (1987) *Private and Fictional Worlds: Canadian Women Novelists of the 1970s and 1980s*, London: Methuen.

Huf, Linda (1985) *A Portrait of the Artist as a Young Woman: the Writer as Heroine in American Literature*, New York: Frederick Ungar.

Huggins, Nathan (1971) *The Harlem Renaissance*, New York: Oxford University Press.

Hull, Gloria T., Patricia Bell Scott and Barbara Smith (eds) (1982) *All the Women Are White, All the Men Are Black, But Some of Us Are Brave: Black Women's Studies*, New York: Feminist Press.

Hurston, Zora Neale (1928, rpt 1979) 'How It Feels To Be Colored Me', in Alice Walker (ed.) *I Love Myself*: 152–5.

—— (1935, rpt 1990) *Mules and Men*, New York: Harper Collins.

Hutchins, Grace (1934a, rpt 1987) 'The Double Burden', in Charlotte Nekola and Paula Rabinowitz (eds) *Writing Red*: 335–9.

—— (1934b) 'Women under Capitalism', in Charlotte Nekola and Paula Rabinowitz (eds) *Writing Red*: 329–34.

Ickstadt, Heinz, Rob Kroes and Brian Lee (eds) (1987) *The Thirties: Politics and Culture in a Time of Broken Dreams*, European Contributions to American Studies XII, Amsterdam: Free University Press.

Ickringill, Steve (ed.) (1990) *Looking Inward Looking Outward: from the 1930s through the 1940s*, European Contributions to American Studies XVIII, Amsterdam: Free University Press.

Inman, Mary (1940a) 'The Code of a Class', in Charlotte Nekola and Paula Rabinowitz (eds) *Writing Red*: 312–15.

—— (1940b) 'Manufacturing Femininity', in Charlotte Nekola and Paula Rabinowitz (eds) *Writing Red*: 304–7.

—— (1940c) 'The Pivot of the System', in Charlotte Nekola and Paula Rabinowitz (eds) *Writing Red*: 308–11.

Isserman, Maurice (1987) *If I Had a Hammer...: the Death of the Old Left and the Birth of the New Left*, New York: Basic Books.

Jacobus, Mary (ed.) (1979) *Women Writing and Writing about Women*, London: Croom Helm.

Jaffe, Harold and John Tytell (eds) (1970) *The American Experience: a Radical Reader*, New York: Harper and Row.

Jameson, Fredric (ed.) (1977) *Aesthetics and Politics*, London: Verso.

—— (1983) *The Political Unconscious: Narrative as a Socially Symbolic Act*, London: Methuen.

—— (1985) 'Periodizing the 60s', in Sonya Sayres et al. (eds) *The 60s Without Apology*: 178–209.

Jardine, Alice (1985) *Gynesis: Configurations of Woman and Modernity*, London: Cornell University Press.

Jelinek, Estelle C. (ed.) (1980) *Women's Autobiography: Essays in Criticism*, London: Indiana University Press.

Johnson, Barbara (1986a) 'Metaphor, Metonymy and Voice in *Their Eyes Were Watching God*', in Harold Bloom (ed.) *Zora Neale Hurston*: 157–73.

—— (1986b) 'Thresholds of Difference: Structures of Address in Zora Neale Hurston', in Henry Louis Gates Jr (ed.) *'Race', Writing and Difference*: 317–28.

Jones, LeRoi (1962, rpt 1969) 'The Myth of a "Negro Literature"', in Addison Gayle Jr (ed.) *Black Expression*: 190–7.

Jordan, Cynthia C. (1989a) 'A Fatherly Character: *Franklin's Autobiography*', in Cynthia Jordan, *Second Stories*: 27–57.

—— (1989b) *Second Stories: the Politics of Language, Form and Gender in Early American Fictions*, London: University of North Carolina Press.

Joseph, Gloria and Jill Lewis (1981) *Common Differences: Conflicts in Black and White Feminist Perspectives*, Boston: South End Press.

Juhasz, Suzanne (1980) 'Towards a Theory of Form in Feminist Autobiography: Kate Millett's *Flying* and *Sita*; Maxine Hong Kingston's *The Woman Warrior*', in Estelle C. Jelinek (ed.) *Women's Autobiography*: 221–37.

Kaplan, Amy (1992) *The Social Construction of American Realism*, London: University of Chicago Press.

Kaplan, Cora (1985) 'Shaping Our New Jerusalems', *New Statesman*, 109, 26 April: 26.

—— (1986) *Sea Changes: Essays on Culture and Feminism*, London: Verso.

—— (1988) 'Between Synchrony and History: Feminist Fiction in the Eighties', unpublished paper, presented at the conference 'Feminist Criticism: the Next Decade', University of Southampton, 2 July.

—— and Maria Lauret (1987) 'Women at War' [interview with Marge Piercy], *Marxism Today*, August: 26–7.

Karl, Frederick R. (1977) 'Doris Lessing in the Sixties: the New Anatomy of Melancholy', in Patricia Meyer Spacks (ed.) *Contemporary Women Novelists*: 55–74.

—— (1983) *American Fiction 1940–1980: a Comprehensive History and Critical Evaluation*, New York: Harper and Row.

Kennedy, Flo (1984, rpt 1985) '"It's Damn Slick Out There"', in Sonya Sayres et al. (eds) *The 60s Without Apology*: 346–58.

Kerman, Cynthia Earl and Richard Eldridge (1987) *The Lives of Jean Toomer: a Hunger for Wholeness*, London: Louisiana State University Press.

Klehr, Harvey (1973) 'Marxist Theory in Search of America', *Journal of Politics* 35: 311–31.

Klinkowitz, Jerome (1980) *The American 1960s: Imaginative Acts in a Decade of Change*, Ames: Iowa State University Press.

Koedt, Anne (1970, rpt 1973) 'The Myth of the Vaginal Orgasm', in Anne Koedt et al. (eds) *Radical Feminism*: 198–207.

—— ,Ellen Levine and Anita Rapone (eds) (1973) *Radical Feminism*, New York: Quadrangle.

Kolodny, Annette (1980) 'The Lady's Not for Spurning: Kate Millett and the Critics', in Estelle C. Jelinek (ed.) *Women's Autobiography*: 238–59.

Kristeva, Julia (1981, rpt 1989) 'Women's Time', *Signs* 7, 1: 13–35, rpt in Catherine Belsey and Jane Moore (eds) *The Feminist Reader*, London: Macmillan, pp. 212–33.

—— (1989) 'A Question of Subjectivity: an Interview' [with Susan Sellers], in Philip Rice and Patricia Waugh (eds) *Literary Theory*: 128–34.

Krouse, Agathe Nesoule (1979) 'Toward a Definition of Literary Feminism', in Cheryl L. Brown and Karen Olson (eds) *Feminist Criticism*: 279–90.

Kruger, Barbara and Phil Mariani (eds) (1989) *Remaking History*, Dia Art Foundation Discussions in Contemporary Culture 4, Seattle: Bay Press.

Kurzweil, Edith and William Phillips (eds) (1983) *Writers and Politics: a Partisan Review Reader*, London: Routledge and Kegan Paul.

Lacey, Candida Ann (1985) 'Engendering conflict: American women and the making of a proletarian fiction (with particular reference to the period 1929 to 1935)', Unpublished Ph.D. thesis, University of Sussex.

Langer, Elinor (1984) 'Afterword', in Josephine Herbst, *Rope of Gold*: 431–49.

Lasch, Christopher (1979, rpt 1980) *The Culture of Narcissism: American Life in an Age of Diminishing Expectations*, London: Abacus.

Lauret, Maria (1989) 'Seizing Time and Making New: Feminist Criticism, Politics, and Contemporary Feminist Fiction', *Feminist Review* 31: 94–106.

—— (1991) 'Feminism and Culture – the Movie: a Critical Overview of Writing on Women and Cinema', *Women: a Cultural Review* 2, 1: 52–69.

—— (1994) '"It's My Party": Fictions of the Sexual Revolution', in Gina Wisker (ed.) *It's My Party: Reading Twentieth Century Women's Writing*: 30–45.

Lefanu, Sarah (1988) *In the Chinks of the World Machine: Feminism and Science Fiction*, London: Women's Press.

Lejeune, Philippe (1977) 'Autobiography in the Third Person', *New Literary History* 9, 1: 26–50.

Lenz, Günter (1990) 'The Radical Imagination: Revisionary Modes of Radical Cultural Criticism in Thirties America', in Steve Ickringill (ed.) *Looking Inward Looking Outward*: 94–126.

Leonard, John (1976) 'Pop Goes the Novel' [review of Lisa Alther's *Kinflicks*], *New York Times Book Review*, 14 March: 4.

—— (1980) [review of Marge Piercy's *Vida*], *International Herald Tribune*, 23 January: 23.

Lerner, Gerda (ed.) (1972) *Black Women in White America: a Documentary History*, New York: Panther.

Lerner, Michael (1982) 'Recapturing the Family Issue', *The Nation*, 6 February: 141–3.

LeSueur, Meridel (1935b, rpt 1987) 'The Fetish of Being Outside', in Charlotte Nekola and Paula Rabinowitz (eds) *Writing Red*: 299–303.

—— (1956, rpt 1982a, 1982b) 'The Dark of the Time', in Meridel LeSueur *Harvest & Song for My Time*: 122 and in *Ripening*: 239.

Levine, Lawrence W. (1978) *Black Culture and Black Consciousness: Afro-American Folk Thought from Slavery to Freedom*, Oxford: Oxford University Press.

Lewis, David Levering (1981) *When Harlem Was in Vogue*, New York: Oxford University Press.

Livingstone, Rodney (ed.) (1981) *Georg Lukacs: Essays on Realism*, transl. David Fernbach, Cambridge, Mass.: MIT Press.

Locke, Alain (1925, rpt 1968) 'The New Negro', in Abraham Chapman (ed.) *Black Voices*: 512–23.

Lorde, Audre (1979, rpt 1983) 'The Master's Tools Will Never Dismantle the Master's House', in Cherríe Moraga and Gloria Anzaldúa (eds) *This Bridge Called My Back*: 98–101.

—— (1983, rpt 1985) 'My Words Will Be There', in Mari Evans (ed.) *Black Women Writers*: 261–8.

—— (1990) 'Foreword' in Joanne Braxton and Andrée McLaughlin (eds) *Wild Women in the Whirlwind*, London: Serpent's Tail.

Lovell, Terry (1983a) *Pictures of Reality: Aesthetics, Politics and Pleasure*, London: British Film Institute.

—— (1983b) 'Writing Like a Woman: a Question of Politics', in Francis Barker et al. (eds) *The Politics of Theory*: 15–25.

—— (1987) *Consuming Fiction*, London: Verso.

Lukács, Georg (1932, rpt 1981) 'Reportage or Portrayal?' in Georg Lukacs, *Essays on Realism*: 45–75.

—— (1981) *Essays on Realism*, ed. Rodney Livingstone, transl. David Fernbach, Cambridge, Mass.: MIT Press.

Lucas, J. Anthony (1971) *Don't Shoot – We Are Your Children!*, New York: Random House.

McDowell, Deborah E. (1985) 'Introduction: a Question of Power or, the Rear Guard Faces Front', in Jessie Redmon Fauset, *Plum Bun*: ix–xxiv.

McKay, Nellie Y. (1990) 'The Autobiographies of Zora Neale Hurston and Gwendolyn Brooks: Alternate Versions of the Black Female Self', in Joanne M. Braxton and Andrée Nicola McLaughlin (eds) *Wild Women in the Whirlwind*: 264–81.

MacKinnon, Catherine A. (1987) *Feminism Unmodified*, Boston: Harvard University Press.

MacKinnon, Janice R. and Stephen R. (1988) *Agnes Smedley: the Life and Times of an American Radical*, London: Virago.

Mailer, Norman (1957, rpt 1984) 'The White Negro', in Judith Clavir Albert and Stewart Edward Albert (eds) *The 60s Papers*: 93–104.

—— (1963, rpt 1977) 'The Case against McCarthy: a Review of *The Group*', in Patricia Meyer Spacks (ed.) *Contemporary Women Novelists*: 74–84.

Major, Clarence (1967, rpt 1968) 'A Black Criterion', in Abraham Chapman (ed.) *Black Voices*: 698–9.

Marable, Manning (1984) *Race, Reform and Rebellion: the Second Reconstruction in Black America 1945–1982*, London: Macmillan.

—— (1985) *Black American Politics: from the Washington Marches to Jesse Jackson*, London: Verso.

Martin, Biddy (1988) 'Lesbian Identity and Autobiographical Difference[s]', in Bella Brodzki and Celeste Schenck (eds) *Life/Lines*: 77–103.

Martin, Reginald (1988) *Ishmael Reed and the New Black Aesthetic Critics*, London: Macmillan.

Matusow, Allen J. (1986) *The Unraveling of America: a History of Liberalism in the 1960s*, London: Harper and Row.

Miller, James (1987) *Democracy Is in the Streets: from Port Huron to the Siege of Chicago*, New York: Simon and Schuster.

Miller, Nancy (1988) *Subject to Change: Reading Feminist Writing*, New York: Columbia University Press.

Millett, Kate (1971, rpt 1977) *Sexual Politics*, London: Virago.

Mills, C. Wright (1960, rpt 1984) 'Letter to the New Left', in Judith Clavir Albert and Stewart Edward Albert (eds) *The 60s Papers*: 86–92.

Mitchell, Juliet (1966, rpt 1984) 'Women, the Longest Revolution', in Juliet Mitchell, *Women: the Longest Revolution*: 18–54.

—— (1971) *Woman's Estate*, Harmondsworth: Penguin.

—— (1984) *Women: the Longest Revolution: Essays in Feminism, Literature and Psychoanalysis*, London: Virago.

—— and Ann Oakley (eds) (1986) *What is Feminism?*, Oxford: Basil Blackwell.

—— and Jacqueline Rose (eds) (1982) *Feminine Sexuality: Jacques Lacan and the Ecole Freudienne*, London: Macmillan.

Modleski, Tania (1984) *Loving with a Vengeance*, London: Methuen.

Moers, Ellen (1977) *Literary Women: the Great Writers*, New York: Anchor Doubleday.

Moi, Toril (1985) *Sexual/Textual Politics: Feminist Literary Theory*, New Accents, London: Methuen.

Moraga, Cherríe and Gloria Anzaldúa (eds) (1983) *This Bridge Called My Back: Radical Writings by Radical Women of Color*, New York: Kitchen Table Women of Color Press.

Moretti, Franco (1987) *The Way of the World: the Bildungsroman in European Culture*, London: Verso.

Morgan, Ellen (1973) 'Humanbecoming: Form and Focus in the Neo-Feminist Novel', in Susan Koppelman Cornillon (ed.) *Images of Women in Fiction*: 183–205.

—— (1978) 'Alienation of the Woman Writer in *The Golden Notebook*', in Cheryl L. Brown and Karen Olson (eds) *Feminist Criticism*: 301–11.

Morgan, Robin (ed.) (1970a, rpt 1984) 'Goodbye to All That', in Judith Clavir Albert and Stewart Edward Albert (eds) *The 60s Papers*: 509–16.

—— (1970b) *Sisterhood Is Powerful: an Anthology of Writings from the Women's Liberation Movement*, New York: Vintage.

Morris, Meaghan (1988a) 'The Pirate's Fiancée', in Meaghan Morris, *The Pirate's Fiancée*: 51–69.

—— (1988b) *The Pirate's Fiancée: Feminism, Reading, Postmodernism*, London: Verso.

Morrison, Toni (1984, rpt 1985) 'Rootedness: the Ancestor as Foundation', in Mari Evans (ed.) *Black Women Writers*: 339–45.

—— (1988) 'Unspeakable Things Unspoken: the Afro-American Presence in American Literature', *Michigan Quarterly Review*, Winter: 1–34.

Moylan, Tom (1986) *Demand the Impossible: Science Fiction and the Utopian Imagination*, London: Methuen.

Mulhern, Francis (1985) 'Writing for the Future: the Politics of Literature', *New Statesman*, 109, 22 March: 24–6.

Nekola, Charlotte (1987) 'Worlds Unseen: Political Women Journalists and the 1930s', in Charlotte Nekola and Paula Rabinowitz (eds) *Writing Red*: 189–98.

—— and Paula Rabinowitz (eds) (1987) *Writing Red: an Anthology of American Women Writers 1930–1940*, New York: Feminist Press at the City University of New York.

Newton, Judith (1987) 'Making – and Remaking History: Another Look at Patriarchy', in Shari Benstock (ed.) *Issues in Feminist Literary Scholarship*: 124–40.

—— and Deborah Rosenfelt (eds) (1985) *Feminist Criticism and Social Change: Sex, Class and Race in Literature and Culture*, London: Methuen.

Nilsen, Helge Normann (1984) 'Tillie Olsen's *Tell Me a Riddle*: the Political Theme', *Etudes Anglaises* T., xxxvii, 2: 163–9.

Norton, Eleonor Holmes (1970) 'For Sadie and Maude', in Robin Morgan (ed.) *Sisterhood Is Powerful*: 397–403.

Norton, Mary Beth (ed.) (1989) *Major Problems in American Women's History: Documents and Essays*, Lexington, Mass.: D. C. Heath.

O'Brien, John (ed.) (1973) *Interviews with Black Writers*, New York: Liveright.

Olney, James (1980) *Autobiography: Essays Theoretical and Critical*, Princeton: Princeton University Press.

Olsen, Tillie (1934, rpt 1987) 'The Strike', in Charlotte Nekola and Paula Rabinowitz (eds) *Writing Red*: 245–51.

—— (1971, 1972, rpt 1980) 'Rebecca Harding Davis', in Tillie Olsen, *Silences*: 47–118.

—— (1980b) *Silences*, London: Virago.

O'Neale, Sondra (1984) 'Reconstruction of the Composite Self: New Images of Black Women in Maya Angelou's Continuing Autobiography', in Mari Evans (ed.) *Black Women Writers*: 25–36.

Palmer, Paulina (1989) *Contemporary Women's Fiction: Narrative Practice and Feminist Theory*, Hemel Hempstead: Harvester Wheatsheaf.

Petschesky, Rosalind Pollack (1984, rpt 1986) *Abortion and Woman's Choice: the State, Sexuality and Reproductive Freedom*, London: Verso.

Piercy, Marge (1970b) 'The Grand Coolie Damn', in Robin Morgan (ed.) *Sisterhood Is Powerful*: 472–93.

—— (1974a) 'Reconsideration: Agnes Smedley, Dirt-Poor Daughter of Earth', *New Republic* 171, 14 December: 19–20.

—— (1974b, rpt 1982) 'Through the Cracks: Growing Up in the Fifties', in Marge Piercy, *Parti-Colored Blocks for a Quilt*: 113–28.

—— (1976b) '*Meridian*, by Alice Walker', *The New York Times Book Review*, 23 May: 5, 12.

—— (1977, rpt 1982) 'An Interview with *Sandscript*', in Marge Piercy, *Parti-Colored Blocks for a Quilt*: 99–112.

—— (1980b, rpt 1982) 'An Interview with Alison Platt of *Sojourner*', in Marge Piercy, *Parti- Colored Blocks for a Quilt*: 175–81.

——— (1981, rpt 1982) 'The City as Battleground', in Marge Piercy, *Parti-Colored Blocks for a Quilt*: 161–71.

——— (1981–1982, rpt 1982) 'An Interview with Peggy Friedmann and Ruthann Robson of *Kalliope*', in Marge Piercy, *Parti-Colored Blocks for a Quilt*: 131–40.

——— (1982b) *Parti-Colored Blocks for a Quilt*, Ann Arbor: University of Michigan Press.

——— (1989) 'A Dark Thread in the Weave', in David Rosenberg (ed.) *Testimony: Contemporary Writers Make the Holocaust Personal*, New York: Random House.

——— and Dick Lourie (1972) 'Tom Eliot Meets the Hulk at Little Big Horn: the Political Economy of Poetry', *Triquarterly*, special issue *Literature in Revolution*, 23/24: 57–91.

Plamondon, Genie (n.d., rpt 1984) 'Hello to All That', in Judith Clavir Albert and Stewart Edward Albert (eds) *The 60s Papers*: 520–3.

Polenberg, Richard (1980, rpt 1984) *One Nation Divisible: Class, Race and Ethnicity in the United States Since 1938*, Harmondsworth: Penguin.

Popkin, Ann (1979) 'The Personal Is Political: the Women's Liberation Movement', in Dick Cluster (ed.) *They Should Have Served That Cup of Coffee*: 181–222.

Powell, Linda (1983) 'Black Macho and Black Feminism', in Barbara Smith (ed.) *Home Girls*: 283–92.

Rabinowitz, Paula (1991) *Labor and Desire: Women's Revolutionary Fiction in Depression America*, Chapel Hill: University of North Carolina Press.

Radicalesbians (1973) 'The Woman Identified Woman', in Anne Koedt et al. (eds) *Radical Feminism*: 240–5.

Radstone, Susannah (ed.) (1989) *Sweet Dreams: Sexuality, Gender and Popular Fiction*, London: Lawrence and Wishart.

Rainwater, Lee and William L. Yancey (eds) (1967) *The Moynihan Report and the Politics of Controversy*, London: MIT Press.

Raynaud, Claudine (1988) '"A Nutmeg Nestled Inside Its Covering of Mace": Audre Lorde's *Zami*', in Bella Brodzki and Celeste Schenck (eds) *Life/Lines*: 221–42.

Reagon, Bernice Johnson (1983) 'Coalition Politics: Turning the Century', in Barbara Smith (ed.) *Home Girls*: 356–68.

Redstockings (1978) *Feminist Revolution*, New York: Random House.

Rice, Philip and Patricia Waugh (eds) (1989) *Literary Theory: a Reader*, London: Edward Arnold.

Rich, Adrienne (1976) *Of Woman Born: Motherhood as Experience and Institution*, New York: W. W. Norton.

——— (1979, rpt 1980) *On Lies, Secrets and Silence: Selected Prose 1966–1978*, London: Virago.

——— (1980, rpt 1984) 'Compulsory Heterosexuality and Lesbian Existence', in Ann Barr Snitow et al. (eds) *Desire*: 212–41.

Rich, B. Ruby (1983) 'Anti-Porn: Soft Issue, Hard World', *Feminist Review* 13: 56–67.

Rideout, Walter B. (1956) *The Radical Novel in the United States 1900–1954*, Cambridge, Mass.: Harvard University Press.

Riese, Utz (1987) 'Neither High Nor Low: Michael Gold's Concept of Proletarian Literature', in Heinz Ickstadt et al. (eds) *The Thirties*: 143–66.

Rigney, Barbara Hill (1978) *Madness and Sexual Politics in the Feminist Novel: Studies in Brontë, Woolf, Lessing and Atwood*, Madison: University of Wisconsin Press.

Robinson, Lillian S. (1978) *Sex, Class and Culture*, London: Indiana University Press.

Roe, Sue (ed.) (1989) *Women Reading Women's Writing*, Hemel Hempstead: Harvester Wheatsheaf.

Rohrlich, Ruby and Elaine Hoffman Baruch (eds) (1984) *Women in Search of Utopia: Mavericks and Mythmakers*, New York: Schocken.

Rosenberg, David (ed.) (1989) *Testimony: Contemporary Writers Make the Holocaust Personal*, New York: Random House.

Rosenfelt, Deborah (1985) 'From the Thirties: Tillie Olsen and the Radical Tradition', in Judith Newton and Deborah Rosenfelt (eds) *Feminist Criticism and Social Change*: 216–48.

Rothschild, Mary Aikin (1979) 'White Women Volunteers in the Freedom Summers: Their Life and Work in a Movement for Social Change', *Feminist Studies* 5, 3: 466–95.

Russ, Joanna (1973a) 'The Image of Women in Science Fiction', in Susan Koppelman Cornillon (ed.) *Images of Women in Fiction*: 79–96.

—— (1973b) 'What Can a Heroine Do? Or Why Women Can't Write', in Susan Koppelman Cornillon (ed.) *Images of Women in Fiction*: 3–20.

—— (1984) *How to Suppress Women's Writing*, London: Women's Press.

Rutherford, Jonathan (ed.) (1990) *Identity: Community, Culture, Difference*, London: Lawrence and Wishart.

Ryan, Mary P. (1983) *Womanhood in America from Colonial Times to the Present*, 3rd edn, New York: Franklin Watts.

Sale, Kirkpatrick (1973) *SDS*, New York: Random House.

Sapiro, Virginia (1986) 'The Women's Movement, Politics and Policy in the Reagan Era', in Drude Dahlerup (ed.) *The New Women's Movement*: 122–8.

Sarachild, Kathie (1971) 'Feminist "Organizing" and Consciousness-Raising', in Leslie B. Tanner (ed.) *Voices from Women's Liberation*: 154–7.

Sayre, Nora (1973, rpt 1974) *Sixties Going on Seventies*, London: Constable.

Sayres, Sonya, Anders Stephanson, Stanley Aronowitz and Fredric Jameson (eds) (1985) *The 60s Without Apology*, Minneapolis: University of Minnesota with *Social Text*.

Schachner, E. A. (1934) 'Revolutionary Literature in the US Today', *Windsor Quarterly*, Spring: 27–64.

Scharf, Lois and Joan M. Jensen (eds) (1983) *Decades of Discontent: the Women's Movement 1920–1949*, Contributions in Women's Studies 28, Westport, Conn.: Greenwood Press.

Schultz, Elizabeth (1981) 'To Be Black and Blue: the Blues Genre in Afro-American Autobiography', in Albert E. Stone (ed.) *The American Autobiography*: 109–32.

Schwartz, Larry (1977) 'On the Problem of Criticizing Political Fiction', *Polit* 1, 1: 109–19.

Scott, Bonnie Kime (ed.) (1990) *The Gender of Modernism: a Critical Anthology*, Bloomington: Indiana University Press.

Segal, Lynne (1991) 'Whose Left? Socialism, Feminism and the Future', *New Left Review* 185: 81–91.

Seiter, Ellen (1986) 'The Personal Is Political: Margarethe von Trotta's "Marianne und Juliane"', in Charlotte Brunsdon (ed.) *Films for Women*: 109–16.

Sellers, Susan (1989) 'A Question of Subjectivity: an Interview' [with Julia Kristeva], in Philip Rice and Patricia Waugh (eds) *Literary Theory*: 128–34.

Shaffer, Robert (1979) 'Women and the Communist Party USA, 1930–1940', *Socialist Review*: 73–118.

Sheridan, Susan (ed.) (1990) *Grafts: Feminist Cultural Criticism*, London: Verso.

Showalter, Elaine (1977, rpt 1978) *A Literature of Their Own: British Women Novelists from Brontë to Lessing*, London: Virago.

—— (ed.) (1985, rpt 1986) *The New Feminist Criticism: Essays on Women, Literature and Theory*, London: Virago.

Shulman, Alix Kates (1980) 'Sex and Power: Sexual Bases of Radical Feminism', in Catherine Stimpson and Ethel Spector Person (eds) *Women: Sex and Sexuality*: 21–35.

Simson, Rennie (1984) 'The Afro-American Female: the Historical Context of the Construction of Sexual Identity', in Ann Barr Snitow et al. (eds) *Desire*: 43–9.

Smith, Barbara (ed.) (1983) *Home Girls: a Black Feminist Anthology*, New York: Kitchen Table Women of Color Press.

—— (1990) 'The Truth That Never Hurts: Black Lesbians in the Fiction of the 1980s', in Joanne M. Braxton and Andrée Nicola McLaughlin (eds) *Wild Women in the Whirlwind*: 213–45.

—— and Cenen (1983) 'The Blood Yes the Blood: a Conversation', in Barbara Smith (ed.) *Home Girls*: 31–51.

Smith, Sidonie (1987) *A Poetics of Women's Autobiography: Marginality and the Fiction of Self-Representation*, Bloomington: Indiana University Press.

Smith, Valerie (1987) *Self-Discovery and Authority in Afro-American Narrative*, Cambridge, Mass.: Harvard University Press.

—— (1990) 'Split Affinities: the Case of Interracial Rape', in Marianne Hirsch and Evelyn Fox-Keller (eds) *Conflicts in Feminism*: 271–87.

SNCC (Student Non-Violent Coordinating Committee) (n.d., rpt 1984) 'SNCC: Founding Statement', in Judith Clavir Albert and Stewart Edward Albert (eds) *The 60s Papers*: 113.

—— (1964, rpt 1984) 'SNCC Position Paper: Women in the Movement', in Judith Clavir Albert and Stewart Edward Albert (eds) *The 60s Papers*: 114–16.

—— (1966, rpt 1984) 'What We Want', in Judith Clavir Albert and Stewart Edward Albert (eds) *The 60s Papers*: 117–18.

Snitow, Ann Barr (1980) 'The Front Line: Notes on Sex in Novels by Women, 1969–1979', in Catherine Stimpson and Ethel Spector Person (eds) *Women: Sex and Sexuality*: 158–74.

—— , Christine Stansell and Sharon Thompson (eds) (1984) *Desire: the Politics of Sexuality*, London: Virago.

Sochen, June (ed.) (1971) *The New Feminism in Twentieth Century America*, Lexington: D. C. Heath.

Sollors, Werner (1990) 'Anthropological and Sociological Tendencies in American Literature of the 1930s and 1940s: Richard Wright, Zora Neale Hurston, and American Culture', in Steve Ickringill (ed.) *Looking Inward Looking Outward*: 22–75.

Solomon, Irwin D. (1989) *Feminism and Black Activism in Contemporary America: an Ideological Assessment*, New York: Greenwood Press.

Spacks, Patricia Meyer (ed.) (1977) *Contemporary Women Novelists: a Collection of Critical Essays*, Englewood Cliffs, NJ: Prentice Hall.

—— (1980) 'Selves in Hiding', in Estelle C. Jelinek (ed.) *Women's Autobiography*: 102–32.

Spelman, Elizabeth V. (1988, rpt 1990) *Inessential Woman: Problems of Exclusion in Feminist Thought*, London: Women's Press.

Sprinker, Michael (1987) *Imaginary Relations: Aesthetics and Ideology in the Theory of Historical Materialism*, London: Verso.

Stacey, Judith (1986) 'Are Feminists Afraid to Leave Home? The Challenge of Conservative Pro-Family Feminism', in Juliet Mitchell and Ann Oakley (eds) *What is Feminism?*: 219–48.

Stanton, Domna C. (ed.) (1987) *The Female Autograph: Theory and Practice of Autobiography from the Tenth to the Twentieth Century*, Chicago: University of Chicago Press.

Stimpson, Catherine R. and Ethel Spector Person (eds) (1980) *Women: Sex and Sexuality*, London: University of Chicago Press.

Stone, Albert E. (ed.) (1980, rpt 1981) *The American Autobiography: a Collection of Critical Essays*, Englewood Cliffs, NJ: Prentice Hall.

Suleiman, Susan Rubin (1983) *Authoritarian Fictions: the Ideological Novel as Literary Genre*, New York: Columbia University Press.

Tallis, Raymond (1988) *In Defence of Realism*, London: Edward Arnold.

Tambling, Jeremy (1990) *Confession: Sexuality, Sin, the Subject*, Manchester: Manchester University Press.

Tanner, Leslie B. (ed.) (1971) *Voices from Women's Liberation*, New York: Mentor.

Tate, Claudia (ed.) (1983, rpt 1985) *Black Women Writers at Work*, Harpenden: Oldcastle Books.

Taylor, Gordon O. (1986) *Studies in American Autobiography*, London: Macmillan.

Teichler, Paula A. (1987) 'Escaping the Sentence: Diagnosis and Discourse in "The Yellow Wallpaper"', in Shari Benstock (ed.) *Issues in Feminist Literary Scholarship*: 62–78.

Teish, Luisah (1983) 'Women's Spirituality: a Household Act', in Barbara Smith (ed.) *Home Girls*: 331–51.

Teodori, Massimo (ed.) (1970) *The New Left: a Documentary History*, London: Jonathan Cape.

Trimberger, Ellen Kay (1979) 'Women in the Old and New Left: the Evolution of a Politics of Personal Life', *Feminist Studies* 5, 3: 432–50.

Van Gelder, Lindsy (1970) 'The Trials of Lois Lane: Women in Journalism', in Robin Morgan (ed.) *Sisterhood Is Powerful*: 88–93.

Vance, Carole S. (ed.) (1984, rpt 1992) *Pleasure and Danger: Exploring Female Sexuality*, 2nd edn, London: Pandora.

Walker, Alice (1975, rpt 1984) 'Looking for Zora', in Alice Walker, *In Search of Our Mothers' Gardens*: 93–116.

—— (1976b, rpt 1984) 'Saving the Life That Is Your Own: the Importance of Models in the Artist's Life', in Alice Walker, *In Search of Our Mothers' Gardens*: 3–14.

—— (1979b) 'Dedication: On Refusing to Be Humbled by Second Place in a Contest You Did Not Design: a Tradition by Now', in Alice Walker (ed.) *I Love Myself*: 1–6.

—— (1979c, rpt 1984) '*One* Child of One's Own: a Meaningful Digression within the Work(s)', in Alice Walker, *In Search of Our Mothers' Gardens*: 361–83.

—— (1979d, rpt 1984) 'Zora Neale Hurston: a Cautionary Tale and a Partisan View', in Alice Walker, *In Search of Our Mothers' Gardens*: 83–92.

—— (1983a) 'Only Justice Can Stop a Curse', in Barbara Smith (ed.) *Home Girls*: 352–5.

—— (1983b, rpt 1984) *In Search of Our Mothers' Gardens: Womanist Prose*, London: Women's Press.

—— (1984, rpt 1988) 'On *Seeing Red*', in Alice Walker, *Living by the Word*: 125–9.

—— (1987, rpt 1988) 'In the Closet of the Soul', in Alice Walker, *Living by the Word*: 78–92.

—— (1988) *Living by the Word: Selected Writings 1973–1987*, London: Women's Press.

Walker, Melissa (1991) *Down from the Mountaintop: Black Women's Novels in the Wake of the Civil Rights Movement, 1966–1989*, New Haven: Yale University Press.

Wall, Cheryl A. (ed.) (1989, rpt 1990) *Changing Our Own Words: Essays on Criticism, Theory and Writing by Black Women*, London: Routledge.

Wallace, Michele (1975, rpt 1982) 'A Black Feminist's Search for Sisterhood', in Gloria T. Hull et al. (eds) *All the Women Are White*: 63–8.

—— (1979) *Black Macho and the Myth of the Superwoman*, New York: Dial Press.

—— (1989) 'Reading 1968 and the Great American Whitewash', in Barbara Kruger and Phil Mariani (eds) *Remaking History*: 97–109.

—— (1990a) *Invisibility Blues: from Pop to Theory*, London: Verso.

—— (1990b) 'Who Owns Zora Neale Hurston? Critics Carve Up the Legend', in Michele Wallace, *Invisibility Blues*: 172–86.

Ware, Cellestine (1970) *Woman Power: the Movement for Women's Liberation*, New York: Tower.

BIBLIOGRAPHY

Ware, Susan (1982) *Holding Their Own: American Women in the 1930s*, Boston: Twayne.

Washington, Mary Helen (1979) 'Zora Neale Hurston: a Woman Half in Shadow', in Alice Walker (ed.) *I Love Myself*: 7–25.

—— (1989a) '"I Love the Way Janie Crawford Left Her Husbands": Zora Neale Hurston's Emergent Female Hero', in Mary Helen Washington (ed.) *Invented Lives*: 237–54.

—— (1989b) '"Infidelity Becomes Her": the Ambivalent Woman in the Fiction of Ann Petry and Dorothy West', in Mary Helen Washington (ed.) *Invented Lives*: 297–306.

—— (ed.) (1989c) *Invented Lives: Narratives of Black Women 1860–1960*, London: Virago.

Waugh, Patricia (1984) *Metafiction: the Theory and Practice of Self-Conscious Fiction*, London: Methuen.

—— (1989) *Feminine Fictions: Revisiting the Postmodern*, London: Routledge.

Weems, Renita (1983) 'Artists without an Art Form', in Barbara Smith (ed.) *Home Girls*: 94–105.

West, Cornel (1985) 'The Paradox of the Afro-American Rebellion', in Sonya Sayres et al. (eds) *The 60s without Apology*: 44–58.

Williams, Raymond (1961, rpt 1965) *The Long Revolution*, Harmondsworth: Penguin.

—— (1981) *Culture*, London: Fontana.

Willis, Susan (1987) *Specifying: Black Women Writing the American Experience*, London: University of Wisconsin Press.

Wilson, Elisabeth (1982b) 'Interview with Andrea Dworkin', *Feminist Review* 11: 23–9.

—— (1983) 'The Context of "Between Pleasure and Danger": the Barnard Conference on Sexuality', *Feminist Review* 13: 35–41.

—— (1989) 'Telling It Like It Is: Women and Confessional Writing', in Susannah Radstone (ed.) *Sweet Dreams*: 21–45.

Winston, Elizabeth (1980) 'The Autobiographer and Her Readers: from Apology to Affirmation', in Estelle C. Jelinek (ed.) *Women's Autobiography*: 93–111.

Wisker, Gina (ed.) (1993a) *Black Women's Writing*, London: Macmillan.

—— (1993b) '"Disremembered and Unaccounted for": Reading Toni Morrison's *Beloved* and Alice Walker's *The Temple of My Familiar*', in Gina Wisker (ed.) *Black Women's Writing*: 78–95.

—— (ed.) (1994) *It's My Party: Reading Twentieth Century Women's Writing*, London: Pluto.

Wollstonecraft, Mary (1972, rpt 1975) *Vindication of the Rights of Woman*, Harmondsworth: Penguin.

Woolf, Virginia (1924, rpt 1986, 1992) 'Mr. Bennett and Mrs. Brown', in Peter Faulkner (ed.) *A Modernist Reader*: 112–128 and in Virginia Woolf, *A Woman's Essays*: 69–87.

—— (1929, rpt 1957) *A Room of One's Own*, London: Harcourt Brace Jovanovich.

—— (1992) *A Woman's Essays* Vol. I, Harmondsworth: Penguin.

Wright, Elizabeth (1984) *Psychoanalytic Criticism: Theory in Practice*, New Accents, London: Methuen.

Wright, Richard (1937) 'Between Laughter and Tears' [review of Zora Neale Hurston's *Their Eyes Were Watching God*], *New Masses*, 5 October: 25–6.

Yee, Carol Zonis (1973) 'Why Aren't We Writing about Ourselves?', in Susan Koppelman Cornillon (ed.) *Images of Women in Fiction*: 131–4.

Zimmerman, Bonnie (1983) 'Exiting from Patriarchy: the Lesbian Novel of Development', in Elizabeth Abel et al. (eds) *The Voyage in*: 244–57.

INDEX

Aaron, Daniel 161
Abel, Elizabeth 100; *The Voyage In* 90
abortion rights 169, 170, 172–6
activism: in *Meridian* 126–9; and
personal life 33–5, 61; *see also*
personal politics
Adams, Louise 70
African-American historiography: and
the novel 135–6; as trauma 126–9,
139; *see also* political history
African-American womanhood 134–9;
see also black feminism; black
masculinity
African-American writing:
appropriation of, by Atwood 182;
and autobiography 116–23; and
feminist fiction 79; and Hurston 13,
36–8; *see also* black women's writing
Albert, Judith and Stewart, *The 60s
Papers* 163
Allende, Isabel 140
Alpert, Jane 154; *Growing Up
Underground* 207 n15
Alther, Lisa: and feminist criticism 91,
92, 93; *Kinflicks* 85, 90
American dream, critique of 40–1
American Women 52
Americanism: in Hurston 39; and New
Left 152; respiritualisation of 140,
143
Ames, Lois 210 n20
Angelou, Maya 142, 166; *All God's
Children Need Travelling* 118;
autobiography 8, 97, 98, 107,
118–21, 122; *Gather Together in My
Name* 118, 119, 120; *The Heart of a
Woman* 118, 119, 121; *I Know Why the
Caged Bird Sings* 118, 119; and 1930s

42, 43; *Singin' and Swingin' and
Gettin' Merry Like Christmas* 118, 119,
121
Antin, Mary, *The Promised Land* 207 n21
Arnold, June, *Sister Gin* 94
Aronowitz, Stanley 152
Atwood, Margaret: *Cat's Eye* 177; and
feminist criticism 43; *The Handmaid's
Tale* 9, 88, 168, 171, 172, 176–83,
184, 185, 186
autobiography 80, 97–100, 105–8,
110–11, 113–23, 173, 177; African-
American 116–23
autonomy, female 183–4

backlash 'feminism' 66, 71–2, 165–86
Baker, Ella 48, 67, 125
Baldwin, James 143; *Nobody Knows My
Name* 121
Barrett, Michèle 162
Barth, John 14, 78
Barthelme, Donald 78
Battersby, Christine 188
Bell, Bernard 40, 41, 138, 139, 140; *The
Afro-American Novel and Its Tradition*
128, 129
Belsey, Catherine 76, 137
Benveniste, Emile 107, 108
Bernal, Martin, *Black Athena* 205 n20
Bethel, Lorraine 4, 5
Bettelheim, Bruno 186
Black Arts Movement 141, 142
black feminism 54, 67–71, 142; *see also*
African-American womanhood
black masculinity 131, 141–2
black nationalism 141, 143
black women's writing 35–42, 116–23,
126, 142–3; and white readers

womanism 125, 132, 134, 137, 143
Women's Liberation 8, 51–77, 122,
    152–3; and Civil Rights 124, 125;
    and feminist fiction 84–6; and New
    Left 45–7, 51–61, 144, 146–7; in *Vida*
    144–7, 150, 152–3, 159
Women's Press 197 n15
women's writing, and feminist criticism

2–3, 6, 74–5
Woolf, Virginia 3, 19, 30, 81, 82; *A
    Room of One's Own* 11, 97, 113; *The
    Waves* 113
Wright, Richard 36, 142, 143, 192 n29;
    Native Son 40, 207 n21

Zimmerman, Bonnie 90, 123